133

THE
GOLDEN TREASURY
OF THE BEST SONGS AND
LYRICAL POEMS IN
THE ENGLISH LANGUAGE

Oxford University Press, Amen House, London E.C.4

GLASGOW NEW YORK TORONTO MELBOURNE WELLINGTON
BOMBAY CALCUTTA MADRAS KARACHI LAHORE DACCA
CAPE TOWN SALISBURY NAIROBI IBADAN ACCRA
KUALA LUMPUR HONG KONG

CONTENTS

Εἰς τὸν λειμῶνα καθίσας,
ἔδρεπεν ἕτερον ἐφ' ἑτέρῳ
αἰρόμενος ἄγρευμ' ἀνθέων
ἁδομένᾳ ψυχᾷ.

[Eurip. *frag.* 754.]

[' He sat in the meadow and plucked
with glad heart the spoil of the
flowers, gathering them one by one.']

TO ALFRED TENNYSON
POET LAUREATE

THIS book in its progress has recalled often to my memory a man with whose friendship we were once honoured, to whom no region of English Literature was unfamiliar, and who, whilst rich in all the noble gifts of Nature, was most eminently distinguished by the noblest and the rarest,—just judgement and high-hearted patriotism. It would have been hence a peculiar pleasure and pride to dedicate what I have endeavoured to make a true national Anthology of three centuries to Henry Hallam. But he is beyond the reach of any human tokens of love and reverence ; and I desire therefore to place before it a name united with his by associations which, whilst Poetry retains her hold on the minds of Englishmen, are not likely to be forgotten.

Your encouragement, given while traversing the wild scenery of Treryn Dinas, led me to begin the work ; and it has been completed under your advice and assistance. For the favour now asked I have thus a second reason : and to this I may add, the homage which is your right as Poet, and the gratitude due to a Friend, whose regard I rate at no common value.

Permit me then to inscribe to yourself a book which, I hope, may be found by many a lifelong fountain of innocent and exalted pleasure; a source of animation to friends when they meet; and able to sweeten solitude itself with best society, —with the companionship of the wise and the good, with the beauty which the eye cannot see, and the music only heard in silence. If this Collection proves a storehouse of delight to Labour and to Poverty,—if it teaches those indifferent to the Poets to love them, and those who love them to love them more, the aim and the desire entertained in framing it will be fully accomplished.

F. T. P.

May, 1861.

PREFACE

THIS little Collection differs, it is believed, from others in the attempt made to include in it all the best original Lyrical pieces and Songs in our language, by writers not living,—and none beside the best. Many familiar verses will hence be met with ; many also which should be familiar :—the Editor will regard as his fittest readers those who love Poetry so well, that he can offer them nothing not already known and valued.

The Editor is acquainted with no strict and exhaustive definition of Lyrical Poetry ; but he has found the task of practical decision increase in clearness and in facility as he advanced with the work, whilst keeping in view a few simple principles. Lyrical has been here held essentially to imply that each Poem shall turn on some single thought, feeling, or situation. In accordance with this, narrative, descriptive, and didactic poems,—unless accompanied by rapidity of movement, brevity, and the colouring of human passion,—have been excluded. Humorous poetry, except in the very unfrequent instances where a truly poetical tone pervades the whole, with what is strictly personal, occasional, and religious, has been considered foreign to the idea of the book. Blank verse and the ten-syllable couplet, with all pieces markedly dramatic, have been rejected as alien from what is commonly understood by Song, and rarely conforming to Lyrical conditions in treatment. But it is not anticipated, nor is it possible, that all readers shall think the line accurately drawn. Some poems, as Gray's 'Elegy,' the 'Allegro' and 'Penseroso,' Wordsworth's 'Ruth' or Campbell's 'Lord Ullin,' might be claimed with perhaps equal justice for a narrative or descriptive selection : whilst with reference especially to Ballads and Sonnets, the Editor can only state that he has taken his utmost pains to decide without caprice or partiality.

This also is all he can plead in regard to a point even more liable to question ;—what degree of merit should give rank among the Best. That a Poem shall be worthy of the writer's genius,—that it shall reach a perfection commensurate with its aim,—that we should require finish in proportion to brevity,—that passion, colour, and originality cannot atone for serious imperfections in clearness, unity, or truth,—that a few good lines do not make a good poem,—that popular estimate is serviceable as a guidepost more than as a compass,—above all, that Excellence should be looked for rather in the Whole than in the Parts,—such and other such canons have been always steadily regarded. He may however add that the pieces chosen, and a far larger number rejected, have been carefully and repeatedly considered ; and that he has been aided throughout by two friends of independent and exercised judgement, besides the distinguished person addressed in the Dedication. It is hoped that by this procedure the volume has been freed from that onesidedness which must beset individual decisions :—but for the final choice the Editor is alone responsible.

It would obviously have been invidious to apply the standard aimed at in this Collection to the Living. Nor, even in the cases where this might be done without offence, does it appear wise to attempt to anticipate the verdict of the Future on our contemporaries. Should the book last, poems by Tennyson, Bryant, Clare, Lowell, and others, will no doubt claim and obtain their place among the best. But the Editor trusts that this will be effected by other hands, and in days far distant.

Chalmers' vast collection, with the whole works of all accessible poets not contained in it, and the best Anthologies of different periods, have been twice systematically read through : and it is hence improbable that any omissions which may be regretted are due to oversight. The poems are printed entire, except in a very few instances (specified in the notes) where a stanza has been omitted. The omissions have been risked only when the piece could be thus brought to a closer lyrical unity : and, as essentially opposed to this unity, extracts, obviously such, are excluded. In regard to the text, the purpose of the book has appeared to justify the choice of the most poetical version, wherever more than one exists : and much labour has been given to present each poem, in disposition, spelling, and punctuation, to the greatest advantage.

For the permission under which the copyright pieces are inserted, thanks are due to the respective Proprietors, without whose liberal concurrence the scheme of the collection would have been defeated.

In the arrangement, the most poetically-effective order has been attempted. The English mind has passed through phases of thought and cultivation so various and so opposed during these three centuries of Poetry, that a rapid passage between Old and New, like rapid alteration of the eye's focus in looking at the landscape, will always be wearisome and hurtful to the sense of Beauty. The poems have been therefore distributed into Books corresponding, I to the ninety years closing about 1616, II thence to 1700, III to 1800, IV to the half-century just ended. Or, looking at the Poets who more or less give each portion its distinctive character, they might be called the Books of Shakespeare, Milton, Gray, and Wordsworth. The volume, in this respect, so far as the limitations of its range allow, accurately reflects the natural growth and evolution of our Poetry.

A rigidly chronological sequence, however, rather fits a collection aiming at instruction than at pleasure, and the Wisdom which comes through Pleasure :—within each book the pieces have therefore been arranged in gradations of feeling or subject. The development of the symphonies of Mozart and Beethoven has been here thought of as a model, and nothing placed without careful consideration. And it is hoped that the contents of this Anthology will thus be found to present a certain unity, ' as episodes,' in the noble language of Shelley, ' to that great Poem which all poets, like the co-operating thoughts of one great mind, have built up since the beginning of the world.'

As he closes his long survey, the Editor trusts he may add without egotism, that he has found the vague general verdict of popular Fame more just than those have thought, who, with too severe a criticism, would confine judgements on Poetry to ' the selected few of many generations.' Not many appear to have gained reputation without some gift or performance that, in due degree, deserved it : and if no verses by certain writers who show less strength than sweetness, or more thought than mastery in expression, are printed in this volume, it should not be imagined that they have been excluded without much hesitation and regret,— far less that they have been slighted. Throughout this vast and pathetic array of Singers now silent, few have been honoured with the name Poet, and have not possessed a skill in words, a sympathy with beauty, a tenderness of feeling, or seriousness in reflection, which render their works, although never perhaps attaining that loftier and finer excellence here required,—better worth reading than much of what fills the scanty hours that most men spare for self-improvement, or for pleasure in any of its more elevated and permanent forms.— And if this be true of even mediocre poetry, for

how much more are we indebted to the best!
Like the fabled fountain of the Azores, but with
a more various power, the magic of this Art can
confer on each period of life its appropriate blessing:
on early years Experience, on maturity Calm, on
age Youthfulness. Poetry gives treasures ' more
golden than gold,' leading us in higher and healthier
ways than those of the world, and interpreting to
us the lessons of Nature. But she speaks best
for herself. Her true accents, if the plan has been
executed with success, may be heard throughout
the following pages :—wherever the Poets of
England are honoured, wherever the dominant
language of the world is spoken, it is hoped that
they will find fit audience.

F. T. P.

NOTE

Samuel Rogers, who died in 1855, was the last
poet included in *The Golden Treasury*. In this re-
print additional poems are given representing the
poets since then to the present day. None but
Mr. Palgrave could have grouped the newer poems
in ' the most poetically-effective order ', as he con-
ceived it, so they have been added in the chronological order of their authors. A few dates in the
original selection have been corrected. Acknow-
ledgements for leave to include copyright poems
are due to Mr. Lascelles Abercrombie and Messrs.
John Lane for permission to include ' Margaret's
Song ' (from *Interludes and Poems*) ; Messrs. George
Bell & Sons for Mr. Coventry Patmore's ' The
Toys ' ; Mr. Laurence Binyon and The Times Pub-
lishing Co. for ' For the Fallen ' ; Messrs. William
Blackwood & Sons for George Eliot's ' O may I
join the choir invisible ' ; to Mr. Edmund Blunden
and Messrs. Sidgwick & Jackson for ' Alms-

women'; Mr. Robert Bridges for 'Gird on thy Sword', 'I have loved Flowers that Fade', and 'Nightingales'; Messrs. Burns, Oates & Washbourne, for Alice Meynell's 'Veneration of Images' and 'Unto Us', and for Francis Thompson's 'In No Strange Land'; Messrs. Chatto & Windus for Arthur O'Shaughnessy's ode and R. L. Stevenson's 'In Memoriam F. A. S.'; Mr. G. K. Chesterton and Messrs. Methuen for 'Before the Roman came to Rye' (from *The Flying Inn*); Messrs. Constable & Co. and Messrs. Charles Scribner's Sons, New York, for the four sonnets from George Meredith's 'Modern Love'; Messrs. John Lane for John Davidson's 'In Romney Marsh' (from *Ballads and Songs*); Mr. W. H. Davies and Messrs. Jonathan Cape for 'Sweet Stay-at-Home' (from *Collected Poems*); Mr. Walter de la Mare for 'Arabia' and 'Trees'; Mr. Alban Dobson for Austin Dobson's 'A Ballad to Queen Elizabeth'; Mr. John Drinkwater and Messrs. Sidgwick & Jackson for 'The Town Window'; Messrs. Elkin Mathews & Marrot for Lionel Johnson's 'Cadgwith'; the executors of the late Mr. J. E. Flecker and Messrs. Martin Secker for 'The Golden Journey to Samarkand'; Mrs. Henley and Mr. Nutt for Mr. W. E. Henley's 'Out of the night that covers me'; the family of Gerard Manley Hopkins and the Oxford University Press for 'Pied Beauty' and 'The Starlight Night'; Mr. A. E. Housman and Messrs. Grant Richards for 'An Epitaph on an Army of Mercenaries' (from *Last Poems*); Mr. Rudyard Kipling and Messrs. Methuen for 'Recessional' (from *The Five Nations*), 'The Last Chantey' (from *The Seven Seas*), and 'The Coward' (from *The Years Between*); Mr. John Masefield and Messrs. Heinemann for 'Sea-Fever' (from *Collected Poems*); Sir Henry Newbolt for 'Drake's Drum' and Mary Coleridge's 'We were Young'; Mr. J. D. C. Pellow and the Oxford University Press for 'London Bridge'; Mr. Siegfried Sassoon and Messrs. William Heinemann for 'Everyone Sang';

Messrs. Sidgwick & Jackson for Rupert Brooke's 'The Soldier'; the late Mr. Watts-Dunton for the four poems by Swinburne; Mrs. Thomas for 'Adlestrop' by Edward Thomas; Mr. Charles Williams for 'After Ronsard'; Mr. W. B. Yeats and Messrs. Macmillan for 'The Folly of being Comforted' (from *Later Poems*); and Mr. W. B. Yeats and Messrs. Ernest Benn for 'The Lake Isle of Innisfree' (from *Poems*).

Additional thanks for other poems added in the latest edition are due to: Mr. W. H. Auden and Messrs. Faber & Faber for 'Out on the Lawn', 'Look, Stranger' and 'A Shilling Life'; Mr. George Barker and Messrs. Faber & Faber for 'The Seal Boy' and 'The Chimera'; Mr. T. S. Eliot and Messrs. Faber & Faber for 'Gerontion', 'Whispers of Immortality' and 'Animula'; Mr. William Empson and Messrs. Chatto & Windus for 'Description of a View' and 'Note on Local Flora'; Mr. Cecil Day Lewis and the Hogarth Press for 'The Flight' from *A Time to Dance*; Mr. Louis MacNeice and Messrs. Faber & Faber for 'Spring Voices' and 'Trapeze'; Mr. Wilfred Owen and Messrs. Chatto & Windus for 'Futility' and 'Strange Meeting'; Mr. Ezra Pound for 'Lament of the Frontier Guard' and 'Villanelle: The Psychological Hour'; Mr. John Crowe Ransom and Alfred A. Knopf Inc. for 'Necrological' and 'Captain Carpenter' from *Chills and Fevers*; Mr. Stephen Spender and Messrs. Faber & Faber for 'How Strangely this Sun' and 'New Year'; Mr. Dylan Thomas for 'When once the Twilight' and 'This Bread I Break'; Mrs. Yeats and Messrs. Macmillan for 'A Prayer for my son', 'The Hawk', 'Byzantium', 'The Delphic Oracle Upon Plotinus', 'Two Songs of a Fool, II', 'From the "Antigone"' (from *The Collected Poems of W. B. Yeats*).

THE GOLDEN TREASURY

BOOK FIRST

1

SPRING

Spring, the sweet Spring, is the year's pleasant
        king ;
Then blooms each thing, then maids dance in a ring,
Cold doth not sting, the pretty birds do sing,
    Cuckoo, jug-jug, pu-we, to-witta-woo !

The palm and may make country houses gay,   5
Lambs frisk and play, the shepherds pipe all day,
And we hear ay birds tune this merry lay,
    Cuckoo, jug-jug, pu-we, to-witta-woo !

The fields breathe sweet, the daisies kiss our feet,
Young lovers meet, old wives a-sunning sit,   10
In every street these tunes our ears do greet,
    Cuckoo, jug-jug, pu-we, to-witta-woo !
        Spring ! the sweet Spring !

                                    T. NASH.

2

SUMMONS TO LOVE

        Phoebus, arise !
        And paint the sable skies
        With azure, white, and red :
Rouse Memnon's mother from her Tithon's bed
That she thy càreer may with roses spread :   5
The nightingales thy coming each-where sing :

Make an eternal spring,
Give life to this dark world which lieth dead ;
Spread forth thy golden hair
In larger locks than thou wast wont before,   10
And emperor-like decore
With diadem of pearl thy temples fair :
Chase hence the ugly night
Which serves but to make dear thy glorious light.

—This is that happy morn,   15
That day, long-wishèd day
Of all my life so dark,
(If cruel stars have not my ruin sworn
And fates my hopes betray),
Which, purely white, deserves   20
An everlasting diamond should it mark.
This is the morn should bring unto this grove
My Love, to hear and recompense my love.
Fair King, who all preserves,
But show thy blushing beams,   25
And thou two sweeter eyes
Shalt see than those which by Peneüs' streams
Did once thy heart surprise.
Now, Flora, deck thyself in fairest guise :
If that ye, winds, would hear   30
A voice surpassing far Amphion's lyre,
Your furious chiding stay ;
Let Zephyr only breathe,
And with her tresses play.
—The winds all silent are,   35
And Phoebus in his chair
Ensaffroning sea and air
Makes vanish every star :
Night like a drunkard reels
Beyond the hills, to shun his flaming wheels :   40
The fields with flowers are deck'd in every hue,
The clouds with orient gold spangle their blue ;
Here is the pleasant place—
And nothing wanting is, save She, alas !

W. DRUMMOND OF HAWTHORNDEN.

3
TIME AND LOVE

I

When I have seen by Time's fell hand defaced
  The rich proud cost of out-worn buried age ;
When sometime lofty towers I see down-razed,
  And brass eternal slave to mortal rage ;

When I have seen the hungry ocean gain   5
  Advantage on the kingdom of the shore,
And the firm soil win of the watery main,
  Increasing store with loss, and loss with store ;

When I have seen such interchange of state,
  Or state itself confounded to decay,   10
Ruin hath taught me thus to ruminate—
  That Time will come and take my Love away :

—This thought is as a death, which cannot choose
But weep to have that which it fears to lose.

W. SHAKESPEARE.

4
II

Since brass, nor stone, nor earth, nor boundless sea,
  But sad mortality o'ersways their power,
How with this rage shall beauty hold a plea,
  Whose action is no stronger than a flower ?

O how shall summer's honey breath hold out   5
  Against the wreckful siege of battering days,
When rocks impregnable are not so stout
  Nor gates of steel so strong, but time decays ?

O fearful meditation ! where, alack !   9
  Shall Time's best jewel from Time's chest lie hid?
Or what strong hand can hold his swift foot back,
  Or who his spoil of beauty can forbid ?

O ! none, unless this miracle have might,
That in black ink my love may still shine bright.

W. SHAKESPEARE.

5

THE PASSIONATE SHEPHERD TO HIS LOVE

Come live with me and be my Love,
And we will all the pleasures prove
That hills and valleys, dale and field,
And all the craggy mountains yield.

There will we sit upon the rocks   5
And see the shepherds feed their flocks,
By shallow rivers, to whose falls
Melodious birds sing madrigals.

There will I make thee beds of roses
And a thousand fragrant posies,   10
A cap of flowers, and a kirtle
Embroider'd all with leaves of myrtle.

A gown made of the finest wool,
Which from our pretty lambs we pull,
Fair linéd slippers for the cold,   15
With buckles of the purest gold.

A belt of straw and ivy buds
With coral clasps and amber studs :
And if these pleasures may thee move,
Come live with me and be my Love.   20

Thy silver dishes for thy meat
As precious as the gods do eat,
Shall on an ivory table be
Prepared each day for thee and me.

The shepherd swains shall dance and sing   25
For thy delight each May-morning :
If these delights thy mind may move,
Then live with me and be my Love.

C. MARLOWE.

6

A MADRIGAL

Crabbed Age and Youth
Cannot live together :
   Youth is full of pleasance,
Age is full of care ;
   Youth like summer morn,   5
Age like winter weather,
   Youth like summer brave,
Age like winter bare :
   Youth is full of sport,
   Age's breath is short,   10
Youth is nimble, Age is lame :
   Youth is hot and bold,
   Age is weak and cold,
Youth is wild, and Age is tame :—
   Age, I do abhor thee,   15
   Youth, I do adore thee ;
O ! my Love, my Love is young !
   Age, I do defy thee—
   O sweet shepherd, hie thee,
For methinks thou stay'st too long.   20

         W. SHAKESPEARE.

7

Under the greenwood tree
Who loves to lie with me,
And turn his merry note
Unto the sweet bird's throat—
Come hither, come hither, come hither !   5
     Here shall he see
     No enemy
But winter and rough weather.

Who doth ambition shun
And loves to live i' the sun,   10

Seeking the food he eats
    And pleased with what he gets—
Come hither, come hither, come hither !
        Here shall he see
        No enemy   15
But winter and rough weather.

                            W. SHAKESPEARE.

8

It was a lover and his lass
    With a hey and a ho, and a hey-nonino !
That o'er the green cornfield did pass
In the spring time, the only pretty ring time,
When birds do sing hey ding a ding ding :   5
    Sweet lovers love the Spring.

Between the acres of the rye
These pretty country folks would lie :

This carol they began that hour,
How that a life was but a flower :   10

And therefore take the present time
    With a hey and a ho, and a hey-nonino !
For love is crownéd with the prime
In spring time, the only pretty ring time,
When birds do sing hey ding a ding ding :
    Sweet lovers love the Spring.   16

                            W. SHAKESPEARE.

9

PRESENT IN ABSENCE

Absence, hear thou my protestation
    Against thy strength,
    Distance, and length ;
Do what thou canst for alteration :

For hearts of truest mettle   5
Absence doth join, and Time doth settle.

Who loves a mistress of such quality,
    He soon hath found
    Affection's ground
Beyond time, place, and all mortality.   10
    To hearts that cannot vary
    Absence is Present, Time doth tarry.

By absence this good means I gain,
    That I can catch her,
    Where none can watch her,   15
In some close corner of my brain :
    There I embrace and kiss her ;
    And so I both enjoy and miss her.

                                    ANON.

10

ABSENCE

Being your slave, what should I do but tend
    Upon the hours and times of your desire ?
I have no precious time at all to spend
    Nor services to do, till you require :

Nor dare I chide the world-without-end hour   5
    Whilst I, my sovereign, watch the clock for you,
Nor think the bitterness of absence sour
    When you have bid your servant once adieu :

Nor dare I question with my jealous thought
    Where you may be, or your affairs suppose,   10
But like a sad slave, stay and think of nought
    Save, where you are, how happy you make
        those ;—

So true a fool is love, that in your will,
Though you do anything, he thinks no ill.

                            W SHAKESPEARE.

11

How like a winter hath my absence been
　　From Thee, the pleasure of the fleeting year !
What freezings have I felt, what dark days seen,
　　What old December's bareness everywhere !

And yet this time removed was summer's time ;　5
　　The teeming autumn, big with rich increase,
Bearing the wanton burden of the prime
　　Like widow'd wombs after their lords' decease :

Yet this abundant issue seem'd to me
　　But hope of orphans, and unfather'd fruit ;　10
For summer and his pleasures wait on thee,
　　And, thou away, the very birds are mute ;

Or if they sing, 'tis with so dull a cheer,
That leaves look pale, dreading the winter's near.
　　　　　　　　　　　　W. SHAKESPEARE.

12

A CONSOLATION

When in disgrace with fortune and men's eyes
　　I all alone beweep my outcast state,
And trouble deaf heaven with my bootless cries,
　　And look upon myself, and curse my fate ;

Wishing me like to one more rich in hope,　5
　　Featured like him, like him with friends possest,
Desiring this man's art, and that man's scope,
　　With what I most enjoy contented least ;

Yet in these thoughts myself almost despising,
　　Haply I think on Thee—and then my state,　10
Like to the lark at break of day arising
　　From sullen earth, sings hymns at heaven's gate ;

For thy sweet love remember'd such wealth brings,
That then I scorn to change my state with kings.
　　　　　　　　　　　　W. SHAKESPEARE.

13
THE UNCHANGEABLE

O never say that I was false of heart,
　　Though absence seem'd my flame to qualify :
As easy might I from myself depart
　　As from my soul, which in thy breast doth lie ;

That is my home of love ; if I have ranged, 5
　　Like him that travels, I return again,
Just to the time, not with the time exchanged,
　　So that myself bring water for my stain.

Never believe, though in my nature reign'd
　　All frailties that besiege all kinds of blood, 10
That it could so preposterously be stain'd
　　To leave for nothing all thy sum of good :

For nothing this wide universe I call,
Save thou, my rose : in it thou art my all.
　　　　　　　　　　　W. SHAKESPEARE.

14

To me, fair Friend, you never can be old,
　　For as you were when first your eye I eyed
Such seems your beauty still. Three winters cold
　　Have from the forests shook three summers'
　　　pride ;

Three beauteous springs to yellow autumn turn'd 5
　　In process of the seasons have I seen,
Three April perfumes in three hot Junes burn'd,
　　Since first I saw you fresh, which yet are green.

Ah ! yet doth beauty, like a dial-hand,
　　Steal from his figure, and no pace perceived ; 10
So your sweet hue, which methinks still doth stand,
　　Hath motion, and mine eye may be deceived :

For fear of which, hear this, thou age unbred,—
Ere you were born, was beauty's summer dead.
　　　　　　　　　　　W. SHAKESPEARE.

15

DIAPHENIA

Diaphenia like the daffadowndilly,
White as the sun, fair as the lily,
Heigh ho, how I do love thee !
   I do love thee as my lambs
   Are belovéd of their dams ;   5
How blest were I if thou would'st prove me.

Diaphenia like the spreading roses,
That in thy sweets all sweets encloses,
Fair sweet, how I do love thee !
   I do love thee as each flower   10
   Loves the sun's life-giving power ;
For dead, thy breath to life might move me.

Diaphenia like to all things blesséd
When all thy praises are expresséd,
Dear joy, how I do love thee !   15
   As the birds do love the spring,
   Or the bees their careful king :
Then in requite, sweet virgin, love me !

H. CONSTABLE.

16

ROSALYNDE

Like to the clear in highest sphere
Where all imperial glory shines,
Of selfsame colour is her hair
   Whether unfolded, or in twines :
      Heigh ho, fair Rosalynde !   5
Her eyes are sapphires set in snow,
   Resembling heaven by every wink ;
The Gods do fear whenas they glow,
   And I do tremble when I think
      Heigh ho, would she were mine !   10

Her cheeks are like the blushing cloud
  That beautifies Aurora's face,
Or like the silver crimson shroud
  That Phoebus' smiling looks doth grace ;
      Heigh ho, fair Rosalynde !   15
Her lips are like two budded roses
  Whom ranks of lilies neighbour nigh,
Within which bounds she balm encloses
  Apt to entice a deity :
      Heigh ho, would she were mine !   20

Her neck is like a stately tower
  Where Love himself imprison'd lies,
To watch for glances every hour
  From her divine and sacred eyes :
      Heigh ho, for Rosalynde !   25
Her paps are centres of delight,
  Her breasts are orbs of heavenly frame,
Where Nature moulds the dew of light
  To feed perfection with the same :
      Heigh ho, would she were mine !   30

With orient pearl, with ruby red,
  With marble white, with sapphire blue
Her body every way is fed,
  Yet soft in touch and sweet in view :
      Heigh ho, fair Rosalynde !   35
Nature herself her shape admires ;
  The Gods are wounded in her sight ;
And Love forsakes his heavenly fires
  And at her eyes his brand doth light :
      Heigh ho, would she were mine ! 40

Then muse not, Nymphs, though I bemoan
  The absence of fair Rosalynde,
Since for a fair there's fairer none,
  Nor for her virtues so divine :
      Heigh ho, fair Rosalynde ;   45
Heigh ho, my heart ! would God that she were
mine !
                T. LODGE.

17

COLIN

Beauty sat bathing by a spring
  Where fairest shades did hide her ;
The winds blew calm, the birds did sing,
  The cool streams ran beside her.
My wanton thoughts enticed mine eye   5
  To see what was forbidden :
But better memory said, fie !
    So vain desire was chidden :—
        Hey nonny nonny O !
        Hey nonny nonny !   10

Into a slumber then I fell,
  When fond imagination
Seem'd to see, but could not tell
  Her feature or her fashion.
But ev'n as babes in dreams do smile,   15
  And sometimes fall a-weeping,
So I awaked, as wise this while
  As when I fell a-sleeping :—
        Hey nonny nonny O !
        Hey nonny nonny !   20
           THE SHEPHERD TONY.

18

TO HIS LOVE

Shall I compare thee to a summer's day ?
  Thou art more lovely and more temperate :
Rough winds do shake the darling buds of May,
  And summer's lease hath all too short a date :

Sometime too hot the eye of heaven shines,   5
  And often is his gold complexion dimm'd :
And every fair from fair sometime declines,
    By chance, or nature's changing course, un-
      trimm'd.

But thy eternal summer shall not fade
  Nor lose possession of that fair thou owest ; 10
Nor shall death brag thou wanderest in his shade,
  When in eternal lines to time thou growest :

So long as men can breathe, or eyes can see,
So long lives this, and this gives life to thee.

                    W. SHAKESPEARE.

19

TO HIS LOVE

When in the chronicle of wasted time
  I see descriptions of the fairest wights,
And beauty making beautiful old rhyme
  In praise of ladies dead, and lovely knights ;

Then in the blazon of sweet beauty's best   5
  Of hand, of foot, of lip, of eye, of brow,
I see their antique pen would have exprest
  Ev'n such a beauty as you master now.

So all their praises are but prophecies
  Of this our time, all you prefiguring ;   10
And, for they look'd but with divining eyes,
  They had not skill enough your worth to sing :

For we, which now behold these present days,
Have eyes to wonder but lack tongues to praise.

                    W. SHAKESPEARE.

20

LOVE'S PERJURIES

    On a day, alack the day !
    Love, whose month is ever May,
    Spied a blossom passing fair
    Playing in the wanton air :
    Through the velvet leaves the wind,   5
    All unseen, 'gan passage find ;

That the lover, sick to death,
Wish'd himself the heaven's breath.
Air, quoth he, thy cheeks may blow ;
Air, would I might triumph so !   10
But, alack, my hand is sworn
Ne'er to pluck thee from thy thorn :
Vow, alack, for youth unmeet ;
Youth so apt to pluck a sweet.
Do not call it sin in me   15
That I am forsworn for thee :
Thou for whom Jove would swear
Juno but an Ethiope were,
And deny himself for Jove,
Turning mortal for thy love.   20

W. SHAKESPEARE.

21

A SUPPLICATION

Forget not yet the tried intent
Of such a truth as I have meant ;
My great travail so gladly spent,
    Forget not yet !

Forget not yet when first began   5
The weary life ye know, since whan
The suit, the service none tell can ;
    Forget not yet !

Forget not yet the great assays,
The cruel wrong, the scornful ways,   10
The painful patience in delays,
    Forget not yet !

Forget not ! O, forget not this,
How long ago hath been, and is
The mind that never meant amiss—   15
    Forget not yet !

Forget not then thine own approved
The which so long hath thee so loved,
Whose steadfast faith yet never moved—
                    Forget not this !   20
                SIR T. WYATT.

22

TO AURORA

O if thou knew'st how thou thyself dost harm,
   And dost prejudge thy bliss, and spoil my rest ;
   Then thou would'st melt the ice out of thy breast
And thy relenting heart would kindly warm.

O if thy pride did not our joys controul,   5
   What world of loving wonders should'st thou see!
   For if I saw thee once transform'd in me,
Then in thy bosom I would pour my soul ;

Then all my thoughts should in thy visage shine,
   And if that aught mischanced thou should'st not
     moan   10
   Nor bear the burthen of thy griefs alone ;
No, I would have my share in what were thine :

And whilst we thus should make our sorrows one,
This happy harmony would make them none.

    W. ALEXANDER, EARL OF STERLINE.

23

TRUE LOVE

Let me not to the marriage of true minds
   Admit impediments. Love is not love
Which alters when it alteration finds,
   Or bends with the remover to remove :—

O no ! it is an ever-fixéd mark   5
   That looks on tempests, and is never shaken ;
It is the star to every wandering bark,
   Whose worth's unknown, although his height be
    taken.

Love's not Time's fool, though rosy lips and cheeks
　　Within his bending sickle's compass come ;　　10
Love alters not with his brief hours and weeks,
　　But bears it out ev'n to the edge of doom :—

If this be error, and upon me proved,
I never writ, nor no man ever loved.

　　　　　　　　　　　W. SHAKESPEARE.

24

A DITTY

My true-love hath my heart, and I have his,
　　By just exchange one for another given :
I hold his dear, and mine he cannot miss,
　　There never was a better bargain driven :
　　　My true-love hath my heart, and I have his.　5

His heart in me keeps him and me in one,
　　My heart in him his thoughts and senses guides :
He loves my heart, for once it was his own,
　　I cherish his because in me it bides :
　　　My true-love hath my heart, and I have his.　10

　　　　　　　　　　　SIR P. SIDNEY.

25

LOVE'S OMNIPRESENCE

Were I as base as is the lowly plain,
　　And you, my Love, as high as heaven above,
Yet should the thoughts of me your humble swain
　　Ascend to heaven, in honour of my Love.

Were I as high as heaven above the plain,　　5
　　And you, my Love, as humble and as low
As are the deepest bottoms of the main,
　　Wheresoe'er you were, with you my love should go.

Were you the earth, dear Love, and I the skies,
  My love should shine on you like to the sun,   10
And look upon you with ten thousand eyes
  Till heaven wax'd blind, and till the world were
     done.

Wheresoe'er I am, below, or else above you,
Wheresoe'er you are, my heart shall truly love you.
J. SYLVESTER.

26

CARPE DIEM

O Mistress mine, where are you roaming?
O stay and hear! your true-love's coming
  That can sing both high and low;
Trip no further, pretty sweeting,
Journeys end in lovers' meeting—   5
  Every wise man's son doth know.

What is love? 'tis not hereafter;
Present mirth hath present laughter;
  What's to come is still unsure:
In delay there lies no plenty,—   10
Then come kiss me, Sweet-and-twenty,
  Youth's a stuff will not endure.
W. SHAKESPEARE.

27

WINTER

When icicles hang by the wall
  And Dick the shepherd blows his nail,
And Tom bears logs into the hall,
  And milk comes frozen home in pail;
When blood is nipt, and ways be foul,   5
Then nightly sings the staring owl
     Tuwhoo!
Tuwhit! tuwhoo! A merry note!
While greasy Joan doth keel the pot.

When all aloud the wind doth blow,   10
   And coughing drowns the parson's saw,
And birds sit brooding in the snow,
   And Marian's nose looks red and raw ;
When roasted crabs hiss in the bowl—
Then nightly sings the staring owl   15
      Tuwhoo !
Tuwhit ! tuwhoo ! A merry note !
While greasy Joan doth keel the pot.

              W. SHAKESPEARE.

28

That time of year thou may'st in me behold
   When yellow leaves, or none, or few, do hang
Upon those boughs which shake against the cold,
   Bare ruin'd choirs, where late the sweet birds
     sang.

In me thou see'st the twilight of such day   5
   As after sunset fadeth in the west,
Which by and by black night doth take away,
   Death's second self, that seals up all in rest.

In me thou see'st the glowing of such fire,
   That on the ashes of his youth doth lie   10
As the death-bed whereon it must expire,
   Consumed with that which it was nourish'd by :

—This thou perceiv'st, which makes thy love more
    strong,
To love that well which thou must leave ere long.

              W. SHAKESPEARE.

29

REMEMBRANCE

When to the sessions of sweet silent thought
   I summon up remembrance of things past,
I sigh the lack of many a thing I sought,
   And with old woes new wail my dear time's
    waste ;

Then can I drown an eye, unused to flow,   5
  For precious friends hid in death's dateless night,
And weep afresh love's long-since-cancell'd woe,
  And moan the expense of many a vanish'd sight.

Then can I grieve at grievances foregone,
  And heavily from woe to woe tell o'er   10
The sad account of fore-bemoanéd moan,
  Which I new pay as if not paid before :

—But if the while I think on thee, dear friend,
All losses are restored, and sorrows end.

                    W. SHAKESPEARE.

30

REVOLUTIONS

Like as the waves make towards the pebbled shore,
  So do our minutes hasten to their end ;
Each changing place with that which goes before,
  In sequent toil all forwards do contend.

Nativity, once in the main of light,   5
  Crawls to maturity, wherewith being crown'd,
Crooked eclipses 'gainst his glory fight,
  And Time that gave doth now his gift confound.

Time doth transfix the flourish set on youth,
  And delves the parallels in beauty's brow ;   10
Feeds on the rarities of nature's truth,
  And nothing stands but for his scythe to mow :

And yet, to times in hope, my verse shall stand
Praising thy worth, despite his cruel hand.

                    W. SHAKESPEARE.

31

Farewell ! thou art too dear for my possessing,
  And like enough thou know'st thy estimate ;
The charter of thy worth gives thee releasing ;
  My bonds in thee are all determinate.

For how do I hold thee but by thy granting ?   5
    And for that riches where is my deserving ?
The cause of this fair gift in me is wanting,
    And so my patent back again is swerving.

Thyself thou gav'st, thy own worth then not
        knowing,   9
    Or me, to whom thou gav'st it, else mistaking ;
So thy great gift, upon misprision growing,
    Comes home again, on better judgement making.

Thus have I had thee as a dream doth flatter ;
In sleep, a king ; but waking, no such matter.
                  W. SHAKESPEARE.

32

THE LIFE WITHOUT PASSION

They that have power to hurt, and will do none,
    That do not do the thing they most do show,
Who, moving others, are themselves as stone,
    Unmovéd, cold, and to temptation slow,—

They rightly do inherit Heaven's graces,   5
    And husband nature's riches from expense ;
They are the lords and owners of their faces,
    Others, but stewards of their excellence.

The summer's flower is to the summer sweet,
    Though to itself it only live and die ;   10
But if that flower with base infection meet,
    The basest weed outbraves his dignity :

For sweetest things turn sourest by their deeds ;
Lilies that fester smell far worse than weeds.
                  W. SHAKESPEARE.

33

THE LOVER'S APPEAL

And wilt thou leave me thus ?
  Say nay ! say nay ! for shame !
  To save thee from the blame
  Of all my grief and grame.
And wilt thou leave me thus ?   5
  Say nay ! say nay !

And wilt thou leave me thus,
  That hath loved thee so long
  In wealth and woe among ?
  And is thy heart so strong   10
As for to leave me thus ?
  Say nay ! say nay !

And wilt thou leave me thus,
  That hath given thee my heart
  Never for to depart   15
  Neither for pain nor smart ?
And wilt thou leave me thus ?
  Say nay ! say nay !

And wilt thou leave me thus,
  And have no more pity   20
  Of him that loveth thee ?
  Alas ! thy cruelty !
And wilt thou leave me thus ?
  Say nay ! say nay !

Sir T. Wyatt.

34

THE NIGHTINGALE

As it fell upon a day
In the merry month of May,
Sitting in a pleasant shade
Which a grove of myrtles made,

Beasts did leap and birds did sing,   5
Trees did grow and plants did spring,
Every thing did banish moan
Save the Nightingale alone.
She, poor bird, as all forlorn,
Lean'd her breast up-till a thorn,   10
And there sung the dolefull'st ditty
That to hear it was great pity.
Fie, fie, fie, now would she cry ;
Tereu, tereu, by and by :
That to hear her so complain   15
Scarce I could from tears refrain ;
For her griefs so lively shown
Made me think upon mine own.
—Ah, thought I, thou mourn'st in vain,
None takes pity on thy pain :   20
Senseless trees, they cannot hear thee,
Ruthless beasts, they will not cheer thee ;
King Pandion, he is dead,
All thy friends are lapp'd in lead :
All thy fellow birds do sing   25
Careless of thy sorrowing :
Even so, poor bird, like thee
None alive will pity me.

                           R. BARNFIELD.

35

Care-charmer Sleep, son of the sable Night,
  Brother to Death, in silent darkness born,
Relieve my languish, and restore the light ;
  With dark forgetting of my care return.

  And let the day be time enough to mourn   5
The shipwreck of my ill-adventured youth :
  Let waking eyes suffice to wail their scorn,
Without the torment of the night's untruth.

Cease, dreams, the images of day-desires,   9
  To model forth the passions of the morrow ;

Never let rising Sun approve you liars
  To add more grief to aggravate my sorrow:
Still let me sleep, embracing clouds in vain,
And never wake to feel the day's disdain.

S. DANIEL.

36
MADRIGAL

Take, O take those lips away
  That so sweetly were forsworn,
And those eyes, the break of day,
  Lights that do mislead the morn:
But my kisses bring again,   5
      Bring again—
Seals of love, but seal'd in vain,
      Seal'd in vain!

W. SHAKESPEARE.

37
LOVE'S FAREWELL

Since there's no help, come let us kiss and part,—
  Nay I have done, you get no more of me;
And I am glad, yea, glad with all my heart,
  That thus so cleanly I myself can free;

Shake hands for ever, cancel all our vows,   5
  And when we meet at any time again,
Be it not seen in either of our brows
  That we one jot of former love retain.

Now at the last gasp of love's latest breath,
  When, his pulse failing, passion speechless lies, 10
When faith is kneeling by his bed of death,
  And innocence is closing up his eyes,

—Now if thou would'st, when all have given him
    over,
From death to life thou might'st him yet recover!

M. DRAYTON.

38

TO HIS LUTE

My lute, be as thou wert when thou didst grow
  With thy green mother in some shady grove,
  When immelodious winds but made thee move,
And birds their ramage did on thee bestow.

  Since that dear Voice which did thy sounds
    approve,   5
Which wont in such harmonious strains to flow,
  Is reft from Earth to tune those spheres above,
What art thou but a harbinger of woe?

Thy pleasing notes be pleasing notes no more,
  But orphans' wailings to the fainting ear;   10
  Each stroke a sigh, each sound draws forth a
    tear;
For which be silent as in woods before:

Or if that any hand to touch thee deign,
Like widow'd turtle still her loss complain.

W. DRUMMOND.

39

BLIND LOVE

O me! what eyes hath love put in my head
  Which have no correspondence with true sight:
Or if they have, where is my judgement fled
  That censures falsely what they see aright?

If that be fair whereon my false eyes dote,   5
  What means the world to say it is not so?
If it be not, then love doth well denote
  Love's eye is not so true as all men's: No,

How can it? O how can love's eye be true,   9
  That is so vex'd with watching and with tears?
No marvel then though I mistake my view:
  The sun itself sees not till heaven clears.

O cunning Love! with tears thou keep'st me blind,
Lest eyes well-seeing thy foul faults should find!

W. SHAKESPEARE.

40

THE UNFAITHFUL SHEPHERDESS

While that the sun with his beams hot
  Scorchéd the fruits in vale and mountain,
Philon the shepherd, late forgot,
    Sitting beside a crystal fountain,
      In shadow of a green oak tree   5
      Upon his pipe this song play'd he :
Adieu Love, adieu Love, untrue Love,
Untrue Love, untrue Love, adieu Love ;
Your mind is light, soon lost for new love.

So long as I was in your sight   10
  I was your heart, your soul, and treasure ;
And evermore you sobb'd and sigh'd
    Burning in flames beyond all measure :
      —Three days endured your love to me,
      And it was lost in other three !   15
Adieu Love, adieu Love, untrue Love,
Untrue Love, untrue Love, adieu Love ;
Your mind is light, soon lost for new love.

Another Shepherd you did see
  To whom your heart was soon enchainéd ;
Full soon your love was leapt from me,   21
    Full soon my place he had obtainéd.
      Soon came a third, your love to win,
      And we were out and he was in.
Adieu Love, adieu Love, untrue Love,   25
Untrue Love, untrue Love, adieu Love ;
Your mind is light, soon lost for new love.

Sure you have made me passing glad
  That you your mind so soon removéd,
Before that I the leisure had   30
    To choose you for my best belovéd :

For all your love was past and done
   Two days before it was begun :—
Adieu Love, adieu Love, untrue Love,
Untrue Love, untrue Love, adieu Love ;   35
Your mind is light, soon lost for new love.

ANON.

41

A RENUNCIATION

If women could be fair, and yet not fond,
   Or that their love were firm, not fickle still,
I would not marvel that they make men bond
   By service long to purchase their good will ;
But when I see how frail those creatures are,   5
I muse that men forget themselves so far.

To mark the choice they make, and how they change,
   How oft from Phoebus they do flee to Pan ;
Unsettled still, like haggards wild they range,
   These gentle birds that fly from man to man ;   10
Who would not scorn and shake them from the fist,
And let them fly, fair fools, which way they list ?

Yet for disport we fawn and flatter both,
   To pass the time when nothing else can please,
And train them to our lure with subtle oath,   15
   Till, weary of their wiles, ourselves we ease ;
And then we say when we their fancy try,
To play with fools, O what a fool was I !

E. VERE, EARL OF OXFORD.

42

Blow, blow, thou winter wind,
   Thou art not so unkind
      As man's ingratitude ;
Thy tooth is not so keen
Because thou art not seen,   5
   Although thy breath be rude.

Heigh ho ! sing heigh ho ! unto the green holly :
Most friendship is feigning, most loving mere folly :
  Then, heigh ho ! the holly !
  This life is most jolly.   10

  Freeze, freeze, thou bitter sky,
  That dost not bite so nigh
   As benefits forgot :
  Though thou the waters warp,
  Thy sting is not so sharp   15
   As friend remember'd not.
Heigh ho ! sing heigh ho ! unto the green holly :
Most friendship is feigning, most loving mere folly :
  Then, heigh ho ! the holly !
  This life is most jolly.   20

      W. SHAKESPEARE.

43

MADRIGAL

My thoughts hold mortal strife
I do detest my life,
And with lamenting cries,
Peace to my soul to bring,
Oft call that prince which here doth monarchize : 5
—But he, grim grinning King,
Who caitiffs scorns, and doth the blest surprise,
Late having deck'd with beauty's rose his tomb,
Disdains to crop a weed, and will not come.

      W. DRUMMOND.

44

DIRGE OF LOVE

Come away, come away, Death,
And in sad cypres let me be laid ;
Fly away, fly away, breath ;
I am slain by a fair cruel maid.

My shroud of white, stuck all with yew,   5
    O prepare it !
My part of death, no one so true
    Did share it.

Not a flower, not a flower sweet
On my black coffin let there be strown ;   10
    Not a friend, not a friend greet
My poor corpse, where my bones shall be thrown :
A thousand thousand sighs to save,
    Lay me, O where
Sad true lover never find my grave,   15
    To weep there.
                 W. SHAKESPEARE.

45

FIDELE

Fear no more the heat o' the sun
    Nor the furious winter's rages ;
Thou thy worldly task hast done,
    Home art gone and ta'en thy wages :
Golden lads and girls all must,   5
As chimney-sweepers, come to dust.

Fear no more the frown o' the great,
    Thou art past the tyrant's stroke ;
Care no more to clothe and eat ;
    To thee the reed is as the oak :   10
The sceptre, learning, physic, must
All follow this, and come to dust.

Fear no more the lightning-flash
    Nor the all-dreaded thunder-stone ;
Fear not slander, censure rash ;   15
    Thou hast finish'd joy and moan :
All lovers young, all lovers must
Consign to thee, and come to dust.
                 W. SHAKESPEARE.

46

A SEA DIRGE

Full fathom five thy father lies :
 Of his bones are coral made ;
Those are pearls that were his eyes :
 Nothing of him that doth fade
But doth suffer a sea-change   5
Into something rich and strange.
Sea-nymphs hourly ring his knell :
Hark ! now I hear them,—
  Ding, dong, bell.

W. SHAKESPEARE.

47

A LAND DIRGE

Call for the robin-redbreast and the wren,
 Since o'er shady groves they hover
 And with leaves and flowers do cover
The friendless bodies of unburied men.
 Call unto his funeral dole   5
 The ant, the field-mouse, and the mole,
To rear him hillocks that shall keep him warm
And (when gay tombs are robb'd) sustain no harm ;
But keep the wolf far thence, that's foe to men,
For with his nails he'll dig them up again.   10

J. WEBSTER.

48

POST MORTEM

If thou survive my well-contented day
 When that churl Death my bones with dust shall
  cover,
And shalt by fortune once more re-survey
 These poor rude lines of thy deceasèd lover ;

Compare them with the bettering of the time,   5
  And though they be outstripp'd by every pen,
Reserve them for my love, not for their rhyme
  Exceeded by the height of happier men.

O then vouchsafe me but this loving thought—
  ' Had my friend's muse grown with this growing
    age,   10
A dearer birth than this his love had brought,
  To march in ranks of better equipage :

But since he died, and poets better prove,
Theirs for their style I'll read, his for his love.'

W. SHAKESPEARE.

49

THE TRIUMPH OF DEATH

No longer mourn for me when I am dead
  Than you shall hear the surly sullen bell
Give warning to the world, that I am fled
  From this vile world, with vilest worms to dwell ;

Nay, if you read this line, remember not   5
  The hand that writ it ; for I love you so,
That I in your sweet thoughts would be forgot
  If thinking on me then should make you woe.

O if, I say, you look upon this verse
  When I perhaps compounded am with clay,   10
Do not so much as my poor name rehearse,
  But let your love even with my life decay ;

Lest the wise world should look into your moan,
And mock you with me after I am gone.

W. SHAKESPEARE.

50

MADRIGAL

  Tell me where is Fancy bred,
  Or in the heart, or in the head ?
  How begot, how nourishéd ?
    Reply, reply.

It is engender'd in the eyes,　　　　　　5
With gazing fed ; and Fancy dies
In the cradle where it lies :
　　Let us all ring Fancy's knell ;
　　I'll begin it,—Ding, dong, bell.
　　　　—Ding, dong, bell.　　　　　10
　　　　　　　　　W. SHAKESPEARE.

51

CUPID AND CAMPASPE

Cupid and my Campaspe play'd
At cards for kisses ; Cupid paid :
He stakes his quiver, bow, and arrows,
His mother's doves, and team of sparrows ;
Loses them too ; then down he throws　　5
The coral of his lip, the rose
Growing on 's cheek (but none knows how) ;
With these, the crystal of his brow,
And then the dimple of his chin ;
All these did my Campaspe win :　　　　10
At last he set her both his eyes—
She won, and Cupid blind did rise.
　　O Love ! has she done this to thee ?
　　What shall, alas ! become of me ?
　　　　　　　　　J. LYLY.

52

Pack, clouds, away, and welcome day,
　　With night we banish sorrow ;
Sweet air blow soft, mount lark aloft
　　To give my Love good-morrow !
Wings from the wind to please her mind　　5
　　Notes from the lark I'll borrow ;
Bird prune thy wing, nightingale sing,
　　To give my Love good-morrow ;
　　　　To give my Love good-morrow
　　　　Notes from them all I'll borrow.　　10

Wake from thy nest, Robin-red-breast,
　　Sing birds in every furrow ;
And from each bill, let music shrill
　　Give my fair Love good-morrow !
Blackbird and thrush in every bush,　　　　　　15
　　Stare, linnet, and cock-sparrow,
You pretty elves, amongst yourselves
　　Sing my fair Love good-morrow !
　　　　To give my Love good-morrow
　　　　Sing birds in every furrow !　　　　　20

　　　　　　　　　　　　　　　T. HEYWOOD.

53

PROTHALAMION

Calm was the day, and through the trembling air
　　Sweet-breathing Zephyrus did softly play—
　　A gentle spirit, that lightly did delay
Hot Titan's beams, which then did glister fair ;
　　When I (whom sullen care,　　　　　　5
Through discontent of my long fruitless stay
　　In princes' court, and expectation vain
Of idle hopes, which still do fly away
　　Like empty shadows, did afflict my brain)
　　　Walk'd forth to ease my pain　　　　　10
Along the shore of silver-streaming Thames ;
Whose rutty bank, the which his river hems,
　　Was painted all with variable flowers,
And all the meads adorn'd with dainty gems
　　　Fit to deck maidens' bowers,　　　　　15
　　　And crown their paramours
Against the bridal day, which is not long :
Sweet Thames ! run softly, till I end my song.

There in a meadow by the river's side
　　A flock of nymphs I chancéd to espy,　　　　20
　　All lovely daughters of the flood thereby,
With goodly greenish locks all loose untied
　　　As each had been a bride ;

And each one had a little wicker basket
　　Made of fine twigs, entrailéd curiously,　25
In which they gather'd flowers to fill their flasket,
　　And with fine fingers cropt full feateously
　　　　The tender stalks on high.
Of every sort which in that meadow grew
They gather'd some ;　the violet, pallid blue,　30
　　The little daisy that at evening closes,
The virgin lily and the primrose true,
　　　　With store of vermeil roses,
　　　　To deck their bridegrooms' posies
Against the bridal day, which was not long :　35
Sweet Thames ! run softly, till I end my song.

With that I saw two swans of goodly hue
　　Come softly swimming down along the lee ;
　　Two fairer birds I yet did never see ;
The snow which doth the top of Pindus strow　40
　　　　Did never whiter show,
Nor Jove himself, when he a swan would be
　　For love of Leda, whiter did appear ;
Yet Leda was (they say) as white as he,　44
　　Yet not so white as these, nor nothing near ;
　　　　So purely white they were,
That even the gentle stream, the which them bare,
Seem'd foul to them, and bade his billows spare
　　To wet their silken feathers, lest they might
Soil their fair plumes with water not so fair,　50
　　　　And mar their beauties bright,
　　　　That shone as Heaven's light
Against their bridal day, which was not long :
Sweet Thames ! run softly, till I end my song.

Eftsoons the nymphs, which now had flowers their fill,
　　Ran all in haste to see that silver brood　56
　　As they came floating on the crystal flood ;
Whom when they saw, they stood amazéd still
　　Their wondering eyes to fill ;
Them seem'd they never saw a sight so fair　60
　　Of fowls, so lovely, that they sure did deem
Them heavenly born, or to be that same pair

Which through the sky draw Venus' silver team ;
  For sure they did not seem
To be begot of any earthly seed, 65
But rather angels, or of angels' breed ;
  Yet were they bred of summer's heat, they say,
In sweetest season, when each flower and weed
    The earth did fresh array ;
    So fresh they seem'd as day, 70
Even as their bridal day, which was not long :
Sweet Thames ! run softly, till I end my song.

Then forth they all out of their baskets drew
  Great store of flowers, the honour of the field,
  That to the sense did fragrant odours yield, 75
All which upon those goodly birds they threw
    And all the waves did strew,
That like old Peneus' waters they did seem
  When down along by pleasant Tempe's shore
Scatter'd with flowers, through Thessaly they
    stream, 80
  That they appear, through lilies' plenteous store,
    Like a bride's chamber-floor.
Two of those nymphs meanwhile two garlands bound
Of freshest flowers which in that mead they found,
  The which presenting all in trim array, 85
Their snowy foreheads therewithal they crown'd ;
    Whilst one did sing this lay
    Prepared against that day,
Against their bridal day, which was not long :
Sweet Thames ! run softly, till I end my song. 90

' Ye gentle birds ! the world's fair ornament,
  And Heaven's glory, whom this happy hour
  Doth lead unto your lovers' blissful bower,
Joy may you have, and gentle heart's content
    Of your love's couplement ; 95
And let fair Venus, that is queen of love,
  With her heart-quelling son upon you smile,
Whose smile, they say, hath virtue to remove
  All love's dislike, and friendship's faulty guile
    For ever to assoil. 100

Let endless peace your steadfast hearts accord,
And blessed plenty wait upon your board ;
   And let your bed with pleasures chaste abound,
That fruitful issue may to you afford
      Which may your foes confound,   105
      And make your joys redound
Upon your bridal day, which is not long :
Sweet Thames ! run softly, till I end my song.'

So ended she ; and all the rest around
   To her redoubled that her undersong,   110
   Which said their bridal day should not be long :
And gentle Echo from the neighbour ground
   Their accents did resound.
So forth those joyous birds did pass along   114
   Adown the lee that to them murmur'd low,
As he would speak but that he lack'd a tongue,
   Yet did by signs his glad affection show,
      Making his stream run slow.
And all the fowl which in his flood did dwell
'Gan flock about these twain, that did excel   120
   The rest, so far as Cynthia doth shend
The lesser stars. So they, enrangéd well,
      Did on those two attend,
      And their best service lend   124
Against their wedding day, which was not long :
Sweet Thames ! run softly, till I end my song.

At length they all to merry London came,
   To merry London, my most kindly nurse,
   That to me gave this life's first native source,
Though from another place I take my name,   130
      An house of ancient fame :
There when they came whereas those bricky towers
   The which on Thames' broad aged back do ride,
Where now the studious lawyers have their bowers,
   There whilome wont the Templar-knights to
      bide,   135
      Till they decay'd through pride ;
Next whereunto there stands a stately place,
Where oft I gainéd gifts and goodly grace

Of that great lord, which therein wont to dwell,
Whose want too well now feels my friendless case ;
    But ah ! here fits not well   141
    Old woes, but joys, to tell
Against the bridal day, which is not long :
Sweet Thames ! run softly, till I end my song.

Yet therein now doth lodge a noble peer,   145
    Great England's glory and the world's wide
        wonder,
  Whose dreadful name late through all Spain did
        thunder,
And Hercules' two pillars standing near
    Did make to quake and fear :
Fair branch of honour, flower of chivalry !   150
    That fillest England with thy triumphs' fame,
Joy have thou of thy noble victory,
    And endless happiness of thine own name
      That promiseth the same ;
That through thy prowess and victorious arms 155
Thy country may be freed from foreign harms,
  And great Eliza's glorious name may ring
Through all the world, fill'd with thy wide alarms,
    Which some brave Muse may sing
      To ages following,   160
Upon the bridal day, which is not long :
Sweet Thames ! run softly, till I end my song.

From those high towers this noble lord issúing
    Like radiant Hesper, when his golden hair
    In th' ocean billows he hath bathéd fair,   165
Descended to the river's open viewing
    With a great train ensuing.
Above the rest were goodly to be seen
    Two gentle knights of lovely face and feature,
Beseeming well the bower of any queen,   170
    With gifts of wit and ornaments of nature,
      Fit for so goodly stature,
That like the twins of Jove they seem'd in sight
Which deck the baldric of the Heavens bright ;

    They two, forth pacing to the river's side,   175
Received those two fair brides, their love's delight ;
      Which, at th' appointed tide,
      Each one did make his bride
Against their bridal day, which is not long :   179
Sweet Thames ! run softly, till I end my song.

                       E. SPENSER.

54

THE HAPPY HEART

Art thou poor, yet hast thou golden slumbers ?
      O sweet content !
Art thou rich, yet is thy mind perplexed ?
      O punishment !
Dost thou laugh to see how fools are vexed   5
To add to golden numbers, golden numbers ?
O sweet content ! O sweet, O sweet content !
    Work apace, apace, apace, apace ;
    Honest labour bears a lovely face ;
Then hey nonny nonny, hey nonny nonny !   10

Canst drink the waters of the crispéd spring ?
      O sweet content !
Swimm'st thou in wealth, yet sink'st in thine own
           tears ?
      O punishment !
Then he that patiently want's burden bears   15
No burden bears, but is a king, a king !
O sweet content ! O sweet, O sweet content !
    Work apace, apace, apace, apace ;
    Honest labour bears a lovely face ;
Then hey nonny nonny, hey nonny nonny !   20

                     T. DEKKER.

55

This Life, which seems so fair,
Is like a bubble blown up in the air
 By sporting children's breath,
  Who chase it everywhere   4
And strive who can most motion it bequeath.
And though it sometime seem of its own might

 Like to an eye of gold, to be fix'd there,
And firm to hover in that empty height,
That only is because it is so light.   9
 —But in that pomp it doth not long appear ;
For, when 'tis most admired, in a thought,
Because it erst was nought, it turns to nought.
         W. DRUMMOND.

56

SOUL AND BODY

Poor Soul, the centre of my sinful earth,
 [Fool'd by] those rebel powers that thee array,
Why dost thou pine within, and suffer dearth,
 Painting thy outward walls so costly gay ?

Why so large cost, having so short a lease, 5
 Dost thou upon thy fading mansion spend ?
Shall worms, inheritors of this excess,
 Eat up thy charge ? is this thy body's end ?

Then, Soul, live thou upon thy servant's loss,
 And let that pine to aggravate thy store ; 10
Buy terms divine in selling hours of dross ;
 Within be fed, without be rich no more :—

So shalt thou feed on death, that feeds on men,
And death once dead, there's no more dying then.
         W. SHAKESPEARE.

57

LIFE

The World's a bubble, and the Life of Man
        Less than a span :
In his conception wretched, from the womb
        So to the tomb ;
Curst from the cradle, and brought up to years
        With cares and fears.   6
Who then to frail mortality shall trust,
But limns the water, or but writes in dust.

Yet since with sorrow here we live opprest,
        What life is best ?   10
Courts are but only superficial schools
        To dandle fools :
The rural parts are turn'd into a den
        Of savage men :
And where's a city from all vice so free,   15
But may be term'd the worst of all the three ?

Domestic cares afflict the husband's bed,
        Or pains his head :
Those that live single, take it for a curse,
        Or do things worse :   20
Some would have children : those that have them
        moan
        Or wish them gone :
What is it, then, to have, or have no wife,
But single thraldom, or a double strife ?

Our own affections still at home to please   25
        Is a disease :
To cross the sea to any foreign soil,
        Perils and toil :
Wars with their noise affright us ; when they cease,
        We are worse in peace ;—   30
What then remains, but that we still should cry
Not to be born, or, being born, to die ?

                        LORD BACON.

58

THE LESSONS OF NATURE

Of this fair volume which we World do name
  If we the sheets and leaves could turn with care,
Of Him who it corrects, and did it frame,
  We clear might read the art and wisdom rare :

Find out His power which wildest powers doth
    tame,   5
  His providence extending everywhere,
  His justice which proud rebels doth not spare,
In every page, no period of the same.

But silly we, like foolish children, rest
  Well pleased with colour'd vellum, leaves of gold,
Fair dangling ribbands, leaving what is best,   11
  On the great Writer's sense ne'er taking hold ;

Or if by chance we stay our minds on aught,
It is some picture on the margin wrought.

W. DRUMMOND.

59

Doth then the world go thus, doth all thus move ?
  Is this the justice which on Earth we find ?
  Is this that firm decree which all both bind ?
Are these your influences, Powers above ?   4

Those souls which vice's moody mists most blind,
Blind Fortune, blindly, most their friend doth prove ;
And they who thee, poor idol, Virtue ! love,
  Ply like a feather toss'd by storm and wind.

Ah ! if a Providence doth sway this all,
  Why should best minds groan under most dis-
    tress ?   10
Or why should pride humility make thrall,
  And injuries the innocent oppress ?

Heavens ! hinder, stop this fate ; or grant a time
When good may have, as well as bad, their prime.

W. DRUMMOND.

60
THE WORLD'S WAY

Tired with all these, for restful death I cry—
    As, to behold desert a beggar born,
And needy nothing trimm'd in jollity,
    And purest faith unhappily forsworn,

And gilded honour shamefully misplaced,   5
    And maiden virtue rudely strumpeted,
And right perfection wrongfully disgraced,
    And strength by limping sway disabled,

And art made tongue-tied by authority,
    And folly, doctor-like, controlling skill,   10
And simple truth miscall'd simplicity,
    And captive Good attending captain Ill :—
—Tired with all these, from these would I be gone,
Save that, to die, I leave my Love alone.

                      W. SHAKESPEARE.

61
SAINT JOHN BAPTIST

The last and greatest Herald of Heaven's King
    Girt with rough skins, hies to the deserts wild,
Among that savage brood the woods forth bring,
    Which he more harmless found than man, and
        mild.   4

His food was locusts, and what there doth spring,
    With honey that from virgin hives distill'd ;
Parch'd body, hollow eyes, some uncouth thing
    Made him appear, long since from earth exiled.

There burst he forth : ' All ye whose hopes rely
    On God, with me amidst these deserts mourn,
    Repent, repent, and from old errors turn ! '   11
—Who listen'd to his voice, obey'd his cry ?

Only the echoes, which he made relent,
Rung from their flinty caves, Repent ! Repent !

                      W. DRUMMOND.

THE GOLDEN TREASURY

BOOK SECOND

62

ODE ON THE
MORNING OF CHRIST'S NATIVITY

This is the month, and this the happy morn
   Wherein the Son of Heaven's Eternal King
Of wedded maid and virgin mother born,
   Our great redemption from above did bring ;
   For so the holy sages once did sing   5
That He our deadly forfeit should release,
And with His Father work us a perpetual peace.

That glorious Form, that Light unsufferable,
   And that far-beaming blaze of Majesty
Wherewith He wont at Heaven's high council-
     table   10
   To sit the midst of Trinal Unity,
   He laid aside ; and, here with us to be,
Forsook the courts of everlasting day,
And chose with us a darksome house of mortal clay.

Say, heavenly Muse, shall not thy sacred vein
   Afford a present to the Infant God ?   16
Hast thou no verse, no hymn, or solemn strain
   To welome Him to this His new abode,
   Now while the heaven, by the sun's team un-
     trod,
Hath took no print of the approaching light,   20
And all the spangled host keep watch in squadrons
   bright ?

See how from far, upon the eastern road,
   The star-led wizards haste with odours sweet :
O run, prevent them with thy humble ode
   And lay it lowly at His blessed feet ;   25

Have thou the honour first thy Lord to greet,
And join thy voice unto the angel quire
From out His secret altar touch'd with hallow'd fire.

The Hymn

    It was the winter wild
    While the heaven-born Child   30
All meanly wrapt in the rude manger lies ;
      Nature in awe to Him
      Had doff'd her gaudy trim,
With her great Master so to sympathize :
    It was no season then for her   35
To wanton with the sun, her lusty paramour.

    Only with speeches fair
    She woos the gentle air
To hide her guilty front with innocent snow ;
      And on her naked shame,   40
      Pollute with sinful blame,
The saintly veil of maiden white to throw ;
    Confounded, that her Maker's eyes
Should look so near upon her foul deformities.

    But He, her fears to cease,   45
    Sent down the meek-eyed Peace ;
She, crown'd with olive green, came softly sliding
      Down through the turning sphere,
      His ready harbinger,
With turtle wing the amorous clouds dividing ;
    And waving wide her myrtle wand,   51
She strikes a universal peace through sea and land.

    No war, or battle's sound
    Was heard the world around :
The idle spear and shield were high uphung ;   55
      The hooked chariot stood
      Unstain'd with hostile blood ;
The trumpet spake not to the arméd throng ;
    And kings sat still with awful eye,
As if they surely knew their sovran Lord was by. 60

But peaceful was the night
Wherein the Prince of Light
His reign of peace upon the earth began :
  The winds, with wonder whist,
  Smoothly the waters kist,   65
Whispering new joys to the mild ocean—
Who now hath quite forgot to rave,
While birds of calm sit brooding on the charméd
    wave.

  The stars, with deep amaze,
  Stand fix'd in steadfast gaze,   70
Bending one way their precious influence ;
  And will not take their flight
  For all the morning light,
Or Lucifer that often warn'd them thence ;
  But in their glimmering orbs did glow   75
Until their Lord Himself bespake, and bid them go.

  And though the shady gloom
  Had given day her room,
The sun himself withheld his wonted speed,
  And hid his head for shame,   80
  As his inferior flame
The new-enlighten'd world no more should need :
  He saw a greater Sun appear
Than his bright throne or burning axletree could
    bear.

  The shepherds on the lawn   85
  Or ere the point of dawn
Sate simply chatting in a rustic row ;
  Full little thought they than
  That the mighty Pan
Was kindly come to live with them below ;   90
  Perhaps their loves, or else their sheep
Was all that did their silly thoughts so busy keep.

  When such music sweet
  Their hearts and ears did greet
As never was by mortal finger strook—   95
  Divinely-warbled voice

Answering the stringéd noise,
As all their souls in blissful rapture took :
The air, such pleasure loth to lose,
With thousand echoes still prolongs each heavenly
close.   100

Nature that heard such sound
Beneath the hollow round
Of Cynthia's seat the airy region thrilling,
Now was almost won
To think her part was done,   105
And that her reign had here its last fulfilling ;
She knew such harmony alone
Could hold all heaven and earth in happier union.

At last surrounds their sight
A globe of circular light,   110
That with long beams the shamefaced night
array'd ;
The helméd Cherubim
And sworded Seraphim
Are seen in glittering ranks with wings display'd,
Harping in loud and solemn quire   115
With unexpressive notes, to Heaven's new-born
Heir.

Such music (as 'tis said)
Before was never made
But when of old the sons of morning sung,
While the Creator great   120
His constellations set
And the well-balanced world on hinges hung ;
And cast the dark foundations deep,
And bid the weltering waves their oozy channel
keep.

Ring out, ye crystal spheres !   125
Once bless our human ears,
If ye have power to touch our senses so ;
And let your silver chime
Move in melodious time ;
And let the bass of heaven's deep organ blow ;

And with your ninefold harmony   131
Make up full consort to the angelic symphony.

  For if such holy song,
  Enwrap our fancy long,
Time will run back, and fetch the age of gold ;
  And speckled vanity   136
  Will sicken soon and die,
And leprous sin will melt from earthly mould ;
  And Hell itself will pass away,
And leave her dolorous mansions to the peering day.

  Yea, Truth and Justice then   141
  Will down return to men,
Orb'd in a rainbow ; and, like glories wearing,
  Mercy will sit between
  Throned in celestial sheen,   145
With radiant feet the tissued clouds down
   steering ;
  And Heaven, as at some festival,
Will open wide the gates of her high palace hall.

  But wisest Fate says No ;
  This must not yet be so ;   150
The Babe yet lies in smiling infancy
  That on the bitter cross
  Must redeem our loss ;
So both Himself and us to glorify :
  Yet first, to those ychain'd in sleep   155
The wakeful trump of doom must thunder through
   the deep,

  With such a horrid clang
  As on mount Sinai rang
While the red fire and smouldering clouds out-
   brake :
  The aged Earth aghast   160
  With terror of that blast
Shall from the surface to the centre shake,
  When, at the world's last sessión,
The dreadful Judge in middle air shall spread His
   throne.

And then at last our bliss   165
Full and perfect is,
But now begins ; for from this happy day
The old Dragon under ground,
In straiter limits bound,
Not half so far casts his usurpéd sway ;   170
And, wroth to see his kingdom fail,
Swinges the scaly horror of his folded tail.

The oracles are dumb ;
No voice or hideous hum
Runs through the archéd roof in words deceiving:
Apollo from his shrine   176
Can no more divine,
With hollow shriek the steep of Delphos leaving :
No nightly trance or breathéd spell
Inspires the pale-eyed priest from the prophetic cell.

The lonely mountains o'er   181
And the resounding shore
A voice of weeping heard, and loud lament ;
From haunted spring and dale
Edged with poplar pale   185
The parting Genius is with sighing sent ;
With flower-inwoven tresses torn
The nymphs in twilight shade of tangled thickets
        mourn.

In consecrated earth
And on the holy hearth   190
The Lars and Lemures moan with midnight
        plaint ;
In urns, and altars round
A drear and dying sound
Affrights the Flamens at their service quaint ;
And the chill marble seems to sweat,   195
While each peculiar Power forgoes his wonted seat.

Peor and Baalim
Forsake their temples dim,
With that twice-batter'd god of Palestine ;
And moonéd Ashtaroth   200
Heaven's queen and mother both,

Now sits not girt with tapers' holy shine ;
  The Lybic Hammon shrinks his horn,
In vain the Tyrian maids their wounded Thammuz
    mourn.

    And sullen Moloch, fled,   205
    Hath left in shadows dread
His burning idol all of blackest hue ;
    In vain with cymbals' ring
    They call the grisly king,
In dismal dance about the furnace blue ;   210
  The brutish gods of Nile as fast,
Isis, and Orus, and the dog Anubis, haste.

    Nor is Osiris seen
    In Memphian grove, or green,
Trampling the unshower'd grass with lowings
    loud :   215
    Nor can he be at rest
    Within his sacred chest ;
Nought but profoundest hell can be his shroud ;
  In vain with timbrell'd anthems dark
The sable-stoléd sorcerers bear his worshipt ark.

    He feels from Juda's land   221
    The dreaded infant's hand ;
The rays of Bethlehem blind his dusky eyn ;
    Nor all the gods beside
    Longer dare abide,   225
Not Typhon huge ending in snaky twine :
  Our Babe, to show his Godhead true,
Can in His swaddling bands control the damnéd
    crew.

    So, when the sun in bed
    Curtain'd with cloudy red   230
Pillows his chin upon an orient wave,
    The flocking shadows pale
    Troop to the infernal jail,
Each fetter'd ghost slips to his several grave ;
  And the yellow-skirted fays   235
Fly after the night-steeds, leaving their moon-loved
    maze.

But see, the Virgin blest
    Hath laid her Babe to rest ;
Time is, our tedious song should here have
    ending :
    Heaven's youngest-teeméd star   240
    Hath fix'd her polish'd car,
Her sleeping Lord with hand-maid lamp attend-
    ing :
    And all about the courtly stable
Bright-harness'd angels sit in order serviceable.

                            J. MILTON.

63

SONG FOR SAINT CECILIA'S DAY, 1687

From Harmony, from heavenly Harmony
    This universal frame began :
  When Nature underneath a heap
    Of jarring atoms lay
  And could not heave her head,   5
The tuneful voice was heard from high
    Arise, ye more than dead !
Then cold, and hot, and moist, and dry
In order to their stations leap,
    And Music's power obey.   10
From harmony, from heavenly harmony
    This universal frame began :
    From harmony to harmony
Through all the compass of the notes it ran,
The diapason closing full in Man.   15

What passion cannot Music raise and quell ?
    When Jubal struck the chorded shell
  His listening brethren stood around,
    And, wondering, on their faces fell
  To worship that celestial sound.   20
Less than a god they thought there could not
    dwell
    Within the hollow of that shell
    That spoke so sweetly and so well.
What passion cannot Music raise and quell ?

The trumpet's loud clangor   25
  Excites us to arms,
With shrill notes of anger
  And mortal alarms.
The double double double beat
  Of the thundering drum   30
  Cries ' Hark ! the foes come ;
Charge, charge, 'tis too late to retreat !'

The soft complaining flute
  In dying notes discovers
  The woes of hopeless lovers,   35
Whose dirge is whisper'd by the warbling lute.

Sharp violins proclaim
Their jealous pangs and desperation,
Fury, frantic indignation,
Depth of pains, and height of passion   40
  For the fair disdainful dame.

But oh ! what art can teach,
What human voice can reach
  The sacred organ's praise ?
Notes inspiring holy love,   45
  Notes that wing their heavenly ways
To mend the choirs above.

Orpheus could lead the savage race,
And trees unrooted left their place
  Sequacious of the lyre :   50
But bright Cecilia raised the wonder higher :
When to her Organ vocal breath was given,
An Angel heard, and straight appear'd—
  Mistaking Earth for Heaven !

Grand Chorus

As from the power of sacred lays   55
  The spheres began to move,
And sung the great Creator's praise
  To all the blest above ;

So when the last and dreadful hour
  This crumbling pageant shall devour   60
The trumpet shall be heard on high,
The dead shall live, the living die,
And Music shall untune the sky.

J. DRYDEN.

64

ON THE LATE MASSACRE IN PIEDMONT

Avenge, O Lord ! Thy slaughter'd Saints, whose
    bones
  Lie scatter'd on the Alpine mountains cold ;
  Even them who kept Thy truth so pure of old,
When all our fathers worshipt stocks and stones,

Forget not : in Thy book record their groans   5
  Who were Thy sheep, and in their ancient fold
  Slain by the bloody Piemontese, that roll'd
Mother with infant down the rocks. Their moans

The vales redoubled to the hills, and they   9
  To Heaven. Their martyr'd blood and ashes sow
O'er all the Italian fields, where still doth sway

  The triple tyrant : that from these may grow
A hundred-fold, who, having learnt Thy way,
  Early may fly the Babylonian woe.

J. MILTON.

65

HORATIAN ODE UPON CROMWELL'S
RETURN FROM IRELAND

The forward youth that would appear,
Must now forsake his Muses dear,
    Nor in the shadows sing
    His numbers languishing.

'Tis time to leave the books in dust,   5
And oil th' unuséd armour's rust,
    Removing from the wall
    The corslet of the hall.

So restless Cromwell could not cease
In the inglorious arts of peace,   10
    But through adventurous war
    Urgéd his active star :

And like the three-fork'd lightning, first
Breaking the clouds where it was nurst,
    Did thorough his own side   15
    His fiery way divide :

(For 'tis all one to courage high
The emulous, or enemy ;
    And with such, to enclose
    Is more than to oppose ;)   20

Then burning through the air he went
And palaces and temples rent ;
    And Caesar's head at last
    Did through his laurels blast.

'Tis madness to resist or blame   25
The face of angry heaven's flame ;
    And if we would speak true,
    Much to the man is due

Who, from his private gardens, where
He lived reservéd and austere   30
    (As if his highest plot
    To plant the bergamot),

Could by industrious valour climb
To ruin the great work of Time,
    And cast the Kingdoms old   35
    Into another mould ;

Though Justice against Fate complain,
And plead the ancient Rights in vain—
    But those do hold or break
    As men are strong or weak.   40

Nature, that hateth emptiness,
Allows of penetration less,
    And therefore must make room
    Where greater spirits come.

What field of all the Civil War 45
Where his were not the deepest scar ?
    And Hampton shows what part
    He had of wiser art ;

Where, twining subtle fears with hope,
He wove a net of such a scope 50
    That Charles himself might chase
    To Carisbrook's narrow case ;

That thence the Royal actor borne
The tragic scaffold might adorn :
    While round the armèd bands 55
    Did clap their bloody hands ;

He nothing common did or mean
Upon that memorable scene,
    But with his keener eye
    The axe's edge did try ; 60

Nor call'd the Gods, with vulgar spite,
To vindicate his helpless right ;
    But bow'd his comely head
    Down, as upon a bed.

—This was that memorable hour 65
Which first assured the forcèd power
    So when they did design
    The Capitol's first line,

A Bleeding Head, where they begun,
Did fright the architects to run ; 70
    And yet in that the State
    Foresaw its happy fate !

And now the Irish are ashamed
To see themselves in one year tamed :
    So much one man can do 75
    That does both act and know.

They can affirm his praises best,
And have, though overcome, confest
    How good he is, how just
    And fit for highest trust ; 80

Nor yet grown stiffer with command,
But still in the Republic's hand—
    How fit he is to sway
    That can so well obey !—

He to the Commons' feet presents   85
A Kingdom for his first year's rents.
    And (what he may) forbears
    His fame, to make it theirs :

And has his sword and spoils ungirt
To lay them at the Public's skirt.   90
    So when the falcon high
    Falls heavy from the sky,

She, having kill'd, no more does search
But on the next green bough to perch,
    Where, when he first does lure,   95
    The falconer has her sure.

—What may not then our Isle presume
While victory his crest does plume ?
    What may not others fear
    If thus he crowns each year ?   100

As Caesar he, ere long, to Gaul,
To Italy an Hannibal,
    And to all states not free
    Shall climacteric be.

The Pict no shelter now shall find   105
Within his parti-colour'd mind,
    But from this valour sad,
    Shrink underneath the plaid—

Happy, if in the tufted brake
The English hunter him mistake,   110
    Nor lay his hounds in near
    The Caledonian deer.

But thou, the War's and Fortune's son,
March indefatigably on ;
    And for the last effect   115
    Still keep the sword erect :

Besides the force it has to fright
The spirits of the shady night,
 The same arts that did gain
 A power, must it maintain. 120

A. MARVELL.

66

LYCIDAS

Elegy on a Friend drowned in the Irish Channel

Yet once more, O ye laurels, and once more
Ye myrtles brown, with ivy never sere,
I come to pluck your berries harsh and crude,
And with forced fingers rude
Shatter your leaves before the mellowing year. 5
Bitter constraint, and sad occasion dear
Compels me to disturb your season due :
For Lycidas is dead, dead ere his prime,
Young Lycidas, and hath not left his peer :
Who would not sing for Lycidas ? he knew 10
Himself to sing, and build the lofty rhyme.
He must not float upon his watery bier
Unwept, and welter to the parching wind,
Without the meed of some melodious tear.

Begin then, Sisters of the sacred well 15
That from beneath the seat of Jove doth spring,
Begin, and somewhat loudly sweep the string.
Hence with denial vain and coy excuse :
So may some gentle Muse
With lucky words favour my destined urn ; 20
And as he passes, turn
And bid fair peace be to my sable shroud.

For we were nursed upon the self-same hill,
Fed the same flock by fountain, shade, and rill.
Together both, ere the high lawns appear'd 25
Under the opening eye-lids of the morn,
We drove a-field, and both together heard
What time the gray-fly winds her sultry horn,
Battening our flocks with the fresh dews of night,
Oft till the star, that rose at evening bright, 30

Toward heaven's descent had sloped his westering
    wheel.
Meanwhile the rural ditties were not mute,
Temper'd to the oaten flute ;
Rough Satyrs danced, and Fauns with cloven heel
From the glad sound would not be absent long ;
And old Damoetas loved to hear our song.   36

But O the heavy change, now thou art gone,
Now thou art gone, and never must return !
Thee, Shepherd, thee the woods, and desert caves,
With wild thyme and the gadding vine o'ergrown,
And all their echoes, mourn :   41
The willows and the hazel copses green
Shall now no more be seen
Fanning their joyous leaves to thy soft lays.
As killing as the canker to the rose,   45
Or taint-worm to the weanling herds that graze,
Or frost to flowers, that their gay wardrobe wear
When first the white-thorn blows ;
Such, Lycidas, thy loss to shepherd's ear.

Where were ye, Nymphs, when the remorseless
    deep   50
Closed o'er the head of your loved Lycidas ?
For neither were ye playing on the steep
Where your old bards, the famous Druids, lie,
Nor on the shaggy top of Mona high,
Nor yet where Deva spreads her wizard stream :
Ay me ! I fondly dream—   56
Had ye been there—for what could that have done?
What could the Muse herself that Orpheus bore,
The Muse herself, for her enchanting son,
Whom universal nature did lament,   60
When by the rout that made the hideous roar
His gory visage down the stream was sent,
Down the swift Hebrus to the Lesbian shore ?

Alas ! what boots it with uncessant care
To tend the homely, slighted, shepherd's trade
And strictly meditate the thankless Muse ?   66
Were it not better done, as others use,

To sport with Amaryllis in the shade,
Or with the tangles of Neaera's hair ?   69
Fame is the spur that the clear spirit doth raise
(That last infirmity of noble mind)
To scorn delights, and live laborious days ;
But the fair guerdon when we hope to find,
And think to burst out into sudden blaze,   74
Comes the blind Fury with the abhorréd shears
And slits the thin-spun life. ' But not the praise '
Phoebus replied, and touch'd my trembling ears :
' Fame is no plant that grows on mortal soil,
Nor in the glistering foil   79
Set off to the world, nor in broad rumour lies :
But lives and spreads aloft by those pure eyes
And perfect witness of all-judging Jove ;
As he pronounces lastly on each deed,
Of so much fame in heaven expect thy meed.'   84

O fountain Arethuse, and thou honour'd flood
Smooth-sliding Mincius, crown'd with vocal reeds,
That strain I heard was of a higher mood :
But now my oat proceeds,
And listens to the herald of the sea
That came in Neptune's plea ;   90
He ask'd the waves, and ask'd the felon winds,
What hard mishap hath doom'd this gentle swain ?
And question'd every gust of rugged wings
That blows from off each beakéd promontory :
They knew not of his story ;   95
And sage Hippotades their answer brings,
That not a blast was from his dungeon stray'd ;
The air was calm, and on the level brine
Sleek Panope with all her sisters play'd.
It was that fatal and perfidious bark   100
Built in the eclipse, and rigg'd with curses dark,
That sunk so low that sacred head of thine.

Next Camus, reverend sire, went footing slow,
His mantle hairy, and his bonnet sedge,
Inwrought with figures dim, and on the edge   105
Like to that sanguine flower inscribed with woe :

'Ah ! who hath reft,' quoth he, 'my dearest
  pledge ? '
Last came, and last did go
The pilot of the Galilean lake ;
Two massy keys he bore of metals twain   110
(The golden opes, the iron shuts amain) ;
He shook his mitred locks, and stern bespake :
' How well could I have spared for thee, young
  swain,
Enow of such as for their bellies' sake
Creep and intrude and climb into the fold !   115
Of other care they little reckoning make
Than how to scramble at the shearers' feast,
And shove away the worthy bidden guest.
Blind mouths ! that scarce themselves know how
  to hold
A sheep-hook, or have learn'd aught else the least
That to the faithful herdman's art belongs !   121
What recks it them ? What need they ? They
  are sped ;
And when they list, their lean and flashy songs
Grate on their scrannel pipes of wretched straw ;
The hungry sheep look up, and are not fed,   125
But swoln with wind and the rank mist they draw
Rot inwardly, and foul contagion spread :
Besides what the grim wolf with privy paw
Daily devours apace, and nothing said :
—But that two-handed engine at the door   130
Stands ready to smite once, and smite no more.'

    Return, Alpheus, the dread voice is past
That shrunk thy streams ; return, Sicilian Muse,
And call the vales, and bid them hither cast
Their bells and flowerets of a thousand hues.   135
Ye valleys low, where the mild whispers use
Of shades, and wanton winds, and gushing brooks,
On whose fresh lap the swart star sparely looks,
Throw hither all your quaint enamell'd eyes   139
That on the green turf suck the honey'd showers
And purple all the ground with vernal flowers.

Bring the rathe primrose that forsaken dies,
The tufted crow-toe, and pale jessamine,
The white pink, and the pansy freak'd with jet,
The glowing violet, 145
The musk-rose, and the well-attired woodbine,
With cowslips wan that hang the pensive head,
And every flower that sad embroidery wears :
Bid amarantus all his beauty shed,
And daffadillies fill their cups with tears 150
To strew the laureat hearse where Lycid lies.
For, so to interpose a little ease,
Let our frail thoughts dally with false surmise ;
Ay me ! whilst thee the shores and sounding seas
Wash far away,—where'er thy bones are hurl'd, 156
Whether beyond the stormy Hebrides
Where thou perhaps, under the whelming tide,
Visitest the bottom of the monstrous world ;
Or whether thou, to our moist vows denied,
Sleep'st by the fable of Bellerus old, 160
Where the great Vision of the guarded mount
Looks toward Namancos and Bayona's hold,
—Look homeward, Angel, now, and melt with
    ruth :
—And, O ye dolphins, waft the hapless youth !

  Weep no more, woeful shepherds, weep no
    more, 165
For Lycidas, your sorrow, is not dead,
Sunk though he be beneath the watery floor ;
So sinks the day-star in the ocean-bed,
And yet anon repairs his drooping head
And tricks his beams, and with new-spangled ore
Flames in the forehead of the morning sky : 171
So Lycidas sunk low, but mounted high
Through the dear might of Him that walk'd the
    waves ;
Where, other groves and other streams along,
With nectar pure his oozy locks he laves, 175
And hears the unexpressive nuptial song
In the blest kingdoms meek of joy and love.

There entertain him all the saints above
In solemn troops, and sweet societies,
That sing, and singing in their glory move,　　180
And wipe the tears for ever from his eyes.
Now, Lycidas, the shepherds weep no more ;
Henceforth thou art the Genius of the shore
In thy large recompense, and shalt be good
To all that wander in that perilous flood.　　185

Thus sang the uncouth swain to the oaks and rills,
While the still morn went out with sandals grey ;
He touch'd the tender stops of various quills,
With eager thought warbling his Doric lay :
And now the sun had stretch'd out all the hills,
And now was dropt into the western bay :　　191
At last he rose, and twitch'd his mantle blue :
To-morrow to fresh woods, and pastures new.

　　　　　　　　　　　　　J. MILTON.

67

ON THE TOMBS IN WESTMINSTER ABBEY

Mortality, behold and fear,
What a change of flesh is here !
Think how many royal bones
Sleep within these heaps of stones ;
Here they lie, had realms and lands,　　5
Who now want strength to stir their hands,
Where from their pulpits seal'd with dust
They preach, ' In greatness is no trust.'
Here's an acre sown indeed
With the richest royallest seed　　10
That the earth did e'er suck in
Since the first man died for sin :
Here the bones of birth have cried
' Though gods they were, as men they died ! '
Here are sands, ignoble things,　　15
Dropt from the ruin'd sides of kings :
Here's a world of pomp and state
Buried in dust, once dead by fate.

　　　　　　　　　　　　　F. BEAUMONT.

68

THE LAST CONQUEROR

Victorious men of earth, no more
 Proclaim how wide your empires are ;
Though you bind-in every shore,
 And your triumphs reach as far
  As night or day,
 Yet you, proud monarchs, must obey
And mingle with forgotten ashes, when
Death calls ye to the crowd of common men.

Devouring Famine, Plague, and War,
 Each able to undo mankind,
Death's servile emissaries are ;
 Nor to these alone confined,
  He hath at will
 More quaint and subtle ways to kill ;
A smile or kiss, as he will use the art,
Shall have the cunning skill to break a heart.
       J. SHIRLEY.

69

DEATH THE LEVELLER

The glories of our blood and state
 Are shadows, not substantial things ;
There is no armour against fate ;
 Death lays his icy hand on kings :
  Sceptre and Crown
  Must tumble down,
And in the dust be equal made
With the poor crooked scythe and spade.

Some men with swords may reap the field,
 And plant fresh laurels where they kill :
But their strong nerves at last must yield ;
 They tame but one another still :

Early or late
They stoop to fate,
And must give up their murmuring breath   15
When they, pale captives, creep to death.

The garlands wither on your brow ;
Then boast no more your mighty deeds ;
Upon Death's purple altar now
See where the victor-victim bleeds :   20
Your heads must come
To the cold tomb ;
Only the actions of the just
Smell sweet, and blossom in their dust.

J. SHIRLEY.

70

WHEN THE ASSAULT WAS INTENDED TO THE CITY

Captain, or Colonel, or Knight in arms,
Whose chance on these defenceless doors may
seize,
If deed of honour did thee ever please,
Guard them, and him within protect from harms.

He can requite thee ; for he knows the charms
That call fame on such gentle acts as these,   6
And he can spread thy name o'er lands and seas,
Whatever clime the sun's bright circle warms.

Lift not thy spear against the Muses' bower :
The great Emathian conqueror bid spare   10
The house of Pindarus, when temple and tower

Went to the ground : and the repeated air
Of sad Electra's poet had the power
To save the Athenian walls from ruin bare.

J. MILTON.

71

ON HIS BLINDNESS

When I consider how my light is spent
  Ere half my days, in this dark world and wide,
  And that one talent which is death to hide
Lodged with me useless, though my soul more bent

To serve therewith my Maker, and present   5
  My true account, lest He returning chide,—
  Doth God exact day-labour, light denied?
I fondly ask:—But Patience, to prevent

That murmur, soon replies; God doth not need
  Either man's work, or His own gifts: who best
    Bear His mild yoke, they serve Him best: His
      state   11

Is kingly; thousands at His bidding speed
  And post o'er land and ocean without rest:—
  They also serve who only stand and wait.
                                    J. MILTON.

72

CHARACTER OF A HAPPY LIFE

How happy is he born or taught
  That serveth not another's will;
Whose armour is his honest thought,
  And silly truth his highest skill!

Whose passions not his masters are,   5
  Whose soul is still prepared for death;
Untied unto the world with care
  Of princely love or vulgar breath;

Who hath his life from rumours freed,
  Whose conscience is his strong retreat   10
Whose state can neither flatterers feed,
  Nor ruin make accusers great;

Who envieth none whom chance doth raise
　　Or vice ; who never understood　　　　　　14
How deepest wounds are given with praise ;
　　Nor rules of state, but rules of good :

Who God doth late and early pray
　　More of his grace than gifts to lend ;
Who entertains the harmless day
　　With a well-chosen book or friend ;　　　　20

—This man is free from servile bands
　　Of hope to rise, or fear to fall ;
Lord of himself, though not of lands ;
　　And having nothing, he hath all.
　　　　　　　　　　　　Sir H. Wotton.

73

THE NOBLE NATURE

　　It is not growing like a tree
　　In bulk, doth make Man better be ;
Or standing long an oak, three hundred year,
To fall a log at last, dry, bald, and sere :
　　　　A lily of a day　　　　　　　　　　5
　　　　Is fairer far in May,
　　Although it fall and die that night ;
　　It was the plant and flower of Light.
In small proportions we just beauties see ;
And in short measures life may perfect be.　　10
　　　　　　　　　　　　B. Jonson.

74

THE GIFTS OF GOD

When God at first made Man,
Having a glass of blessings standing by ;
Let us (said He) pour on him all we can :
Let the world's riches, which dispersèd lie,
　　Contract into a span.　　　　　　　　5

So strength first made a way ;
Then beauty flow'd, then wisdom, honour, pleasure :
When almost all was out, God made a stay,
Perceiving that alone, of all His treasure,
    Rest in the bottom lay.   10

For if I should (said He)
Bestow this jewel also on my creature,
He would adore my gifts instead of me,
And rest in Nature, not the God of Nature :
    So both should losers be.   15

Yet let him keep the rest,
But keep them with repining restlessness :
Let him be rich and weary, that at least,
If goodness lead him not, yet weariness
    May toss him to my breast.   20
                G. HERBERT.

75

THE RETREAT

Happy those early days, when I
Shined in my Angel-infancy !
Before I understood this place
Appointed for my second race,
Or taught my soul to fancy aught   5
But a white, celestial thought ;
When yet I had not walk'd above
A mile or two from my first Love,
And looking back, at that short space
Could see a glimpse of His bright face ;   10
When on some gilded cloud or flower
My gazing soul would dwell an hour,
And in those weaker glories spy
Some shadows of eternity ;
Before I taught my tongue to wound   15
My conscience with a sinful sound,
Or had the black art to dispense
A several sin to every sense,

But felt through all this fleshly dress
Bright shoots of everlastingness.   20

O how I long to travel back,
And tread again that ancient track !
That I might once more reach that plain,
Where first I left my glorious train ;
From whence th' enlighten'd spirit sees   25
That shady City of Palm trees !
But ah ! my soul with too much stay
Is drunk, and staggers in the way :—
Some men a forward motion love,
But I by backward steps would move ;   30
And when this dust falls to the urn,
In that state I came, return.

H. VAUGHAN.

76

TO MR. LAWRENCE

Lawrence, of virtuous father virtuous son,
  Now that the fields are dank and ways are mire,
  Where shall we sometimes meet, and by the fire
Help waste a sullen day, what may be won

From the hard season gaining ? Time will run   6
  On smoother, till Favonius re-inspire
  The frozen earth, and clothe in fresh attire
The lily and rose, that neither sow'd nor spun.

What neat repast shall feast us, light and choice,
  Of Attic taste, with wine, whence we may rise
To hear the lute well touch'd, or artful voice   11

  Warble immortal notes and Tuscan air ?
  He who of those delights can judge, and spare
To interpose them oft, is not unwise.

J. MILTON.

77

TO CYRIACK SKINNER

Cyriack, whose grandsire, on the royal bench
  Of British Themis, with no mean applause
  Pronounced, and in his volumes taught, our laws,
Which others at their bar so often wrench ;   4

To-day deep thoughts resolve with me to drench
  In mirth, that after no repenting draws ;
  Let Euclid rest, and Archimedes pause,
And what the Swede intend, and what the French.

To measure life learn thou betimes, and know   9
  Toward solid good what leads the nearest way ;
  For other things mild Heaven a time ordains,

And disapproves that care, though wise in show,
  That with superfluous burden loads the day,
  And, when God sends a cheerful hour, refrains.

                        J. MILTON.

78

HYMN TO DIANA

Queen and Huntress, chaste and fair,
  Now the sun is laid to sleep,
Seated in thy silver chair
    State in wonted manner keep :
      Hesperus entreats thy light,   5
    Goddess excellently bright.

Earth, let not thy envious shade
  Dare itself to interpose ;
Cynthia's shining orb was made
    Heaven to clear when day did close :   10
      Bless us then with wishéd sight,
    Goddess excellently bright.

Lay thy bow of pearl apart
  And thy crystal-shining quiver ;
Give unto the flying hart   15
    Space to breathe, how short soever :
        Thou that mak'st a day of night,
        Goddess excellently bright !

                                    B. JONSON.

79

WISHES FOR THE SUPPOSED MISTRESS

  Whoe'er she be,
  That not impossible She
That shall command my heart and me ;

  Where'er she lie,
  Lock'd up from mortal eye   5
In shady leaves of destiny :

  Till that ripe birth
  Of studied Fate stand forth,
And teach her fair steps tread our earth ;

  Till that divine   10
  Idea take a shrine
Of crystal flesh, through which to shine :

  —Meet you her, my Wishes,
  Bespeak her to my blisses,
And be ye call'd, my absent kisses.   15

  I wish her beauty
  That owes not all its duty
To gaudy tire, or glist'ring shoe-tie :

  Something more than
  Taffata or tissue can,   20
Or rampant feather, or rich fan.

  A face that's best
  By its own beauty drest,
And can alone commend the rest :

A face made up 25
Out of no other shop
Than what Nature's white hand sets ope.

Sidneian showers
Of sweet discourse, whose powers
Can crown old Winter's head with flowers.

Whate'er delight 31
Can make day's forehead bright
Or give down to the wings of night.

Soft silken hours,
Open suns, shady bowers ; 35
'Bove all, nothing within that lowers.

Days, that need borrow
No part of their good morrow
From a fore-spent night of sorrow :

Days, that in spite 40
Of darkness, by the light
Of a clear mind are day all night.

Life, that dares send
A challenge to his end, 44
And when it comes, say, ' Welcome, friend.'

I wish her store
Of worth may leave her poor
Of wishes ; and I wish——no more.

—Now, if Time knows
That Her, whose radiant brows 50
Weave them a garland of my vows ;

Her that dares be
What these lines wish to see :
I seek no further, it is She.

'Tis She, and here 55
Lo ! I unclothe and clear
My wishes' cloudy character.

Such worth as this is
Shall fix my flying wishes,
And determine them to kisses. 60

Let her full glory,
My fancies, fly before ye ;
Be ye my fictions :—but her story.

R. CRASHAW.

80

THE GREAT ADVENTURER

Over the mountains
    And over the waves,
Under the fountains
    And under the graves ;
Under floods that are deepest,   5
    Which Neptune obey ;
Over rocks that are steepest
    Love will find out the way.

Where there is no place
    For the glow-worm to lie ;   10
Where there is no space
    For receipt of a fly ;
Where the midge dares not venture
    Lest herself fast she lay ;
If love come, he will enter   15
    And soon find out his way.

You may esteem him
    A child for his might ;
Or you may deem him
    A coward from his flight ;   20
But if she whom love doth honour
    Be conceal'd from the day,
Set a thousand guards upon her,
    Love will find out the way.

Some think to lose him   25
    By having him confined ;
And some do suppose him,
    Poor thing, to be blind ;

But if ne'er so close ye wall him,
　　Do the best that you may,　　　　　　30
Blind love, if so ye call him,
　　Will find out his way.

You may train the eagle
　　To stoop to your fist ;
Or you may inveigle　　　　　　　　　　35
　　The phoenix of the east ;
The lioness, ye may move her
　　To give o'er her prey ;
But you'll ne'er stop a lover :
　　He will find out his way.　　　　　　　40

ANON.

81

CHILD AND MAIDEN

Ah, Chloris ! that I now could sit
　　As unconcern'd as when
Your infant beauty could beget
　　No pleasure, nor no pain !
When I the dawn used to admire,　　　　5
　　And praised the coming day,
I little thought the growing fire
　　Must take my rest away.

Your charms in harmless childhood lay
　　Like metals in the mine ;　　　　　　10
Age from no face took more away
　　Than youth conceal'd in thine.
But as your charms insensibly
　　To their perfection prest,
Fond love as unperceived did fly,　　　　15
　　And in my bosom rest.

My passion with your beauty grew,
　　And Cupid at my heart,
Still as his mother favour'd you,
　　Threw a new flaming dart :　　　　　20

Each gloried in their wanton part ;
　　To make a lover, he
Employ'd the utmost of his art—
　　To make a beauty, she.

SIR C. SEDLEY.

82

COUNSEL TO GIRLS

Gather ye rose-buds while ye may,
　　Old Time is still a-flying :
And this same flower that smiles to-day,
　　To-morrow will be dying.

The glorious Lamp of Heaven, the Sun,　　5
　　The higher he 's a-getting
The sooner will his race be run,
　　And nearer he 's to setting.

That age is best which is the first,
　　When youth and blood are warmer ;　　10
But being spent, the worse, and worst
　　Times, still succeed the former.

Then be not coy, but use your time ;
　　And while ye may, go marry :
For having lost but once your prime,　　15
　　You may for ever tarry.

R. HERRICK.

83

TO LUCASTA, ON GOING TO THE WARS

Tell me not, Sweet, I am unkind
　　That from the nunnery
Of thy chaste breast and quiet mind
　　To war and arms I fly.

True, a new mistress now I chase,   5
  The first foe in the field ;
And with a stronger faith embrace
  A sword, a horse, a shield.

Yet this inconstancy is such
  As you too shall adore ;   10
I could not love thee, Dear, so much,
  Loved I not Honour more.

COLONEL LOVELACE.

84

ELIZABETH OF BOHEMIA

You meaner beauties of the night,
  That poorly satisfy our eyes
More by your number than your light,
  You common people of the skies,
What are you, when the Moon shall rise ?   5

You curious chanters of the wood
  That warble forth dame Nature's lays,
Thinking your passions understood
  By your weak accents ; what 's your praise
When Philomel her voice shall raise ?   10

You violets that first appear,
  By your pure purple mantles known
Like the proud virgins of the year,
  As if the spring were all your own,—
What are you, when the Rose is blown ?   15

So when my Mistress shall be seen
  In form and beauty of her mind,
By virtue first, then choice, a Queen,
  Tell me, if she were not design'd
Th' eclipse and glory of her kind ?   20

SIR H. WOTTON.

85

TO THE LADY MARGARET LEY

Daughter to that good Earl, once President
  Of England's Council and her Treasury,
  Who lived in both, unstain'd with gold or fee,
And left them both, more in himself content,

Till the sad breaking of that Parliament   5
  Broke him, as that dishonest victory
  At Chaeronea, fatal to liberty,
Kill'd with report that old man eloquent ;—

Though later born than to have known the days
  Wherein your father flourish'd, yet by you,   10
    Madam, methinks I see him living yet ;

So well your words his noble virtues praise,
  That all both judge you to relate them true,
    And to possess them, honour'd Margaret.

                                J. MILTON.

86

THE LOVELINESS OF LOVE

It is not Beauty I demand,
  A crystal brow, the moon's despair,
Nor the snow's daughter, a white hand,
  Nor mermaid's yellow pride of hair :

Tell me not of your starry eyes,   5
  Your lips that seem on roses fed,
Your breasts, where Cupid trembling lies
  Nor sleeps for kissing of his bed :—

A bloomy pair of vermeil cheeks
  Like Hebe's in her ruddiest hours,   10
A breath that softer music speaks
  Than summer winds a-wooing flowers,

These are but gauds : nay, what are lips ?
  Coral beneath the ocean-stream,
Whose brink when your adventurer sips   15
  Full oft he perisheth on them.

And what are cheeks, but ensigns oft
  That wave hot youth to fields of blood ?
Did Helen's breast, though ne'er so soft,
  Do Greece or Ilium any good ?   20

Eyes can with baleful ardour burn ;
  Poison can breath, that erst perfumed ;
There's many a white hand holds an urn
  With lovers' hearts to dust consumed.

For crystal brows—there's nought within ;   25
  They are but empty cells for pride ;
He who the Syren's hair would win
  Is mostly strangled in the tide.

Give me, instead of Beauty's bust,
  A tender heart, a loyal mind   30
Which with temptation I could trust,
  Yet never link'd with error find,—

One in whose gentle bosom I
  Could pour my secret heart of woes,
Like the care-burthen'd honey-fly   35
  That hides his murmurs in the rose,—

My earthly Comforter ! whose love
  So indefeasible might be
That, when my spirit won above,
  Hers could not stay, for sympathy.   40

G. DARLEY.

87

THE TRUE BEAUTY

He that loves a rosy cheek
  Or a coral lip admires,
Or from star-like eyes doth seek
  Fuel to maintain his fires ;

As old Time makes these decay,   5
So his flames must waste away.

But a smooth and steadfast mind,
    Gentle thoughts, and calm desires,
Hearts with equal love combined,
    Kindle never-dying fires :—   10
Where these are not, I despise
Lovely cheeks or lips or eyes.

                              T. CAREW.

88

TO DIANEME

Sweet, be not proud of those two eyes
Which starlike sparkle in their skies ;
Nor be you proud, that you can see
All hearts your captives ; yours yet free :
Be you not proud of that rich hair   5
Which wantons with the lovesick air ;
Whenas that ruby which you wear,
Sunk from the tip of your soft ear,
Will last to be a precious stone
When all your world of beauty 's gone.   10

                              R. HERRICK.

89

      Go, lovely Rose !
Tell her, that wastes her time and me,
      That now she knows,
When I resemble her to thee,
How sweet and fair she seems to be.   5

      Tell her that's young
And shuns to have her graces spied,
      That hadst thou sprung
In deserts, where no men abide,
Thou must have uncommended died.   10

Small is the worth
Of beauty from the light retired :
    Bid her come forth,
Suffer herself to be desired,
And not blush so to be admired.   15

    Then die ! that she
The common fate of all things rare
    May read in thee :
How small a part of time they share
That are so wondrous sweet and fair !   20

                              E. WALLER.

90

TO CELIA

Drink to me only with thine eyes,
    And I will pledge with mine ;
Or leave a kiss but in the cup
    And I'll not look for wine.
The thirst that from the soul doth rise   5
    Doth ask a drink divine ;
But might I of Jove's nectar sup,
    I would not change for thine.

I sent thee late a rosy wreath,
    Not so much honouring thee   10
As giving it a hope that there
    It could not wither'd be ;
But thou thereon didst only breathe
    And sent'st it back to me ;
Since when it grows, and smells, I swear, 15
    Not of itself but thee !

                              B. JONSON.

91

CHERRY-RIPE

There is a garden in her face
    Where roses and white lilies grow ;
A heavenly paradise is that place,
    Wherein all pleasant fruits do flow ;

There cherries grow which none may buy,　　5
Till ' Cherry-Ripe ' themselves do cry.

Those cherries fairly do enclose
　Of orient pearl a double row,
Which when her lovely laughter shows,
　They look like rose-buds fill'd with snow :　10
Yet them nor peer nor prince can buy,
Till ' Cherry-Ripe ' themselves do cry.

Her eyes like angels watch them still ;
　Her brows like bended bows do stand,
Threat'ning with piercing frowns to kill　15
　All that attempt with eye or hand
Those sacred cherries to come nigh,
—Till ' Cherry-Ripe ' themselves do cry !

T. CAMPION.

92

THE POETRY OF DRESS

I

A sweet disorder in the dress
Kindles in clothes a wantonness :—
A lawn about the shoulders thrown
Into a fine distractión,—
An erring lace, which here and there　5
Enthrals the crimson stomacher —
A cuff neglectful, and thereby
Ribbands to flow confusedly,—
A winning wave, deserving note,
In the tempestuous petticoat,—　10
A careless shoe-string, in whose tie
I see a wild civility,—
Do more bewitch me, than when art
Is too precise in every part.

R. HERRICK.

93

II

Whenas in silks my Julia goes
Then, then (methinks) how sweetly flows
That liquefaction of her clothes.

Next, when I cast mine eyes and see
That brave vibration each way free ;   5
O how that glittering taketh me !

R. HERRICK.

94

III

My Love in her attire doth shew her wit,
　　It doth so well become her :
For every season she hath dressings fit,
　　For Winter, Spring, and Summer.
　　No beauty she doth miss   5
　　　When all her robes are on :
　　But Beauty's self she is
　　　When all her robes are gone.

ANON.

95

ON A GIRDLE

That which her slender waist confined
Shall now my joyful temples bind :
No monarch but would give his crown
His arms might do what this has done.

It was my Heaven's extremest sphere,   5
The pale which held that lovely deer :
My joy, my grief, my hope, my love
Did all within this circle move.

A narrow compass ! and yet there
Dwelt all that's good, and all that's fair :　10
Give me but what this ribband bound,
Take all the rest the Sun goes round.

E. WALLER.

96

TO ANTHEA WHO MAY COMMAND HIM ANY THING

Bid me to live, and I will live
　Thy Protestant to be :
Or bid me love, and I will give
　A loving heart to thee.

A heart as soft, a heart as kind,　　　5
　A heart as sound and free
As in the whole world thou canst find,
　That heart I'll give to thee.

Bid that heart stay, and it will stay,
　To honour thy decree :　　　　　10
Or bid it languish quite away,
　And 't shall do so for thee.

Bid me to weep, and I will weep
　While I have eyes to see :
And, having none, yet I will keep　　15
　A heart to weep for thee.

Bid me despair, and I'll despair
　Under that cypress tree :
Or bid me die, and I will dare
　E'en Death, to die for thee.　　　20

Thou art my life, my love, my heart,
　The very eyes of me,
And hast command of every part,
　To live and die for thee.

R. HERRICK.

97

Love not me for comely grace,
For my pleasing eye or face,
Nor for any outward part,
No, nor for my constant heart,—
    For those may fail, or turn to ill,   5
      So thou and I shall sever :
Keep therefore a true woman's eye,
And love me still, but know not why—
    So hast thou the same reason still
      To doat upon me ever !   10
                ANON.

98

Not, Celia, that I juster am
  Or better than the rest ;
For I would change each hour, like them,
  Were not my heart at rest.

But I am tied to very thee   5
  By every thought I have ;
Thy face I only care to see,
  Thy heart I only crave.

All that in woman is adored
  In thy dear self I find—   10
For the whole sex can but afford
  The handsome and the kind.

Why then should I seek further store,
  And still make love anew ?
When change itself can give no more,   15
  'Tis easy to be true.
             SIR C. SEDLEY.

99

TO ALTHEA FROM PRISON

When Love with unconfinéd wings
  Hovers within my gates,
And my divine Althea brings
  To whisper at the grates ;
When I lie tangled in her hair   5
  And fetter'd to her eye,
The Gods that wanton in the air
  Know no such liberty.

When flowing cups run swiftly round
  With no allaying Thames,   10
Our careless heads with roses crown'd,
  Our hearts with loyal flames ;
When thirsty grief in wine we steep,
  When healths and draughts go free—
Fishes that tipple in the deep   15
  Know no such liberty.

When, like committed linnets, I
  With shriller throat shall sing
The sweetness, mercy, majesty
  And glories of my King ;   20
When I shall voice aloud how good
  He is, how great should be,
Enlargéd winds, that curl the flood,
  Know no such liberty.

Stone walls do not a prison make,   25
  Nor iron bars a cage ;
Minds innocent and quiet take
  That for an hermitage :
If I have freedom in my love
  And in my soul am free,   30
Angels alone, that soar above,
  Enjoy such liberty.

COLONEL LOVELACE.

100

TO LUCASTA, ON GOING BEYOND THE SEAS

If to be absent were to be
  Away from thee ;
 Or that when I am gone
 You or I were alone ;
Then, my Lucasta, might I crave   5
Pity from blustering wind, or swallowing wave.

Though seas and land betwixt us both,
  Our faith and troth,
 Like separated souls,
 All time and space controls :   10
Above the highest sphere we meet
Unseen, unknown, and greet as Angels greet.

So then we do anticipate
  Our after-fate,
 And are alive i' the skies,   15
 If thus our lips and eyes
Can speak like spirits unconfined
In Heaven, their earthy bodies left behind.

      COLONEL LOVELACE.

101

ENCOURAGEMENTS TO A LOVER

Why so pale and wan, fond lover ?
  Prythee, why so pale ?
Will, when looking well can't move her,
  Looking ill prevail ?
  Prythee, why so pale ?   5

Why so dull and mute, young sinner ?
　　Prythee, why so mute ?
Will, when speaking well can't win her,
　　Saying nothing do't ?
　　Prythee, why so mute ?　　　　　10

Quit, quit, for shame ! this will not move,
　　This cannot take her ;
If of herself she will not love,
　　Nothing can make her :
　　The devil take her !　　　　　15

SIR J. SUCKLING.

102

A SUPPLICATION

Awake, awake, my Lyre !
And tell thy silent master's humble tale
　　In sounds that may prevail ;
Sounds that gentle thoughts inspire :
　　Though so exalted she　　　　　5
　　And I so lowly be,
Tell her, such different notes make all thy harmony.

Hark ! how the strings awake :
And, though the moving hand approach not near,
　　Themselves with awful fear　　　　10
A kind of numerous trembling make.
　　Now all thy forces try ;
　　Now all thy charms apply ;
Revenge upon her ear the conquests of her eye.

Weak Lyre ! thy virtue sure　　　　15
Is useless here, since thou art only found
　　To cure, but not to wound,
And she to wound, but not to cure.
　　Too weak too wilt thou prove
　　My passion to remove ;　　　　20
Physic to other ills, thou'rt nourishment to love.

Sleep, sleep again, my Lyre !
For thou canst never tell my humble tale
  In sounds that will prevail,
 Nor gentle thoughts in her inspire ;   25
  All thy vain mirth lay by,
  Bid thy strings silent lie,
Sleep, sleep again, my Lyre, and let thy master die.
        A. COWLEY.

103

THE MANLY HEART

 Shall I, wasting in despair,
 Die because a woman's fair ?
 Or make pale my cheeks with care
 'Cause another's rosy are ?
 Be she fairer than the day   5
 Or the flowery meads in May—
  If she think not well of me,
  What care I how fair she be ?

 Shall my silly heart be pined
 'Cause I see a woman kind ;   10
 Or a well disposèd nature
 Joinèd with a lovely feature ?
 Be she meeker, kinder, than
 Turtle-dove or pelican,
  If she be not so to me,   15
  What care I how kind she be ?

 Shall a woman's virtues move
 Me to perish for her love ?
 Or her well-deservings known
 Make me quite forget mine own ?   20
 Be she with that goodness blest
 Which may merit name of Best ;
  If she be not such to me,
  What care I how good she be ?

'Cause her fortune seems too high, 25
Shall I play the fool and die ?
She that bears a noble mind
If not outward helps she find,
Thinks what with them he would do
That without them dares her woo ; 30
    And unless that mind I see,
    What care I how great she be ?

Great or good, or kind or fair,
I will ne'er the more despair ;
If she love me, this believe, 35
I will die ere she shall grieve ;
If she slight me when I woo,
I can scorn and let her go ;
    For if she be not for me,
    What care I for whom she be ? 40

G. WITHER.

104

MELANCHOLY

Hence, all you vain delights,
As short as are the nights
    Wherein you spend your folly :
There's nought in this life sweet,
If man were wise to see't, 5
    But only melancholy,
    O sweetest melancholy !
Welcome, folded arms, and fixéd eyes,
A sigh that piercing mortifies,
A look that's fasten'd to the ground, 10
A tongue chain'd up without a sound !
Fountain heads and pathless groves,
Places which pale passion loves !
Moonlight walks, when all the fowls
Are warmly housed, save bats and owls ! 15

A midnight bell, a parting groan—
    These are the sounds we feed upon ;
Then stretch our bones in a still gloomy valley ;
Nothing 's so dainty sweet as lovely melancholy.

J. Fletcher.

105

TO A LOCK OF HAIR

Thy hue, dear pledge, is pure and bright
As in that well-remember'd night
When first thy mystic braid was wove,
And first my Agnes whisper'd love.

Since then how often hast thou prest   5
The torrid zone of this wild breast,
Whose wrath and hate have sworn to dwell
With the first sin that peopled hell ;
A breast whose blood 's a troubled ocean,
Each throb the earthquake's wild commotion ! 10
O if such clime thou canst endure
Yet keep thy hue unstain'd and pure,
What conquest o'er each erring thought
Of that fierce realm had Agnes wrought !
I had not wander'd far and wide   15
With such an angel for my guide ;
Nor heaven nor earth could then reprove me
If she had lived, and lived to love me.

Not then this world's wild joys had been
To me one savage hunting scene,   20
My sole delight the headlong race
And frantic hurry of the chase ;
To start, pursue, and bring to bay,
Rush in, drag down, and rend my prey,
Then—from the carcass turn away !   25
Mine ireful mood had sweetness tamed,
And soothed each wound which pride inflamed :—
Yes, God and man might now approve me
If thou hadst lived, and lived to love me !

Sir W. Scott.

106

THE FORSAKEN BRIDE

O waly waly up the bank,
  And waly waly down the brae,
And waly waly yon burn-side
  Where I and my Love wont to gae !
I leant my back unto an aik,   5
  I thought it was a trusty tree ;
But first it bow'd, and syne it brak,
  Sae my true Love did lichtly me.

O waly waly, but love be bonny
  A little time while it is new ;   10
But when 'tis auld, it waxeth cauld
  And fades awa' like morning dew.
O wherefore should I busk my head ?
  Or wherefore should I kame my hair ?
For my true Love has me forsook,   15
  And says he'll never loe me mair.

Now Arthur-seat sall be my bed ;
  The sheets shall ne'er be 'fil'd by me :
Saint Anton's well sall be my drink,
  Since my true Love has forsaken me.   20
Marti'mas wind, when wilt thou blaw
  And shake the green leaves aff the tree ?
O gentle Death, when wilt thou come ?
  For of my life I am wearie.

'Tis not the frost, that freezes fell,   25
  Nor blawing snaw's inclemencie ;
'Tis not sic cauld that makes me cry,
  But my Love's heart grown cauld to me.
When we came in by Glasgow town
  We were a comely sight to see ;   30
My Love was clad in the black velvét,
  And I myself in cramasie.

But had I wist, before I kist,
    That love had been sae ill to win ;
I had lockt my heart in a case of gowd   35
    And pinn'd it with a siller pin.
And, O ! if my young babe were born,
    And set upon the nurse's knee,
And I mysell were dead and gane,
    For a maid again I'll never be.   40

ANON.

107

FAIR HELEN

I wish I were where Helen lies ;
Night and day on me she cries ;
O that I were where Helen lies
    On fair Kirconnell lea !

Curst be the heart that thought the thought,
And curst the hand that fired the shot,   6
When in my arms burd Helen dropt,
    And died to succour me !

O think na but my heart was sair
When my Love dropt down and spak nae mair !
I laid her down wi' meikle care   11
    On fair Kirconnell lea.

As I went down the water-side,
None but my foe to be my guide,
None but my foe to be my guide,   15
    On fair Kirconnell lea ;

I lighted down my sword to draw,
I hackéd him in pieces sma',
I hackéd him in pieces sma',
    For her sake that died for me.   20

O Helen fair, beyond compare !
I'll make a garland of thy hair
Shall bind my heart for evermair
    Until the day I die.

O that I were where Helen lies !   25
Night and day on me she cries ;
Out of my bed she bids me rise,
    Says, ' Haste and come to me ! '

O Helen fair ! O Helen chaste !
If I were with thee, I were blest,   30
Where thou lies low and takes thy rest
    On fair Kirconnell lea.

I wish my grave were growing green,
A winding-sheet drawn ower my een,
And I in Helen's arms lying,   35
    On fair Kirconnell lea.

I wish I were where Helen lies ;
Night and day on me she cries ;
And I am weary of the skies,
    Since my Love died for me.   40

                      ANON.

108

THE TWA CORBIES

As I was walking all alane
I heard twa corbies making a mane ;
The tane unto the t'other say,
' Where sall we gang and dine to-day ? '

' —In behint yon auld fail dyke,   5
I wot there lies a new-slain Knight ;
And naebody kens that he lies there,
But his hawk, his hound, and lady fair.

' His hound is to the hunting gane,
His hawk to fetch the wild-fowl hame,   10
His lady's ta'en another mate,
So we may make our dinner sweet.

' Ye'll sit on his white hause-bane,
And I'll pick out his bonny blue een :
Wi' ae lock o' his gowden hair   15
We'll theek our nest when it grows bare.

' Mony a one for him makes mane,
But nane sall ken where he is gane ;
O'er his white banes, when they are bare,
The wind sall blaw for evermair.'   20

ANON.

109

TO BLOSSOMS

Fair pledges of a fruitful tree,
    Why do ye fall so fast ?
    Your date is not so past,
But you may stay yet here awhile
    To blush and gently smile,   5
      And go at last.

What, were ye born to be
    An hour or half's delight,
    And so to bid good-night ?
'Twas pity Nature brought ye forth   10
    Merely to show your worth,
      And lose you quite.

But you are lovely leaves, where we
    May read how soon things have
    Their end, though ne'er so brave :   15
And after they have shown their pride
    Like you awhile, they glide
      Into the grave.

R. HERRICK.

110

TO DAFFODILS

Fair Daffodils, we weep to see
    You haste away so soon :
As yet the early-rising Sun
    Has not attain'd his noon.

Stay, stay,   5
Until the hasting day
Has run
But to the even-song;
And, having pray'd together, we
Will go with you along.   10

We have short time to stay, as you,
We have as short a Spring;
As quick a growth to meet decay
As you, or any thing.
We die,   15
As your hours do, and dry
Away
Like to the Summer's rain;
Or as the pearls of morning's dew,
Ne'er to be found again.   20

R. HERRICK.

111

THOUGHTS IN A GARDEN

How vainly men themselves amaze
To win the palm, the oak, or bays,
And their uncessant labours see
Crown'd from some single herb or tree,
Whose short and narrow-vergéd shade   5
Does prudently their toils upbraid;
While all the flowers and trees do close
To weave the garlands of repose.

Fair Quiet, have I found thee here,
And Innocence thy sister dear!   10
Mistaken long, I sought you then
In busy companies of men:
Your sacred plants, if here below,
Only among the plants will grow:
Society is all but rude   15
To this delicious solitude.

No white nor red was ever seen
So amorous as this lovely green.
Fond lovers, cruel as their flame,
Cut in these trees their mistress' name :   20
Little, alas, they know or heed
How far these beauties hers exceed !
Fair trees ! where's'e'er your barks I wound,
No name shall but your own be found.

When we have run our passions' heat   25
Love hither makes his best retreat :
The gods, that mortal beauty chase,
Still in a tree did end their race :
Apollo hunted Daphne so,
Only that she might laurel grow :   30
And Pan did after Syrinx speed
Not as a nymph, but for a reed.

What wondrous life in this I lead !
Ripe apples drop about my head ;
The luscious clusters of the vine   35
Upon my mouth do crush their wine ;
The nectarine and curious peach
Into my hands themselves do reach ;
Stumbling on melons, as I pass,
Ensnared with flowers, I fall on grass.   40

Meanwhile the mind, from pleasure less,
Withdraws into its happiness ;
The mind, that ocean where each kind
Does straight its own resemblance find ;
Yet it creates, transcending these,   45
Far other worlds, and other seas ;
Annihilating all that 's made
To a green thought in a green shade.

Here at the fountain's sliding foot
Or at some fruit-tree's mossy root,   50
Casting the body's vest aside,
My soul into the boughs does glide ;

There, like a bird, it sits and sings,
Then whets and combs its silver wings,
And, till prepared for longer flight,   55
Waves in its plumes the various light.

Such was that happy Garden-state
While man there walk'd without a mate :
After a place so pure and sweet,
What other help could yet be meet !   60
But 'twas beyond a mortal's share
To wander solitary there :
Two paradises 'twere in one,
To live in Paradise alone.

How well the skilful gardener drew   65
Of flowers and herbs this dial new !
Where, from above, the milder sun
Does through a fragrant zodiac run :
And, as it works, th' industrious bee
Computes its time as well as we.   70
How could such sweet and wholesome hours
Be reckon'd, but with herbs and flowers !

                                    A. MARVELL.

112

L'ALLÉGRO

Hence, loathéd Melancholy,
Of Cerberus and blackest Midnight born
    In Stygian cave forlorn
'Mongst horrid shapes, and shrieks, and sights un-
        holy !
    Find out some uncouth cell,   5
Where brooding Darkness spreads his jealous wings
    And the night-raven sings ;
There, under ebon shades and low-brow'd rocks
    As ragged as thy locks,
In dark Cimmerian desert ever dwell.   10

        But come, thou Goddess fair and free,
        In heaven yclep'd Euphrosyne,

And by men, heart-easing Mirth,
Whom lovely Venus at a birth
With two sister Graces more   15
To ivy-crownéd Bacchus bore :
Or whether (as some sager sing)
The frolic wind that breathes the spring,
Zephyr, with Aurora playing,
As he met her once a-Maying—   20
There on beds of violets blue
And fresh-blown roses wash'd in dew
Fill'd her with thee, a daughter fair,
So buxom, blithe, and debonair.

Haste thee, Nymph, and bring with thee
Jest, and youthful jollity,   26
Quips, and cranks, and wanton wiles,
Nods, and becks, and wreathéd smiles,
Such as hang on Hebe's cheek,
And love to live in dimple sleek ;   30
Sport that wrinkled Care derides,
And Laughter holding both his sides.
Come, and trip it as you go
On the light fantastic toe ;
And in thy right hand lead with thee   35
The mountain nymph, sweet Liberty ;
And if I give thee honour due,
Mirth, admit me of thy crew,
To live with her, and live with thee
In unreprovéd pleasures free ;   40
To hear the lark begin his flight
And singing startle the dull night
From his watch-tower in the skies,
Till the dappled dawn doth rise ;
Then to come, in spite of sorrow,   45
And at my window bid good-morrow
Through the sweetbriar, or the vine,
Or the twisted eglantine :
While the cock with lively din
Scatters the rear of darkness thin,   50
And to the stack, or the barn-door,
Stoutly struts his dames before :

Oft listening how the hounds and horn
Cheerly rouse the slumbering morn,
From the side of some hoar hill,   55
Through the high wood echoing shrill.
Sometime walking, not unseen,
By hedge-row elms, on hillocks green,
Right against the eastern gate
Where the great Sun begins his state   60
Robed in flames and amber light
The clouds in thousand liveries dight ;
While the ploughman, near at hand,
Whistles o'er the furrow'd land,
And the milkmaid singeth blithe,   65
And the mower whets his scythe,
And every shepherd tells his tale
Under the hawthorn in the dale.
   Straight mine eye hath caught new pleasures
Whilst the landscape round it measures ;   70
Russet lawns, and fallows grey,
Where the nibbling flocks do stray ;
Mountains, on whose barren breast
The labouring clouds do often rest ;
Meadows trim with daisies pied,   75
Shallow brooks, and rivers wide ;
Towers and battlements it sees
Bosom'd high in tufted trees,
Where perhaps some Beauty lies,
The Cynosure of neighbouring eyes.   80
   Hard by, a cottage chimney smokes
From betwixt two aged oaks,
Where Corydon and Thyrsis, met,
Are at their savoury dinner set
Of herbs, and other country messes   85
Which the neat-handed Phillis dresses ;
And then in haste her bower she leaves
With Thestylis to bind the sheaves ;
Or, if the earlier season lead,
To the tann'd haycock in the mead.   90
   Sometimes with secure delight
The upland hamlets will invite,

When the merry bells ring round,
And the jocund rebecks sound
To many a youth and many a maid, 95
Dancing in the chequer'd shade ;
And young and old come forth to play
On a sunshine holy-day,
Till the live-long daylight fail :
Then to the spicy nut-brown ale, 100
With stories told of many a feat,
How Faery Mab the junkets eat ;
She was pinch'd, and pull'd, she said ;
And he, by Friar's lantern led ;
Tells how the drudging Goblin sweat 105
To earn his cream-bowl duly set,
When in one night, ere glimpse of morn,
His shadowy flail hath thresh'd the corn
That ten day-labourers could not end ;
Then lies him down the lubber fiend, 110
And, stretch'd out all the chimney's length,
Basks at the fire his hairy strength ;
And crop-full out of doors he flings,
Ere the first cock his matin rings.
Thus done the tales, to bed they creep, 115
By whispering winds soon lull'd asleep.
    Tower'd cities please us then
And the busy hum of men,
Where throngs of knights and barons bold,
In weeds of peace high triumphs hold, 120
With store of ladies, whose bright eyes
Rain influence, and judge the prize
Of wit or arms, while both contend
To win her grace, whom all commend.
There let Hymen oft appear 125
In saffron robe, with taper clear,
And pomp, and feast, and revelry,
With mask, and antique pageantry ;
Such sights as youthful poets dream
On summer eves by haunted stream. 130
Then to the well-trod stage anon,
If Jonson's learned sock be on,

Or sweetest Shakespeare, Fancy's child,
Warble his native wood-notes wild.
    And ever against eating cares   135
Lap me in soft Lydian airs
Married to immortal verse,
Such as the meeting soul may pierce
In notes, with many a winding bout
Of linkéd sweetness long drawn out,   140
With wanton heed and giddy cunning,
The melting voice through mazes running,
Untwisting all the chains that tie
The hidden soul of harmony;
That Orpheus' self may heave his head   145
From golden slumber, on a bed
Of heap'd Elysian flowers, and hear
Such strains as would have won the ear
Of Pluto, to have quite set free
His half-regain'd Eurydice.   150

    These delights if thou canst give,
Mirth, with thee I mean to live.

                       J. MILTON.

<h2 style="text-align:center">113</h2>

<h1 style="text-align:center">IL PENSEROSO</h1>

Hence, vain deluding Joys,
The brood of Folly without father bred!
    How little you bestead
Or fill the fixéd mind with all your toys!
    Dwell in some idle brain,   5
And fancies fond with gaudy shapes possess
    As thick and numberless
As the gay motes that people the sunbeams,
    Or likest hovering dreams
The fickle pensioners of Morpheus' train.   10

    But hail, thou goddess sage and holy,
  Hail, divinest Melancholy!

Whose saintly visage is too bright
To hit the sense of human sight,
And therefore to our weaker view 15
O'erlaid with black, staid Wisdom's hue:
Black, but such as in esteem
Prince Memnon's sister might beseem,
Or that starr'd Ethiop queen that strove
To set her beauty's praise above 20
The sea-nymphs, and their powers offended:
Yet thou art higher far descended:
Thee bright-hair'd Vesta, long of yore,
To solitary Saturn bore;
His daughter she; in Saturn's reign 25
Such mixture was not held a stain:
Oft in glimmering bowers and glades
He met her, and in secret shades
Of woody Ida's inmost grove,
Whilst yet there was no fear of Jove. 30
    Come, pensive nun, devout and pure,
Sober, steadfast, and demure,
All in a robe of darkest grain
Flowing with majestic train,
And sable stole of cypres lawn 35
Over thy decent shoulders drawn
Come, but keep thy wonted state,
With even step, and musing gait,
And looks commercing with the skies,
Thy rapt soul sitting in thine eyes: 40
There, held in holy passion still,
Forget thyself to marble, till
With a sad leaden downward cast
Thou fix them on the earth as fast: 44
And join with thee calm Peace, and Quiet,
Spare Fast, that oft with gods doth diet,
And hears the Muses in a ring
Ay round about Jove's altar sing:
And add to these retired Leisure 49
That in trim gardens takes his pleasure:—
But first, and chiefest, with thee bring
Him that yon soars on golden wing

Guiding the fiery-wheeléd throne,
The cherub Contemplatión ;
And the mute Silence hist along,   55
'Less Philomel will deign a song
In her sweetest saddest plight,
Smoothing the rugged brow of Night,
While Cynthia checks her dragon yoke
Gently o'er the accustom'd oak.   60
—Sweet bird, that shunn'st the noise of folly,
Most musical, most melancholy !
Thee, chauntress, oft, the woods among
I woo, to hear thy even-song ;
And missing thee, I walk unseen   65
On the dry smooth-shaven green,
To behold the wandering Moon
Riding near her highest noon,
Like one that had been led astray
Through the heaven's wide pathless way,   70
And oft, as if her head she bow'd,
Stooping through a fleecy cloud.
    Oft, on a plat of rising ground
I hear the far-off curfeu sound
Over some wide-water'd shore,   75
Swinging slow with sullen roar :
Or, if the air will not permit,
Some still removéd place will fit,
Where glowing embers through the room
Teach light to counterfeit a gloom ;   80
Far from all resort of mirth,
Save the cricket on the hearth,
Or the bellman's drowsy charm
To bless the doors from nightly harm.
    Or let my lamp at midnight hour   85
Be seen in some high lonely tower,
Where I may oft out-watch the Bear
With thrice-great Hermes, or unsphere
The spirit of Plato, to unfold
What worlds or what vast regions hold   90
The immortal mind, that hath forsook
Her mansion in this fleshly nook :

And of those demons that are found
In fire, air, flood, or under ground,
Whose power hath a true consent 95
With planet, or with element.
Sometime let gorgeous Tragedy
In scepter'd pall come sweeping by,
Presenting Thebes, or Pelops' line,
Or the tale of Troy divine ; 100
Or what (though rare) of later age
Ennobled hath the buskin'd stage.
   But, O sad Virgin, that thy power
Might raise Musaeus from his bower,
Or bid the soul of Orpheus sing 105
Such notes as, warbled to the string,
Drew iron tears down Pluto's cheek
And made Hell grant what Love did seek !
Or call up him that left half-told
The story of Cambuscan bold, 110
Of Camball, and of Algarsife,
And who had Canacé to wife,
That own'd the virtuous ring and glass ;
And of the wondrous horse of brass
On which the Tartar king did ride : 115
And if aught else great bards beside
In sage and solemn tunes have sung
Of turneys, and of trophies hung,
Of forests, and enchantments drear, 119
Where more is meant than meets the ear.
   Thus, Night, oft see me in thy pale career,
Till civil-suited Morn appear,
Not trick'd and frounced as she was wont
With the Attic Boy to hunt,
But kercheft in a comely cloud 125
While rocking winds are piping loud,
Or usher'd with a shower still,
When the gust hath blown his fill,
Ending on the rustling leaves
With minute drops from off the eaves. 130
And when the sun begins to fling
His flaring beams, me, goddess, bring

To archéd walks of twilight groves,
And shadows brown, that Sylvan loves,
Of pine, or monumental oak,   135
Where the rude axe, with heavéd stroke,
Was never heard the nymphs to daunt
Or fright them from their hallow'd haunt.
There in close covert by some brook
Where no profaner eye may look,   140
Hide me from day's garish eye,
While the bee with honey'd thigh,
That at her flowery work doth sing,
And the waters murmuring,
With such consort as they keep   145
Entice the dewy-feather'd Sleep ;
And let some strange mysterious dream
Wave at his wings in airy stream
Of lively portraiture display'd,
Softly on my eyelids laid :   150
And, as I wake, sweet music breathe
Above, about, or underneath,
Sent by some Spirit to mortals good,
Or the unseen Genius of the wood.
    But let my due feet never fail   155
To walk the studious cloister's pale,
And love the high-embowéd roof,
With antique pillars massy-proof,
And storied windows richly dight
Casting a dim religious light :   160
There let the pealing organ blow
To the full-voiced quire below
In service high and anthems clear,
As may with sweetness, through mine ear,
Dissolve me into ecstasies,   165
And bring all Heaven before mine eyes.
    And may at last my weary age
Find out the peaceful hermitage,
The hairy gown and mossy cell
Where I may sit and rightly spell   170
Of every star that heaven doth show,
And every herb that sips the dew ;

Till old experience do attain
To something like prophetic strain.

These pleasures, Melancholy, give,   175
And I with thee will choose to live.

J. MILTON.

114

SONG OF THE EMIGRANTS IN BERMUDA

Where the remote Bermudas ride
In the ocean's bosom unespied,
From a small boat that row'd along
The listening winds received this song :
   ' What should we do but sing His praise 5
That led us through the watery maze
Unto an isle so long unknown,
And yet far kinder than our own ?
Where He the huge sea-monsters wracks,
That lift the deep upon their backs,   10
He lands us on a grassy stage,
Safe from the storms and prelate's rage :
He gave us this eternal spring
Which here enamels everything,
And sends the fowls to us in care   15
On daily visits through the air ;
He hangs in shades the orange bright
Like golden lamps in a green night,
And does in the pomegranates close
Jewels more rich than Ormus shows :   20
He makes the figs our mouths to meet,
And throws the melons at our feet ;
But apples plants of such a price,
No tree could ever bear them twice.
With cedars chosen by His hand   25
From Lebanon He stores the land ;
And makes the hollow seas that roar
Proclaim the ambergris on shore.
He cast (of which we rather boast)
The Gospel's pearl upon our coast ;   30

And in these rocks for us did frame
A temple where to sound His name.
Oh ! let our voice His praise exalt
Till it arrive at Heaven's vault,   34
Which thence (perhaps) rebounding may
Echo beyond the Mexique bay ! '
Thus sung they in the English boat
An holy and a cheerful note :
And all the way, to guide their chime,
With falling oars they kept the time.   40

A. MARVELL.

115

AT A SOLEMN MUSIC

Blest pair of Sirens, pledges of Heaven's joy,
   Sphere-born harmonious Sisters, Voice and Verse!
Wed your divine sounds, and mixt power employ
   Dead things with inbreathed sense able to pierce;
And to our high-raised phantasy present   5
That undisturbéd Song of pure concent
Ay sung before the sapphire-colour'd throne
     To Him that sits thereon,
With saintly shout and solemn jubilee ;
Where the bright Seraphim in burning row   10
Their loud uplifted angel-trumpets blow ;
And the Cherubic host in thousand quires
Touch their immortal harps of golden wires,
With those just Spirits that wear victorious palms,
     Hymns devout and holy psalms   15
     Singing everlastingly :
That we on earth, with undiscording voice
May rightly answer that melodious noise ;
As once we did, till disproportion'd sin
Jarr'd against nature's chime, and with harsh din
Broke the fair music that all creatures made   21
To their great Lord, whose love their motion sway'd
In perfect diapason, whilst they stood
In first obedience, and their state of good.

O may we soon again renew that Song,   25
And keep in tune with Heaven, till God ere long
To His celestial consort us unite,
To live with Him, and sing in endless morn of light.

J. MILTON.

116

ALEXANDER'S FEAST, OR, THE POWER OF MUSIC

'Twas at the royal feast for Persia won
    By Philip's warlike son—
    Aloft in awful state
    The godlike hero sate
    On his imperial throne ;   5
His valiant peers were placed around,
Their brows with roses and with myrtles bound
    (So should desert in arms be crown'd) ;
    The lovely Thais by his side
    Sate like a blooming eastern bride   10
    In flower of youth and beauty's pride :—
    Happy, happy, happy pair !
      None but the brave
      None but the brave
    None but the brave deserves the fair !   15

    Timotheus placed on high
    Amid the tuneful quire
With flying fingers touch'd the lyre :
The trembling notes ascend the sky
    And heavenly joys inspire.   20
    The song began from Jove
Who left his blissful seats above—
Such is the power of mighty love !
A dragon's fiery form belied the god ;
Sublime on radiant spires he rode   25
When he to fair Olympia prest,
And while he sought her snowy breast,

Then round her slender waist he curl'd,
And stamp'd an image of himself, a sovereign of the
      world.   29
—The listening crowd admire the lofty sound ;
 A present deity ! they shout around :
A present deity ! the vaulted roofs rebound :
      With ravish'd ears
      The monarch hears,
      Assumes the god,   35
      Affects to nod
    And seems to shake the spheres.

The praise of Bacchus then the sweet musician sung,
 Of Bacchus ever fair and ever young :
    The jolly god in triumph comes !   40
    Sound the trumpets, beat the drums !
      Flush'd with a purple grace
      He shows his honest face :
Now give the hautboys breath ; he comes, he comes!
    Bacchus, ever fair and young,   45
    Drinking joys did first ordain ;
    Bacchus' blessings are a treasure,
    Drinking is the soldier's pleasure :
      Rich the treasure,
      Sweet the pleasure,   50
    Sweet is pleasure after pain.

Soothed with the sound, the king grew vain ;
Fought all his battles o'er again,
And thrice he routed all his foes, and thrice he slew
      the slain.
    The master saw the madness rise,   55
    His glowing cheeks, his ardent eyes ;
And while he Heaven and Earth defied
Changed his hand and check'd his pride.
      He chose a mournful Muse
      Soft pity to infuse :   60
He sung Darius great and good,
    By too severe a fate
Fallen, fallen, fallen, fallen,
    Fallen from his high estate,

And weltering in his blood ;   65
Deserted, at his utmost need,
By those his former bounty fed ;
On the bare earth exposed he lies
With not a friend to close his eyes.
—With downcast looks the joyless victor sate,
Revolving in his alter'd soul   71
   The various turns of Chance below ;
And now and then a sigh he stole,
   And tears began to flow.

The mighty master smiled to see   75
That love was in the next degree ;
'Twas but a kindred-sound to move,
For pity melts the mind to love.
Softly sweet, in Lydian measures
Soon he soothed his soul to pleasures.   80
War, he sung, is toil and trouble,
Honour but an empty bubble ;
Never ending, still beginning,
   Fighting still, and still destroying ;
If the world be worth thy winning,   85
   Think, O think, it worth enjoying :
Lovely Thais sits beside thee,
Take the good the gods provide thee !
—The many rend the skies with loud applause ;
So Love was crown'd, but Music won the cause.
The prince, unable to conceal his pain,   91
     Gazed on the fair
    Who caused his care,
And sigh'd and look'd, sigh'd and look'd,
Sigh'd and look'd, and sigh'd again :   95
At length with love and wine at once opprest
The vanquish'd victor sunk upon her breast.

Now strike the golden lyre again :
A louder yet, and yet a louder strain !
Break his bands of sleep asunder   100
And rouse him like a rattling peal of thunder.
Hark, hark ! the horrid sound
   Has raised up his head :

As awaked from the dead
And amazed he stares around.   105
Revenge, revenge, Timotheus cries,
See the Furies arise !
　　See the snakes that they rear
　　How they hiss in their hair,
And the sparkles that flash from their eyes !   110
　　　　Behold a ghastly band,
　　　　Each a torch in his hand !
Those are Grecian ghosts, that in battle were slain
　　　　And unburied remain
　　　　Inglorious on the plain :   115
　　　　Give the vengeance due
　　　　To the valiant crew !
Behold how they toss their torches on high,
How they point to the Persian abodes
And glittering temples of their hostile gods.   120
—The princes applaud with a furious joy :
And the King seized a flambeau with zeal to destroy ;
　　　　Thais led the way
　　　　To light him to his prey,
And like another Helen, fired another Troy !   125

　　　　—Thus, long ago,
Ere heaving bellows learn'd to blow,
　　While organs yet were mute,
　　Timotheus, to his breathing flute
　　　　And sounding lyre,   130
Could swell the soul to rage, or kindle soft desire.
　　At last divine Cecilia came,
　　Inventress of the vocal frame ;
The sweet enthusiast from her sacred store
　　Enlarged the former narrow bounds,   135
　　And added length to solemn sounds,
With Nature's mother-wit, and arts unknown before.
—Let old Timotheus yield the prize
　　Or both divide the crown ;
He raised a mortal to the skies ;   140
　　She drew an angel down !

　　　　　　　　　　　　　　　J DRYDEN.

117

ODE ON THE PLEASURE ARISING FROM VICISSITUDE

Now the golden Morn aloft
　Waves her dew-bespangled wing,
With vermeil cheek and whisper soft
　She woos the tardy Spring :
Till April starts, and calls around 　　5
The sleeping fragrance from the ground,
And lightly o'er the living scene
Scatters his freshest, tenderest green.

New-born flocks, in rustic dance,
　Frisking ply their feeble feet ; 　　10
Forgetful of their wintry trance
　The birds his presence greet :
But chief, the sky-lark warbles high
His trembling thrilling ecstasy ;
And lessening from the dazzled sight, 　　15
Melts into air and liquid light.

Yesterday the sullen year
　Saw the snowy whirlwind fly ;
Mute was the music of the air,
　The herd stood drooping by : 　　20
Their raptures now that wildly flow
No yesterday nor morrow know ;
'Tis Man alone that joy descries
With forward and reverted eyes.

Smiles on past Misfortune's brow   25
  Soft Reflection's hand can trace,
And o'er the cheek of Sorrow throw
  A melancholy grace ;
While Hope prolongs our happier hour,
Or deepest shades, that dimly lour   30
And blacken round our weary way,
Gilds with a gleam of distant day.

Still, where rosy Pleasure leads,
  See a kindred Grief pursue ;
Behind the steps that Misery treads   35
  Approaching Comfort view :
The hues of bliss more brightly glow
Chastised by sabler tints of woe,
And blended form, with artful strife,
The strength and harmony of life.   40

See the wretch that long has tost
  On the thorny bed of pain,
At length repair his vigour lost
  And breathe and walk again :
The meanest floweret of the vale,   45
The simplest note that swells the gale,
The common sun, the air, the skies,
To him are opening Paradise.

                    T. GRAY.

118

THE QUIET LIFE

Happy the man, whose wish and care
  A few paternal acres bound,
Content to breathe his native air
      In his own ground.

Whose herds with milk, whose fields with bread,
  Whose flocks supply him with attire ;   6
Whose trees in summer yield him shade,
      In winter fire.

Blest, who can unconcern'dly find
   Hours, days, and years slide soft away   10
In health of body, peace of mind,
       Quiet by day,

Sound sleep by night ; study and ease
   Together mix'd ; sweet recreation,
And innocence, which most does please   15
       With meditation.

Thus let me live, unseen, unknown ;
   Thus unlamented let me die ;
Steal from the world, and not a stone
       Tell where I lie.   20

A. POPE.

119

THE BLIND BOY

O say what is that thing call'd Light,
   Which I must ne'er enjoy ;
What are the blessings of the sight,
   O tell your poor blind boy !

You talk of wondrous things you see,   5
   You say the sun shines bright ;
I feel him warm, but how can he
   Or make it day or night ?

My day or night myself I make
   Whene'er I sleep or play ;   10
And could I ever keep awake
   With me 'twere always day.

With heavy sighs I often hear
   You mourn my hapless woe ;
But sure with patience I can bear   15
   A loss I ne'er can know.

Then let not what I cannot have
   My cheer of mind destroy ;
Whilst thus I sing, I am a king,
   Although a poor blind boy.   20

C. CIBBER.

120

ON A FAVOURITE CAT, DROWNED IN A TUB OF GOLDFISHES

'Twas on a lofty vase's side,
Where China's gayest art had dyed
  The azure flowers that blow,
Demurest of the tabby kind,
The pensive Selima, reclined, 5
  Gazed on the lake below.

Her conscious tail her joy declared:
The fair round face, the snowy beard,
  The velvet of her paws,
Her coat that with the tortoise vies, 10
Her ears of jet, and emerald eyes,
  She saw; and purr'd applause.

Still had she gazed, but 'midst the tide
Two angel forms were seen to glide,
  The Genii of the stream: 15
Their scaly armour's Tyrian hue
Through richest purple to the view
  Betray'd a golden gleam.

The hapless Nymph with wonder saw:
A whisker first, and then a claw 20
  With many an ardent wish
She stretch'd, in vain, to reach the prize—
What female heart can gold despise?
  What Cat's averse to Fish?

Presumptuous maid! with looks intent 25
Again she stretch'd, again she bent,
  Nor knew the gulf between—
Malignant Fate sat by and smiled—
The slippery verge her feet beguiled;
  She tumbled headlong in! 30

Eight times emerging from the flood
She mew'd to every watery God
   Some speedy aid to send :—
No Dolphin came, no Nereid stirr'd,
Nor cruel Tom nor Susan heard—   35
   A favourite has no friend !

From hence, ye Beauties, undeceived,
Know one false step is ne'er retrieved,
   And be with caution bold :
Not all that tempts your wandering eyes   40
And heedless hearts, is lawful prize,
   Nor all that glisters, gold !

T. GRAY.

121

TO CHARLOTTE PULTENEY

Timely blossom, Infant fair,
Fondling of a happy pair,
Every morn and every night
Their solicitous delight,
Sleeping, waking, still at ease,   5
Pleasing, without skill to please ;
Little gossip, blithe and hale,
Tattling many a broken tale,
Singing many a tuneless song,
Lavish of a heedless tongue ;   10
Simple maiden, void of art,
Babbling out the very heart,
Yet abandon'd to thy will,
Yet imagining no ill,
Yet too innocent to blush ;   15
Like the linnet in the bush
To the mother-linnet's note
Moduling her slender throat ;
Chirping forth thy petty joys,
Wanton in the change of toys,   20
Like the linnet green, in May
Flitting to each bloomy spray ;

Wearied then and glad of rest,
Like the linnet in the nest :—
This thy present happy lot,   25
This, in time will be forgot :
Other pleasures, other cares,
Ever-busy Time prepares ;
And thou shalt in thy daughter see,
This picture, once, resembled thee.   30

A. Philips.

122

RULE, BRITANNIA

When Britain first at Heaven's command
  Arose from out the azure main,
This was the charter of the land,
  And guardian angels sung this strain :
Rule, Britannia ! rule the waves !   5
  Britons never will be slaves.

The nations not so blest as thee
  Must in their turns to tyrants fall,
While thou shalt flourish great and free,
  The dread and envy of them all.   10

Still more majestic shalt thou rise,
  More dreadful from each foreign stroke ;
As the loud blast that tears the skies
  Serves but to root thy native oak.

Thee haughty tyrants ne'er shall tame ;   15
  All their attempts to bend thee down
Will but arouse thy generous flame,
  But work their woe and thy renown.

To thee belongs the rural reign ;
  Thy cities shall with commerce shine ;   20
All thine shall be the subject main,
  And every shore it circles thine !

The Muses, still with Freedom found,
  Shall to thy happy coast repair ;

Blest Isle, with matchless beauty crown'd,   25
  And manly hearts to guard the fair :—
Rule, Britannia ! rule the waves !
  Britons never will be slaves !

J. THOMSON.

123

THE BARD

A Pindaric Ode

' Ruin seize thee, ruthless King !
  Confusion on thy banners wait !
Tho' fann'd by Conquest's crimson wing
  They mock the air with idle state.
Helm, nor hauberk's twisted mail,   5
Nor e'en thy virtues, tyrant, shall avail
To save thy secret soul from nightly fears,
From Cambria's curse, from Cambria's tears ! '
—Such were the sounds that o'er the crested pride
  Of the first Edward scatter'd wild dismay,   10
As down the steep of Snowdon's shaggy side
  He wound with toilsome march his long array :—
Stout Glo'ster stood aghast in speechless trance ;
' To arms ! ' cried Mortimer, and couch'd his
      quivering lance.

On a rock, whose haughty brow   15
Frowns o'er old Conway's foaming flood,
  Robed in the sable garb of woe,
With haggard eyes the Poet stood ;
(Loose his beard and hoary hair
Stream'd like a meteor to the troubled air ;)   20
And with a master's hand and prophet's fire
Struck the deep sorrows of his lyre :
' Hark, how each giant oak and desert cave
  Sighs to the torrent's awful voice beneath !   24
O'er thee, O King ! their hundred arms they wave,
  Revenge on thee in hoarser murmurs breathe ;

Vocal no more, since Cambria's fatal day,
To high-born Hoel's harp, or soft Llewellyn's lay.

'   Cold is Cadwallo's tongue,
      That hush'd the stormy main :   30
Brave Urien sleeps upon his craggy bed :
      Mountains, ye mourn in vain
      Modred, whose magic song
Made huge Plinlimmon bow his cloud-topt head.
      On dreary Arvon's shore they lie   35
Smear'd with gore and ghastly pale :
Far, far aloof the affrighted ravens sail ;
      The famish'd eagle screams, and passes by.
Dear lost companions of my tuneful art,
      Dear as the light that visits these sad eyes,   40
Dear as the ruddy drops that warm my heart,
      Ye died amidst your dying country's cries—
No more I weep.   They do not sleep ;
      On yonder cliffs, a griesly band,
I see them sit ; they linger yet,   45
      Avengers of their native land :
With me in dreadful harmony they join,
And weave with bloody hands the tissue of thy line.'

" Weave the warp and weave the woof,
      The winding-sheet of Edward's race :   50
Give ample room and verge enough
      The characters of hell to trace.
Mark the year and mark the night
When Severn shall re-echo with affright
The shrieks of death thro' Berkley's roofs that ring,
Shrieks of an agonizing king !   56
      She-wolf of France, with unrelenting fangs
That tear'st the bowels of thy mangled mate,
      From thee be born, who o'er thy country hangs
The scourge of Heaven !   What terrors round him
      wait !   60
Amazement in his van, with Flight combined,
And Sorrow's faded form, and Solitude behind.

" Mighty victor, mighty lord,
      Low on his funeral couch he lies !

No pitying heart, no eye, afford   65
   A tear to grace his obsequies.
Is the sable warrior fled ?
Thy son is gone.   He rests among the dead.
The swarm that in thy noon-tide beam were born ?
—Gone to salute the rising morn.   70
Fair laughs the Morn, and soft the zephyr blows,
   While proudly riding o'er the azure realm
In gallant trim the gilded Vessel goes :
   Youth on the prow, and Pleasure at the helm :
Regardless of the sweeping Whirlwind's sway,   75
That, hush'd in grim repose, expects his evening prey.

   " Fill high the sparkling bowl,
The rich repast prepare ;
   Reft of a crown, he yet may share the feast :
Close by the regal chair   80
   Fell Thirst and Famine scowl
A baleful smile upon their baffled guest.
Heard ye the din of battle bray,
   Lance to lance, and horse to horse ?   84
   Long years of havoc urge their destined course,
And thro' the kindred squadrons mow their way.
Ye towers of Julius, London's lasting shame,
With many a foul and midnight murder fed,
   Revere his Consort's faith, his Father's fame,
And spare the meek usurper's holy head !   90
Above, below, the rose of snow,
   Twined with her blushing foe, we spread :
The bristled boar in infant-gore
   Wallows beneath the thorny shade.   94
Now, brothers, bending o'er the accursèd loom,
Stamp we our vengeance deep, and ratify his doom.

   " Edward, lo ! to sudden fate
   (Weave we the woof ; The thread is spun ;)
Half of thy heart we consecrate.
   (The web is wove ; The work is done.) "   100
' Stay, O stay ! nor thus forlorn
Leave me unbless'd, unpitied, here to mourn :

In yon bright track that fires the western skies
They melt, they vanish from my eyes.   104
But O ! what solemn scenes on Snowdon's height
   Descending slow their glittering skirts unroll ?
Visions of glory, spare my aching sight,
   Ye unborn ages, crowd not on my soul !
No more our long-lost Arthur we bewail :—   109
All hail, ye genuine kings ! Britannia's issue, hail !

   ' Girt with many a baron bold
Sublime their starry fronts they rear ;
   And gorgeous dames, and statesmen old
In bearded majesty, appear.
In the midst a form divine !   115
Her eye proclaims her of the Briton-Line :
Her lion-port, her awe-commanding face
Attemper'd sweet to virgin-grace.
What strings symphonious tremble in the air,
   What strains of vocal transport round her play ?
Hear from the grave, great Taliessin, hear ;   121
   They breathe a soul to animate thy clay.
Bright Rapture calls, and soaring as she sings,
Waves in the eye of Heaven her many-colour'd
     wings.

   The verse adorn again   125
   Fierce War, and faithful Love,
And Truth severe, by fairy Fiction drest.
   In buskin'd measures move
Pale Grief, and pleasing Pain,
With Horror, tyrant of the throbbing breast.   130
A voice as of the cherub-choir
   Gales from blooming Eden bear,
   And distant warblings lessen on my ear,
That lost in long futurity expire.   134
Fond impious man, think'st thou yon sanguine cloud
   Raised by thy breath, has quench'd the orb of day?
To-morrow he repairs the golden flood
   And warms the nations with redoubled ray.
Enough for me : with joy I see
   The different doom our fates assign :   140

Be thine Despair and sceptred Care ;
  To triumph and to die are mine.'
—He spoke, and headlong from the mountain's
  height
Deep in the roaring tide he plunged to endless night.

T. GRAY.

124

ODE WRITTEN IN MDCCXLVI

How sleep the Brave who sink to rest
By all their Country's wishes blest !
When Spring, with dewy fingers cold,
Returns to deck their hallow'd mould,
She there shall dress a sweeter sod   5
Than Fancy's feet have ever trod.

By fairy hands their knell is rung,
By forms unseen their dirge is sung :
There Honour comes, a pilgrim grey,   9
To bless the turf that wraps their clay ;
And Freedom shall awhile repair
To dwell, a weeping hermit, there !

W. COLLINS.

125

LAMENT FOR CULLODEN

The lovely lass o' Inverness,
  Nae joy nor pleasure can she see ;
For e'en and morn she cries, Alas !
  And ay the saut tear blin's her ee :
Drumossie moor—Drumossie day—   5
  A waefu' day it was to me !
For there I lost my father dear,
  My father dear, and brethren three.

Their winding-sheet the bluidy clay,
  Their graves are growing green to see :   10

And by them lies the dearest lad
　　That ever blest a woman's ee !
Now wae to thee, thou cruel lord,
　　A bluidy man I trow thou be ;
For mony a heart thou hast made sair　　15
　　That ne'er did wrang to thine or thee.

R. Burns.

126

LAMENT FOR FLODDEN

I've heard them lilting at the ewe-milking,
　　Lasses a' lilting before dawn of day ;
But now they are moaning on ilka green loaning—
　　The Flowers of the Forest are a' wede away.

At bughts, in the morning, nae blythe lads are
　　　　scorning,　　　　　　　　　　　　　　　　5
　　Lasses are lonely and dowie and wae ;
Nae daffing, nae gabbing, but sighing and sabbing,
　　Ilk ane lifts her leglin and hies her away.

In har'st, at the shearing, nae youths now are jeering,
　　Bandsters are runkled, and lyart, or grey ;　　10
At fair or at preaching, nae wooing, nae fleeching—
　　The Flowers of the Forest are a' wede away.

At e'en, in the gloaming, nae younkers are roaming
　　'Bout stacks with the lasses at bogle to play ;
But ilk maid sits dreary, lamenting her dearie—　　15
　　The Flowers of the Forest are weded away.

Dool and wae for the order, sent our lads to the
　　　　Border !
　　The English, for ance, by guile wan the day ;
The Flowers of the Forest, that fought aye the fore-
　　　　most,　　　　　　　　　　　　　　　　　19
　　The prime of our land, are cauld in the clay.

We'll hear nae mair lilting at the ewe-milking ;
　　Women and bairns are heartless and wae ;
Sighing and moaning on ilka green loaning—
　　The Flowers of the Forest are a' wede away.

J. Elliot.

127

THE BRAES OF YARROW

' Thy braes were bonny, Yarrow stream,
　　When first on them I met my lover ;
Thy braes how dreary, Yarrow stream,
　　When now thy waves his body cover !
For ever now, O Yarrow stream,　　　　　　　5
　　Thou art to me a stream of sorrow ;
For never on thy banks shall I
　　Behold my love, the flower of Yarrow.

' He promised me a milk-white steed
　　To bear me to his father's bowers ;　　　10
He promised me a little page
　　To squire me to his father's towers ;
He promised me a wedding-ring,—
　　The wedding-day was fix'd to-morrow ;—
Now he is wedded to his grave,　　　　　　15
　　Alas, his watery grave, in Yarrow !

' Sweet were his words when last we met ;
　　My passion I as freely told him ;
Clasp'd in his arms, I little thought
　　That I should never more behold him !　20
Scarce was he gone, I saw his ghost ;
　　It vanish'd with a shriek of sorrow ;
Thrice did the water-wraith ascend,
　　And gave a doleful groan thro' Yarrow.

' His mother from the window look'd　　　25
　　With all the longing of a mother ;
His little sister weeping walk'd
　　The green-wood path to meet her brother ;
They sought him east, they sought him west,
　　They sought him all the forest thorough ;　30
They only saw the cloud of night,
　　They only heard the roar of Yarrow.

'No longer from thy window look—
  Thou hast no son, thou tender mother !
No longer walk, thou lovely maid ;   35
  Alas, thou hast no more a brother !
No longer seek him east or west
  And search no more the forest thorough ;
For, wandering in the night so dark,
  He fell a lifeless corpse in Yarrow.   40

'The tear shall never leave my cheek,
  No other youth shall be my marrow—
I'll seek thy body in the stream,
  And then with thee I'll sleep in Yarrow.'
—The tear did never leave her cheek,   45
  No other youth became her marrow ;
She found his body in the stream,
  And now with him she sleeps in Yarrow.

                                    J. LOGAN.

128

WILLY DROWNED IN YARROW

Down in yon garden sweet and gay
  Where bonnie grows the lily,
I heard a fair maid sighing say,
  'My wish be wi' sweet Willie !

'Willie's rare, and Willie's fair,   5
  And Willie's wondrous bonny ;
And Willie hecht to marry me
  Gin e'er he married ony.

'O gentle wind, that bloweth south
  From where my Love repaireth,   10
Convey a kiss frae his dear mouth
  And tell me how he fareth !

'O tell sweet Willie to come doun
  And hear the mavis singing,
And see the birds on ilka bush   15
  And leaves around them hinging.

‘ The lav’rock there, wi’ her white breast
   And gentle throat sae narrow ;
There’s sport eneuch for gentlemen
   On Leader haughs and Yarrow.   20

‘ O Leader haughs are wide and braid
   And Yarrow haughs are bonny ;
There Willie hecht to marry me
   If e’er he married ony.

‘ But Willie’s gone, whom I thought on,   25
   And does not hear me weeping ;
Draws many a tear frae ’s true love’s e’e
   When other maids are sleeping.

‘ Yestreen I made my bed fu’ braid,
   The night I’ll mak’ it narrow,   30
For a’ the live-lang winter night
   I lie twined o’ my marrow.

‘ O came ye by yon water-side ?
   Pou’d you the rose or lily ?
Or came you by yon meadow green,   35
   Or saw you my sweet Willie ? ’

She sought him up, she sought him down,
   She sought him braid and narrow ;
Syne, in the cleaving of a craig,
   She found him drown’d in Yarrow !   40

                             ANON.

129

LOSS OF THE ROYAL GEORGE

    Toll for the Brave !
    The brave that are no more !
      All sunk beneath the wave
    Fast by their native shore !

      Eight hundred of the brave,   5
    Whose courage well was tried,
      Had made the vessel heel
    And laid her on her side.

A land-breeze shook the shrouds
And she was overset ;   10
    Down went the Royal George,
With all her crew complete.

    Toll for the brave !
Brave Kempenfelt is gone ;
    His last sea-fight is fought,   15
His work of glory done.

    It was not in the battle ;
No tempest gave the shock ;
    She sprang no fatal leak,
She ran upon no rock.   20

    His sword was in the sheath,
His fingers held the pen,
    When Kempenfelt went down
With twice four hundred men.

    Weigh the vessel up   25
Once dreaded by our foes,
    And mingle with your cup
The tears that England owes.

    Her timbers yet are sound,
And she may float again   30
    Full charged with England's thunder,
And plough the distant main :

    But Kempenfelt is gone,
His victories are o'er ;
    And he and his eight hundred   35
Must plough the wave no more.

                                        W. COWPER.

130
BLACK-EYED SUSAN

All in the Downs the fleet was moor'd,
    The streamers waving in the wind,
When black-eyed Susan came aboard ;
    ' O ! where shall I my true-love find ?

Tell me, ye jovial sailors, tell me true
If my sweet William sails among the crew.'

William, who high upon the yard
　　Rock'd with the billow to and fro,
Soon as her well-known voice he heard,
　　He sigh'd, and cast his eyes below :　　10
The cord slides swiftly through his glowing hands,
And quick as lightning on the deck he stands.

So the sweet lark, high poised in air,
　　Shuts close his pinions to his breast
If chance his mate's shrill call he hear,　　15
　　And drops at once into her nest :—
The noblest captain in the British fleet
Might envy William's lips those kisses sweet.

' O Susan, Susan, lovely dear,
　　My vows shall ever true remain ;　　20
Let me kiss off that falling tear ;
　　We only part to meet again.
Change as ye list, ye winds ; my heart shall be
The faithful compass that still points to thee.

' Believe not what the landmen say　　25
　　Who tempt with doubts thy constant mind :
They'll tell thee, sailors, when away,
　　In every port a mistress find :
Yes, yes, believe them when they tell thee so,
For Thou art present wheresoe'er I go.　　30

' If to far India's coast we sail,
　　Thy eyes are seen in diamonds bright,
Thy breath is Afric's spicy gale,
　　Thy skin is ivory so white.
Thus every beauteous object that I view　　35
Wakes in my soul some charm of lovely Sue.

' Though battle call me from thy arms
　　Let not my pretty Susan mourn ;
Though cannons roar, yet safe from harms
　　William shall to his Dear return.　　40
Love turns aside the balls that round me fly,
Lest precious tears should drop from Susan's eye.'

The boatswain gave the dreadful word,
  The sails their swelling bosom spread ;
No longer must she stay aboard ;   45
  They kiss'd, she sigh'd, he hung his head.
Her lessening boat unwilling rows to land ;
'Adieu !' she cries ; and waved her lily hand.

J. GAY.

131

SALLY IN OUR ALLEY

Of all the girls that are so smart
  There's none like pretty Sally ;
She is the darling of my heart,
  And she lives in our alley.
There is no lady in the land   5
  Is half so sweet as Sally ;
She is the darling of my heart,
  And she lives in our alley.

Her father he makes cabbage-nets
  And through the streets does cry 'em ;
Her mother she sells laces long   11
  To such as please to buy 'em :
But sure such folks could ne'er beget
  So sweet a girl as Sally !
She is the darling of my heart,   15
  And she lives in our alley.

When she is by, I leave my work,
  I love her so sincerely ;
My master comes like any Turk,
  And bangs me most severely—   20
But let him bang his bellyful,
  I'll bear it all for Sally ;
She is the darling of my heart,
  And she lives in our alley.

Of all the days that 's in the week   25
  I dearly love but one day—

And that's the day that comes betwixt
  A Saturday and Monday ;
For then I'm drest all in my best
  To walk abroad with Sally ;   30
She is the darling of my heart,
  And she lives in our alley.

My master carries me to church,
  And often am I blamed
Because I leave him in the lurch   35
  As soon as text is named ;
I leave the church in sermon-time
  And slink away to Sally ;
She is the darling of my heart,
  And she lives in our alley.   40

When Christmas comes about again
  O then I shall have money ;
I'll hoard it up, and box and all,
  I'll give it to my honey :
I would it were ten thousand pound,   45
  I'd give it all to Sally ;
She is the darling of my heart,
  And she lives in our alley.

My master and the neighbours all
  Make game of me and Sally,   50
And, but for her, I'd better be
  A slave and row a galley ;
But when my seven long years are out
  O then I'll marry Sally,—
O then we'll wed, and then we'll bed,   55
  But not in our alley !

H. CAREY.

132

A FAREWELL

Go fetch to me a pint o' wine,
  An' fill it in a silver tassie ;
That I may drink before I go
  A service to my bonnie lassie :

The boat rocks at the pier o' Leith,   5
  Fu' loud the wind blaws frae the Ferry,
The ship rides by the Berwick-law,
  And I maun leave my bonnie Mary.

The trumpets sound, the banners fly,
  The glittering spears are rankéd ready ;
The shouts o' war are heard afar,   11
  The battle closes thick and bloody ;
But it 's not the roar o' sea or shore
  Wad make me langer wish to tarry ;
Nor shout o' war that 's heard afar—   15
  It 's leaving thee, my bonnie Mary.

R. BURNS.

133

If doughty deeds my lady please
  Right soon I'll mount my steed ;
And strong his arm, and fast his seat,
  That bears frae me the meed.
I'll wear thy colours in my cap,   5
  Thy picture in my heart ;
And he that bends not to thine eye
  Shall rue it to his smart.
    Then tell me how to woo thee, love ;
      O tell me how to woo thee !   10
    For thy dear sake, nae care I'll take,
    Tho' ne'er another trow me.

If gay attire delight thine eye
  I'll dight me in array ;
I'll tend thy chamber door all night,   15
  And squire thee all the day.
If sweetest sounds can win thine ear,
  These sounds I'll strive to catch ;
Thy voice I'll steal to woo thysell,
  That voice that nane can match.   20

But if fond love thy heart can gain,
  I never broke a vow ;

Nae maiden lays her skaith to me,
  I never loved but you.
For you alone I ride the ring,   25
  For you I wear the blue ;
For you alone I strive to sing,
  O tell me how to woo !
    Then tell me how to woo thee, love ;
      O tell me how to woo thee !   30
    For thy dear sake, nae care I'll take,
      Tho' ne'er another trow me.

   R. GRAHAM OF GARTMORE.

134

TO A YOUNG LADY

Sweet stream, that winds through yonder glade,
Apt emblem of a virtuous maid—
Silent and chaste she steals along,
Far from the world's gay busy throng :
With gentle yet prevailing force,   5
Intent upon her destined course ;
Graceful and useful all she does,
Blessing and blest where'er she goes ;
Pure-bosom'd as that watery glass,
And Heaven reflected in her face.   10

   W. COWPER.

135

THE SLEEPING BEAUTY

Sleep on, and dream of Heaven awhile—
  Tho' shut so close thy laughing eyes,
Thy rosy lips still wear a smile
  And move, and breathe delicious sighs !

Ah, now soft blushes tinge her cheeks   5
  And mantle o'er her neck of snow :
Ah, now she murmurs, now she speaks
  What most I wish—and fear to know !

She starts, she trembles, and she weeps !
  Her fair hands folded on her breast :   10
—And now, how like a saint she sleeps !
  A seraph in the realms of rest !

Sleep on secure ! Above control
  Thy thoughts belong to Heaven and thee :
And may the secret of thy soul   15
  Remain within its sanctuary !

S. ROGERS.

136

For ever, Fortune, wilt thou prove
An unrelenting foe to Love,
And when we meet a mutual heart
Come in between, and bid us part ?

Bid us sigh on from day to day,   5
And wish and wish the soul away ;
Till youth and genial years are flown,
And all the life of life is gone ?

But busy, busy, still art thou,
To bind the loveless joyless vow,   10
The heart from pleasure to delude,
And join the gentle to the rude.

For once, O Fortune, hear my prayer,
And I absolve thy future care ;
All other blessings I resign,   15
Make but the dear Amanda mine.

J. THOMSON.

137

The merchant, to secure his treasure,
  Conveys it in a borrow'd name :
Euphelia serves to grace my measure,
  But Cloe is my real flame.

My softest verse, my darling lyre   5
  Upon Euphelia's toilet lay—
When Cloe noted her desire
  That I should sing, that I should play.

My lyre I tune, my voice I raise,
  But with my numbers mix my sighs ;   10
And whilst I sing Euphelia's praise,
  I fix my soul on Cloe's eyes.

Fair Cloe blush'd : Euphelia frown'd :
  I sung, and gazed ; I play'd, and trembled :
And Venus to the Loves around   15
  Remark'd how ill we all dissembled.

M. PRIOR.

138

When lovely woman stoops to folly
  And finds too late that men betray,—
What charm can soothe her melancholy,
  What art can wash her guilt away ?

The only art her guilt to cover,   5
  To hide her shame from every eye,
To give repentance to her lover
  And wring his bosom, is—to die.

O. GOLDSMITH.

139

Ye flowery banks o' bonnie Doon,
  How can ye bloom sae fair !
How can ye chant, ye little birds,
  And I sae fu' o' care !

Thou'll break my heart, thou bonnie bird   5
  That sings upon the bough ;
Thou minds me o' the happy days
  When my fause Luve was true.

Thou'lt break my heart, thou bonnie bird
   That sings beside thy mate ;   10
For sae I sat, and sae I sang,
   And wist na o' my fate.

Aft hae I roved by bonnie Doon
   To see the woodbine twine ;
And ilka bird sang o' its love,   15
   And sae did I o' mine.

Wi' lightsome heart I pu'd a rose,
   Frae aff its thorny tree ;
And my fause luver staw the rose,
   But left the thorn wi' me.   20
                 R. BURNS.

140

THE PROGRESS OF POESY

A Pindaric Ode

Awake, Aeolian lyre, awake,
And give to rapture all thy trembling strings.
From Helicon's harmonious springs
   A thousand rills their mazy progress take :
The laughing flowers that round them blow   5
Drink life and fragrance as they flow.
Now the rich stream of Music winds along
Deep, majestic, smooth, and strong,
Through verdant vales and Ceres' golden reign ;
Now rolling down the steep amain,   10
Headlong, impetuous, see it pour :
The rocks and nodding groves rebellow to the roar.

O Sovereign of the willing soul,
Parent of sweet and solemn-breathing airs,
Enchanting shell ! the sullen Cares   15
   And frantic Passions hear thy soft control.
On Thracia's hills the Lord of War
Has curb'd the fury of his car

And dropt his thirsty lance at thy command.
Perching on the sceptred hand 20
Of Jove, thy magic lulls the feather'd king
With ruffled plumes, and flagging wing :
Quench'd in dark clouds of slumber lie
The terror of his beak, and lightnings of his eye.

Thee the voice, the dance, obey 25
Temper'd to thy warbled lay.
  O'er Idalia's velvet green
  The rosy-crownéd Loves are seen
On Cytherea's day,
  With antic Sports, and blue-eyed Pleasures, 30
  Frisking light in frolic measures ;
Now pursuing, now retreating,
  Now in circling troops they meet :
To brisk notes in cadence beating
  Glance their many-twinkling feet. 35
Slow melting strains their Queen's approach declare:
  Where'er she turns the Graces homage pay :
With arms sublime that float upon the air
  In gliding state she wins her easy way :
O'er her warm cheek and rising bosom move 40
The bloom of young Desire and purple light of
    Love.

  Man's feeble race what ills await !
Labour, and Penury, the racks of Pain,
Disease, and Sorrow's weeping train, 44
  And Death, sad refuge from the storms of Fate !
The fond complaint, my song, disprove,
And justify the laws of Jove.
Say, has he given in vain the heavenly Muse ?
Night, and all her sickly dews,
Her spectres wan, and birds of boding cry 50
He gives to range the dreary sky :
Till down the eastern cliffs afar
Hyperion's march they spy, and glittering shafts of
    war.

    In climes beyond the solar road,
Where shaggy forms o'er ice-built mountains roam,
The Muse has broke the twilight gloom   56
    To cheer the shivering native's dull abode.
And oft, beneath the odorous shade
Of Chili's boundless forests laid,
She deigns to hear the savage youth repeat   60
In loose numbers wildly sweet
Their feather-cinctured chiefs, and dusky loves.
Her track, where'er the Goddess roves,
Glory pursue, and generous Shame,
Th' unconquerable Mind, and Freedom's holy
    flame.   65

Woods, that wave o'er Delphi's steep,
Isles, that crown th' Aegean deep,
    Fields that cool Ilissus laves,
    Or where Maeander's amber waves
In lingering lab'rinths creep,   70
    How do your tuneful echoes languish,
    Mute, but to the voice of anguish !
Where each old poetic mountain
    Inspiration breath'd around ;
Every shade and hallow'd fountain   75
    Murmur'd deep a solemn sound :
Till the sad Nine, in Greece's evil hour,
    Left their Parnassus for the Latian plains.
Alike they scorn the pomp of tyrant Power,
    And coward Vice, that revels in her chains.   80
When Latium had her lofty spirit lost,
They sought, O Albion, next thy sea-encircled
    coast.

    Far from the sun and summer-gale
In thy green lap was Nature's Darling laid,
What time, where lucid Avon stray'd,   85
    To him the mighty Mother did unveil
Her awful face : the dauntless Child
Stretch'd forth his little arms, and smiled.

This pencil take (she said), whose colours clear
Richly paint the vernal year : 90
Thine, too, these golden keys, immortal Boy !
This can unlock the gates of Joy ;
Of Horror that, and thrilling Fears,
Or ope the sacred source of sympathetic Tears.

Nor second He, that rode sublime 95
Upon the seraph-wings of Ecstasy,
The secrets of the Abyss to spy :
 He pass'd the flaming bounds of Place and Time:
The living Throne, the sapphire-blaze,
Where Angels tremble while they gaze, 100
He saw ; but blasted with excess of light,
Closed his eyes in endless night.
Behold where Dryden's less presumptuous car
Wide o'er the fields of Glory bear
Two coursers of ethereal race 105
With necks in thunder clothed, and long-resounding
  pace.

Hark, his hands the lyre explore !
Bright-eyed Fancy, hovering o'er,
 Scatters from her pictur'd urn 109
 Thoughts that breathe, and words that burn.
But ah ! 'tis heard no more——
 O ! Lyre divine, what daring Spirit
 Wakes thee now ? Tho' he inherit
Nor the pride, nor ample pinion,
 That the Theban Eagle bear, 115
Sailing with supreme dominion
 Thro' the azure deep of air :
Yet oft before his infant eyes would run
 Such forms as glitter in the Muse's ray
With orient hues, unborrow'd of the sun : 120
 Yet shall he mount, and keep his distant way
Beyond the limits of a vulgar fate :
Beneath the Good how far—but far above the Great.

T. GRAY.

141

THE PASSIONS

An Ode for Music

When Music, heavenly maid, was young,
While yet in early Greece she sung,
The Passions oft, to hear her shell,
Throng'd around her magic cell
Exulting, trembling, raging, fainting,   5
Possest beyond the Muse's painting;
By turns they felt the glowing mind
Disturb'd, delighted, rais'd, refin'd:
Till once, 'tis said, when all were fir'd,
Fill'd with fury, rapt, inspir'd,   10
From the supporting myrtles round
They snatch'd her instruments of sound,
And, as they oft had heard apart
Sweet lessons of her forceful art,
Each, for Madness ruled the hour,   15
Would prove his own expressive power.

First Fear his hand, its skill to try,
   Amid the chords bewilder'd laid,
And back recoil'd, he knew not why,
   E'en at the sound himself had made.   20

Next Anger rush'd, his eyes on fire,
   In lightnings own'd his secret stings;
In one rude clash he struck the lyre
   And swept with hurried hand the strings.

With woeful measures wan Despair,   25
   Low sullen sounds, his grief beguiled,
A solemn, strange, and mingled air,
   'Twas sad by fits, by starts 'twas wild.

But thou, O Hope, with eyes so fair,
   What was thy delightful measure?   30
Still it whisper'd promised pleasure
   And bade the lovely scenes at distance hail!

Still would her touch the strain prolong ;
    And from the rocks, the woods, the vale,
She call'd on Echo still through all the song ; 35
    And, where her sweetest theme she chose,
    A soft responsive voice was heard at every close ;
And Hope enchanted smiled, and waved her golden
      hair.

And longer had she sung,—but with a frown
    Revenge impatient rose :   40
He threw his blood-stain'd sword in thunder down ;
      And with a withering look
    The war-denouncing trumpet took,
And blew a blast so loud and dread,
Were ne'er prophetic sounds so full of woe. 45
      And ever and anon he beat
    The doubling drum with furious heat ;
And, though sometimes, each dreary pause between,
    Dejected Pity at his side
    Her soul-subduing voice applied,   50
Yet still he kept his wild unalter'd mien,
While each strain'd ball of sight seem'd bursting
      from his head.

Thy numbers, Jealousy, to nought were fix'd :
    Sad proof of thy distressful state !
Of differing themes the veering song was mix'd ; 55
    And now it courted Love, now raving call'd on
      Hate.

With eyes up-rais'd, as one inspir'd,
Pale Melancholy sat retir'd ;
And from her wild sequester'd seat,
In notes by distance made more sweet,   60
Pour'd through the mellow horn her pensive soul :
    And dashing soft from rocks around
    Bubbling runnels join'd the sound ;
Through glades and glooms the mingled measure
      stole,
    Or. o'er some haunted stream, with fond delay,
    Round an holy calm diffusing,   66
    Love of peace and lonely musing,
In hollow murmurs died away.

But O ! how alter'd was its sprightlier tone,
When Cheerfulness, a nymph of healthiest hue, 70
　　Her bow across her shoulder flung,
　　Her buskins gemm'd with morning dew,
Blew an inspiring air, that dale and thicket rung,
　　The hunter's call to Faun and Dryad known !
The oak-crown'd Sisters and their chaste-eyed Queen, 75
　　Satyrs and Sylvan Boys, were seen
　　Peeping from forth their alleys green :
Brown Exercise rejoic'd to hear ;
　　And Sport leap'd up, and seiz'd his beechen spear.

Last came Joy's ecstatic trial : 80
He, with viny crown advancing,
　　First to the lively pipe his hand addrest :
But soon he saw the brisk awak'ning viol,
　　Whose sweet entrancing voice he lov'd the best :
They would have thought who heard the strain 85
　　　They saw, in Tempe's vale, her native maids
　　　Amidst the festal-sounding shades
To some unwearied minstrel dancing ;
While, as his flying fingers kiss'd the strings, 89
　　Love fram'd with Mirth a gay fantastic round :
　　Loose were her tresses seen, her zone unbound ;
　　And he, amidst his frolic play,
　　As if he would the charming air repay,
Shook thousand odours from his dewy wings.

O Music ! sphere-descended maid, 95
Friend of Pleasure, Wisdom's aid !
Why, goddess, why, to us denied,
Lay'st thou thy ancient lyre aside ?
As in that lov'd Athenian bower
You learn'd an all-commanding power, 100
Thy mimic soul, O nymph endear'd,
Can well recall what then it heard.
Where is thy native simple heart
Devote to Virtue, Fancy, Art ?
Arise, as in that elder time, 105

Warm, energic, chaste, sublime !
Thy wonders in that god-like age
Fill thy recording Sister's page ;—
'Tis said, and I believe the tale,
Thy humblest reed could more prevail,   110
Had more of strength, diviner rage,
Than all which charms this laggard age,
E'en all at once together found,
Cecilia's mingled world of sound :—
O bid our vain endeavours cease :   115
Revive the just designs of Greece :
Return in all thy simple state !
Confirm the tales her sons relate !

W. COLLINS.

142

ODE ON THE SPRING

Lo ! where the rosy-bosom'd Hours,
  Fair Venus' train, appear,
Disclose the long-expecting flowers
  And wake the purple year !
The Attic warbler pours her throat   5
Responsive to the cuckoo's note,
The untaught harmony of Spring :
  While, whispering pleasure as they fly,
  Cool Zephyrs through the clear blue sky
Their gather'd fragrance fling.   10

Where'er the oak's thick branches stretch
  A broader, browner shade,
Where'er the rude and moss-grown beech
  O'er-canopies the glade,
Beside some water's rushy brink   15
With me the Muse shall sit, and think
(At ease reclined in rustic state)
  How vain the ardour of the Crowd,
  How low, how little are the Proud,
How indigent the Great !   20

Still is the toiling hand of Care ;
 The panting herds repose :
Yet hark, how through the peopled air
 The busy murmur glows !
The insect youth are on the wing, 25
Eager to taste the honied spring
And float amid the liquid noon :
 Some lightly o'er the current skim,
 Some show their gaily-gilded trim
Quick-glancing to the sun. 30

To Contemplation's sober eye
 Such is the race of Man :
And they that creep, and they that fly,
 Shall end where they began.
Alike the busy and the gay 35
But flutter through life's little day,
In Fortune's varying colours drest :
 Brush'd by the hand of rough Mischance,
 Or chill'd by Age, their airy dance
They leave, in dust to rest. 40

Methinks I hear in accents low
 The sportive kind reply :
Poor moralist ! and what art thou ?
 A solitary fly !
Thy joys no glittering female meets, 45
No hive hast thou of hoarded sweets,
No painted plumage to display :
 On hasty wings thy youth is flown ;
 Thy sun is set, thy spring is gone—
We frolic while 'tis May. 50

T. GRAY.

143

THE POPLAR FIELD

The poplars are fell'd ; farewell to the shade
And the whispering sound of the cool colonnade ;
The winds play no longer and sing in the leaves,
Nor Ouse on his bosom their image receives. 4

Twelve years have elapsed since I first took a view
Of my favourite field, and the bank where they
  grew :
And now in the grass behold they are laid,
And the tree is my seat that once lent me a shade.

The blackbird has fled to another retreat, 9
Where the hazels afford him a screen from the heat;
And the scene where his melody charm'd me before
Resounds with his sweet-flowing ditty no more.

My fugitive years are all hasting away,
And I must ere long lie as lowly as they, 14
With a turf on my breast and a stone at my head,
Ere another such grove shall arise in its stead.

'Tis a sight to engage me, if anything can,
To muse on the perishing pleasures of man ;
Though his life be a dream, his enjoyments, I see,
Have a being less durable even than he. 20

W. COWPER.

144

TO A MOUSE

*On turning her up in her nest with the plough,
November 1785.*

Wee, sleekit, cow'rin', tim'rous beastie,
O what a panic 's in thy breastie !
Thou need na start awa sae hasty,
  Wi' bickering brattle !
I wad be laith to rin an' chase thee 5
  Wi' murd'ring pattle !

I'm truly sorry man's dominion
Has broken nature's social union,
An' justifies that ill opinion
  Which makes thee startle 10
At me, thy poor earth-born companion,
  An' fellow-mortal !

I doubt na, whiles, but thou may thieve ;
What then ? poor beastie, thou maun live !

A daimen-icker in a thrave   15
   'S a sma' request :
I'll get a blessin' wi' the lave,
   And never miss't !

Thy wee bit housie, too, in ruin !
Its silly wa's the win's are strewin' :   20
And naething, now, to big a new ane,
   O' foggage green !
An' bleak December's winds ensuin'
   Baith snell an' keen !

Thou saw the fields laid bare and waste   25
An' weary winter comin' fast,
An' cozie here, beneath the blast,
   Thou thought to dwell,
Till, crash ! the cruel coulter past
   Out thro' thy cell.   30

That wee bit heap o' leaves an' stibble
Has cost thee mony a weary nibble !
Now thou's turn'd out, for a' thy trouble,
   But house or hald,
To thole the winter's sleety dribble   35
   An' cranreuch cauld !

But, Mousie, thou art no thy lane
In proving foresight may be vain :
The best laid schemes o' mice an' men
   Gang aft a-gley,   40
An' lea'e us nought but grief an' pain,
   For promised joy.

Still thou art blest, compared wi' me !
The present only toucheth thee :
But, och ! I backward cast my e'e   45
   On prospects drear !
An' forward, tho' I canna see,
   I guess an' fear !

                    R. BURNS.

145

A WISH

Mine be a cot beside the hill ;
　A bee-hive's hum shall soothe my ear ;
A willowy brook that turns a mill,
　With many a fall shall linger near.

The swallow, oft, beneath my thatch　　5
　Shall twitter from her clay-built nest ;
Oft shall the pilgrim lift the latch,
　And share my meal, a welcome guest.

Around my ivied porch shall spring
　Each fragrant flower that drinks the dew ; 10
And Lucy, at her wheel, shall sing
　In russet gown and apron blue.

The village-church among the trees,
　Where first our marriage-vows were given,
With merry peals shall swell the breeze　　15
　And point with taper spire to Heaven.

S. ROGERS.

146

TO EVENING

If aught of oaten stop or pastoral song
May hope, O pensive Eve, to soothe thine ear,
　Like thy own brawling springs,
　Thy springs, and dying gales ;

O Nymph reserved,—while now the bright-hair'd
　　sun　　5
Sits in yon western tent, whose cloudy skirts
　With brede ethereal wove
　O'erhang his wavy bed :

Now air is hush'd, save where the weak-ey'd bat
With short shrill shriek flits by on leathern wing,
　Or where the beetle winds　　11
　His small but sullen horn,

As oft he rises 'midst the twilight path,
Against the pilgrim borne in heedless hum,—
    Now teach me, maid composed,   15
    To breathe some soften'd strain,

Whose numbers, stealing through thy dark'ning vale,
May not unseemly with its stillness suit ;
    As musing slow I hail
    Thy genial loved return.   20

For when thy folding-star arising shows
His paly circlet, at his warning lamp
    The fragrant Hours, and Elves
    Who slept in buds the day,

And many a Nymph who wreathes her brows with
    sedge   25
And sheds the freshening dew, and lovelier still
    The pensive Pleasures sweet,
    Prepare thy shadowy car.

Then let me rove some wild and heathy scene ;
Or find some ruin midst its dreary dells,   30
    Whose walls more awful nod
    By thy religious gleams.

Or if chill blustering winds or driving rain
Prevent my willing feet, be mine the hut
    That, from the mountain's side,   35
    Views wilds and swelling floods,

And hamlets brown, and dim-discover'd spires :
And hears their simple bell ; and marks o'er all
    Thy dewy fingers draw
    The gradual dusky veil.   40

While Spring shall pour his showers, as oft he wont,
And bathe thy breathing tresses, meekest Eve !
    While Summer loves to sport
    Beneath thy lingering light ;

While sallow Autumn fills thy lap with leaves ;
Or Winter, yelling through the troublous air,   46
    Affrights thy shrinking train
    And rudely rends thy robes ;

So long, regardful of thy quiet rule,   49
Shall Fancy, Friendship, Science, smiling Peace,
    Thy gentlest influence own,
      And love thy favourite name !

                      W. COLLINS.

147

ELEGY

WRITTEN IN A COUNTRY CHURCH-YARD

The curfew tolls the knell of parting day,
    The lowing herd wind slowly o'er the lea,
The ploughman homeward plods his weary way,
    And leaves the world to darkness, and to me.

Now fades the glimmering landscape on the sight, 5
    And all the air a solemn stillness holds,
Save where the beetle wheels his droning flight,
    And drowsy tinklings lull the distant folds :

Save that from yonder ivy-mantled tower
    The moping owl does to the moon complain   10
Of such as, wandering near her secret bower,
    Molest her ancient solitary reign.

Beneath those rugged elms, that yew-tree's shade,
    Where heaves the turf in many a mouldering heap,
Each in his narrow cell for ever laid,   15
    The rude Forefathers of the hamlet sleep.

The breezy call of incense-breathing morn,
    The swallow twittering from the straw-built shed,
The cock's shrill clarion, or the echoing horn,   19
    No more shall rouse them from their lowly bed.

For them no more the blazing hearth shall burn,
    Or busy housewife ply her evening care :
No children run to lisp their sire's return,
    Or climb his knees the envied kiss to share.

Oft did the harvest to their sickle yield,   25
    Their furrow oft the stubborn glebe has broke ;
How jocund did they drive their team afield !
    How bow'd the woods beneath their sturdy stroke!

Let not Ambition mock their useful toil,
　　Their homely joys, and destiny obscure ;　　30
Nor Grandeur hear with a disdainful smile
　　The short and simple annals of the Poor.

The boast of heraldry, the pomp of power,
　　And all that beauty, all that wealth e'er gave,
Awaits alike th' inevitable hour :—　　　　35
　　The paths of glory lead but to the grave.

Nor you, ye Proud, impute to these the fault
　　If Memory o'er their tomb no trophies raise,
Where through the long-drawn aisle and fretted
　　　　vault
　　The pealing anthem swells the note of praise.

Can storied urn or animated bust　　　　41
　　Back to its mansion call the fleeting breath ?
Can Honour's voice provoke the silent dust,
　　Or Flattery soothe the dull cold ear of Death ?

Perhaps in this neglected spot is laid　　　45
　　Some heart once pregnant with celestial fire ;
Hands, that the rod of empire might have sway'd,
　　Or waked to ecstasy the living lyre :

But Knowledge to their eyes her ample page
　　Rich with the spoils of time, did ne'er unroll ;
Chill Penury repress'd their noble rage,　　51
　　And froze the genial current of the soul.

Full many a gem of purest ray serene
　　The dark unfathom'd caves of ocean bear :
Full many a flower is born to blush unseen,　　55
　　And waste its sweetness on the desert air.

Some village-Hampden, that with dauntless breast
　　The little tyrant of his fields withstood,
Some mute inglorious Milton here may rest,　　59
　　Some Cromwell, guiltless of his country's blood.

Th' applause of list'ning senates to command,
　　The threats of pain and ruin to despise,
To scatter plenty o'er a smiling land,
　　And read their history in a nation's eyes,

Their lot forbad : nor circumscribed alone   65
 Their growing virtues, but their crimes confined ;
Forbad to wade through slaughter to a throne,
 And shut the gates of mercy on mankind,

The struggling pangs of conscious truth to hide,
 To quench the blushes of ingenuous shame,   70
Or heap the shrine of Luxury and Pride
 With incense kindled at the Muse's flame.

Far from the madding crowd's ignoble strife,
 Their sober wishes never learn'd to stray ;
Along the cool sequester'd vale of life   75
 They kept the noiseless tenour of their way.

Yet e'en these bones from insult to protect
 Some frail memorial still erected nigh,
With uncouth rhymes and shapeless sculpture
 deck'd,
 Implores the passing tribute of a sigh.   80

Their name, their years, spelt by th' unletter'd Muse,
 The place of fame and elegy supply :
And many a holy text around she strews,
 That teach the rustic moralist to die.

For who, to dumb forgetfulness a prey,   85
 This pleasing anxious being e'er resign'd,
Left the warm precincts of the cheerful day,
 Nor cast one longing lingering look behind ?

On some fond breast the parting soul relies,
 Some pious drops the closing eye requires ;   90
E'en from the tomb the voice of Nature cries,
 E'en in our ashes live their wonted fires.

For thee, who, mindful of th' unhonour'd dead,
 Dost in these lines their artless tale relate ;
If chance, by lonely contemplation led,   95
 Some kindred spirit shall inquire thy fate,

Haply some hoary-headed swain may say,
 ' Oft have we seen him at the peep of dawn
Brushing with hasty steps the dews away,
 To meet the sun upon the upland lawn ;   100

' There at the foot of yonder nodding beech
    That wreathes its old fantastic roots so high,
His listless length at noontide would he stretch,
    And pore upon the brook that babbles by.

' Hard by yon wood, now smiling as in scorn,   105
    Muttering his wayward fancies he would rove ;
Now drooping, woeful wan, like one forlorn,
    Or crazed with care, or cross'd in hopeless love.

' One morn I miss'd him on the custom'd hill,
    Along the heath, and near his favourite tree ;
Another came ; nor yet beside the rill,   111
    Nor up the lawn, nor at the wood was he ;

' The next with dirges due in sad array
    Slow through the church-way path we saw him
        borne,—   114
Approach and read (for thou canst read) the lay
    Graved on the stone beneath yon aged thorn.'

THE EPITAPH

Here rests his head upon the lap of Earth
    A Youth, to Fortune and to Fame unknown ;
Fair Science frown'd not on his humble birth,
    And Melancholy mark'd him for her own.   120

Large was his bounty, and his soul sincere ;
    Heaven did a recompense as largely send :
He gave to Misery all he had, a tear,
    He gain'd from Heaven, 'twas all he wish'd, a
        friend.

No farther seek his merits to disclose,   125
    Or draw his frailties from their dread abode,
(There they alike in trembling hope repose,)
    The bosom of his Father and his God.

                                        T. GRAY.

148

MARY MORISON

O Mary, at thy window be,
  It is the wish'd, the trysted hour !
Those smiles and glances let me see
  That make the miser's treasure poor :
  How blythely wad I bide the stoure,   5
A weary slave frae sun to sun,
  Could I the rich reward secure,
The lovely Mary Morison.

Yestreen, when to the trembling string
  The dance gaed thro' the lighted ha',   10
To thee my fancy took its wing,—
  I sat, but neither heard nor saw :
  Tho' this was fair, and that was braw,
And yon the toast of a' the town,
  I sigh'd, and said amang them a',   15
' Ye arena Mary Morison.'

O Mary, canst thou wreck his peace
  Wha for thy sake wad gladly dee ?
Or canst thou break that heart of his,
  Whase only faut is loving thee ?   20
  If love for love thou wiltna gie,
At least be pity to me shown ;
  A thought ungentle canna be
The thought o' Mary Morison.
                                R. Burns.

149

BONNIE LESLEY

O saw ye bonnie Lesley
  As she gaed o'er the border ?
She 's gane, like Alexander,
  To spread her conquests farther.

    To see her is to love her,   5
      And love but her for ever ;
    For nature made her what she is,
      And never made anither !

    Thou art a queen, fair Lesley,
      Thy subjects we, before thee ;   10
    Thou art divine, fair Lesley,
      The hearts o' men adore thee.

    The deil he couldna scaith thee,
      Or aught that wad belang thee ;
    He'd look into thy bonnie face,   15
      And say ' I canna wrang thee ! '

    The Powers aboon will tent thee ;
      Misfortune sha'na steer thee ;
    Thou'rt like themselves sae lovely,
      That ill they'll ne'er let near thee.   20

    Return again, fair Lesley,
      Return to Caledonie !
    That we may brag we hae a lass
      There 's nane again sae bonnie.

                    R. Burns.

150

    O my Luve 's like a red, red rose
      That 's newly sprung in June :
    O my Luve 's like the melodie
      That 's sweetly play'd in tune.

    As fair art thou, my bonnie lass,   5
      So deep in luve am I :
    And I will luve thee still, my dear,
      Till a' the seas gang dry :

    Till a' the seas gang dry, my dear,
      And the rocks melt wi' the sun ;   10
    I will luve thee still, my dear,
      While the sands o' life shall run.

And fare thee weel, my only Luve !
   And fare thee weel a while !
And I will come again, my Luve,   15
   Tho' it were ten thousand mile.

                  R. BURNS.

151

HIGHLAND MARY

Ye banks and braes and streams around
   The castle o' Montgomery,
Green be your woods, and fair your flowers,
   Your waters never drumlie !
There simmer first unfauld her robes,   5
   And there the langest tarry ;
For there I took the last fareweel
   O' my sweet Highland Mary.

How sweetly bloom'd the gay green birk,
   How rich the hawthorn's blossom,   10
As underneath their fragrant shade
   I clasp'd her to my bosom !
The golden hours on angel wings
   Flew o'er me and my dearie ;
For dear to me as light and life   15
   Was my sweet Highland Mary.

Wi' mony a vow and lock'd embrace
   Our parting was fu' tender ;
And pledging aft to meet again,
   We tore oursels asunder ;   20
But, oh ! fell Death's untimely frost,
   That nipt my flower sae early !
Now green's the sod, and cauld's the clay,
   That wraps my Highland Mary !

O pale, pale now, those rosy lips,   25
   I aft hae kiss'd sae fondly !
And closed for ay the sparkling glance
   That dwelt on me sae kindly ;

And mouldering now in silent dust
  That heart that lo'ed me dearly !   30
But still within my bosom's core
  Shall live my Highland Mary.

R. BURNS.

152

AULD ROBIN GRAY

When the sheep are in the fauld, and the kye at hame,
And a' the warld to rest are gane,
The waes o' my heart fa' in showers frae my e'e,
While my gudeman lies sound by me.

Young Jamie lo'ed me weel, and sought me for his
  bride ;   5
But saving a croun he had naething else beside :
To make the croun a pund, young Jamie gaed to sea;
And the croun and the pund were baith for me.

He hadna been awa' a week but only twa,
When my father brak his arm, and the cow was
  stown awa ;   10
My mother she fell sick, and my Jamie at the sea—
And auld Robin Gray came a-courtin' me.

My father couldna work, and my mother couldna spin;
I toil'd day and night, but their bread I couldna win;
Auld Rob maintain'd them baith, and wi' tears in
  his e'e   15
Said, Jennie, for their sakes, O, marry me !

My heart it said nay ; I look'd for Jamie back ;
But the wind it blew high, and the ship it was a
  wrack ;
His ship it was a wrack—why didna Jamie dee ?
Or why do I live to cry, Wae's me ?   20

My father urgit sair : my mother didna speak ;
But she look'd in my face till my heart was like to
  break :
They gi'ed him my hand, but my heart was at the sea ;
Sae auld Robin Gray he was gudeman to me.

I hadna been a wife a week but only four,   25
When mournfu' as I sat on the stane at the door,
I saw my Jamie's wraith, for I couldna think it he—
Till he said, I'm come hame to marry thee.

O sair, sair did we greet, and muckle did we say ;
We took but ae kiss, and I bad him gang away :
I wish that I were dead, but I'm no like to dee ;
And why was I born to say, Wae's me !   32

I gang like a ghaist, and I carena to spin ;
I daurna think on Jamie, for that wad be a sin ;
But I'll do my best a gude wife ay to be,   35
For auld Robin Gray he is kind unto me.

LADY A. LINDSAY.

153

DUNCAN GRAY

Duncan Gray cam here to woo,
    Ha, ha, the wooing o't,
On blythe Yule night when we were fou,
    Ha, ha, the wooing o't :
Maggie coost her head fu' high,   5
Look'd asklent and unco skeigh,
Gart poor Duncan stand abeigh ;
    Ha, ha, the wooing o't !

Duncan fleech'd, and Duncan pray'd ;
Meg was deaf as Ailsa Craig ;   10
Duncan sigh'd baith out and in,
Grat his een baith bleer't and blin',
Spak o' lowpin ower a linn !

Time and chance are but a tide,
Slighted love is sair to bide ;   15
Shall I, like a fool, quoth he,
For a haughty hizzie dee ?
She may gae to—France for me !

How it comes let doctors tell,
Meg grew sick—as he grew heal ;　20
Something in her bosom wrings,
For relief a sigh she brings ;
And O, her een, they spak sic things !

Duncan was a lad o' grace ;
　Ha, ha, the wooing o't !　25
Maggie's was a piteous case ;
　Ha, ha, the wooing o't !
Duncan couldna be her death,
Swelling pity smoor'd his wrath ;
Now they're crouse and canty baith :　30
　Ha, ha, the wooing o't !

R. BURNS.

154

THE SAILOR'S WIFE

And are ye sure the news is true ?
　And are ye sure he 's weel ?
Is this a time to think o' wark ?
　Ye jades, lay by your wheel ;
Is this the time to spin a thread,　5
　When Colin 's at the door ?
Reach down my cloak, I'll to the quay,
　And see him come ashore.
For there 's nae luck about the house,
　There 's nae luck at a' ;　10
There's little pleasure in the house
　When our gudeman 's awa'.

And gie to me my bigonet,
　My bishop's satin gown ;
For I maun tell the baillie's wife　15
　That Colin 's in the town.
My Turkey slippers maun gae on,
　My stockins pearly blue ;
It 's a' to pleasure our gudeman,
　For he 's baith leal and true.　20

Rise, lass, and mak a clean fireside,
    Put on the muckle pot ;
Gie little Kate her button gown
    And Jock his Sunday coat ;
And mak their shoon as black as slaes,   25
    Their hose as white as snaw ;
It 's a' to please my ain gudeman,
    For he 's been long awa'.

There 's twa fat hens upo' the coop
    Been fed this month and mair ;   30
Mak haste and thraw their necks about,
    That Colin weel may fare ;
And spread the table neat and clean,
    Gar ilka thing look braw,
For wha can tell how Colin fared   35
    When he was far awa' ?

Sae true his heart, sae smooth his speech,
    His breath like caller air ;
His very foot has music in 't
    As he comes up the stair—   40
And will I see his face again ?
    And will I hear him speak ?
I'm downright dizzy wi' the thought,
    In troth I'm like to greet !

If Colin 's weel, and weel content,   45
    I hae nae mair to crave :
And gin I live to keep him sae,
    I'm blest aboon the lave :
And will I see his face again,
    And will I hear him speak ?   50
I'm downright dizzy wi' the thought,
    In troth I'm like to greet.
For there 's nae luck about the house,
    There 's nae luck at a' ;
There 's little pleasure in the house   55
    When our gudeman 's awa'.

W. J. MICKLE.

155

JEAN

Of a' the airts the wind can blaw
  I dearly like the West,
For there the bonnie lassie lives,
  The lassie I lo'e best:
There's wild woods grow, and rivers row,   5
  And mony a hill between;
But day and night my fancy's flight
  Is ever wi' my Jean.

I see her in the dewy flowers,
  I see her sweet and fair: 10
I hear her in the tunefu' birds,
  I hear her charm the air:
There 's not a bonnie flower that springs
  By fountain, shaw, or green,
There 's not a bonnie bird that sings   15
  But minds me o' my Jean.

O blaw ye westlin winds, blaw saft
  Amang the leafy trees;
Wi' balmy gale, frae hill and dale
  Bring hame the laden bees;   20
And bring the lassie back to me
  That 's ay sae neat and clean;
Ae smile o' her wad banish care,
  Sae charming is my Jean.

What sighs and vows amang the knowes
  Hae pass'd atween us twa!   26
How fond to meet, how wae to part
  That night she gaed awa!
The Powers aboon can only ken
  To whom the heart is seen,   30
That nane can be sae dear to me
  As my sweet lovely Jean!

                R. Burns.

156

JOHN ANDERSON

John Anderson my jo, John,
   When we were first acquent
Your locks were like the raven,
   Your bonnie brow was brent ;
But now your brow is beld, John,   5
   Your locks are like the snow ;
But blessings on your frosty pow,
   John Anderson my jo.

John Anderson my jo, John,
   We clamb the hill thegither,   10
And mony a canty day, John,
   We've had wi' ane anither :
Now we maun totter down, John,
   But hand in hand we'll go,
And sleep thegither at the foot,   15
   John Anderson my jo.

R. BURNS.

157

THE LAND O' THE LEAL

I'm wearing awa', Jean,
Like snaw when it 's thaw, Jean,
I'm wearing awa'
   To the land o' the leal.
There 's nae sorrow there, Jean,   5
There 's neither cauld nor care, Jean,
The day is ay fair
   In the land o' the leal.

Ye were ay leal and true, Jean,
Your task 's ended noo, Jean,   10
And I'll welcome you
   To the land o' the leal.

Our bonnie bairn 's there, Jean,
  She was baith guid and fair, Jean ;
O we grudged her right sair   15
  To the land o' the leal !

Then dry that tearfu' e'e, Jean,
  My soul langs to be free, Jean,
And angels wait on me
  To the land o' the leal.   20
Now fare ye weel, my ain Jean,
  This warld's care is vain, Jean ;
We'll meet and ay be fain
  In the land o' the leal.

LADY NAIRNE.

158

ODE ON A DISTANT PROSPECT OF
ETON COLLEGE

Ye distant spires, ye antique towers
  That crown the watery glade,
Where grateful Science still adores
  Her Henry's holy shade ;
And ye, that from the stately brow   5
Of Windsor's heights th' expanse below
  Of grove, of lawn, of mead survey,
Whose turf, whose shade, whose flowers among
Wanders the hoary Thames along
  His silver-winding way :   10

Ah happy hills ! ah pleasing shade !
  Ah fields beloved in vain !
Where once my careless childhood stray'd,
  A stranger yet to pain !
I feel the gales that from ye blow   15
A momentary bliss bestow,
  As waving fresh their gladsome wing
My weary soul they seem to soothe,
And, redolent of joy and youth,
  To breathe a second spring.   20

Say, Father Thames, for thou hast seen
  Full many a sprightly race
Disporting on thy margent green
  The paths of pleasure trace ;
Who foremost now delight to cleave   25
With pliant arm, thy glassy wave ?
  The captive linnet which enthral ?
What idle progeny succeed
To chase the rolling circle's speed
  Or urge the flying ball ?   30

While some on earnest business bent
  Their murmuring labours ply
'Gainst graver hours, that bring constraint
  To sweeten liberty :
Some bold adventurers disdain   35
The limits of their little reign
  And unknown regions dare descry :
Still as they run they look behind,
They hear a voice in every wind,
  And snatch a fearful joy.   40

Gay hope is theirs by fancy fed,
  Less pleasing when possest ;
The tear forgot as soon as shed,
  The sunshine of the breast :
Theirs buxom health, of rosy hue,   45
Wild wit, invention ever new,
  And lively cheer, of vigour born ;
The thoughtless day, the easy night,
The spirits pure, the slumbers light
  That fly th' approach of morn.   50

Alas ! regardless of their doom
  The little victims play !
No sense have they of ills to come
  Nor care beyond to-day :
Yet see how all around them wait   55
The Ministers of human fate
  And black Misfortune's baleful train !

Ah show them where in ambush stand
To seize their prey, the murderous band !
  Ah, tell them they are men !　　　　60

These shall the fury Passions tear,
  The vultures of the mind,
Disdainful Anger, pallid Fear,
  And Shame that skulks behind ;
Or pining Love shall waste their youth,　　65
Or Jealousy with rankling tooth
  That inly gnaws the secret heart,
And Envy wan, and faded Care,
Grim-visaged comfortless Despair,
  And Sorrow's piercing dart.　　　　70

Ambition this shall tempt to rise,
  Then whirl the wretch from high,
To bitter Scorn a sacrifice
  And grinning Infamy.
The stings of Falsehood those shall try,　　75
And hard Unkindness' alter'd eye,
  That mocks the tear it forced to flow ;
And keen Remorse with blood defiled,
And moody Madness laughing wild
  Amid severest woe.　　　　80

Lo, in the vale of years beneath
  A griesly troop are seen,
The painful family of Death,
  More hideous than their Queen :
This racks the joints, this fires the veins,　　85
That every labouring sinew strains,
  Those in the deeper vitals rage :
Lo, Poverty, to fill the band,
That numbs the soul with icy hand,
  And slow-consuming Age.　　　　90

To each his sufferings : all are men,
  Condemn'd alike to groan ;
The tender for another's pain,
  Th' unfeeling for his own.　　　　94
Yet, ah ! why should they know their fate,
Since sorrow never comes too late,

And happiness too swiftly flies ?
Thought would destroy their paradise.
No more ;—where ignorance is bliss,
'Tis folly to be wise.   100

T. GRAY.

159

HYMN TO ADVERSITY

Daughter of Jove, relentless power,
    Thou tamer of the human breast,
Whose iron scourge and torturing hour
    The bad affright, afflict the best !
Bound in thy adamantine chain   5
The proud are taught to taste of pain,
And purple tyrants vainly groan
With pangs unfelt before, unpitied and alone.

When first thy Sire to send on earth
    Virtue, his darling child, design'd,   10
To thee he gave the heavenly birth
    And bade to form her infant mind.
Stern, rugged Nurse ! thy rigid lore
With patience many a year she bore :
What sorrow was, thou bad'st her know, 15
And from her own she learn'd to melt at others' woe.

Scared at thy frown terrific, fly
    Self-pleasing Folly's idle brood,
Wild Laughter, Noise, and thoughtless Joy,
    And leave us leisure to be good.   20
Light they disperse, and with them go
The summer Friend, the flattering Foe ;
By vain Prosperity received,
To her they vow their truth, and are again believed.

Wisdom in sable garb array'd   25
    Immersed in rapturous thought profound,
And Melancholy, silent maid,
    With leaden eye, that loves the ground,

Still on thy solemn steps attend :
   Warm Charity, the general friend,   30
   With Justice, to herself severe,
And Pity dropping soft the sadly-pleasing tear.

O, gently on thy suppliant's head
   Dread Goddess, lay thy chastening hand !
Not in thy Gorgon terrors clad,   35
   Nor circled with the vengeful band
(As by the impious thou art seen)
With thundering voice, and threatening mien,
   With screaming Horror's funeral cry,
Despair, and fell Disease, and ghastly Poverty :

Thy form benign, O Goddess, wear.   41
   Thy milder influence impart,
Thy philosophic train be there
   To soften, not to wound my heart.
The generous spark extinct revive,   45
   Teach me to love and to forgive,
Exact my own defects to scan,
What others are to feel, and know myself a Man.

                      T. GRAY.

160

THE SOLITUDE OF ALEXANDER SELKIRK

I am monarch of all I survey,
   My right there is none to dispute ;
From the centre all round to the sea
   I am lord of the fowl and the brute.
O solitude ! where are the charms   5
   That sages have seen in thy face ?
Better dwell in the midst of alarms
   Than reign in this horrible place.

I am out of humanity's reach
   I must finish my journey alone,   10
Never hear the sweet music of speech ;
   I start at the sound of my own.

The beasts that roam over the plain
  My form with indifference see ;
They are so unacquainted with man,   15
  Their tameness is shocking to me.

Society, friendship, and love
  Divinely bestow'd upon man,
O had I the wings of a dove
  How soon would I taste you again !   20
My sorrows I then might assuage
  In the ways of religion and truth,
Might learn from the wisdom of age,
  And be cheer'd by the sallies of youth.

Ye winds that have made me your sport,   25
  Convey to this desolate shore
Some cordial endearing report
  Of a land I shall visit no more :
My friends, do they now and then send
  A wish or a thought after me ?   30
O tell me I yet have a friend,
  Though a friend I am never to see.

How fleet is a glance of the mind !
  Compared with the speed of its flight,
The tempest itself lags behind,   35
  And the swift-wingéd arrows of light.
When I think of my own native land
  In a moment I seem to be there ;
But, alas ! recollection at hand
  Soon hurries me back to despair.   40

But the seafowl is gone to her nest,
  The beast is laid down in his lair ;
Even here is a season of rest,
  And I to my cabin repair.
There is mercy in every place,   45
  And mercy, encouraging thought !
Gives even affliction a grace
  And reconciles man to his lot.

               W. COWPER.

161

TO MARY UNWIN

Mary ! I want a lyre with other strings,
　　Such aid from heaven as some have feign'd they
　　　　drew,
　An eloquence scarce given to mortals, new
And undebased by praise of meaner things,

That ere through age or woe I shed my wings　　5
　I may record thy worth with honour due,
　In verse as musical as thou art true,
Verse that immortalizes whom it sings :—

But thou hast little need. There is a Book
　By seraphs writ with beams of heavenly light,　10
On which the eyes of God not rarely look,
　A chronicle of actions just and bright—

There all thy deeds, my faithful Mary, shine ;
And since thou own'st that praise, I spare thee mine.

　　　　　　　　　　　　W. COWPER.

162

TO THE SAME

　The twentieth year is well-nigh past
　Since first our sky was overcast ;
　Ah, would that this might be the last !
　　　My Mary !

　Thy spirits have a fainter flow,　　　　　　5
　I see thee daily weaker grow—
　'Twas my distress that brought thee low,
　　　My Mary !

　Thy needles, once a shining store,
　For my sake restless heretofore,　　　　　10
　Now rust disused, and shine no more ;
　　　My Mary !

For though thou gladly wouldst fulfil
The same kind office for me still,
Thy sight now seconds not thy will,   15
    My Mary !

But well thou play'dst the housewife's part,
And all thy threads with magic art
Have wound themselves about this heart,
    My Mary !   20

Thy indistinct expressions seem
Like language utter'd in a dream ;
Yet me they charm, whate'er the theme,
    My Mary !

Thy silver locks, once auburn bright,   25
Are still more lovely in my sight
Than golden beams of orient light,
    My Mary !

For could I view nor them nor thee,
What sight worth seeing could I see ?   30
The sun would rise in vain for me,
    My Mary !

Partakers of thy sad decline
Thy hands their little force resign ;
Yet, gently press'd, press gently mine,   35
    My Mary !

Such feebleness of limbs thou prov'st
That now at every step thou mov'st
Upheld by two ; yet still thou lov'st,
    My Mary !   40

And still to love, though press'd with ill,
In wintry age to feel no chill,
With me is to be lovely still,
    My Mary !

But ah ! by constant heed I know   45
How oft the sadness that I show
Transforms thy smiles to looks of woe,
    My Mary !

And should my future lot be cast
With much resemblance of the past,   50
Thy worn-out heart will break at last—
    My Mary !

                                    W. COWPER.

                    163

THE DYING MAN IN HIS GARDEN

Why, Damon, with the forward day
Dost thou thy little spot survey,
From tree to tree, with doubtful cheer,
Observe the progress of the year,
What winds arise, what rains descend,   5
When thou before that year shalt end ?

What do thy noonday walks avail,
 To clear the leaf, and pick the snail
Then wantonly to death decree
An insect usefuller than thee ?   10
Thou and the worm are brother-kind,
As low, as earthy, and as blind.

Vain wretch ! canst thou expect to see
The downy peach make court to thee ?
Or that thy sense shall ever meet   15
The bean-flower's deep-embosom'd sweet
Exhaling with an evening's blast ?
Thy evenings then will all be past !

Thy narrow pride, thy fancied green
(For vanity 's in little seen),   20
All must be left when Death appears,
In spite of wishes, groans, and tears ;
Nor one of all thy plants that grow
But Rosemary will with thee go.

                                    G. SEWELL.

164

TO-MORROW

In the downhill of life, when I find I'm declining,
    May my lot no less fortunate be
Than a snug elbow-chair can afford for reclining,
    And a cot that o'erlooks the wide sea ;
With an ambling pad-pony to pace o'er the lawn,
    While I carol away idle sorrow,   6
And blithe as the lark that each day hails the dawn
    Look forward with hope for to-morrow.

With a porch at my door, both for shelter and shade
    too,
    As the sunshine or rain may prevail ;   10
And a small spot of ground for the use of the spade
    too,
    With a barn for the use of the flail :
A cow for my dairy, a dog for my game,
    And a purse when a friend wants to borrow ;
I'll envy no nabob his riches or fame,   15
    Nor what honours await him to-morrow.

From the bleak northern blast may my cot be
    completely
    Secured by a neighbouring hill ;
And at night may repose steal upon me more sweetly
    By the sound of a murmuring rill :   20
And while peace and plenty I find at my board,
    With a heart free from sickness and sorrow,
With my friends may I share what to-day may
    afford,
    And let them spread the table to-morrow.   24

And when I at last must throw off this frail covering
    Which I've worn for three-score years and ten,
On the brink of the grave I'll not seek to keep
    hovering,
    Nor my thread wish to spin o'er again :

But my face in the glass I'll serenely survey,   29
   And with smiles count each wrinkle and furrow ;
As this old worn-out stuff, which is threadbare
    to-day,
   May become everlasting to-morrow.

                  J. COLLINS.

165

Life ! I know not what thou art,
But know that thou and I must part ;
And when, or how, or where we met
I own to me 's a secret yet.

   Life ! we've been long together   5
Through pleasant and through cloudy weather ;
'Tis hard to part when friends are dear—
Perhaps 'twill cost a sigh, a tear ;
—Then steal away, give little warning,
   Choose thine own time ;   10
Say not Good Night,—but in some brighter clime
   Bid me Good Morning.

             A. L. BARBAULD.

THE GOLDEN TREASURY

BOOK FOURTH

166

ON FIRST LOOKING INTO CHAPMAN'S HOMER

Much have I travell'd in the realms of gold
  And many goodly states and kingdoms seen ;
  Round many western islands have I been
Which bards in fealty to Apollo hold.

Oft of one wide expanse had I been told   5
  That deep-brow'd Homer ruled as his demesne ;
  Yet did I never breathe its pure serene
Till I heard Chapman speak out loud and bold :

Then felt I like some watcher of the skies
  When a new planet swims into his ken ;   10
Or like stout Cortez, when with eagle eyes

  He stared at the Pacific—and all his men
Look'd at each other with a wild surmise—
  Silent, upon a peak in Darien.

J. KEATS.

167

ODE ON THE POETS

Bards of Passion and of Mirth
Ye have left your souls on earth !
Have ye souls in heaven too,
Double-lived in regions new ?

Yes, and those of heaven commune 5
With the spheres of sun and moon ;
With the noise of fountains wond'rous
And the parle of voices thund'rous ;
With the whisper of heaven's trees
And one another, in soft ease 10
Seated on Elysian lawns
Brows'd by none but Dian's fawns ;
Underneath large blue-bells tented,
Where the daisies are rose-scented,
And the rose herself has got 15
Perfume which on earth is not ;
Where the nightingale doth sing
Not a senseless, trancéd thing,
But divine melodious truth ;
Philosophic numbers smooth ; 20
Tales and golden histories
Of heaven and its mysteries.

Thus ye live on high, and then
On the earth ye live again ;
And the souls ye left behind you 25
Teach us, here, the way to find you,
Where your other souls are joying,
Never slumber'd, never cloying.
Here, your earth-born souls still speak
To mortals, of their little week ; 30
Of their sorrows and delights ;
Of their passions and their spites ;
Of their glory and their shame ;
What doth strengthen and what maim :—
Thus ye teach us, every day, 35
Wisdom, though fled far away.

Bards of Passion and of Mirth
Ye have left your souls on earth !
Ye have souls in heaven too,
Double-lived in regions new ! 40

J. KEATS.

168

LOVE

All thoughts, all passions, all delights,
  Whatever stirs this mortal frame,
All are but ministers of Love,
    And feed his sacred flame.

Oft in my waking dreams do I   5
  Live o'er again that happy hour,
When midway on the mount I lay
    Beside the ruin'd tower.

The moonshine stealing o'er the scene
  Had blended with the lights of eve ;   10
And she was there, my hope, my joy,
    My own dear Genevieve !

She lean'd against the arméd man,
  The statue of the arméd knight ;
She stood and listen'd to my lay,   15
    Amid the lingering light.

Few sorrows hath she of her own,
  My hope ! my joy ! my Genevieve !
She loves me best whene'er I sing
    The songs that make her grieve.   20

I play'd a soft and doleful air,
  I sang an old and moving story—
An old rude song, that suited well
    That ruin wild and hoary.

She listen'd with a flitting blush,   25
  With downcast eyes and modest grace ;
For well she knew I could not choose
    But gaze upon her face.

I told her of the Knight that wore
  Upon his shield a burning brand ;   30
And that for ten long years he woo'd
    The Lady of the Land.

I told her how he pined ; and ah !
 The deep, the low, the pleading tone
With which I sang another's love   35
  Interpreted my own.

She listen'd with a flitting blush,
 With downcast eyes and modest grace ;
And she forgave me, that I gazed
  Too fondly on her face.   40

But when I told the cruel scorn
 That crazed that bold and lovely Knight,
And that he cross'd the mountain-woods,
  Nor rested day nor night ;

That sometimes from the savage den, 45
 And sometimes from the darksome shade,
And sometimes starting up at once
  In green and sunny glade

There came and look'd him in the face
 An angel beautiful and bright ; 50
And that he knew it was a Fiend,
  This miserable Knight !

And that, unknowing what he did,
 He leap'd amid a murderous band,
And saved from outrage worse than death 55
  The Lady of the Land ;

And how she wept, and clasp'd his knees
 And how she tended him in vain ;
And ever strove to expiate
  The scorn that crazed his brain ; 60

And that she nursed him in a cave,
 And how his madness went away,
When on the yellow forest leaves
  A dying man he lay ;

—His dying words—but when I reach'd 65
 That tenderest strain of all the ditty,
My faltering voice and pausing harp
  Disturb'd her soul with pity !

All impulses of soul and sense
 Had thrill'd my guileless Genevieve; 70
The music and the doleful tale,
 The rich and balmy eve;

And hopes, and fears that kindle hope,
 An undistinguishable throng,
And gentle wishes long subdued, 75
 Subdued and cherish'd long!

She wept with pity and delight,
 She blush'd with love and virgin shame;
And like the murmur of a dream,
 I heard her breathe my name. 80

Her bosom heaved—she stepp'd aside,
 As conscious of my look she stept—
Then suddenly, with timorous eye
 She fled to me and wept.

She half enclosed me with her arms, 85
 She press'd me with a meek embrace;
And bending back her head, look'd up,
 And gazed upon my face.

'Twas partly love, and partly fear,
 And partly 'twas a bashful art, 90
That I might rather feel, than see,
 The swelling of her heart.

I calm'd her fears, and she was calm,
 And told her love with virgin pride;
And so I won my Genevieve, 95
 My bright and beauteous Bride.

S. T. Coleridge.

169

ALL FOR LOVE

O talk not to me of a name great in story;
The days of our youth are the days of our glory;
And the myrtle and ivy of sweet two-and-twenty
Are worth all your laurels, though ever so plenty.

What are garlands and crowns to the brow that is
    wrinkled ?   5
'Tis but as a dead flower with May-dew besprinkled:
Then away with all such from the head that is hoary—
What care I for the wreaths that can only give glory?

O Fame !—if I e'er took delight in thy praises,   9
'Twas less for the sake of thy high-sounding phrases,
Than to see the bright eyes of the dear one discover
She thought that I was not unworthy to love her.

There chiefly I sought thee, there only I found thee;
Her glance was the best of the rays that surround
    thee ;
When it sparkled o'er aught that was bright in my
    story,   15
I knew it was love, and I felt it was glory.

                      LORD BYRON.

170

THE OUTLAW

O Brignall banks are wild and fair,
    And Greta woods are green,
And you may gather garlands there
    Would grace a summer queen.
And as I rode by Dalton Hall   5
    Beneath the turrets high,
A Maiden on the castle-wall
    Was singing merrily :
' O Brignall banks are fresh and fair,
    And Greta woods are green ;   10
I'd rather rove with Edmund there
    Than reign our English queen.'

' If, Maiden, thou wouldst wend with me,
    To leave both tower and town,
Thou first must guess what life lead we   15
    That dwell by dale and down.
And if thou canst that riddle read,
    As read full well you may,
Then to the greenwood shalt thou speed
    As blithe as Queen of May.'   20

Yet sung she, ' Brignall banks are fair
  And Greta woods are green ;
I'd rather rove with Edmund there
  Than reign our English queen.

' I read you by your bugle-horn   25
  And by your palfrey good,
I read you for a ranger sworn
  To keep the king's greenwood.'
' A ranger, lady, winds his horn,
  And 'tis at peep of light ;   30
His blast is heard at merry morn,
  And mine at dead of night.'
Yet sung she, ' Brignall banks are fair,
  And Greta woods are gay ;
I would I were with Edmund there   35
  To reign his Queen of May !

' With burnish'd brand and musketoon
  So gallantly you come,
I read you for a bold Dragoon
  That lists the tuck of drum.'   40
' I list no more the tuck of drum,
  No more the trumpet hear ;
But when the beetle sounds his hum
  My comrades take the spear.
And O ! though Brignall banks be fair   45
  And Greta woods be gay,
Yet mickle must the maiden dare
  Would reign my Queen of May !

' Maiden ! a nameless life I lead,
  A nameless death I'll die ;   50
The fiend whose lantern lights the mead
  Were better mate than I !
And when I'm with my comrades met
  Beneath the greenwood bough,—
What once we were we all forget,   55
  Nor think what we are now.'

Chorus

Yet Brignall banks are fresh and fair,
  And Greta woods are green,
And you may gather garlands there
  Would grace a summer queen.   60

                              SIR W. SCOTT.

171

There be none of Beauty's daughters
  With a magic like thee ;
And like music on the waters
  Is thy sweet voice to me :
When, as if its sound were causing   5
  The charméd ocean's pausing,
The waves lie still and gleaming,
And the lull'd winds seem dreaming :

And the midnight moon is weaving
  Her bright chain o'er the deep,   10
Whose breast is gently heaving
  As an infant's asleep :
So the spirit bows before thee
  To listen and adore thee ;
With a full but soft emotion,   15
Like the swell of Summer's ocean.

                              LORD BYRON.

172

LINES TO AN INDIAN AIR

I arise from dreams of thee
  In the first sweet sleep of night,
When the winds are breathing low
  And the stars are shining bright :
I arise from dreams of thee,   5
  And a spirit in my feet
Has led me—who knows how ?
  To thy chamber-window, sweet !

The wandering airs they faint
  On the dark, the silent stream—   10
The champak odours fail
  Like sweet thoughts in a dream ;
The nightingale's complaint
  It dies upon her heart,
As I must die on thine,   15
  O belovéd as thou art !

O lift me from the grass !
  I die, I faint, I fail !
Let thy love in kisses rain
  On my lips and eyelids pale.   20
My cheek is cold and white, alas !
  My heart beats loud and fast ;
O ! press it close to thine again
  Where it will break at last.

P. B. SHELLEY.

173

She walks in beauty, like the night
  Of cloudless climes and starry skies,
And all that 's best of dark and bright
  Meet in her aspect and her eyes,
Thus mellow'd to that tender light   5
  Which heaven to gaudy day denies.

One shade the more, one ray the less,
  Had half impair'd the nameless grace
Which waves in every raven tress,
  Or softly lightens o'er her face,   10
Where thoughts serenely sweet express
  How pure, how dear their dwelling-place.

And on that cheek and o'er that brow
  So soft, so calm, yet eloquent,
The smiles that win, the tints that glow   15
  But tell of days in goodness spent,
A mind at peace with all below,
  A heart whose love is innocent.

LORD BYRON.

174

She was a phantom of delight
When first she gleam'd upon my sight;
A lovely apparition, sent
To be a moment's ornament;
Her eyes as stars of Twilight fair;   5
Like Twilight's, too, her dusky hair;
But all things else about her drawn
From May-time and the cheerful dawn;
A dancing shape, an image gay,
To haunt, to startle, and waylay.   10

I saw her upon nearer view,
A spirit, yet a woman too!
Her household motions light and free,
And steps of virgin-liberty;
A countenance in which did meet   15
Sweet records, promises as sweet;
A creature not too bright or good
For human nature's daily food,
For transient sorrows, simple wiles,
Praise, blame, love, kisses, tears, and smiles.

And now I see with eye serene   21
The very pulse of the machine;
A being breathing thoughtful breath,
A traveller between life and death:
The reason firm, the temperate will,   25
Endurance, foresight, strength, and skill;
A perfect woman, nobly plann'd
To warn, to comfort, and command;
And yet a Spirit still, and bright
With something of angelic light.   30

W. WORDSWORTH.

175

She is not fair to outward view
As many maidens be;
Her loveliness I never knew
Until she smiled on me.

O then I saw her eye was bright, 5
A well of love, a spring of light.

But now her looks are coy and cold,
  To mine they ne'er reply,
And yet I cease not to behold
  The love-light in her eye : 10
Her very frowns are fairer far
Than smiles of other maidens are.

H. COLERIDGE.

176

I fear thy kisses, gentle maiden ;
  Thou needest not fear mine ;
My spirit is too deeply laden
  Ever to burthen thine.

I fear thy mien, thy tones, thy motion ; 5
  Thou needest not fear mine ;
Innocent is the heart's devotion
  With which I worship thine.

P. B. SHELLEY.

177

THE LOST LOVE

She dwelt among the untrodden ways
  Beside the springs of Dove ;
A maid whom there were none to praise,
  And very few to love :

A violet by a mossy stone 5
  Half hidden from the eye !
—Fair as a star, when only one
  Is shining in the sky.

She lived unknown, and few could know
  When Lucy ceased to be ; 10
But she is in her grave, and oh,
  The difference to me !

W. WORDSWORTH.

178

I travell'd among unknown men
　In lands beyond the sea ;
Nor, England ! did I know till then
　What love I bore to thee.

'Tis past, that melancholy dream ! 　　　5
　Nor will I quit thy shore
A second time ; for still I seem
　To love thee more and more.

Among thy mountains did I feel
　The joy of my desire ; 　　　　　　10
And she I cherish'd turn'd her wheel
　Beside an English fire.

Thy mornings show'd, thy nights conceal'd
　The bowers where Lucy play'd ;
And thine too is the last green field 　　15
　That Lucy's eyes survey'd.

　　　　　　　　　W. WORDSWORTH.

179

THE EDUCATION OF NATURE

Three years she grew in sun and shower ;
Then Nature said, ' A lovelier flower
　On earth was never sown :
This child I to myself will take ;
She shall be mine, and I will make 　　　5
　A lady of my own.

' Myself will to my darling be
Both law and impulse : and with me
　The girl, in rock and plain,
In earth and heaven, in glade and bower, 　10
Shall feel an overseeing power
　To kindle or restrain.

' She shall be sportive as the fawn
That wild with glee across the lawn
 Or up the mountain springs ;   15
And hers shall be the breathing balm,
And hers the silence and the calm
 Of mute insensate things.

' The floating clouds their state shall lend
To her ; for her the willow bend ;   20
 Nor shall she fail to see
E'en in the motions of the storm
Grace that shall mould the maiden's form
 By silent sympathy.

' The stars of midnight shall be dear 25
To her ; and she shall lean her ear
 In many a secret place
Where rivulets dance their wayward round,
And beauty born of murmuring sound
 Shall pass into her face.   30

' And vital feelings of delight
Shall rear her form to stately height,
 Her virgin bosom swell ;
Such thoughts to Lucy I will give
While she and I together live   35
 Here in this happy dell.'

Thus Nature spake—The work was done—
How soon my Lucy's race was run !
She died, and left to me
This heath, this calm and quiet scene ; 40
The memory of what has been,
 And never more will be.

       W. WORDSWORTH.

      180

A slumber did my spirit seal ;
 I had no human fears :
She seem'd a thing that could not feel
 The touch of earthly years.

No motion has she now, no force ;   5
  She neither hears nor sees ;
Roll'd round in earth's diurnal course
  With rocks, and stones, and trees.

W. WORDSWORTH.

181

LORD ULLIN'S DAUGHTER

A Chieftain to the Highlands bound
  Cries ' Boatman, do not tarry !
And I'll give thee a silver pound
  To row us o'er the ferry ! '

' Now who be ye, would cross Lochgyle   5
  This dark and stormy water ? '
' O I'm the chief of Ulva's isle,
  And this, Lord Ullin's daughter.

' And fast before her father's men
  Three days we've fled together,   10
For should he find us in the glen,
  My blood would stain the heather.

' His horsemen hard behind us ride—
  Should they our steps discover,
Then who will cheer my bonny bride   15
  When they have slain her lover ? '

Out spoke the hardy Highland wight,
  ' I'll go, my chief, I'm ready :
It is not for your silver bright,
  But for your winsome lady :—   20

' And by my word ! the bonny bird
  In danger shall not tarry ;
So though the waves are raging white
  I'll row you o'er the ferry.'

By this the storm grew loud apace,   25
  The water-wraith was shrieking ;
And in the scowl of heaven each face
  Grew dark as they were speaking.

But still as wilder blew the wind
   And as the night grew drearer,   30
Adown the glen rode arméd men,
   Their trampling sounded nearer.

'O haste thee, haste!' the lady cries,
   'Though tempests round us gather;
I'll meet the raging of the skies,   35
   But not an angry father.'

The boat has left a stormy land,
   A stormy sea before her,—
When, oh! too strong for human hand
   The tempest gather'd o'er her.   40

And still they row'd amidst the roar
   Of waters fast prevailing:
Lord Ullin reach'd that fatal shore,—
   His wrath was changed to wailing.

For, sore dismay'd, through storm and shade
   His child he did discover:—   46
One lovely hand she stretch'd for aid,
   And one was round her lover.

'Come back! come back!' he cried in grief
   'Across this stormy water: 50
And I'll forgive your Highland chief,
   My daughter!—O my daughter!'

'Twas vain: the loud waves lash'd the shore,
   Return or aid preventing:
The waters wild went o'er his child,   55
   And he was left lamenting.
                T. CAMPBELL.

182

JOCK O' HAZELDEAN

'Why weep ye by the tide, ladie?
   Why weep ye by the tide?
I'll wed ye to my youngest son,
   And ye sall be his bride:

And ye sall be his bride, ladie,　　　　　5
　　Sae comely to be seen '—
But aye she loot the tears down fa'
　　For Jock o' Hazeldean.

'Now let this wilfu' grief be done,
　　And dry that cheek so pale ;　　　　10
Young Frank is chief of Errington
　　And lord of Langley-dale ;
His step is first in peaceful ha',
　　His sword in battle keen '—
But aye she loot the tears down fa'　　15
　　For Jock o' Hazeldean.

'A chain of gold ye sall not lack,
　　Nor braid to bind your hair ;
Nor mettled hound, nor managed hawk,
　　Nor palfrey fresh and fair ;　　　　20
And you, the foremost o' them a',
　　Shall ride our forest queen '—
But aye she loot the tears down fa'
　　For Jock o' Hazeldean.

The kirk was deck'd at morning-tide,　　25
　　The tapers glimmer'd fair ;
The priest and bridegroom wait the bride,
　　And dame and knight are there.
They sought her baith by bower and ha' ;
　　The ladie was not seen !　　　　30
She 's o'er the Border, and awa'
　　Wi' Jock o' Hazeldean
　　　　　　　　　　　　Sir W. Scott.

183

FREEDOM AND LOVE

How delicious is the winning
Of a kiss at love's beginning,
When two mutual hearts are sighing
For the knot there's no untying !

Yet remember, 'midst your wooing,   5
Love has bliss, but Love has ruing ;
Other smiles may make you fickle,
Tears for other charms may trickle.

Love he comes, and Love he tarries,
Just as fate or fancy carries ;   10
Longest stays, when sorest chidden ;
Laughs and flies, when press'd and bidden.

Bind the sea to slumber stilly,
Bind its odour to the lily,
Bind the aspen ne'er to quiver,   15
Then bind Love to last for ever.

Love's a fire that needs renewal
Of fresh beauty for its fuel :
Love's wing moults when caged and captured,
Only free, he soars enraptured.   20

Can you keep the bee from ranging
Or the ringdove's neck from changing ?
No ! nor fetter'd Love from dying
In the knot there's no untying.

                                   T. CAMPBELL.

184

LOVE'S PHILOSOPHY

The fountains mingle with the river
    And the rivers with the ocean,
The winds of heaven mix for ever
    With a sweet emotion ;
Nothing in the world is single,   5
    All things by a law divine
In one another's being mingle—
    Why not I with thine ?

See the mountains kiss high heaven
    And the waves clasp one another ;   10
No sister-flower would be forgiven
    If it disdain'd its brother :

And the sunlight clasps the earth,
　　And the moonbeams kiss the sea—
What are all these kissings worth,　　　15
　　If thou kiss not me?

P. B. SHELLEY.

185

ECHOES

How sweet the answer Echo makes
　　To Music at night,
When, roused by lute or horn, she wakes,
And far away o'er lawns and lakes
　　Goes answering light!　　　5

Yet Love hath echoes truer far
　　And far more sweet
Than e'er, beneath the moonlight's star,
Of horn or lute or soft guitar
　　The songs repeat.　　　10

'Tis when the sigh,—in youth sincere
　　And only then—
The sigh that's breathed for one to hear,
Is by that one, that only Dear
　　Breathed back again.　　　15

T. MOORE.

186

A SERENADE

Ah! County Guy, the hour is nigh,
　　The sun has left the lea,
The orange flower perfumes the bower,
　　The breeze is on the sea.
The lark, his lay who trill'd all day,　　　5
　　Sits hush'd his partner nigh;
Breeze, bird, and flower confess the hour,
　　But where is County Guy?

The village maid steals through the shade
   Her shepherd's suit to hear ;   10
To beauty shy, by lattice high,
   Sings high-born Cavalier.
The star of Love, all stars above,
   Now reigns o'er earth and sky,
And high and low the influence know—   15
   But where is County Guy ?

SIR W. SCOTT.

187

TO THE EVENING STAR

Gem of the crimson-colour'd Even,
   Companion of retiring day,
Why at the closing gates of heaven,
   Belovéd Star, dost thou delay ?

So fair thy pensile beauty burns   5
   When soft the tear of twilight flows ;
So due thy plighted love returns
   To chambers brighter than the rose ;

To Peace, to Pleasure, and to Love
   So kind a star thou seem'st to be,   10
Sure some enamour'd orb above
   Descends and burns to meet with thee.

Thine is the breathing, blushing hour,
   When all unheavenly passions fly,
Chased by the soul-subduing power   15
   Of Love's delicious witchery.

O ! sacred to the fall of day,
   Queen of propitious stars, appear,
And early rise, and long delay,
   When Caroline herself is here !   20

Shine on her chosen green resort,
   Whose trees the sunward summit crown,
And wanton flowers, that well may court
   An angel's feet to tread them down.

Shine on her sweetly-scented road,   25
  Thou star of evening's purple dome,
That lead'st the nightingale abroad,
  And guid'st the pilgrim to his home.

Shine where my charmer's sweeter breath
  Embalms the soft exhaling dew,   30
Where dying winds a sigh bequeath
  To kiss the cheek of rosy hue.

Where, winnow'd by the gentle air,
  Her silken tresses darkly flow,
And fall upon her brow so fair,   35
  Like shadows on the mountain snow.

Thus, ever thus, at day's decline
  In converse sweet to wander far—
O bring with thee my Caroline,
  And thou shalt be my Ruling Star!   40

               T. CAMPBELL.

188

TO THE NIGHT

Swiftly walk over the western wave
      Spirit of Night!
Out of the misty eastern cave,
  Where, all the long and lone daylight,
Thou wovest dreams of joy and fear   5
Which make thee terrible and dear,—
      Swift be thy flight!

Wrap thy form in a mantle grey
      Star-inwrought!
Blind with thine hair the eyes of Day,   10
  Kiss her until she be wearied out,
Then wander o'er city, and sea, and land,
Touching all with thine opiate wand—
      Come, long-sought!

When I arose and saw the dawn,   15
    I sigh'd for thee ;
When light rode high, and the dew was gone,
  And noon lay heavy on flower and tree,
And the weary Day turn'd to his rest,
Lingering like an unloved guest,   20
    I sigh'd for thee.

Thy brother Death came, and cried,
    ' Wouldst thou me ? '
Thy sweet child Sleep, the filmy-eyed,
  Murmur'd like a noontide bee,   25
' Shall I nestle near thy side ?
Wouldst thou me ? '—And I replied,
    ' No, not thee ! '

Death will come when thou art dead,
    Soon, too soon—   30
Sleep will come when thou art fled ;
  Of neither would I ask the boon
I ask of thee, belovéd Night—
Swift be thine approaching flight,
    Come soon, soon !   35

P. B. SHELLEY.

189

TO A DISTANT FRIEND

Why art thou silent ? Is thy love a plant
  Of such weak fibre that the treacherous air
  Of absence withers what was once so fair ?
Is there no debt to pay, no boon to grant ?

Yet have my thoughts for thee been vigilant,   5
  Bound to thy service with unceasing care—
The mind's least generous wish a mendicant
  For nought but what thy happiness could spare.

Speak !—though this soft warm heart, once free to
    hold
  A thousand tender pleasures, thine and mine,
Be left more desolate, more dreary cold   11

Than a forsaken bird's-nest fill'd with snow
  'Mid its own bush of leafless eglantine—
Speak, that my torturing doubts their end may
    know !   W. WORDSWORTH.

190

When we two parted
  In silence and tears,
Half broken-hearted,
  To sever for years,
Pale grew thy cheek and cold,   5
  Colder thy kiss ;
Truly that hour foretold
  Sorrow to this !

The dew of the morning
  Sunk chill on my brow ;   10
It felt like the warning
  Of what I feel now.
Thy vows are all broken,
  And light is thy fame :
I hear thy name spoken   15
  And share in its shame.

They name thee before me,
  A knell to mine ear ;
A shudder comes o'er me—
  Why wert thou so dear ?   20
They know not I knew thee
  Who knew thee too well :
Long, long shall I rue thee
  Too deeply to tell.

In secret we met :   25
  In silence I grieve
That thy heart could forget,
  Thy spirit deceive.
If I should meet thee
  After long years,   30
How should I greet thee ?—
  With silence and tears.
            LORD BYRON.

191

HAPPY INSENSIBILITY

In a drear-nighted December,
  Too happy, happy tree,
Thy branches ne'er remember
  Their green felicity :
The north cannot undo them   5
With a sleety whistle through them,
Nor frozen thawings glue them
  From budding at the prime.

In a drear-nighted December,
  Too happy, happy brook,   10
Thy bubblings ne'er remember
  Apollo's summer look ;
But with a sweet forgetting
They stay their crystal fretting,
Never, never petting   15
  About the frozen time.

Ah, would 'twere so with many
  A gentle girl and boy !
But were there ever any
  Writhed not at passèd joy ?   20
To know the change and feel it,
When there is none to heal it
Nor numbèd sense to steel it—
  Was never said in rhyme.

                              J. KEATS.

192

Where shall the lover rest
  Whom the fates sever
From his true maiden's breast,
  Parted for ever ?
Where, through groves deep and high,   5
  Sounds the far billow,

Where early violets die
   Under the willow.
     Eleu loro !
Soft shall be his pillow.   10

There, through the summer day,
   Cool streams are laving :
There, while the tempests sway,
   Scarce are boughs waving ;
There thy rest shalt thou take,   15
   Parted for ever,
Never again to wake,
   Never, O never !
     Eleu loro !
   Never, O never !   20

Where shall the traitor rest,
   He, the deceiver,
Who could win maiden's breast,
   Ruin, and leave her ?
In the lost battle,   25
   Borne down by the flying,
Where mingles war's rattle
   With groans of the dying ;
     Eleu loro !
   There shall he be lying.   30

Her wing shall the eagle flap
   O'er the falsehearted ;
His warm blood the wolf shall lap
   Ere life be parted :
Shame and dishonour sit   35
   By his grave ever ;
Blessing shall hallow it
   Never, O never !
     Eleu loro !
   Never, O never !   40

SIR W. SCOTT.

193
LA BELLE DAME SANS MERCI

'O what can ail thee, knight-at-arms,
  Alone and palely loitering?
The sedge has wither'd from the Lake,
  And no birds sing.

'O what can ail thee, knight-at-arms!   5
  So haggard and so woebegone?
The squirrel's granary is full,
  And the harvest's done.

'I see a lily on thy brow
  With anguish moist and fever dew,   10
And on thy cheeks a fading rose
  Fast withereth too.'

'I met a Lady in the Meads,
  Full beautiful—a fairy's child,
Her hair was long, her foot was light,   15
  And her eyes were wild.

'I made a garland for her head,
  And bracelets too, and fragrant zone;
She look'd at me as she did love,
  And made sweet moan.   20

'I set her on my pacing steed
  And nothing else saw all day long,
For sidelong would she bend, and sing
  A fairy's song.

'She found me roots of relish sweet,   25
  And honey wild and manna dew,
And sure in language strange she said
  "I love thee true."

'She took me to her elfin grot,
  And there she wept, and sigh'd full sore,   30
And there I shut her wild wild eyes
  With kisses four.

'And there she lulléd me asleep,
   And there I dream'd—Ah ! woe betide !
The latest dream I ever dreamt   35
   On the cold hill side.

'I saw pale Kings and Princes too,
   Pale warriors, death-pale were they all ;
They cried—" La belle Dame sans Merci
   Thee hath in thrall ! "   40

'I saw their starved lips in the gloam
   With horrid warning gapéd wide.
And I awoke and found me here
   On the cold hill's side.

'And this is why I sojourn here   45
   Alone and palely loitering,
Though the sedge is wither'd from the Lake
   And no birds sing.'

J. KEATS.

194

THE ROVER

'A weary lot is thine, fair maid,
   A weary lot is thine !
To pull the thorn thy brow to braid,
   And press the rue for wine.
A lightsome eye, a soldier's mien,   5
   A feather of the blue,
A doublet of the Lincoln green—
   No more of me you knew
           My Love !
No more of me you knew.   10

'This morn is merry June, I trow,
   The rose is budding fain ;
But she shall bloom in winter snow
   Ere we two meet again.'
He turn'd his charger as he spake   15
   Upon the river shore,

He gave his bridle-reins a shake,
  Said ' Adieu for evermore
             My Love !
And adieu for evermore.'   20
                 SIR W. SCOTT.

195

THE FLIGHT OF LOVE

When the lamp is shattered,
  The light in the dust lies dead—
When the cloud is scattered,
  The rainbow's glory is shed.
When the lute is broken,   5
  Sweet tones are remembered not ;
When the lips have spoken,
  Loved accents are soon forgot.

As music and splendour
  Survive not the lamp and the lute,   10
The heart's echoes render
  No song when the spirit is mute—
No song but sad dirges,
  Like the wind through a ruined cell,
Or the mournful surges   15
  That ring the dead seaman's knell.

When hearts have once mingled,
  Love first leaves the well-built nest ;
The weak one is singled
  To endure what it once possest.   20
O Love ! who bewailest
  The frailty of all things here,
Why choose you the frailest
  For your cradle, your home, and your bier ?

Its passions will rock thee   25
  As the storms rock the ravens on high ;
Bright reason will mock thee
  Like the sun from a wintry sky.

From thy nest every rafter
    Will rot, and thine eagle home   30
Leave thee naked to laughter,
    When leaves fall and cold winds come.

P. B. SHELLEY.

196

THE MAID OF NEIDPATH

O lovers' eyes are sharp to see,
    And lovers' ears in hearing ;
And love, in life's extremity,
    Can lend an hour of cheering.
Disease had been in Mary's bower   5
    And slow decay from mourning,
Though now she sits on Neidpath's tower
    To watch her love's returning.

All sunk and dim her eyes so bright,
    Her form decay'd by pining,   10
Till through her wasted hand, at night,
    You saw the taper shining.
By fits a sultry hectic hue
    Across her cheek was flying ;
By fits so ashy pale she grew   15
    Her maidens thought her dying.

Yet keenest powers to see and hear
    Seem'd in her frame residing ;
Before the watch-dog prick'd his ear
    She heard her lover's riding ;   20
Ere scarce a distant form was kenn'd
    She knew and waved to greet him,
And o'er the battlement did bend
    As on the wing to meet him.

He came—he pass'd—an heedless gaze,   25
    As o'er some stranger glancing ;
Her welcome, spoke in faltering phrase,
    Lost in his courser's prancing—

The castle-arch, whose hollow tone
  Returns each whisper spoken,   30
Could scarcely catch the feeble moan
  Which told her heart was broken.
Sir W. Scott.

197

THE MAID OF NEIDPATH

Earl March look'd on his dying child,
  And, smit with grief to view her—
' The youth,' he cried, ' whom I exiled
  Shall be restored to woo her.'

She's at the window many an hour   5
  His coming to discover :
And he look'd up to Ellen's bower
  And she look'd on her lover—

But ah ! so pale, he knew her not,
  Though her smile on him was dwelling—   10
' And am I then forgot—forgot ? '
  It broke the heart of Ellen.

In vain he weeps, in vain he sighs,
  Her cheek is cold as ashes ;
Nor love's own kiss shall wake those eyes   15
  To lift their silken lashes.
T. Campbell.

198

Bright Star, would I were steadfast as thou art—
  Not in lone splendour hung aloft the night,
And watching, with eternal lids apart,
  Like nature's patient sleepless Eremite,

The moving waters at their priestlike task   5
  Of pure ablution round earth's human shores,
Or gazing on the new soft-fallen mask
  Of snow upon the mountains and the moors—

No—yet still steadfast, still unchangeable,   9
    Pillow'd upon my fair love's ripening breast,
To feel for ever its soft fall and swell,
    Awake for ever in a sweet unrest ;

Still, still to hear her tender-taken breath,
And so live ever,—or else swoon to death.

                 J. KEATS.

199

THE TERROR OF DEATH

When I have fears that I may cease to be
    Before my pen has glean'd my teeming brain,
Before high-pilèd books, in charact'ry
    Hold like rich garners the full-ripen'd grain ;

When I behold, upon the night's starr'd face,   5
    Huge cloudy symbols of a high romance,
And think that I may never live to trace
    Their shadows, with the magic hand of chance ;

And when I feel, fair creature of an hour !
    That I shall never look upon thee more,   10
Never have relish in the fairy power
    Of unreflecting love—then on the shore

Of the wide world I stand alone, and think
Till love and fame to nothingness do sink.

                 J. KEATS.

200

DESIDERIA

Surprised by joy—impatient as the wind—
    I turn'd to share the transport—O with whom
    But Thee—deep buried in the silent tomb,
That spot which no vicissitude can find ?

Love, faithful love recall'd thee to my mind—   5
    But how could I forget thee ? Through what
    power

Even for the least division of an hour
Have I been so beguiled as to be blind

To my most grievous loss ?—That thought's return
  Was the worst pang that sorrow ever bore,   10
Save one, one only, when I stood forlorn,

  Knowing my heart's best treasure was no more ;
That neither present time, nor years unborn
  Could to my sight that heavenly face restore.

W. WORDSWORTH.

201

At the mid hour of night, when stars are weeping, I
  fly
To the lone vale we loved, when life shone warm in
  thine eye ;
And I think oft, if spirits can steal from the regions
  of air
To revisit past scenes of delight, thou wilt come to
  me there
And tell me our love is remember'd, even in the
  sky !   5

Then I sing the wild song it once was rapture to hear,
When our voices, commingling, breathed like one on
  the ear ;
And as Echo far off through the vale my sad orison
  rolls,
I think, O my Love ! 'tis thy voice, from the
  Kingdom of Souls
Faintly answering still the notes that once were so
  dear.   10

T. MOORE.

202

ELEGY ON THYRZA

And thou art dead, as young and fair
  As aught of mortal birth ;
And form so soft and charms so rare
  Too soon return'd to Earth !

Though Earth received them in her bed,   5
And o'er the spot the crowd may tread
    In carelessness or mirth,
There is an eye which could not brook
A moment on that grave to look.

I will not ask where thou liest low,   10
    Nor gaze upon the spot ;
There flowers or weeds at will may grow,
    So I behold them not :
It is enough for me to prove
That what I loved and long must love   15
    Like common earth can rot ;
To me there needs no stone to tell
'Tis Nothing that I loved so well.

Yet did I love thee to the last,
    As fervently as thou,   20
Who didst not change through all the past
    And canst not alter now.
The love where Death has set his seal
Nor age can chill, nor rival steal,
    Nor falsehood disavow :   25
And, what were worse, thou canst not see
Or wrong, or change, or fault in me.

The better days of life were ours ;
    The worst can be but mine :
The sun that cheers, the storm that lours,   30
    Shall never more be thine.
The silence of that dreamless sleep
I envy now too much to weep ;
    Nor need I to repine
That all those charms have pass'd away   35
I might have watch'd through long decay.

The flower in ripen'd bloom unmatch'd
    Must fall the earliest prey ;
Though by no hand untimely snatch'd,
    The leaves must drop away.   40
And yet it were a greater grief

To watch it withering, leaf by leaf,
  Than see it pluck'd to-day ;
Since earthly eye but ill can bear
To trace the change to foul from fair.   45

I know not if I could have borne
  To see thy beauties fade ;
The night that follow'd such a morn
  Had worn a deeper shade :
Thy day without a cloud hath past,   50
And thou wert lovely to the last,
  Extinguish'd, not decay'd ;
As stars that shoot along the sky
Shine brightest as they fall from high.

As once I wept, if I could weep,   55
  My tears might well be shed,
To think I was not near, to keep
  One vigil o'er thy bed :
To gaze, how fondly ! on thy face,
To fold thee in a faint embrace,   60
  Uphold thy drooping head ;
And show that love, however vain,
Nor thou nor I can feel again.

Yet how much less it were to gain,
  Though thou hast left me free,   65
The loveliest things that still remain
  Than thus remember thee !
The all of thine that cannot die
Through dark and dread Eternity
  Returns again to me,   70
And more thy buried love endears
Than aught except its living years.

                                   LORD BYRON.

                    203

One word is too often profaned
  For me to profane it,
One feeling too falsely disdain'd
  For thee to disdain it ;

One hope is too like despair 　　　　5
　　For prudence to smother,
And Pity from thee more dear
　　Than that from another.

I can give not what men call love ;
　　But wilt thou accept not 　　　　10
The worship the heart lifts above
　　And the Heavens reject not,—
The desire of the moth for the star,
　　Of the night for the morrow,
The devotion to something afar 　　15
　　From the sphere of our sorrow ?

　　　　　　　　　　P. B. SHELLEY.

204

GATHERING SONG OF DONALD
THE BLACK

Pibroch of Donuil Dhu,
　　Pibroch of Donuil,
Wake thy wild voice anew,
　　Summon Clan Conuil.
Come away, come away, 　　　　5
　　Hark to the summons !
Come in your war-array,
　　Gentles and commons.

Come from deep glen, and
　　From mountain so rocky ; 　　10
The war-pipe and pennon
　　Are at Inverlocky.
Come every hill-plaid, and
　　True heart that wears one,
Come every steel blade, and 　　15
　　Strong hand that bears one.

Leave untended the herd,
　　The flock without shelter ;
Leave the corpse uninterr'd,
　　The bride at the altar ; 　　20

Leave the deer, leave the steer,
  Leave nets and barges :
Come with your fighting gear,
  Broadswords and targes.

Come as the winds come, when   25
  Forests are rended ;
Come as the waves come, when
  Navies are stranded :
Faster come, faster come,
  Faster and faster,   30
Chief, vassal, page and groom,
  Tenant and master.

Fast they come, fast they come ;
  See how they gather !
Wide waves the eagle plume,   35
  Blended with heather.
Cast your plaids, draw your blades,
  Forward each man set !
Pibroch of Donuil Dhu
  Knell for the onset !   40
                        SIR W. SCOTT.

205

A wet sheet and a flowing sea,
  A wind that follows fast
And fills the white and rustling sail
  And bends the gallant mast ;
And bends the gallant mast, my boys,   5
  While like the eagle free
Away the good ship flies, and leaves
  Old England on the lee.

O for a soft and gentle wind !
  I heard a fair one cry ;   10
But give to me the snoring breeze
  And white waves heaving high ;

And white waves heaving high, my lads,
    The good ship tight and free—
The world of waters is our home,   15
    And merry men are we.

There's tempest in yon hornéd moon,
    And lightning in yon cloud ;
But hark the music, mariners !
    The wind is piping loud ;   20
The wind is piping loud, my boys,
    The lightning flashes free—
While the hollow oak our palace is,
    Our heritage the sea.

A. CUNNINGHAM.

206

Ye Mariners of England
    That guard our native seas,
Whose flag has braved, a thousand years,
    The battle and the breeze,
Your glorious standard launch again   5
    To match another foe :
And sweep through the deep,
    While the stormy winds do blow ;
While the battle rages loud and long
    And the stormy winds do blow.   10

The spirits of your fathers
    Shall start from every wave—
For the deck it was their field of fame,
    And Ocean was their grave.
Where Blake and mighty Nelson fell   15
    Your manly hearts shall glow,
As ye sweep through the deep,
    While the stormy winds do blow ;
While the battle rages loud and long
    And the stormy winds do blow.   20

Britannia needs no bulwarks,
    No towers along the steep ;

Her march is o'er the mountain waves,
 Her home is on the deep.
With thunders from her native oak   25
 She quells the floods below—
As they roar on the shore,
 When the stormy winds do blow;
When the battle rages loud and long,
 And the stormy winds do blow. 30

The meteor flag of England
 Shall yet terrific burn;
Till danger's troubled night depart
 And the star of peace return.
Then, then, ye ocean warriors!   35
 Our song and feast shall flow
To the fame of your name,
 When the storm has ceased to blow;
When the fiery fight is heard no more,
 And the storm has ceased to blow. 40

T. CAMPBELL.

207

BATTLE OF THE BALTIC

Of Nelson and the North
Sing the glorious day's renown,
 When to battle fierce came forth
 All the might of Denmark's crown,
And her arms along the deep proudly shone; 5
 By each gun the lighted brand
In a bold, determined hand,
And the Prince of all the land
 Led them on.

 Like leviathans afloat   10
Lay their bulwarks on the brine;
 While the sign of battle flew
 On the lofty British line:
It was ten of April morn by the chime:
 As they drifted on their path 15

There was silence deep as death ;
And the boldest held his breath
   For a time.

But the might of England flush'd
To anticipate the scene ;   20
  And her van the fleeter rush'd
O'er the deadly space between.
' Hearts of oak !' our captains cried, when each gun
  From its adamantine lips
Spread a death-shade round the ships,   25
  Like the hurricane eclipse
   Of the sun.

Again ! again ! again !
  And the havoc did not slack,
  Till a feeble cheer the Dane   30
To our cheering sent us back ;
Their shots along the deep slowly boom :
  Then ceased—and all is wail,
As they strike the shatter'd sail ;
  Or in conflagration pale   35
   Light the gloom.

Out spoke the victor then
  As he hail'd them o'er the wave,
  ' Ye are brothers ! ye are men !
And we conquer but to save :   40
So peace instead of death let us bring :
  But yield, proud foe, thy fleet
With the crews, at England's feet,
  And make submission meet
   To our King.'   45

Then Denmark blest our chief
  That he gave her wounds repose ;
  And the sounds of joy and grief
From her people wildly rose,
As death withdrew his shades from the day : 50
  While the sun look'd smiling bright
O'er a wide and woeful sight,
  Where the fires of funeral light
   Died away.

Now joy, old England, raise 55
For the tidings of thy might,
By the festal cities' blaze,
Whilst the wine cup shines in light ;
And yet amidst that joy and uproar,
Let us think of them that sleep 60
Full many a fathom deep
By thy wild and stormy steep,
Elsinore !

Brave hearts ! to Britain's pride
Once so faithful and so true, 65
On the deck of fame that died
With the gallant good Riou :
Soft sigh the winds of heaven o'er their grave !
While the billow mournful rolls
And the mermaid's song condoles, 70
Singing glory to the souls
Of the brave ! T. CAMPBELL.

208

ODE TO DUTY

Stern Daughter of the Voice of God !
O Duty ! if that name thou love
Who art a light to guide, a rod
To check the erring, and reprove ;
Thou, who art victory and law 5
When empty terrors overawe,
From vain temptations dost set free,
And calm'st the weary strife of frail humanity !

There are who ask not if thine eye
Be on them ; who, in love and truth 10
Where no misgiving is, rely
Upon the genial sense of youth :
Glad hearts ! without reproach or blot,
Who do thy work, and know it not :
O ! if through confidence misplaced 15
They fail, thy saving arms, dread Power ! around
them cast.

Serene will be our days and bright,
   And happy will our nature be,
When love is an unerring light,
   And joy its own security.   20
And they a blissful course may hold
Ev'n now, who, not unwisely bold,
Live in the spirit of this creed,
Yet seek thy firm support, according to their need.

I, loving freedom, and untried,   25
   No sport of every random gust,
Yet being to myself a guide,
   Too blindly have reposed my trust :
And oft, when in my heart was heard
Thy timely mandate, I deferr'd   30
The task, in smoother walks to stray ;
But thee I now would serve more strictly, if I may.

Through no disturbance of my soul
   Or strong compunction in me wrought,
I supplicate for thy control,   35
   But in the quietness of thought :
Me this uncharter'd freedom tires ;
I feel the weight of chance desires :
My hopes no more must change their name ;
I long for a repose that ever is the same.   40

Stern Lawgiver ! yet thou dost wear
   The Godhead's most benignant grace ;
Nor know we anything so fair
   As is the smile upon thy face :
Flowers laugh before thee on their beds,   45
And fragrance in thy footing treads ;
Thou dost preserve the stars from wrong ;
And the most ancient heavens, through thee, are
        fresh and strong.

To humbler functions, awful Power !
   I call thee : I myself commend   50
Unto thy guidance from this hour ;
   O let my weakness have an end !

Give unto me, made lowly wise,
  The spirit of self-sacrifice ;
  The confidence of reason give ;   55
And in the light of Truth thy bondman let me live.
                W. WORDSWORTH.

209

ON THE CASTLE OF CHILLON

Eternal Spirit of the chainless Mind !
  Brightest in dungeons, Liberty, thou art—
  For there thy habitation is the heart—
The heart which love of Thee alone can bind ;

And when thy sons to fetters are consign'd,   5
  To fetters, and the damp vault's dayless gloom,
  Their country conquers with their martyrdom,
And Freedom's fame finds wings on every wind.

Chillon ! thy prison is a holy place
  And thy sad floor an altar, for 'twas trod, 10
Until his very steps have left a trace

  Worn, as if thy cold pavement were a sod,
By Bonnivard ! May none those marks efface !
  For they appeal from tyranny to God.
                LORD BYRON.

210

ENGLAND AND SWITZERLAND

1802

Two Voices are there, one is of the Sea,
  One of the Mountains, each a mighty voice :
  In both from age to age thou didst rejoice,
They were thy chosen music, Liberty !

There came a tyrant, and with holy glee   5
  Thou fought'st against him,—but hast vainly
      striven :
  Thou from thy Alpine holds at length art driven,
Where not a torrent murmurs heard by thee.

Of one deep bliss thine ear hath been bereft ;
Then cleave, O cleave to that which still is left ;
   For, high-soul'd Maid, what sorrow would it be

    That Mountain floods should thunder as before,
     And Ocean bellow from his rocky shore,   13
And neither awful Voice be heard by Thee !

               W. WORDSWORTH.

211

ON THE EXTINCTION OF THE VENETIAN REPUBLIC

Once did She hold the gorgeous East in fee,
   And was the safeguard of the West ; the worth
   Of Venice did not fall below her birth,
Venice, the eldest child of liberty.

She was a maiden city, bright and free ;   5
   No guile seduced, no force could violate ;
   And when she took unto herself a mate,
She must espouse the everlasting Sea.

And what if she had seen those glories fade,
   Those titles vanish, and that strength decay,—
Yet shall some tribute of regret be paid   11

   When her long life hath reach'd its final day :
Men are we, and must grieve when even the shade
   Of that which once was great is pass'd away.

               W. WORDSWORTH.

212

LONDON, MDCCCII

O Friend ! I know not which way I must look
   For comfort, being, as I am, opprest
   To think that now our life is only drest
For show ; mean handiwork of craftsman, cook,

Or groom !—We must run glittering like a brook
   In the open sunshine, or we are unblest ;   6
   The wealthiest man among us is the best :
No grandeur now in Nature or in book

Delights us. Rapine, avarice, expense,
   This is idolatry ; and these we adore :   10
   Plain living and high thinking are no more :

    The homely beauty of the good old cause
Is gone ; our peace, our fearful innocence,
    And pure religion breathing household laws.
               W. WORDSWORTH.

213

THE SAME

Milton ! thou shouldst be living at this hour :
   England hath need of thee : she is a fen
   Of stagnant waters : altar, sword, and pen,
Fireside, the heroic wealth of hall and bower,

Have forfeited their ancient English dower   5
   Of inward happiness. We are selfish men :
   O ! raise us up, return to us again ;
And give us manners, virtue, freedom, power.

Thy soul was like a Star, and dwelt apart :
   Thou hadst a voice whose sound was like the sea,
   Pure as the naked heavens, majestic, free ;   11

    So didst thou travel on life's common way
In cheerful godliness ; and yet thy heart
    The lowliest duties on herself did lay.
               W. WORDSWORTH.

214

When I have borne in memory what has tamed
   Great nations ; how ennobling thoughts depart
   When men change swords for ledgers, and desert
The student's bower for gold,—some fears unnamed

I had, my Country !—am I to be blamed ?   5
  Now, when I think of thee, and what thou art,
    Verily, in the bottom of my heart
Of those unfilial fears I am ashamed.

For dearly must we prize thee ; we who find
  In thee a bulwark for the cause of men ;   10
    And I by my affection was beguiled :

What wonder if a Poet now and then,
Among the many movements of his mind,
    Felt for thee as a lover or a child !

               W. WORDSWORTH.

215

HOHENLINDEN

On Linden, when the sun was low,
All bloodless lay the untrodden snow ;
And dark as winter was the flow
    Of Iser, rolling rapidly.

But Linden saw another sight,   5
When the drum beat at dead of night,
Commanding fires of death to light
    The darkness of her scenery.

By torch and trumpet fast array'd
Each horseman drew his battle blade   10
And furious every charger neigh'd
    To join the dreadful revelry.

Then shook the hills with thunder riven,
Then rush'd the steed, to battle driven,
And louder than the bolts of Heaven   15
    Far flash'd the red artillery.

But redder yet that light shall glow
On Linden's hills of stainéd snow ;
And bloodier yet the torrent flow
    Of Iser, rolling rapidly.   20

'Tis morn ; but scarce yon level sun
Can pierce the war-clouds, rolling dun,
Where furious Frank and fiery Hun
    Shout in their sulphurous canopy.

The combat deepens. On, ye brave   25
Who rush to glory, or the grave !
Wave, Munich, all thy banners wave,
    And charge with all thy chivalry !

Few, few shall part, where many meet !
The snow shall be their winding-sheet,   30
And every turf beneath their feet
    Shall be a soldier's sepulchre.

                  T. CAMPBELL.

216

AFTER BLENHEIM

It was a summer evening,
    Old Kaspar's work was done,
And he before his cottage door
    Was sitting in the sun ;
And by him sported on the green   5
His little grandchild Wilhelmine.

She saw her brother Peterkin
    Roll something large and round
Which he beside the rivulet
    In playing there had found ;   10
He came to ask what he had found
That was so large and smooth and round.

Old Kaspar took it from the boy
    Who stood expectant by ;
And then the old man shook his head,   15
    And with a natural sigh
' 'Tis some poor fellow's skull,' said he,
' Who fell in the great victory.

'I find them in the garden,
  For there's many here about ;   20
And often when I go to plough
  The ploughshare turns them out.
For many thousand men,' said he,
'Were slain in that great victory.'

'Now tell us what 'twas all about,'   25
  Young Peterkin he cries ;
And little Wilhelmine looks up
  With wonder-waiting eyes ;
'Now tell us all about the war,
And what they fought each other for.'   30

'It was the English,' Kaspar cried,
  'Who put the French to rout ;
But what they fought each other for
  I could not well make out.
But everybody said,' quoth he,   35
'That 'twas a famous victory.

'My father lived at Blenheim then,
  Yon little stream hard by ;
They burnt his dwelling to the ground,
  And he was forced to fly :   40
So with his wife and child he fled,
Nor had he where to rest his head.

'With fire and sword the country round
  Was wasted far and wide,
And many a childing mother then   45
  And new-born baby died :
But things like that, you know, must be
At every famous victory.

'They say it was a shocking sight
  After the field was won ;   50
For many thousand bodies here
  Lay rotting in the sun :
But things like that, you know, must be
After a famous victory.

'Great praise the Duke of Marlbro' won
 And our good Prince Eugene ; ' 56
'Why, 'twas a very wicked thing ! '
 Said little Wilhelmine ;
'Nay . . nay . . my little girl,' quoth he,
'It was a famous victory. 60

'And everybody praised the Duke
 Who this great fight did win.'
'But what good came of it at last ? '
 Quoth little Peterkin :—
'Why, that I cannot tell,' said he, 65
'But 'twas a famous victory.'

R. SOUTHEY.

217

PRO PATRIA MORI

When he who adores thee has left but the name
 Of his fault and his sorrows behind,
O ! say wilt thou weep, when they darken the fame
 Of a life that for thee was resign'd ? 4
Yes, weep, and however my foes may condemn,
 Thy tears shall efface their decree ;
For, Heaven can witness, though guilty to them,
 I have been but too faithful to thee.

With thee were the dreams of my earliest love,
 Every thought of my reason was thine : 10
In my last humble prayer to the Spirit above
 Thy name shall be mingled with mine !
O ! blest are the lovers and friends who shall live
 The days of thy glory to see ;
But the next dearest blessing that Heaven can give
 Is the pride of thus dying for thee. 16

T. MOORE.

218

THE BURIAL OF SIR JOHN MOORE
AT CORUNNA

Not a drum was heard, not a funeral note,
    As his corse to the rampart we hurried ;
Not a soldier discharged his farewell shot
    O'er the grave where our Hero we buried.

We buried him darkly at dead of night,   5
    The sods with our bayonets turning ;
By the struggling moonbeam's misty light
    And the lantern dimly burning.

No useless coffin enclosed his breast,
    Not in sheet or in shroud we wound him ;   10
But he lay like a Warrior taking his rest
    With his martial cloak around him.

Few and short were the prayers we said,
    And we spoke not a word of sorrow ;
But we steadfastly gaz'd on the face that was dead,
    And we bitterly thought of the morrow.   16

We thought, as we hollow'd his narrow bed
    And smooth'd down his lonely pillow,
That the Foe and the Stranger would tread o'er his
      head,
    And we far away on the billow !   20

Lightly they'll talk of the Spirit that's gone
    And o'er his cold ashes upbraid him,—
But little he'll reck, if they let him sleep on
    In the grave where a Briton has laid him.

But half of our heavy task was done   25
    When the clock struck the hour for retiring :
And we heard the distant and random gun
    That the foe was sullenly firing.

Slowly and sadly we laid him down,
  From the field of his fame fresh and gory ;   30
We carved not a line, and we raised not a stone—
  But we left him alone with his glory.

C. WOLFE.

219

SIMON LEE THE OLD HUNTSMAN

In the sweet shire of Cardigan,
  Not far from pleasant Ivor Hall,
An old man dwells, a little man,—
  'Tis said he once was tall.
Full five-and-thirty years he lived   5
  A running huntsman merry ;
And still the centre of his cheek
  Is red as a ripe cherry.

No man like him the horn could sound,
  And hill and valley rang with glee   10
When Echo bandied round and round
  The halloo of Simon Lee.
In those proud days he little cared
  For husbandry or tillage ;
To blither tasks did Simon rouse   15
  The sleepers of the village.

He all the country could outrun,
  Could leave both man and horse behind ;
And often, ere the chase was done,
  He reeled and was stone-blind.   20
And still there 's something in the world
  At which his heart rejoices ;
For when the chiming hounds are out,
  He dearly loves their voices !

But O the heavy change !—bereft   25
  Of health, strength, friends, and kindred, see !
Old Simon to the world is left
  In liveried poverty :

His master's dead, and no one now
   Dwells in the Hall of Ivor ;   30
Men, dogs, and horses, all are dead ;
   He is the sole survivor.

And he is lean and he is sick ;
   His body, dwindled and awry,
Rests upon ankles swoln and thick ;   35
   His legs are thin and dry.
One prop he has, and only one,
   His wife, an aged woman,
Lives with him, near the waterfall,
   Upon the village common.   40

Beside their moss-grown hut of clay,
   Not twenty paces from the door,
A scrap of land they have, but they
   Are poorest of the poor.
This scrap of land he from the heath   45
   Enclosed when he was stronger ;
But what to them avails the land
   Which he can till no longer ?

Oft, working by her husband's side,
   Ruth does what Simon cannot do ;   50
For she, with scanty cause for pride,
   Is stouter of the two.
And, though you with your utmost skill
   From labour could not wean them,
'Tis little, very little, all   55
   That they can do between them.

Few months of life has he in store
   As he to you will tell,
For still, the more he works, the more
   Do his weak ankles swell.   60
My gentle reader, I perceive
   How patiently you've waited,
And now I fear that you expect
   Some tale will be related.

O reader ! had you in your mind   65
  Such stores as silent thought can bring,
O gentle reader ! you would find
  A tale in every thing.
What more I have to say is short,
  And you must kindly take it :   70
It is no tale ; but, should you think,
  Perhaps a tale you'll make it.

One summer-day I chanced to see
  This old man doing all he could
To unearth the root of an old tree,   75
  A stump of rotten wood.
The mattock totter'd in his hand ;
  So vain was his endeavour
That at the root of the old tree
  He might have work'd for ever.   80

' You're overtask'd, good Simon Lee,
  Give me your tool,' to him I said ;
And at the word right gladly he
  Received my proffer'd aid.
I struck, and with a single blow   85
  The tangled root I sever'd,
At which the poor old man so long
  And vainly had endeavour'd.

The tears into his eyes were brought,
  And thanks and praises seem'd to run   90
So fast out of his heart, I thought
  They never would have done.
—I've heard of hearts unkind, kind deeds
  With coldness still returning ;
Alas ! the gratitude of men   95
  Hath oftener left me mourning.

W. Wordsworth.

220
THE OLD FAMILIAR FACES

I have had playmates, I have had companions
In my days of childhood, in my joyful school-days;
　All, all are gone, the old familiar faces.

I have been laughing, I have been carousing,
Drinking late, sitting late, with my bosom cronies;
　All, all are gone, the old familiar faces.　　　6

I loved a love once, fairest among women:
Closed are her doors on me, I must not see her—
　All, all are gone, the old familiar faces.

I have a friend, a kinder friend has no man:　　10
Like an ingrate, I left my friend abruptly;
　Left him, to muse on the old familiar faces.

Ghost-like I paced round the haunts of my child-
　　hood;
Earth seem'd a desert I was bound to traverse,
　Seeking to find the old familiar faces.　　　15

Friend of my bosom, thou more than a brother,
Why wert not thou born in my father's dwelling?
　So might we talk of the old familiar faces,

How some they have died, and some they have
　　left me,　　　19
And some are taken from me; all are departed;
　All, all are gone, the old familiar faces.

C. LAMB.

221
THE JOURNEY ONWARDS

As slow our ship her foamy track
　Against the wind was cleaving,
Her trembling pennant still look'd back
　To that dear isle 'twas leaving.
So loth we part from all we love,　　　5
　From all the links that bind us;
So turn our hearts, as on we rove,
　To those we've left behind us!

When, round the bowl, of vanish'd years
  We talk with joyous seeming— 10
With smiles that might as well be tears,
  So faint, so sad their beaming ;
While memory brings us back again
  Each early tie that twined us,
O, sweet's the cup that circles then 15
  To those we've left behind us !

And when in other climes we meet
  Some isle or vale enchanting,
Where all looks flowery, wild, and sweet,
  And nought but love is wanting ; 20
We think how great had been our bliss
  If Heaven had but assign'd us
To live and die in scenes like this,
  With some we've left behind us !

As travellers oft look back at eve 25
  When eastward darkly going,
To gaze upon that light they leave
  Still faint behind them glowing,—
So, when the close of pleasure's day
  To gloom hath near consign'd us, 30
We turn to catch one fading ray
  Of joy that's left behind us.

T. Moore.

222

YOUTH AND AGE

There's not a joy the world can give like that it
  takes away,
When the glow of early thought declines in feeling's
  dull decay ;
'Tis not on youth's smooth cheek the blush alone
  which fades so fast,
But the tender bloom of heart is gone, ere youth
  itself be past.

Then the few whose spirits float above the wreck of
    happiness   5
Are driven o'er the shoals of guilt or ocean of
    excess :
The magnet of their course is gone, or only points
    in vain
The shore to which their shiver'd sail shall never
    stretch again.

Then the mortal coldness of the soul like death
    itself comes down ;
It cannot feel for others' woes, it dare not dream
    its own ;   10
That heavy chill has frozen o'er the fountain of our
    tears,
And though the eye may sparkle still, 'tis where the
    ice appears.

Though wit may flash from fluent lips, and mirth
    distract the breast,
Through midnight hours that yield no more their
    former hope of rest ;
'Tis but as ivy-leaves around the ruin'd turret
    wreathe,   15
All green and wildly fresh without, but worn and
    grey beneath.

O could I feel as I have felt, or be what I have been,
Or weep as I could once have wept o'er many a
    vanish'd scene,—
As springs in deserts found seem sweet, all brackish
    though they be,   19
So midst the wither'd waste of life, those tears
    would flow to me !

LORD BYRON.

223

A LESSON

There is a flower, the Lesser Celandine,
    That shrinks like many more from cold and rain,
And, the first moment that the sun may shine,
    Bright as the sun himself, 'tis out again !

When hailstones have been falling, swarm on
    swarm,   5
Or blasts the green field and the trees distrest,
Oft have I seen it muffled up from harm
    In close self-shelter, like a thing at rest.

But lately, one rough day, this flower I past,
    And recognized it, though an alter'd form,   10
Now standing forth an offering to the blast,
    And buffeted at will by rain and storm.

I stopp'd and said, with inly-mutter'd voice,
    ' It doth not love the shower, nor seek the cold ;
This neither is its courage nor its choice,   15
    But its necessity in being old.

' The sunshine may not cheer it, nor the dew ;
    It cannot help itself in its decay ;
Stiff in its members, wither'd, changed of hue,'
    And, in my spleen, I smiled that it was grey.

To be a prodigal's favourite—then, worse truth,
    A miser's pensioner—behold our lot !   22
O Man ! that from thy fair and shining youth
Age might but take the things Youth needed not !

                        W. WORDSWORTH.

224

PAST AND PRESENT

I remember, I remember
    The house where I was born,
The little window where the sun
    Came peeping in at morn ;
He never came a wink too soon   5
    Nor brought too long a day ;
But now, I often wish the night
    Had borne my breath away.

I remember, I remember
    The roses, red and white,   10
The violets, and the lily-cups—
    Those flowers made of light !

The lilacs where the robin built,
　　And where my brother set
The laburnum on his birth-day,—　　15
　　The tree is living yet !

I remember, I remember
　　Where I was used to swing,
And thought the air must rush as fresh
　　To swallows on the wing ;　　20
My spirit flew in feathers then
　　That is so heavy now,
And summer pools could hardly cool
　　The fever on my brow.

I remember, I remember　　25
　　The fir trees dark and high ;
I used to think their slender tops
　　Were close against the sky :
It was a childish ignorance,
　　But now 'tis little joy　　30
To know I'm farther off from Heaven
　　Than when I was a boy.

T. Hood.

225

THE LIGHT OF OTHER DAYS

Oft in the stilly night,
　　Ere slumber's chain has bound me,
Fond Memory brings the light
　　Of other days around me :
　　　The smiles, the tears　　5
　　　Of boyhood's years,
The words of love then spoken ;
　　　The eyes that shone,
　　　Now dimm'd and gone,
The cheerful hearts now broken !　　10
Thus in the stilly night,
　　Ere slumber's chain has bound me,
Sad Memory brings the light
　　Of other days around me.

When I remember all   15
 The friends so link'd together
I've seen around me fall
 Like leaves in wintry weather,
  I feel like one
  Who treads alone   20
 Some banquet-hall deserted,
  Whose lights are fled
  Whose garlands dead,
 And all but he departed !
Thus in the stilly night,   25
 Ere slumber's chain has bound me,
Sad Memory brings the light
 Of other days around me.

T. MOORE.

226

INVOCATION

Rarely, rarely, comest thou,
 Spirit of Delight !
Wherefore hast thou left me now
 Many a day and night ?
Many a weary night and day   5
'Tis since thou art fled away.

How shall ever one like me
 Win thee back again ?
With the joyous and the free
 Thou wilt scoff at pain.   10
Spirit false ! thou hast forgot
All but those who need thee not.

As a lizard with the shade
 Of a trembling leaf,
Thou with sorrow art dismay'd ;   15
 Even the sighs of grief
Reproach thee, that thou art not near,
And reproach thou wilt not hear.

Let me set my mournful ditty
  To a merry measure ;   20
Thou wilt never come for pity,
  Thou wilt come for pleasure ;
Pity then will cut away
Those cruel wings, and thou wilt stay.

I love all that thou lovest,   25
  Spirit of Delight !
The fresh Earth in new leaves drest
  And the starry night ;
Autumn evening, and the morn
When the golden mists are born.   30

I love snow and all the forms
  Of the radiant frost ;
I love waves, and winds, and storms,
  Everything almost
Which is Nature's, and may be   35
Untainted by man's misery.

I love tranquil solitude,
  And such society
As is quiet, wise, and good ;
  Between thee and me   40
What diff'rence ? but thou dost possess
The things I seek, not love them less.

I love Love—though he has wings,
  And like light can flee,
But above all other things,   45
  Spirit, I love thee—
Thou art love and life ! O come !
Make once more my heart thy home !

                                P. B. SHELLEY.

227

STANZAS WRITTEN IN DEJECTION NEAR NAPLES

The sun is warm, the sky is clear,
　　The waves are dancing fast and bright,
Blue isles and snowy mountains wear
　　The purple noon's transparent might :
　　The breath of the moist earth is light　　5
Around its unexpanded buds ;
　　Like many a voice of one delight—
The winds, the birds, the ocean-floods—
The City's voice itself is soft like Solitude's.

I see the Deep's untrampled floor　　　10
　　With green and purple seaweeds strown ;
I see the waves upon the shore,
　　Like light dissolved in star-showers, thrown :
　　I sit upon the sands alone ;
The lightning of the noontide ocean　　15
　　Is flashing round me, and a tone
Arises from its measured motion—
How sweet! did any heart now share in my emotion.

Alas ! I have nor hope nor health,
　　Nor peace within nor calm around,　　20
Nor that content, surpassing wealth,
　　The sage in meditation found,
　　And walked with inward glory crowned—
Nor fame, nor power, nor love, nor leisure ;
　　Others I see whom these surround—　　25
Smiling they live, and call life pleasure ;
To me that cup has been dealt in another measure.

Yet now despair itself is mild
　　Even as the winds and waters are ;
I could lie down like a tired child,　　30
　　And weep away the life of care

Which I have borne, and yet must bear,
Till death like sleep might steal on me,
And I might feel in the warm air
My cheek grow cold, and hear the sea   35
Breathe o'er my dying brain its last monotony.

P. B. SHELLEY.

228

THE SCHOLAR

My days among the Dead are past ;
    Around me I behold,
Where'er these casual eyes are cast,
    The mighty minds of old :
My never-failing friends are they,   5
With whom I converse day by day.

With them I take delight in weal
    And seek relief in woe ;
And while I understand and feel
    How much to them I owe,   10
My cheeks have often been bedew'd
With tears of thoughtful gratitude.

My thoughts are with the Dead ; with them
    I live in long-past years,
Their virtues love, their faults condemn,   15
    Partake their hopes and fears,
And from their lessons seek and find
Instruction with an humble mind.

My hopes are with the Dead ; anon
    My place with them will be,   20
And I with them shall travel on
    Through all Futurity ;
Yet leaving here a name, I trust,
That will not perish in the dust.

R. SOUTHEY.

229
THE MERMAID TAVERN

Souls of Poets dead and gone,
What Elysium have ye known,
Happy field or mossy cavern,
Choicer than the Mermaid Tavern ?
Have ye tippled drink more fine   5
Than mine host's Canary wine ?
Or are fruits of Paradise
Sweeter than those dainty pies
Of venison ? O generous food !
Drest as though bold Robin Hood   10
Would, with his Maid Marian,
Sup and bowse from horn and can.

I have heard that on a day
Mine host's signboard flew away
Nobody knew whither, till   15
An astrologer's old quill
To a sheepskin gave the story—
Said he saw you in your glory
Underneath a new-old Sign
Sipping beverage divine,   20
And pledging with contented smack
The Mermaid in the Zodiac.

Souls of Poets dead and gone,
What Elysium have ye known—
Happy field or mossy cavern—   25
Choicer than the Mermaid Tavern ?

                                    J. KEATS.

230
THE PRIDE OF YOUTH

Proud Maisie is in the wood,
    Walking so early ;
Sweet Robin sits on the bush
    Singing so rarely.

'Tell me, thou bonny bird,   5
    When shall I marry me?'
—'When six braw gentlemen
    Kirkward shall carry ye.'

'Who makes the bridal bed,
    Birdie, say truly?'   10
—'The grey-headed sexton
    That delves the grave duly.

'The glow-worm o'er grave and stone
    Shall light thee steady;
The owl from the steeple sing   15
    Welcome, proud lady.'
                                        SIR W SCOTT.

231
THE BRIDGE OF SIGHS

One more Unfortunate
    Weary of breath,
Rashly importunate,
    Gone to her death!

Take her up tenderly,   5
    Lift her with care;
Fashion'd so slenderly,
    Young, and so fair!

Look at her garments
    Clinging like cerements;   10
Whilst the wave constantly
    Drips from her clothing;
Take her up instantly,
    Loving, not loathing.

Touch her not scornfully;   15
Think of her mournfully,
    Gently and humanly;
Not of the stains of her—
All that remains of her
    Now is pure womanly.   20

Make no deep scrutiny
Into her mutiny
  Rash and undutiful :
Past all dishonour,
Death has left on her   25
  Only the beautiful.

Still, for all slips of hers,
  One of Eve's family—
Wipe those poor lips of hers
  Oozing so clammily.   30

Loop up her tresses
  Escaped from the comb,
Her fair auburn tresses ;
Whilst wonderment guesses
  Where was her home ?   35

Who was her father ?
  Who was her mother ?
Had she a sister ?
  Had she a brother ?
Or was there a dearer one   40
Still, and a nearer one
  Yet, than all other ?

Alas ! for the rarity
Of Christian charity
  Under the sun !   45
O ! it was pitiful !
Near a whole city full,
  Home she had none.

Sisterly, brotherly,
Fatherly, motherly   50
  Feelings had changed :
Love, by harsh evidence,
Thrown from its eminence,
Even God's providence
  Seeming estranged.   55

Where the lamps quiver
So far in the river,
  With many a light
From window and casement,
From garret to basement,   60
She stood, with amazement,
  Houseless by night.
The bleak wind of March
  Made her tremble and shiver ;
But not the dark arch,   65
  Or the black flowing river :
Mad from life's history,
Glad to death's mystery
  Swift to be hurl'd—
Any where, any where   70
  Out of the world !

In she plunged boldly,
No matter how coldly
  The rough river ran,
Over the brink of it,—   75
Picture it, think of it,
  Dissolute Man !
Lave in it, drink of it
  Then, if you can !

Take her up tenderly,   80
  Lift her with care ;
Fashion'd so slenderly,
  Young, and so fair !

Ere her limbs frigidly
Stiffen too rigidly,   85
  Decently, kindly,
Smooth and compose them ;
And her eyes, close them,
  Staring so blindly !

Dreadfully staring   90
  Thro' muddy impurity,
As when with the daring
Last look of despairing
  Fix'd on futurity

Perishing gloomily,   95
Spurr'd by contumely,
Cold inhumanity,
Burning insanity,
   Into her rest.
—Cross her hands humbly,   100
As if praying dumbly,
   Over her breast !

Owning her weakness,
   Her evil behaviour,
And leaving, with meekness,   105
   Her sins to her Saviour !

T. Hood.

232

ELEGY

O snatch'd away in beauty's bloom !
On thee shall press no ponderous tomb ;
   But on thy turf shall roses rear
   Their leaves, the earliest of the year,
And the wild cypress wave in tender gloom :   5

And oft by yon blue gushing stream
   Shall Sorrow lean her drooping head,
And feed deep thought with many a dream,
   And lingering pause and lightly tread ;   9
Fond wretch ! as if her step disturb'd the dead !

Away ! we know that tears are vain,
   That Death nor heeds nor hears distress :
Will this unteach us to complain ?
   Or make one mourner weep the less ?
And thou, who tell'st me to forget,   15
Thy looks are wan, thine eyes are wet.

Lord Byron.

233

HESTER

When maidens such as Hester die,
Their place ye may not well supply,
Though ye among a thousand try
    With vain endeavour.
A month or more hath she been dead,   5
Yet cannot I by force be led
To think upon the wormy bed
    And her together.

A springy motion in her gait,
A rising step, did indicate   10
Of pride and joy no common rate
    That flush'd her spirit :
I know not by what name beside
I shall it call : if 'twas not pride,
It was a joy to that allied   15
    She did inherit.

Her parents held the Quaker rule,
Which doth the human feeling cool ;
But she was train'd in Nature's school,
    Nature had blest her.   20
A waking eye, a prying mind,
A heart that stirs, is hard to bind ;
A hawk's keen sight ye cannot blind,
    Ye could not Hester.

My sprightly neighbour ! gone before   25
To that unknown and silent shore,
Shall we not meet, as heretofore
    Some summer morning—
When from thy cheerful eyes a ray
Hath struck a bliss upon the day,   30
A bliss that would not go away,
    A sweet fore-warning ?

                         C. LAMB.

234

CORONACH

He is gone on the mountain,
  He is lost to the forest,
Like a summer-dried fountain,
  When our need was the sorest.
The font reappearing   5
  From the raindrops shall borrow,
But to us comes no cheering,
  To Duncan no morrow !

The hand of the reaper
  Takes the ears that are hoary,   10
But the voice of the weeper
  Wails manhood in glory.
The autumn winds rushing
  Waft the leaves that are serest,
But our flower was in flushing   15
  When blighting was nearest.

Fleet foot on the correi,
  Sage counsel in cumber,
Red hand in the foray,
  How sound is thy slumber !   20
Like the dew on the mountain,
  Like the foam on the river,
Like the bubble on the fountain,
  Thou art gone, and for ever !

SIR W. SCOTT.

235

THE DEATH-BED

We watch'd her breathing thro' the night,
  Her breathing soft and low,
As in her breast the wave of life
  Kept heaving to and fro.

But when the morn came dim and sad   5
  And chill with early showers,
Her quiet eyelids closed—she had
  Another morn than ours.

                  T. HOOD.

236

ROSABELLE

O listen, listen, ladies gay !
  No haughty feat of arms I tell ;
Soft is the note, and sad the lay
  That mourns the lovely Rosabelle.

Moor, moor the barge, ye gallant crew !   5
  And, gentle ladye, deign to stay !
Rest thee in Castle Ravensheuch,
  Nor tempt the stormy firth to-day.

' The blackening wave is edged with white ;
  To inch and rock the sea-mews fly ;   10
The fishers have heard the Water-Sprite,
  Whose screams forebode that wreck is nigh.

' Last night the gifted Seer did view
  A wet shroud swathed round ladye gay ;
Then stay thee, Fair, in Ravensheuch ;   15
  Why cross the gloomy firth to-day ? '

' 'Tis not because Lord Lindesay's heir
  To-night at Roslin leads the ball,
But that my ladye-mother there
  Sits lonely in her castle-hall.   20

' 'Tis not because the ring they ride,
  And Lindesay at the ring rides well,
But that my sire the wine will chide
  If 'tis not fill'd by Rosabelle.'

—O'er Roslin all that dreary night   25
  A wondrous blaze was seen to gleam ;
'Twas broader than the watch-fire's light,
  And redder than the bright moonbeam.

It glared on Roslin's castled rock,
  It ruddied all the copse-wood glen ;   30
'Twas seen from Dryden's groves of oak,
  And seen from cavern'd Hawthornden.

Seem'd all on fire that chapel proud,
  Where Roslin's chiefs uncoffin'd lie,
Each Baron, for a sable shroud,   35
  Sheath'd in his iron panoply.

Seem'd all on fire within, around,
  Deep sacristy and altar's pale ;
Shone every pillar foliage-bound,
  And glimmer'd all the dead men's mail.   40

Blazed battlement and pinnet high,
  Blazed every rose-carved buttress fair—
So still they blaze, when fate is nigh
  The lordly line of high St. Clair.

There are twenty of Roslin's barons bold   45
  Lie buried within that proud chapelle ;
Each one the holy vault doth hold,
  But the sea holds lovely Rosabelle !

And each St. Clair was buried there
  With candle, with book, and with knell ;   50
But the sea-caves rung, and the wild winds sung
  The dirge of lovely Rosabelle.

                                    SIR W. SCOTT.

237

ON AN INFANT DYING AS SOON AS BORN

I saw where in the shroud did lurk
  A curious frame of Nature's work ;
A flow'ret crushéd in the bud,
A nameless piece of Babyhood,
Was in her cradle-coffin lying ;   5
Extinct, with scarce the sense of dying :
So soon to exchange the imprisoning womb
For darker closets of the tomb !

She did but ope an eye, and put
A clear beam forth, then straight up shut   10
For the long dark : ne'er more to see
Through glasses of mortality.
Riddle of destiny, who can show
What thy short visit meant, or know
What thy errand here below ?   15
Shall we say, that Nature blind
Check'd her hand, and changed her mind,
Just when she had exactly wrought
A finish'd pattern without fault ?
Could she flag, or could she tire,   20
Or lack'd she the Promethean fire
(With her nine moons' long workings sicken'd)
That should thy little limbs have quicken'd ?
Limbs so firm, they seem'd to assure
Life of health, and days mature ;   25
Woman's self in miniature !
Limbs so fair, they might supply
(Themselves now but cold imagery)
The sculptor to make Beauty by.
Or did the stern-eyed Fate descry   30
That babe or mother, one must die ;
So in mercy left the stock
And cut the branch ; to save the shock
Of young years widow'd, and the pain
When Single State comes back again   35
To the lone man who, 'reft of wife,
Thenceforward drags a maiméd life ?
The economy of Heaven is dark,
And wisest clerks have miss'd the mark,
Why human buds, like this, should fall   40
More brief than fly ephemeral
That has his day ; while shrivell'd crones
Stiffen with age to stocks and stones ;
And crabbéd use the conscience sears
In sinners of an hundred years.   45
—Mother's prattle, mother's kiss,
Baby fond, thou ne'er wilt miss :
Rites which custom does impose,

Silver bells, and baby clothes ;
Coral redder than those lips   50
Which pale death did late eclipse ;
Music framed for infants' glee,
Whistle never tuned for thee ;
Though thou want'st not, thou shalt have them,
Loving hearts were they which gave them.   55
Let not one be missing ; nurse,
See them laid upon the hearse
Of infant slain by doom perverse.
Why should kings and nobles have
Pictured trophies to their grave,   60
And we, churls, to thee deny
Thy pretty toys with thee to lie—
A more harmless vanity ?

C. LAMB.

238

THE AFFLICTION OF MARGARET

Where art thou, my beloved Son,
   Where art thou, worse to me than dead ?
O find me, prosperous or undone !
   Or, if the grave be now thy bed,
Why am I ignorant of the same   5
That I may rest ; and neither blame
Nor sorrow may attend thy name ?

Seven years, alas ! to have received
   No tidings of an only child ;
To have despaired, have hoped, believed,   10
   And been for evermore beguiled,—
Sometimes with thoughts of very bliss !
I catch at them, and then I miss ;
Was ever darkness like to this ?

He was among the prime in worth,   15
   An object beauteous to behold ;
Well born, well bred ; I sent him forth
   Ingenuous, innocent, and bold :

If things ensued that wanted grace,
  As hath been said, they were not base ;   20
And never blush was on my face.

Ah ! little doth the young one dream,
  When full of play and childish cares,
What power is in his wildest scream
  Heard by his mother unawares !   25
He knows it not, he cannot guess :
Years to a mother bring distress ;
But do not make her love the less.

Neglect me ! no, I suffered long   29
  From that ill thought ; and being blind
Said, ' Pride shall help me in my wrong :
  Kind mother have I been, as kind
As ever breathed :' and that is true ;
I've wet my path with tears like dew,
Weeping for him when no one knew.   35

My Son, if thou be humbled, poor,
  Hopeless of honour and of gain,
O ! do not dread thy mother's door ;
  Think not of me with grief and pain :
I now can see with better eyes ;   40
And worldly grandeur I despise,
And fortune with her gifts and lies.

Alas ! the fowls of heaven have wings,
  And blasts of heaven will aid their flight ;
They mount—how short a voyage brings   45
  The wanderers back to their delight !
Chains tie us down by land and sea ;
And wishes, vain as mine, may be
All that is left to comfort thee.

Perhaps some dungeon hears thee groan,   50
  Maim'd, mangled by inhuman men ;
Or thou upon a desert thrown
  Inheritest the lion's den ;
Or hast been summon'd to the deep,
Thou, thou, and all thy mates, to keep   55
An incommunicable sleep.

I look for ghosts ; but none will force
  Their way to me : 'tis falsely said
That there was ever intercourse
  Between the living and the dead ; 60
For surely then I should have sight
Of him I wait for day and night
With love and longings infinite.

My apprehensions come in crowds ;
  I dread the rustling of the grass ; 65
The very shadows of the clouds
  Have power to shake me as they pass :
I question things, and do not find
One that will answer to my mind ;
And all the world appears unkind. 70

Beyond participation lie
  My troubles, and beyond relief :
If any chance to heave a sigh,
  They pity me, and not my grief.
Then come to me, my Son, or send 75
Some tidings, that my woes may end ;
I have no other earthly friend.

W. WORDSWORTH.

239

HUNTING SONG

Waken, lords and ladies gay !
On the mountain dawns the day ;
All the jolly chase is here
With hawk and horse and hunting-spear ;
Hounds are in their couples yelling, 5
Hawks are whistling, horns are knelling,
Merrily merrily mingle they,
' Waken, lords and ladies gay ! '

Waken, lords and ladies gay !
The mist has left the mountain grey, 10
Springlets in the dawn are steaming,
Diamonds on the brake are gleaming ;

And foresters have busy been
To track the buck in thicket green ;
Now we come to chant our lay,   15
' Waken, lords and ladies gay !'

Waken, lords and ladies gay !
To the greenwood haste away,
We can show you where he lies,
Fleet of foot and tall of size ;   20
We can show the marks he made
When 'gainst the oak his antlers fray'd ;
You shall see him brought to bay ;
' Waken, lords and ladies gay !'

Louder, louder chant the lay,   25
Waken, lords and ladies gay !
Tell them youth and mirth and glee
Run a course as well as we ;
Time, stern huntsman ! who can balk,
Stanch as hound and fleet as hawk ;   30
Think of this, and rise with day,
Gentle lords and ladies gay !

                              SIR W. SCOTT.

240

TO THE SKYLARK

Ethereal minstrel ! pilgrim of the sky !
    Dost thou despise the earth where cares abound ?
Or, while the wings aspire, are heart and eye
    Both with thy nest upon the dewy ground ?
Thy nest which thou canst drop into at will,   5
Those quivering wings composed, that music still !

To the last point of vision, and beyond,
    Mount, daring warbler !—that love-prompted
        strain
('Twixt thee and thine a never-failing bond),
    Thrills not the less the bosom of the plain : 10
Yet might'st thou seem, proud privilege ! to sing
All independent of the leafy spring.

Leave to the nightingale her shady wood ;
  A privacy of glorious light is thine,
Whence thou dost pour upon the world a flood
  Of harmony, with instinct more divine ;   16
Type of the wise, who soar, but never roam—
True to the kindred points of Heaven and Home !

W. WORDSWORTH.

241

TO A SKYLARK

Hail to thee, blithe Spirit !
  Bird thou never wert,
That from heaven, or near it,
  Pourest thy full heart
In profuse strains of unpremeditated art.   5

Higher still and higher
  From the earth thou springest
Like a cloud of fire ;
  The blue deep thou wingest,   9
And singing still dost soar, and soaring ever singest.

In the golden lightning
  Of the sunken sun,
O'er which clouds are brightening,
  Thou dost float and run,   14
Like an unbodied joy whose race is just begun.

The pale purple even
  Melts around thy flight ;
Like a star of heaven
  In the broad daylight   19
Thou art unseen, but yet I hear thy shrill delight :

Keen as are the arrows
  Of that silver sphere,
Whose intense lamp narrows
  In the white dawn clear
Until we hardly see, we feel that it is there.   25

All the earth and air
With thy voice is loud,
As, when night is bare,
From one lonely cloud
The moon rains out her beams, and heaven is over-
flow'd.   30

What thou art we know not ;
What is most like thee ?
From rainbow clouds there flow not
Drops so bright to see   34
As from thy presence showers a rain of melody.

Like a poet hidden
In the light of thought,
Singing hymns unbidden,
Till the world is wrought   39
To sympathy with hopes and fears it heeded not :

Like a high-born maiden
In a palace tower,
Soothing her love-laden
Soul in secret hour   44
With music sweet as love, which overflows her bower:

Like a glow-worm golden
In a dell of dew,
Scattering unbeholden
Its aerial hue
Among the flowers and grass, which screen it from
the view :   50

Like a rose embower'd
In its own green leaves,
By warm winds deflower'd,
Till the scent it gives
Makes faint with too much sweet these heavy-
wingéd thieves.   55

Sound of vernal showers
On the twinkling grass,
Rain-awaken'd flowers,
All that ever was   59
Joyous, and clear, and fresh, thy music doth surpass.

Teach us, sprite or bird,
   What sweet thoughts are thine :
I have never heard
   Praise of love or wine   64
That panted forth a flood of rapture so divine.

Chorus hymeneal,
   Or triumphal chant,
Match'd with thine would be all
   But an empty vaunt—   69
A thing wherein we feel there is some hidden want.

What objects are the fountains
   Of thy happy strain ?
What fields, or waves, or mountains ?
   What shapes of sky or plain ?
What love of thine own kind ? what ignorance of
     pain ?   75

With thy clear keen joyance
   Languor cannot be :
Shadow of annoyance
   Never came near thee :   79
Thou lovest ; but ne'er knew love's sad satiety.

Waking or asleep
   Thou of death must deem
Things more true and deep
   Than we mortals dream,   84
Or how could thy notes flow in such a crystal stream?

We look before and after,
   And pine for what is not :
Our sincerest laughter
   With some pain is fraught ;
Our sweetest songs are those that tell of saddest
     thought.   90

Yet if we could scorn
   Hate, and pride, and fear ;
If we were things born
   Not to shed a tear,   94
I know not how thy joy we ever should come near.

Better than all measures
　　Of delightful sound,
Better than all treasures
　　That in books are found,　　　　99
Thy skill to poet were, thou scorner of the ground!

Teach me half the gladness
　　That thy brain must know,
Such harmonious madness
　　From my lips would flow　　　　104
The world should listen then, as I am listening now!

P. B. SHELLEY.

242

THE GREEN LINNET

Beneath these fruit-tree boughs that shed
Their snow-white blossoms on my head,
With brightest sunshine round me spread
　　Of spring's unclouded weather,
In this sequestered nook how sweet　　　　5
To sit upon my orchard-seat!
And birds and flowers once more to greet,
　　My last year's friends together.

One have I marked, the happiest guest
In all this covert of the blest:　　　　10
Hail to Thee, far above the rest
　　In joy of voice and pinion!
Thou, Linnet! in thy green array,
Presiding Spirit here to-day,
Dost lead the revels of the May,　　　　15
　　And this is thy dominion.

While birds, and butterflies, and flowers,
Make all one band of paramours,
Thou, ranging up and down the bowers,
　　Art sole in thy employment;　　　　20
A Life, a Presence like the Air,
Scattering thy gladness without care,
Too blest with any one to pair,
　　Thyself thy own enjoyment.

Amid yon tuft of hazel trees,   25
That twinkle to the gusty breeze,
Behold him perch'd in ecstasies,
    Yet seeming still to hover ;
There ! where the flutter of his wings
Upon his back and body flings   30
Shadows and sunny glimmerings,
    That cover him all over.

My dazzled sight he oft deceives—
A Brother of the dancing leaves ;
Then flits, and from the cottage-eaves   35
    Pours forth his song in gushes ;
As if by that exulting strain
He mocked and treated with disdain
The voiceless Form he chose to feign,
    While fluttering in the bushes.   40

                        W. WORDSWORTH.

243

TO THE CUCKOO

O blithe new-comer ! I have heard,
    I hear thee and rejoice :
O Cuckoo ! shall I call thee Bird,
    Or but a wandering Voice ?

While I am lying on the grass   5
    Thy twofold shout I hear ;
From hill to hill it seems to pass,
    At once far off and near.

Though babbling only to the vale
    Of sunshine and of flowers,   10
Thou bringest unto me a tale
    Of visionary hours.

Thrice welcome, darling of the Spring !
    Even yet thou art to me
No bird, but an invisible thing,   15
    A voice, a mystery ;

The same whom in my school-boy days
　　I listen'd to ; that Cry
Which made me look a thousand ways
　　In bush, and tree, and sky.　　　　　20

To seek thee did I often rove
　　Through woods and on the green ;
And thou wert still a hope, a love ;
　　Still longed for, never seen.

And I can listen to thee yet ;　　　　25
　　Can lie upon the plain
And listen, till I do beget
　　That golden time again.

O blessèd Bird ! the earth we pace
　　Again appears to be　　　　　　30
An unsubstantial, fairy place,
　　That is fit home for Thee !

W. WORDSWORTH.

244

ODE TO A NIGHTINGALE

My heart aches, and a drowsy numbness pains
　　My sense, as though of hemlock I had drunk,
Or emptied some dull opiate to the drains
　　One minute past, and Lethe-wards had sunk :
'Tis not through envy of thy happy lot,　　　5
　　But being too happy in thine happiness,—
　　　　That thou, light-wingéd Dryad of the trees,
　　　　　　In some melodious plot
　　Of beechen green, and shadows numberless,
　　　　Singest of summer in full-throated ease.　　10

O for a draught of vintage ! that hath been
　　Cool'd a long age in the deep-delvéd earth,
Tasting of Flora and the country green,
　　Dance, and Provençal song, and sunburnt mirth !
O for a beaker full of the warm South,　　　15
　　Full of the true, the blushful Hippocrene,

With beaded bubbles winking at the brim,
  And purple-stainéd mouth ;   18
That I might drink, and leave the world unseen,
  And with thee fade away into the forest dim :

Fade far away, dissolve, and quite forget
  What thou among the leaves hast never known,
The weariness, the fever, and the fret   23
  Here, where men sit and hear each other groan ;
Where palsy shakes a few, sad, last grey hairs,
  Where youth grows pale, and spectre-thin, and dies;
    Where but to think is to be full of sorrow
      And leaden-eyed despairs ;   28
  Where Beauty cannot keep her lustrous eyes,
  Or new Love pine at them beyond to-morrow.

Away ! away ! for I will fly to thee,
  Not charioted by Bacchus and his pards,
But on the viewless wings of Poesy,
  Though the dull brain perplexes and retards :
Already with thee ! tender is the night,   35
  And haply the Queen-Moon is on her throne,
    Cluster'd around by all her starry Fays ;
      But here there is no light,
  Save what from heaven is with the breezes blown
    Through verdurous glooms and winding
      mossy ways.   40

I cannot see what flowers are at my feet,
  Nor what soft incense hangs upon the boughs,
But, in embalméd darkness, guess each sweet
  Wherewith the seasonable month endows   44
The grass, the thicket, and the fruit-tree wild ;
  White hawthorn, and the pastoral eglantine ;
    Fast-fading violets cover'd up in leaves ;
      And mid-May's eldest child
The coming musk-rose, full of dewy wine,   49
  The murmurous haunt of flies on summer eves.

Darkling I listen ; and, for many a time
  I have been half in love with easeful Death,
Call'd him soft names in many a muséd rhyme,
  To take into the air my quiet breath ;

Now more than ever seems it rich to die, 55
  To cease upon the midnight with no pain,
    While thou art pouring forth thy soul abroad
      In such an ecstasy !
  Still wouldst thou sing, and I have ears in vain—
    To thy high requiem become a sod. 60

Thou wast not born for death, immortal Bird !
  No hungry generations tread thee down ;
The voice I hear this passing night was heard
  In ancient days by emperor and clown :
Perhaps the self-same song that found a path 65
  Through the sad heart of Ruth, when, sick for
      home,
    She stood in tears amid the alien corn ;
      The same that oft-times hath
Charm'd magic casements, opening on the foam
  Of perilous seas, in faery lands forlorn. 70

Forlorn ! the very word is like a bell
  To toll me back from thee to my sole self !
Adieu ! the fancy cannot cheat so well
  As she is famed to do, deceiving elf.
Adieu ! adieu ! thy plaintive anthem fades 75
  Past the near meadows, over the still stream,
    Up the hill-side ; and now 'tis buried deep
      In the next valley-glades :
  Was it a vision, or a waking dream ?
    Fled is that music :—do I wake or sleep ? 80

                   J. KEATS.

245
UPON WESTMINSTER BRIDGE,
SEPT. 3, 1802

Earth has not anything to show more fair :
  Dull would he be of soul who could pass by
  A sight so touching in its majesty :
This City now doth like a garment wear

The beauty of the morning : silent, bare,   5
  Ships, towers, domes, theatres, and temples lie
Open unto the fields, and to the sky,
  All bright and glittering in the smokeless air.

Never did sun more beautifully steep   9
  In his first splendour valley, rock, or hill ;
Ne'er saw I, never felt, a calm so deep !

  The river glideth at his own sweet will :
Dear God ! the very houses seem asleep ;
  And all that mighty heart is lying still !

W. WORDSWORTH.

246

OZYMANDIAS OF EGYPT

I met a traveller from an antique land
  Who said : Two vast and trunkless legs of stone
Stand in the desert. Near them on the sand,
  Half sunk, a shatter'd visage lies, whose frown

And wrinkled lip and sneer of cold command   5
  Tell that its sculptor well those passions read
Which yet survive, stamp'd on these lifeless things,
  The hand that mock'd them and the heart that
    fed ;

  And on the pedestal these words appear :
' My name is Ozymandias, king of kings :   10
  Look on my works, ye Mighty, and despair ! '

Nothing beside remains. Round the decay
  Of that colossal wreck, boundless and bare,
The lone and level sands stretch far away.

P. B. SHELLEY.

247

COMPOSED AT NEIDPATH CASTLE, THE PROPERTY OF LORD QUEENSBERRY, 1803

Degenerate Douglas ! O the unworthy lord !
　　Whom mere despite of heart could so far please
　　And love of havoc, (for with such disease
Fame taxes him,) that he could send forth word

To level with the dust a noble horde,　　　　5
　　A brotherhood of venerable trees,
　　Leaving an ancient dome, and towers like these,
Beggar'd and outraged !—Many hearts deplored

The fate of those old trees ; and oft with pain
　　The traveller at this day will stop and gaze　10
　　　　On wrongs, which Nature scarcely seems to
　　　　　　heed :

For sheltered places, bosoms, nooks, and bays,
　　And the pure mountains, and the gentle Tweed,
And the green silent pastures, yet remain.
　　　　　　　　　　　　　W. WORDSWORTH.

248

ADMONITION TO A TRAVELLER

Yes, there is holy pleasure in thine eye !
　　The lovely cottage in the guardian nook
　　Hath stirr'd thee deeply; with its own dear brook,
Its own small pasture, almost its own sky !

But covet not the abode ; forbear to sigh　　5
　　As many do, repining while they look ;
　　Intruders who would tear from Nature's book
This precious leaf with harsh impiety :

Think what the home must be if it were thine,
　　Even thine, though few thy wants !—Roof,
　　　　window, door,　　　　　　　　　　　10
　　The very flowers are sacred to the Poor,

The roses to the porch which they entwine :
  Yea, all that now enchants thee, from the day
  On which it should be touch'd, would melt away !

W. WORDSWORTH.

249

TO THE HIGHLAND GIRL OF INVERSNEYDE

Sweet Highland Girl, a very shower
Of beauty is thy earthly dower !
Twice seven consenting years have shed
Their utmost bounty on thy head :   4
And these grey rocks ; that household lawn ;
Those trees—a veil just half withdrawn ;
This fall of water that doth make
A murmur near the silent lake ;
This little bay ; a quiet road
That holds in shelter thy abode ;   10
In truth together do ye seem
Like something fashion'd in a dream ;
Such forms as from their covert peep
When earthly cares are laid asleep !
But O fair Creature ! in the light   15
Of common day, so heavenly bright,
I bless Thee, Vision as thou art,
I bless thee with a human heart :
God shield thee to thy latest years !
Thee, neither know I, nor thy peers ;   20
And yet my eyes are fill'd with tears.

With earnest feeling I shall pray
For thee when I am far away ;
For never saw I mien or face
In which more plainly I could trace   25
Benignity and home-bred sense
Ripening in perfect innocence.
Here scattered like a random seed,
Remote from men, Thou dost not need
The embarrassed look of shy distress,   30
And maidenly shamefacedness :

Thou wear'st upon thy forehead clear
The freedom of a mountaineer :
A face with gladness overspread ;
Soft smiles, by human kindness bred ;   35
And seemliness complete, that sways
Thy courtesies, about thee plays ;
With no restraint, but such as springs
From quick and eager visitings
Of thoughts that lie beyond the reach   40
Of thy few words of English speech :
A bondage sweetly brook'd, a strife
That gives thy gestures grace and life !
So have I, not unmoved in mind,
Seen birds of tempest-loving kind   45
Thus beating up against the wind.

What hand but would a garland cull
For thee who art so beautiful ?
O happy pleasure ! here to dwell
Beside thee in some heathy dell ;   50
Adopt your homely ways and dress,
A shepherd, thou a shepherdess !
But I could frame a wish for thee
More like a grave reality :
Thou art to me but as a wave   55
Of the wild sea : and I would have
Some claim upon thee, if I could,
Though but of common neighbourhood,
What joy to hear thee, and to see !
Thy elder brother I would be,   60
Thy father—anything to thee !

Now thanks to Heaven ! that of its grace
Hath led me to this lonely place.
Joy have I had ; and going hence
I bear away my recompense.   65
In spots like these it is we prize
Our memory, feel that she hath eyes :
Then why should I be loth to stir ?
I feel this place was made for her ;

To give new pleasure like the past,   70
Continued long as life shall last.
Nor am I loth, though pleased at heart,
Sweet Highland Girl ! from thee to part ;
For I, methinks, till I grow old,
As fair before me shall behold   75
As I do now, the cabin small,
The lake, the bay, the waterfall ;
And Thee, the Spirit of them all !

W. WORDSWORTH.

250

THE REAPER

Behold her, single in the field,
  Yon solitary Highland Lass !
Reaping and singing by herself ;
  Stop here, or gently pass !
Alone she cuts and binds the grain,   5
And sings a melancholy strain ;
O listen ! for the vale profound
Is overflowing with the sound.

No nightingale did ever chant
  More welcome notes to weary bands   10
Of travellers in some shady haunt,
  Among Arabian sands :
A voice so thrilling ne'er was heard
In spring-time from the cuckoo-bird,
Breaking the silence of the seas   15
Among the farthest Hebrides.

Will no one tell me what she sings ?
  Perhaps the plaintive numbers flow
For old, unhappy, far-off things,
  And battles long ago :   20
Or is it some more humble lay,
Familiar matter of to-day ?
Some natural sorrow, loss, or pain,
That has been, and may be again ?

Whate'er the theme, the maiden sang   25
    As if her song could have no ending ;
I saw her singing at her work,
    And o'er the sickle bending ;
I listen'd, motionless and still ;
And, as I mounted up the hill,   30
The music in my heart I bore,
Long after it was heard no more.

               W. WORDSWORTH.

251

THE REVERIE OF POOR SUSAN

At the corner of Wood Street, when daylight
    appears,
Hangs a Thrush that sings loud, it has sung for
    three years :
Poor Susan has pass'd by the spot, and has heard
In the silence of morning the song of the bird.

'Tis a note of enchantment ; what ails her ? She sees
A mountain ascending, a vision of trees ;   6
Bright volumes of vapour through Lothbury glide,
And a river flows on through the vale of Cheapside.

Green pastures she views in the midst of the dale,
Down which she so often has tripp'd with her pail ;
And a single small cottage, a nest like a dove's,
The one only dwelling on earth that she loves.   12

She looks, and her heart is in heaven : but they fade,
The mist and the river, the hill and the shade ;
The stream will not flow, and the hill will not rise,
And the colours have all pass'd away from her eyes !

               W. WORDSWORTH.

252

TO A LADY, WITH A GUITAR

Ariel to Miranda :—Take
This slave of Music, for the sake
Of him who is the slave of thee ;
And teach it all the harmony
In which thou canst, and only thou,   5
Make the delighted spirit glow,
Till joy denies itself again
And, too intense, is turn'd to pain.
For by permission and command
Of thine own Prince Ferdinand,   10
Poor Ariel sends this silent token
Of more than ever can be spoken ;
Your guardian spirit, Ariel, who
From life to life must still pursue
Your happiness ; for thus alone   15
Can Ariel ever find his own.
From Prospero's enchanted cell,
As the mighty verses tell,
To the throne of Naples he
Lit you o'er the trackless sea,   20
Flitting on, your prow before,
Like a living meteor.
When you die, the silent Moon
In her interlunar swoon
Is not sadder in her cell   25
Than deserted Ariel.
When you live again on earth,
Like an unseen star of birth
Ariel guides you o'er the sea
Of life from your nativity.   30
Many changes have been run
Since Ferdinand and you begun
Your course of love, and Ariel still
Has tracked your steps and served your will.
Now in humbler, happier lot,   35
This is all remember'd not ;

And now, alas ! the poor sprite is
Imprisoned for some fault of his
In a body like a grave ;—
From you he only dares to crave,   40
For his service and his sorrow,
A smile to-day, a song to-morrow.

The artist who this idol wrought
To echo all harmonious thought,
Felled a tree, while on the steep   45
The woods were in their winter sleep,
Rocked in that repose divine
On the wind-swept Apennine ;
And dreaming, some of Autumn past,
And some of Spring approaching fast,   50
And some of April buds and showers,
And some of songs in July bowers,
And all of love ; and so this tree,—
O that such our death may be !—
Died in sleep, and felt no pain,   55
To live in happier form again :
From which, beneath Heaven's fairest star,
The artist wrought this loved Guitar ;
And taught it justly to reply
To all who question skilfully   60
In language gentle as thine own ;
Whispering in enamoured tone
Sweet oracles of woods and dells,
And summer winds in sylvan cells ;
—For it had learnt all harmonies   65
Of the plains and of the skies,
Of the forests and the mountains,
And the many-voicèd fountains ;
The clearest echoes of the hills,
The softest notes of falling rills,   70
The melodies of birds and bees,
The murmuring of summer seas,
And pattering rain, and breathing dew,
And airs of evening ; and it knew
That seldom-heard mysterious sound   75

Which, driven on its diurnal round,
As it floats through boundless day,
Our world enkindles on its way :
—All this it knows, but will not tell
To those who cannot question well   80
The Spirit that inhabits it ;
It talks according to the wit
Of its companions ; and no more
Is heard than has been felt before
By those who tempt it to betray   85
These secrets of an elder day.
But, sweetly as its answers will
Flatter hands of perfect skill,
It keeps its highest holiest tone
For our belovéd friend alone.   90

P. B. Shelley.

253

THE DAFFODILS

I wandered lonely as a cloud
    That floats on high o'er vales and hills,
When all at once I saw a crowd,
    A host, of golden daffodils,
Beside the lake, beneath the trees,   5
Fluttering and dancing in the breeze.

Continuous as the stars that shine
    And twinkle on the milky way,
They stretched in never-ending line
    Along the margin of a bay :   10
Ten thousand saw I at a glance
Tossing their heads in sprightly dance.

The waves beside them danced, but they
    Out-did the sparkling waves in glee :
A Poet could not but be gay   15
    In such a jocund company !
I gazed—and gazed—but little thought
What wealth the show to me had brought :

For oft, when on my couch I lie
    In vacant or in pensive mood,   20
They flash upon that inward eye
    Which is the bliss of solitude ;
And then my heart with pleasure fills,
And dances with the daffodils.

                    W. WORDSWORTH.

254

TO THE DAISY

With little here to do or see
Of things that in the great world be,
Daisy ! again I talk to thee,
        For thou art worthy,
Thou unassuming Commonplace   5
Of Nature, with that homely face,
And yet with something of a grace
        Which love makes for thee !

Oft on the dappled turf at ease
I sit and play with similes,   10
Loose types of things through all degrees,
        Thoughts of thy raising ;
And many a fond and idle name
I give to thee, for praise or blame,
As is the humour of the game,   15
        While I am gazing.

A nun demure, of lowly port ;
Or sprightly maiden, of Love's court,
In thy simplicity the sport
        Of all temptations ;   20
A queen in crown of rubies drest ;
A starveling in a scanty vest ;
Are all, as seems to suit thee best,
        Thy appellations.

A little Cyclops, with one eye   25
Staring to threaten and defy,
That thought comes next—and instantly
        The freak is over.

The shape will vanish, and behold !
A silver shield with boss of gold   30
That spreads itself, some fairy bold
  In fight to cover.

I see thee glittering from afar—
And then thou art a pretty star,
Not quite so fair as many are   35
  In heaven above thee !
Yet like a star, with glittering crest,
Self-poised in air thou seem'st to rest ;—
May peace come never to his nest
  Who shall reprove thee !   40

Sweet Flower ! for by that name at last
When all my reveries are past
I call thee, and to that cleave fast,
  Sweet silent creature !
That breath'st with me in sun and air,   45
Do thou, as thou art wont, repair
My heart with gladness, and a share
  Of thy meek nature !

      W. WORDSWORTH.

255

ODE TO AUTUMN

Season of mists and mellow fruitfulness,
 Close bosom-friend of the maturing sun ;
Conspiring with him how to load and bless
 With fruit the vines that round the thatch-eaves
   run ;
To bend with apples the moss'd cottage-trees,   5
 And fill all fruit with ripeness to the core ;
  To swell the gourd, and plump the hazel shells
 With a sweet kernel ; to set budding more,
And still more, later flowers for the bees,
Until they think warm days will never cease ;   10
  For Summer has o'erbrimm'd their clammy
   cells.

Who hath not seen thee oft amid thy store ?
  Sometimes whoever seeks abroad may find
Thee sitting careless on a granary floor,
    Thy hair soft-lifted by the winnowing wind ; 15
Or on a half-reap'd furrow sound asleep,
    Drows'd with the fume of poppies, while thy hook
      Spares the next swath and all its twinéd
        flowers ;
And sometimes like a gleaner thou dost keep
    Steady thy laden head across a brook ; 20
    Or by a cider-press, with patient look,
      Thou watchest the last oozings, hours by hours.

Where are the songs of Spring ? Aye, where are they ?
  Think not of them,—thou hast thy music too,
While barréd clouds bloom the soft-dying day 25
    And touch the stubble-plains with rosy hue ;
Then in a wailful choir the small gnats mourn
    Among the river sallows, borne aloft
      Or sinking as the light wind lives or dies ;
And full-grown lambs loud bleat from hilly bourn; 30
    Hedge-crickets sing, and now with treble soft
    The redbreast whistles from a garden-croft,
      And gathering swallows twitter in the skies.

J. KEATS.

256

ODE TO WINTER

Germany, December 1800

When first the fiery-mantled Sun
  His heavenly race began to run,
  Round the earth and ocean blue
  His children four the Seasons flew :—
    First, in green apparel dancing, 5
    The young Spring smiled with angel-grace ;
    Rosy Summer, next advancing,
    Rush'd into her sire's embrace—
  Her bright-hair'd sire, who bade her keep
    For ever nearest to his smiles. 10

On Calpe's olive-shaded steep
  Or India's citron-cover'd isles.
More remote, and buxom-brown,
  The Queen of vintage bow'd before his throne ;
A rich pomegranate gemm'd her crown,   15
  A ripe sheaf bound her zone.

But howling Winter fled afar
  To hills that prop the polar star ;
And loves on deer-borne car to ride
With barren darkness at his side,   20
Round the shore where loud Lofoden
  Whirls to death the roaring whale.
Round the hall where Runic Odin
  Howls his war-song to the gale—
Save when adown the ravaged globe   25
  He travels on his native storm,
Deflowering Nature's grassy robe
  And trampling on her faded form ;
Till light's returning lord assume
  The shaft that drives him to his polar field,   30
Of power to pierce his raven plume
  And crystal-cover'd shield.

O sire of storms ! whose savage ear
  The Lapland drum delights to hear,
When Frenzy with her bloodshot eye   35
Implores thy dreadful deity—
Archangel ! power of desolation !
  Fast descending as thou art,
Say, hath mortal invocation
  Spells to touch thy stony heart ?   40
Then, sullen Winter ! hear my prayer
And gently rule the ruin'd year ;
Nor chill the wanderer's bosom bare,
Nor freeze the wretch's falling tear :
To shuddering Want's unmantled bed   45
  Thy horror-breathing agues cease to lend,
And gently on the orphan head
  Of innocence descend.

But chiefly spare, O king of clouds !
The sailor on his airy shrouds,   50
When wrecks and beacons strew the steep
And spectres walk along the deep.
Milder yet thy snowy breezes
    Pour on yonder tented shores,
Where the Rhine's broad billow freezes,   55
    Or the dark-brown Danube roars.
O winds of Winter ! list ye there
    To many a deep and dying groan ?
Or start, ye demons of the midnight air,
    At shrieks and thunders louder than your own?
Alas ! e'en your unhallow'd breath   61
    May spare the victim fallen low ;
But man will ask no truce to death,
    No bounds to human woe.

                              T. CAMPBELL.

                         257

                 YARROW UNVISITED

                       1803

From Stirling Castle we had seen
    The mazy Forth unravell'd,
Had trod the banks of Clyde and Tay,
    And with the Tweed had travell'd ;
And when we came to Clovenford,   5
    Then said my ' winsome Marrow,'
' Whate'er betide, we'll turn aside,
    And see the Braes of Yarrow.'

' Let Yarrow folk, frae Selkirk town,
    Who have been buying, selling,   10
Go back to Yarrow, 'tis their own,
    Each maiden to her dwelling !
On Yarrow's banks let herons feed,
    Hares couch, and rabbits burrow,
But we will downward with the Tweed,   15
    Nor turn aside to Yarrow.

' There's Galla Water, Leader Haughs,
    Both lying right before us ;
And Dryburgh, where with chiming Tweed
    The lintwhites sing in chorus ;   20
There's pleasant Tiviot-dale, a land
    Made blithe with plough and harrow :
Why throw away a needful day
    To go in search of Yarrow ?

' What's Yarrow but a river bare   25
    That glides the dark hills under ?
There are a thousand such elsewhere
    As worthy of your wonder.'
—Strange words they seem'd of slight and scorn ;
    My True-love sigh'd for sorrow,   30
And look'd me in the face, to think
    I thus could speak of Yarrow !

' O green,' said I, ' are Yarrow's holms,
    And sweet is Yarrow flowing !
Fair hangs the apple frae the rock,   35
    But we will leave it growing.
O'er hilly path and open Strath
    We'll wander Scotland thorough ;
But, though so near, we will not turn
    Into the dale of Yarrow.   40

' Let beeves and home-bred kine partake
    The sweets of Burn-mill meadow ;
The swan on still St. Mary's Lake
    Float double, swan and shadow !
We will not see them ; will not go   45
    To-day, nor yet to-morrow ;
Enough if in our hearts we know
    There's such a place as Yarrow.

' Be Yarrow stream unseen, unknown !
    It must, or we shall rue it :   50
We have a vision of our own,
    Ah ! why should we undo it ?

The treasured dreams of times long past,
  We'll keep them, winsome Marrow !
For when we're there, although 'tis fair, 55
  'Twill be another Yarrow !

' If Care with freezing years should come,
  And wandering seem but folly,—
Should we be loth to stir from home,
  And yet be melancholy ; 60
Should life be dull, and spirits low,
  'Twill soothe us in our sorrow
That earth has something yet to show,
  The bonny holms of Yarrow ! '

              W. WORDSWORTH.

258

YARROW VISITED

September 1814

And is this—Yarrow ?—*This* the Stream
  Of which my fancy cherish'd
So faithfully, a waking dream,
  An image that hath perish'd ?
O that some Minstrel's harp were near 5
  To utter notes of gladness
And chase this silence from the air,
  That fills my heart with sadness !

Yet why ?—a silvery current flows
  With uncontroll'd meanderings ; 10
Nor have these eyes by greener hills
  Been soothed, in all my wanderings.
And, through her depths, St. Mary's Lake
  Is visibly delighted ;
For not a feature of those hills 15
  Is in the mirror slighted.

A blue sky bends o'er Yarrow Vale,
  Save where that pearly whiteness
Is round the rising sun diffused,
  A tender hazy brightness ; 20

Mild dawn of promise ! that excludes
    All profitless dejection ;
Though not unwilling here to admit
    A pensive recollection.

Where was it that the famous Flower   25
    Of Yarrow Vale lay bleeding ?
His bed perchance was yon smooth mound
    On which the herd is feeding :
And haply from this crystal pool,
    Now peaceful as the morning,   30
The Water-wraith ascended thrice,
    And gave his doleful warning.

Delicious is the Lay that sings
    The haunts of happy lovers,
The path that leads them to the grove,   35
    The leafy grove that covers :
And pity sanctifies the verse
    That paints, by strength of sorrow,
The unconquerable strength of love ;
    Bear witness, rueful Yarrow !   40

But thou, that didst appear so fair
    To fond imagination,
Dost rival in the light of day
    Her delicate creation :
Meek loveliness is round thee spread,   45
    A softness still and holy :
The grace of forest charms decay'd,
    And pastoral melancholy.

That region left, the vale unfolds
    Rich groves of lofty stature,   50
With Yarrow winding through the pomp
    Of cultivated nature ;
And, rising from those lofty groves,
    Behold a ruin hoary,
The shatter'd front of Newark's Towers,   55
    Renown'd in Border story.

Fair scenes for childhood's opening bloom,
    For sportive youth to stray in,
For manhood to enjoy his strength,
    And age to wear away in !   60
Yon cottage seems a bower of bliss,
    A covert for protection
Of tender thoughts, that nestle there—
    The brood of chaste affection.

How sweet on this autumnal day   65
    The wild-wood fruits to gather,
And on my True-love's forehead plant
    A crest of blooming heather !
And what if I enwreathed my own ?
    'Twere no offence to reason ;   70
The sober hills thus deck their brows
    To meet the wintry season.

I see—but not by sight alone,
    Loved Yarrow, have I won thee ;
A ray of Fancy still survives—   75
    Her sunshine plays upon thee !
Thy ever-youthful waters keep
    A course of lively pleasure ;
And gladsome notes my lips can breathe
    Accordant to the measure.   80

The vapours linger round the heights,
    They melt, and soon must vanish ;
One hour is theirs, nor more is mine—
    Sad thought ! which I would banish,
But that I know, where'er I go,   85
    Thy genuine image, Yarrow !
Will dwell with me—to heighten joy,
    And cheer my mind in sorrow.

                    W. WORDSWORTH.

259

THE INVITATION

Best and brightest, come away,
Fairer far than this fair Day,
Which, like thee to those in sorrow,
Comes to bid a sweet good-morrow
To the rough Year just awake   5
In its cradle on the brake.
The brightest hour of unborn Spring
Through the winter wandering,
Found, it seems, the halcyon Morn
To hoar February born ;   10
Bending from Heaven, in azure mirth,
It kiss'd the forehead of the Earth,
And smiled upon the silent sea,
And bade the frozen streams be free,
And waked to music all their fountains,   15
And breathed upon the frozen mountains,
And like a prophetess of May
Strew'd flowers upon the barren way,
Making the wintry world appear
Like one on whom thou smilest, dear.   20

Away, away, from men and towns,
To the wild wood and the downs—
To the silent wilderness
Where the soul need not repress
Its music, lest it should not find   25
An echo in another's mind,
While the touch of Nature's art
Harmonizes heart to heart.

Radiant Sister of the Day
Awake ! arise ! and come away !   30
To the wild woods and the plains,
And the pools where winter rains
Image all their roof of leaves,
Where the pine its garland weaves

Of sapless green and ivy dun   35
Round stems that never kiss the sun ;
Where the lawns and pastures be
And the sandhills of the sea ;
Where the melting hoar-frost wets
The daisy-star that never sets,   40
And wind-flowers and violets,
Which yet join not scent to hue,
Crown the pale year weak and new ;
When the night is left behind
In the deep east, dun and blind,   45
And the blue noon is over us,
And the multitudinous
Billows murmur at our feet,
Where the earth and ocean meet,
And all things seem only one   50
In the universal sun.

P. B. SHELLEY.

260

THE RECOLLECTION

Now the last day of many days,
   All beautiful and bright as thou,
      The loveliest and the last, is dead,
Rise, Memory, and write its praise !
Up,—to thy wonted work ! come, trace   5
   The epitaph of glory fled,
For now the Earth has changed its face,
   A frown is on the Heaven's brow.

We wander'd to the Pine Forest
   That skirts the Ocean's foam ;   10
The lightest wind was in its nest,
   The tempest in its home.
The whispering waves were half asleep,
   The clouds were gone to play,
And on the bosom of the deep   15
   The smile of Heaven lay ;

It seem'd as if the hour were one
   Sent from beyond the skies
Which scatter'd from above the sun
   A light of Paradise.   20

We paused amid the pines that stood
   The giants of the waste,
Tortured by storms to shapes as rude
   As serpents interlaced,
And soothed by every azure breath   25
   That under Heaven is blown
To harmonies and hues beneath,
   As tender as its own :
Now all the tree-tops lay asleep
   Like green waves on the sea,   30
As still as in the silent deep
   The ocean woods may be.

How calm it was !—the silence there
   By such a chain was bound,
That even the busy woodpecker   35
   Made stiller by her sound
The inviolable quietness ;
   The breath of peace we drew
With its soft motion made not less
   The calm that round us grew.   40
There seem'd from the remotest seat
   Of the wide mountain waste,
To the soft flower beneath our feet
   A magic circle traced,—
A spirit interfused around,   45
   A thrilling silent life ;
To momentary peace it bound
   Our mortal nature's strife ;—
And still I felt the centre of
   The magic circle there   50
Was one fair form that fill'd with love
   The lifeless atmosphere.

We paused beside the pools that lie
   Under the forest bough ;

Each seem'd as 'twere a little sky 　　　55
　　Gulf'd in a world below ;
A firmament of purple light
　　Which in the dark earth lay,
More boundless than the depth of night,
　　And purer than the day— 　　　　60
In which the lovely forests grew
　　As in the upper air,
More perfect both in shape and hue
　　Than any spreading there.
There lay the glade and neighbouring lawn, 65
　　And through the dark green wood
The white sun twinkling like the dawn
　　Out of a speckled cloud.
Sweet views which in our world above
　　Can never well be seen 　　　　70
Were imaged by the water's love
　　Of that fair forest green :
And all was interfused beneath
　　With an Elysian glow,
An atmosphere without a breath, 　　75
　　A softer day below.
Like one beloved, the scene had lent
　　To the dark water's breast
Its every leaf and lineament
　　With more than truth exprest ; 　　80
Until an envious wind crept by,
　　Like an unwelcome thought
Which from the mind's too faithful eye
　　Blots one dear image out.
Though thou art ever fair and kind, 　　85
　　The forests ever green,
Less oft is peace in Shelley's mind
　　Than calm in waters seen.

　　　　　　　　　　P. B. SHELLEY.

261

BY THE SEA

It is a beauteous evening, calm and free ;
    The holy time is quiet as a Nun
    Breathless with adoration ; the broad sun
Is sinking down in its tranquillity ;

The gentleness of heaven broods o'er the Sea :   5
    Listen ! the mighty Being is awake,
    And doth with his eternal motion make
A sound like thunder—everlastingly.

Dear child ! dear girl ! that walkest with me here,
    If thou appear untouch'd by solemn thought
        Thy nature is not therefore less divine :   11

Thou liest in Abraham's bosom all the year,
    And worshipp'st at the Temple's inner shrine,
God being with thee when we know it not.

W. WORDSWORTH.

262

TO THE EVENING STAR

Star that bringest home the bee,
And sett'st the weary labourer free !
    If any star shed peace, 'tis thou,
        That send'st it from above,   4
    Appearing when Heaven's breath and brow
        Are sweet as hers we love.

Come to the luxuriant skies,
Whilst the landscape's odours rise,
    Whilst far-off lowing herds are heard,
        And songs when toil is done,   10
    From cottages whose smoke unstirr'd
        Curls yellow in the sun.

Star of love's soft interviews,
Parted lovers on thee muse ;
   Their remembrancer in Heaven   15
   Of thrilling vows thou art,
Too delicious to be riven
   By absence from the heart.

                  T. CAMPBELL.

263

DATUR HORA QUIETI

The sun upon the lake is low,
   The wild birds hush their song,
The hills have evening's deepest glow,
   Yet Leonard tarries long.
Now all whom varied toil and care   5
   From home and love divide,
In the calm sunset may repair
   Each to the loved one's side.

The noble dame on turret high,
   Who waits her gallant knight,   10
Looks to the western beam to spy
   The flash of armour bright.
The village maid, with hand on brow
   The level ray to shade,
Upon the footpath watches now   15
   For Colin's darkening plaid.

Now to their mates the wild swans row,
   By day they swam apart,
And to the thicket wanders slow
   The hind beside the hart.   20
The woodlark at his partner's side
   Twitters his closing song—
All meet whom day and care divide,
   But Leonard tarries long !

                  SIR W. SCOTT.

264

TO THE MOON

Art thou pale for weariness
Of climbing heaven, and gazing on the earth,
 Wandering companionless
Among the stars that have a different birth,— 5
And ever-changing, like a joyless eye
That finds no object worth its constancy?

P. B. SHELLEY.

265

A widow bird sate mourning for her love
 Upon a wintry bough;
The frozen wind crept on above,
 The freezing stream below.

There was no leaf upon the forest bare, 5
 No flower upon the ground,
And little motion in the air
 Except the mill-wheel's sound.

P. B. SHELLEY.

266

TO SLEEP

A flock of sheep that leisurely pass by,
 One after one; the sound of rain, and bees
 Murmuring; the fall of rivers, winds and seas,
Smooth fields, white sheets of water, and pure sky;

I have thought of all by turns, and yet do lie 5
 Sleepless; and soon the small birds' melodies
 Must hear, first uttered from my orchard trees,
And the first cuckoo's melancholy cry.

Even thus last night, and two nights more, I lay,
  And could not win thee, Sleep! by any stealth:
So do not let me wear to-night away :   11
  Without Thee what is all the morning's wealth ?
Come, blessèd barrier between day and day,
  Dear mother of fresh thoughts and joyous health!
                              W. WORDSWORTH.

267

THE SOLDIER'S DREAM

Our bugles sang truce, for the night-cloud had lower'd,
  And the sentinel stars set their watch in the sky;
And thousands had sunk on the ground overpower'd,
  The weary to sleep, and the wounded to die.   4

When reposing that night on my pallet of straw
  By the wolf-scaring faggot that guarded the slain,
At the dead of the night a sweet vision I saw;
  And thrice ere the morning I dreamt it again.

Methought from the battle-field's dreadful array
  Far, far I had roam'd on a desolate track:
'Twas autumn,—and sunshine arose on the way
  To the home of my fathers, that welcomed me back.

I flew to the pleasant fields traversed so oft   13
  In life's morning march, when my bosom was
    young ;
I heard my own mountain-goats bleating aloft,   15
  And knew the sweet strain that the corn-reapers
    sung.

Then pledged we the wine-cup, and fondly I swore
  From my home and my weeping friends never to
    part ;   18
My little ones kiss'd me a thousand times o'er,
  And my wife sobb'd aloud in her fullness of heart.

' Stay—stay with us !—rest !—thou art weary and
    worn ! '—
  And fain was their war-broken soldier to stay ;—
But sorrow return'd with the dawning of morn,
  And the voice in my dreaming ear melted away.
                              T. CAMPBELL.

268

A DREAM OF THE UNKNOWN

I dream'd that as I wander'd by the way
  Bare Winter suddenly was changed to Spring,
And gentle odours led my steps astray,
  Mix'd with a sound of waters murmuring
Along a shelving bank of turf, which lay   5
  Under a copse, and hardly dared to fling
Its green arms round the bosom of the stream,
But kiss'd it and then fled, as thou mightest in
    dream.

There grew pied wind-flowers and violets,
  Daisies, those pearl'd Arcturi of the earth,   10
The constellated flower that never sets ;
  Faint oxlips ; tender blue-bells, at whose birth
The sod scarce heaved ; and that tall flower that
    wets—
Like a child, half in tenderness and mirth—
Its mother's face with heaven's collected tears,   15
When the low wind, its playmate's voice, it hears.

And in the warm hedge grew lush eglantine,
  Green cow-bind and the moonlight-colour'd may,
And cherry-blossoms, and white cups, whose wine
  Was the bright dew yet drain'd not by the day ;
And wild roses, and ivy serpentine   21
  With its dark buds and leaves, wandering astray ;
And flowers azure, black, and streak'd with gold,
Fairer than any waken'd eyes behold.

And nearer to the river's trembling edge   25
  There grew broad flag-flowers, purple prank'd
    with white,
And starry river buds among the sedge,
  And floating water-lilies, broad and bright,
Which lit the oak that overhung the hedge
  With moonlight beams of their own watery light ;
And bulrushes, and reeds of such deep green   31
As soothed the dazzled eye with sober sheen.

Methought that of these visionary flowers
  I made a nosegay, bound in such a way
That the same hues, which in their natural bowers
  Were mingled or opposed, the like array   36
Kept these imprison'd children of the Hours
  Within my hand,—and then, elate and gay,
I hasten'd to the spot whence I had come,
That I might there present it—O ! to Whom ?
                      P. B. SHELLEY.

269

THE INNER VISION

Most sweet it is with unuplifted eyes
  To pace the ground, if path be there or none,
While a fair region round the traveller lies
  Which he forbears again to look upon ;

Pleased rather with some soft ideal scene,   5
  The work of Fancy, or some happy tone
Of meditation, slipping in between
  The beauty coming and the beauty gone.

If Thought and Love desert us, from that day
  Let us break off all commerce with the Muse :
With Thought and Love companions of our way—

Whate'er the senses take or may refuse,—   12
  The Mind's internal heaven shall shed her dews
Of inspiration on the humblest lay.
                    W. WORDSWORTH.

270

THE REALM OF FANCY

Ever let the Fancy roam !
Pleasure never is at home :
At a touch sweet Pleasure melteth,
Like to bubbles when rain pelteth ;

Then let wingéd Fancy wander   5
Through the thought still spread beyond her :
Open wide the mind's cage-door,
She'll dart forth, and cloudward soar.
O sweet Fancy ! let her loose ;
Summer's joys are spoilt by use,   10
And the enjoying of the Spring
Fades as does its blossoming :
Autumn's red-lipp'd fruitage too,
Blushing through the mist and dew,
Cloys with tasting : What do then ?   15
Sit thee by the ingle, when
The sear faggot blazes bright,
Spirit of a winter's night ;
When the soundless earth is muffled,
And the cakéd snow is shuffled   20
From the ploughboy's heavy shoon ;
When the Night doth meet the Noon
In a dark conspiracy
To banish Even from her sky.
—Sit thee there, and send abroad,   25
With a mind self-overawed,
Fancy, high-commission'd :—send her !
She has vassals to attend her ;
She will bring, in spite of frost,
Beauties that the earth hath lost ;   30
She will bring thee, all together,
All delights of summer weather ;
All the buds and bells of May
From dewy sward or thorny spray ;
All the heapéd Autumn's wealth,   35
With a still, mysterious stealth ;
She will mix these pleasures up
Like three fit wines in a cup,
And thou shalt quaff it ;—thou shalt hear
Distant harvest-carols clear ;   40
Rustle of the reapéd corn ;
Sweet birds antheming the morn :
And in the same moment—hark !
'Tis the early April lark,

Or the rooks, with busy caw,   45
Foraging for sticks and straw.
Thou shalt, at one glance, behold
The daisy and the marigold ;
White-plumed lilies, and the first
Hedge-grown primrose that hath burst ;   50
Shaded hyacinth, alway
Sapphire queen of the mid-May ;
And every leaf, and every flower
Pearlèd with the self-same shower.
Thou shalt see the field-mouse peep   55
Meagre from its cellèd sleep ;
And the snake all winter-thin
Cast on sunny bank its skin ;
Freckled nest-eggs thou shalt see
Hatching in the hawthorn-tree,   60
When the hen-bird's wing doth rest
Quiet on her mossy nest ;
Then the hurry and alarm
When the bee-hive casts its swarm ;
Acorns ripe down-pattering   65
While the autumn breezes sing.

O sweet Fancy ! let her loose ;
Everything is spoilt by use :
Where 's the cheek that doth not fade,
Too much gazed at ? Where 's the maid   70
Whose lip mature is ever new ?
Where 's the eye, however blue,
Doth not weary ? Where 's the face
One would meet in every place ?
Where 's the voice, however soft,   75
One would hear so very oft ?
At a touch sweet Pleasure melteth
Like to bubbles when rain pelteth.
Let then wingèd Fancy find
Thee a mistress to thy mind :   80
Dulcet-eyed as Ceres' daughter,
Ere the God of Torment taught her
How to frown and how to chide ;

With a waist and with a side
White as Hebe's, when her zone   85
Slipt its golden clasp, and down
Fell her kirtle to her feet,
While she held the goblet sweet,
And Jove grew languid.—Break the mesh
Of the Fancy's silken leash ;   90
Quickly break her prison-string,
And such joys as these she'll bring.
—Let the wingéd Fancy roam !
Pleasure never is at home.

J. Keats.

271

HYMN TO THE SPIRIT OF NATURE

Life of Life ! thy lips enkindle
    With their love the breath between them ;
And thy smiles before they dwindle
    Make the cold air fire ; then screen them
In those looks, where whoso gazes   5
Faints, entangled in their mazes.

Child of Light ! thy limbs are burning
    Through the vest which seems to hide them,
As the radiant lines of morning   9
    Through the clouds, ere they divide them ;
And this atmosphere divinest
Shrouds thee wheresoe'er thou shinest.

Fair are others : none beholds thee ;
    But thy voice sounds low and tender
Like the fairest, for it folds thee   15
    From the sight, that liquid splendour ;
And all feel, yet see thee never,—
As I feel now, lost for ever !

Lamp of Earth ! where'er thou movest
    Its dim shapes are clad with brightness   20

And the souls of whom thou lovest
  Walk upon the winds with lightness
Till they fail, as I am failing,
Dizzy, lost, yet unbewailing!

P. B. SHELLEY.

272

WRITTEN IN EARLY SPRING

I heard a thousand blended notes
  While in a grove I sat reclined,
In that sweet mood when pleasant thoughts
  Bring sad thoughts to the mind.

To her fair works did Nature link   5
  The human soul that through me ran;
And much it grieved my heart to think
  What man has made of man.

Through primrose tufts, in that green bower,
  The periwinkle trail'd its wreaths;   10
And 'tis my faith that every flower
  Enjoys the air it breathes.

The birds around me hopp'd and play'd,
  Their thoughts I cannot measure—
But the least motion which they made   15
  It seem'd a thrill of pleasure.

The budding twigs spread out their fan
  To catch the breezy air;
And I must think, do all I can,
  That there was pleasure there.   20

If this belief from heaven be sent,
  If such be Nature's holy plan,
Have I not reason to lament
  What man has made of man?

W. WORDSWORTH.

273

RUTH : OR THE INFLUENCES OF NATURE

When Ruth was left half desolate
Her father took another mate ;
   And Ruth, not seven years old,
A slighted child, at her own will
Went wandering over dale and hill,   5
   In thoughtless freedom, bold.

And she had made a pipe of straw,
And music from that pipe could draw
   Like sounds of winds and floods ;
Had built a bower upon the green,   10
As if she from her birth had been
   An infant of the woods.

Beneath her father's roof, alone
She seem'd to live ; her thoughts her own ;
   Herself her own delight :   15
Pleased with herself, nor sad nor gay.
And, passing thus the live-long day,
   She grew to woman's height.

There came a youth from Georgia's shore—
A military casque he wore   20
   With splendid feathers drest ;
He brought them from the Cherokees ;
The feathers nodded in the breeze
   And made a gallant crest.

From Indian blood you deem him sprung :
But no ! he spake the English tongue   26
   And bore a soldier's name ;
And, when America was free
From battle and from jeopardy,
   He 'cross the ocean came.   30

With hues of genius on his cheek,
In finest tones the youth could speak :

　　　　　　　　—While he was yet a boy
The moon, the glory of the sun,
And streams that murmur as they run,　　35
　　　Had been his dearest joy.

He was a lovely youth ! I guess
The panther in the wilderness
　　　Was not so fair as he ;
And when he chose to sport and play,　　40
No dolphin ever was so gay
　　　Upon the tropic sea.

Among the Indians he had fought ;
And with him many tales he brought
　　　Of pleasure and of fear ;　　45
Such tales as, told to any maid
By such a youth, in the green shade,
　　　Were perilous to hear.

He told of girls, a happy rout !
Who quit their fold with dance and shout,
　　　Their pleasant Indian town,　　51
To gather strawberries all day long ;
Returning with a choral song
　　　When daylight is gone down.

He spake of plants that hourly change　　55
Their blossoms, through a boundless range
　　　Of intermingling hues ;
With budding, fading, faded flowers,
They stand the wonder of the bowers
　　　From morn to evening dews.　　60

He told of the magnolia, spread
High as a cloud, high over head !
　　　The cypress and her spire ;
—Of flowers that with one scarlet gleam
Cover a hundred leagues, and seem　　65
　　　To set the hills on fire.

The youth of green savannahs spake,
And many an endless, endless lake

With all its fairy crowds
Of islands, that together lie   70
  As quietly as spots of sky
    Among the evening clouds.

' How pleasant,' then he said, ' it were
A fisher or a hunter there,
  In sunshine or in shade   75
To wander with an easy mind,
And build a household fire, and find
  A home in every glade !

' What days and what bright years ! Ah me !
Our life were life indeed, with thee   80
  So pass'd in quiet bliss ;
And all the while,' said he, ' to know
That we were in a world of woe,
  On such an earth as this ! '

And then he sometimes interwove   85
Fond thoughts about a father's love,
  ' For there,' said he, ' are spun
Around the heart such tender ties,
That our own children to our eyes
  Are dearer than the sun.   90

' Sweet Ruth ! and could you go with me
My helpmate in the woods to be,
  Our shed at night to rear ;
Or run, my own adopted bride,
A sylvan huntress at my side,   95
  And drive the flying deer !

' Beloved Ruth ! '—No more he said.
The wakeful Ruth at midnight shed
  A solitary tear :
She thought again—and did agree   100
With him to sail across the sea,
  And drive the flying deer.

' And now, as fitting is and right,
We in the church our faith will plight,

　　A husband and a wife.'　　　　　　　105
Even so they did ; and I may say
That to sweet Ruth that happy day
　　Was more than human life.

Through dream and vision did she sink,
Delighted all the while to think　　　　110
　　That, on those lonesome floods
And green savannahs, she should share
His board with lawful joy, and bear
　　His name in the wild woods.

But, as you have before been told,　　115
This Stripling, sportive, gay, and bold,
　　And with his dancing crest
So beautiful, through savage lands
Had roam'd about, with vagrant bands
　　Of Indians in the West.　　　　　　120

The wind, the tempest roaring high,
The tumult of a tropic sky
　　Might well be dangerous food
For him, a youth to whom was given
So much of earth—so much of heaven,　125
　　And such impetuous blood.

Whatever in those climes he found
Irregular in sight or sound
　　Did to his mind impart
A kindred impulse, seem'd allied　　　130
To his own powers, and justified
　　The workings of his heart.

Nor less, to feed voluptuous thought,
The beauteous forms of Nature wrought,—
　　Fair trees and gorgeous flowers ;　　135
The breezes their own languor lent ;
The stars had feelings, which they sent
　　Into those favour'd bowers.

Yet, in his worst pursuits, I ween
That sometimes there did intervene　　140

Pure hopes of high intent :
For passions, link'd to forms so fair
  And stately, needs must have their share
    Of noble sentiment.

But ill he lived, much evil saw, 145
With men to whom no better law
  Nor better life was known ;
Deliberately and undeceived
Those wild men's vices he received,
    And gave them back his own. 150

His genius and his moral frame
Were thus impair'd, and he became
  The slave of low desires :
A man who without self-control
Would seek what the degraded soul 155
    Unworthily admires.

And yet he with no feign'd delight
Had woo'd the maiden, day and night
  Had loved her, night and morn :
What could he less than love a maid 160
Whose heart with so much nature play'd—
    So kind and so forlorn ?

Sometimes most earnestly he said,
' O Ruth ! I have been worse than dead ;
  False thoughts, thoughts bold and vain 165
Encompass'd me on every side
When I, in confidence and pride,
    Had cross'd the Atlantic main.

' Before me shone a glorious world
Fresh as a banner bright, unfurl'd 170
  To music suddenly :
I look'd upon those hills and plains,
And seem'd as if let loose from chains
    To live at liberty.

' No more of this—for now, by thee, 175
Dear Ruth ! more happily set free,

With nobler zeal I burn ;
My soul from darkness is released
Like the whole sky when to the east
   The morning doth return.'   180

Full soon that better mind was gone ;
No hope, no wish remain'd, not one,—
   They stirr'd him now no more ;
New objects did new pleasure give,
And once again he wish'd to live   185
   As lawless as before.

Meanwhile, as thus with him it fared,
They for the voyage were prepared,
   And went to the sea-shore :
But, when they thither came, the youth   190
Deserted his poor bride, and Ruth
   Could never find him more.

God help thee, Ruth !—Such pains she had,
That she in half a year was mad,
   And in a prison housed ;   195
And there, with many a doleful song
Made of wild words, her cup of wrong
   She fearfully caroused.

Yet sometimes milder hours she knew,
Nor wanted sun, nor rain, nor dew,   200
   Nor pastimes of the May,
—They all were with her in her cell ;
And a clear brook with cheerful knell
   Did o'er the pebbles play.

When Ruth three seasons thus had lain,   205
There came a respite to her pain ;
   She from her prison fled ;
But of the Vagrant none took thought ;
And where it liked her best she sought
   Her shelter and her bread.   210

Among the fields she breathed again
The master-current of her brain

Ran permanent and free ;
And, coming to the banks of Tone,
There did she rest ; and dwell alone   215
  Under the greenwood tree.

The engines of her pain, the tools
That shaped her sorrow, rocks and pools,
  And airs that gently stir
The vernal leaves—she loved them still,   220
Nor ever tax'd them with the ill
  Which had been done to her.

A barn her winter bed supplies ;
But, till the warmth of summer skies
  And summer days is gone,   225
(And all do in this tale agree)
She sleeps beneath the greenwood tree,
  And other home hath none.

An innocent life, yet far astray !
And Ruth will, long before her day,   230
  Be broken down and old.
Sore aches she needs must have ! but less
Of mind, than body's wretchedness,
  From damp, and rain, and cold.

If she is prest by want of food   235
She from her dwelling in the wood
  Repairs to a road-side ;
And there she begs at one steep place,
Where up and down with easy pace
  The horsemen-travellers ride.   240

That oaten pipe of hers is mute
Or thrown away : but with a flute
  Her loneliness she cheers ;
This flute, made of a hemlock stalk,
At evening in his homeward walk   245
  The Quantock woodman hears.

I, too, have pass'd her on the hills
Setting her little water-mills

By spouts and fountains wild—
Such small machinery as she turn'd   250
Ere she had wept, ere she had mourn'd,
    A young and happy child !

Farewell ! and when thy days are told,
Ill-fated Ruth ! in hallow'd mould
    Thy corpse shall buried be ;   255
For thee a funeral bell shall ring,
And all the congregation sing
    A Christian psalm for thee.

W. WORDSWORTH.

274
WRITTEN IN THE EUGANEAN HILLS, NORTH ITALY

Many a green isle needs must be
In the deep wide sea of misery,
Or the mariner, worn and wan,
Never thus could voyage on
Day and night, and night and day,   5
Drifting on his dreary way,
With the solid darkness black
Closing round his vessel's track ;
Whilst above, the sunless sky,
Big with clouds, hangs heavily,   10
And behind, the tempest fleet
Hurries on with lightning feet,
Riving sail, and cord, and plank,
Till the ship has almost drank
Death from the o'er-brimming deep ;   15
And sinks down, down, like that sleep
When the dreamer seems to be
Weltering through eternity ;
And the dim low line before
Of a dark and distant shore   20
Still recedes, as ever still
Longing with divided will,

But no power to seek or shun,
He is ever drifted on
O'er the unreposing wave,   25
To the haven of the grave.

Aye, many flowering islands lie
In the waters of wide Agony :
To such a one this morn was led
My bark, by soft winds piloted.   30
—'Mid the mountains Euganean
I stood listening to the paean
With which the legion'd rooks did hail
The sun's uprise majestical :
Gathering round with wings all hoar,   35
Through the dewy mist they soar
Like gray shades, till the eastern heaven
Bursts, and then,—as clouds of even,
Fleck'd with fire and azure, lie
In the unfathomable sky,—   40
So their plumes of purple grain
Starr'd with drops of golden rain
Gleam above the sunlight woods,
As in silent multitudes
On the morning's fitful gale   45
Through the broken mist they sail ;
And the vapours cloven and gleaming
Follow down the dark steep streaming,
Till all is bright, and clear, and still
Round the solitary hill.   50

Beneath is spread like a green sea
The waveless plain of Lombardy,
Bounded by the vaporous air,
Islanded by cities fair ;
Underneath Day's azure eyes,   55
Ocean's nursling, Venice lies,—
A peopled labyrinth of walls,
Amphitrite's destined halls,
Which her hoary sire now paves
With his blue and beaming waves.   60

Lo ! the sun upsprings behind,
Broad, red, radiant, half-reclined
On the level quivering line
Of the waters crystalline ;
And before that chasm of light,   65
As within a furnace bright,
Column, tower, and dome, and spire,
Shine like obelisks of fire,
Pointing with inconstant motion
From the altar of dark ocean   70
To the sapphire-tinted skies ;
As the flames of sacrifice
From the marble shrines did rise,
As to pierce the dome of gold
Where Apollo spoke of old.   75

Sun-girt City ! thou hast been
Ocean's child, and then his queen ;
Now is come a darker day,
And thou soon must be his prey,
If the power that raised thee here   80
Hallow so thy watery bier.
A less drear ruin then than now,
With thy conquest-branded brow
Stooping to the slave of slaves
From thy throne, among the waves   85
Wilt thou be,—when the sea-mew
Flies, as once before it flew,
O'er thine isles depopulate,
And all is in its ancient state,
Save where many a palace gate,   90
With green sea-flowers overgrown
Like a rock of ocean's own,
Topples o'er the abandon'd sea
As the tides change sullenly.
The fisher on his watery way   95
Wandering at the close of day,
Will spread his sail and seize his oar
Till he pass the gloomy shore,
Lest thy dead should, from their sleep
Bursting o'er the starlight deep,   100

Lead a rapid masque of death
O'er the waters of his path.

Noon descends around me now :
'Tis the noon of autumn's glow,
When a soft and purple mist   105
Like a vaporous amethyst,
Or an air-dissolvéd star
Mingling light and fragrance, far
From the curved horizon's bound
To the point of Heaven's profound,   110
Fills the overflowing sky ;
And the plains that silent lie
Underneath ; the leaves unsodden
Where the infant Frost has trodden
With his morning-wingéd feet   115
Whose bright print is gleaming yet ;
And the red and golden vines
Piercing with their trellised lines
The rough, dark-skirted wilderness ;
The dun and bladed grass no less,   120
Pointing from this hoary tower
In the windless air ; the flower
Glimmering at my feet ; the line
Of the olive-sandall'd Apennine
In the south dimly islanded ;   125
And the Alps, whose snows are spread
High between the clouds and sun ;
And of living things each one ;
And my spirit, which so long
Darken'd this swift stream of song,—   130
Interpenetrated lie
By the glory of the sky ;
Be it love, light, harmony,
Odour, or the soul of all
Which from Heaven like dew doth fall, 135
Or the mind which feeds this verse
Peopling the lone universe.

Noon descends, and after noon
Autumn's evening meets me soon.

Leading the infantine moon   140
And that one star, which to her
Almost seems to minister
Half the crimson light she brings
From the sunset's radiant springs:
And the soft dreams of the morn   145
(Which like wingéd winds had borne
To that silent isle, which lies
'Mid remember'd agonies,
The frail bark of this lone being),
Pass, to other sufferers fleeing,   150
And its ancient pilot, Pain,
Sits beside the helm again.

Other flowering isles must be
In the sea of Life and Agony:
Other spirits float and flee   155
O'er that gulf: even now, perhaps,
On some rock the wild wave wraps,
With folding wings they waiting sit
For my bark, to pilot it
To some calm and blooming cove,   160
Where for me, and those I love,
May a windless bower be built,
Far from passion, pain, and guilt,
In a dell 'mid lawny hills
Which the wild sea-murmur fills,   165
And soft sunshine, and the sound
Of old forests echoing round,
And the light and smell divine,
Of all flowers that breathe and shine.
—We may live so happy there,   170
That the Spirits of the Air
Envying us, may even entice
To our healing Paradise
The polluting multitude;
But their rage would be subdued   175
By that clime divine and calm,
And the winds whose wings rain balm
On the uplifted soul, and leaves

Under which the bright sea heaves ;
While each breathless interval   180
In their whisperings musical
The inspired soul supplies
With its own deep melodies ;
And the love which heals all strife
Circling, like the breath of life,   185
All things in that sweet abode
With its own mild brotherhood.
They, not it, would change ; and soon
Every sprite beneath the moon
Would repent its envy vain,   190
And the earth grow young again.

P. B. SHELLEY.

275

ODE TO THE WEST WIND

(1)

O wild West Wind, thou breath of Autumn's being,
   Thou, from whose unseen presence the leaves dead
Are driven, like ghosts from an enchanter fleeing,

Yellow, and black, and pale, and hectic red,
   Pestilence-stricken multitudes : O thou   5
Who chariotest to their dark wintry bed

The wingèd seeds, where they lie cold and low,
   Each like a corpse within its grave, until
Thine azure sister of the Spring shall blow

Her clarion o'er the dreaming earth, and fill   10
   (Driving sweet buds like flocks to feed in air)
With living hues and odours plain and hill :

Wild Spirit, which art moving everywhere ;
Destroyer and Preserver ; hear, oh, hear !

(2)

Thou on whose stream, mid the steep sky's com-
    motion,   15
    Loose clouds like earth's decaying leaves are shed,
Shook from the tangled boughs of Heaven and
    Ocean,

Angels of rain and lightning : there are spread
    On the blue surface of thine airy surge,
Like the bright hair uplifted from the head   20

Of some fierce Maenad, even from the dim verge
    Of the horizon to the zenith's height,
The locks of the approaching storm. Thou dirge

Of the dying year, to which this closing night
    Will be the dome of a vast sepulchre,   25
Vaulted with all thy congregated might

Of vapours, from whose solid atmosphere
Black rain, and fire, and hail, will burst : oh, hear

(3)

Thou who didst waken from his summer dreams
    The blue Mediterranean, where he lay,   30
Lull'd by the coil of his crystalline streams,

Beside a pumice isle in Baiae's bay,
    And saw in sleep old palaces and towers
Quivering within the wave's intenser day,

All overgrown with azure moss and flowers   35
    So sweet, the sense faints picturing them ! Thou
For whose path the Atlantic's level powers

Cleave themselves into chasms, while far below
    The sea-blooms and the oozy woods which wear
The sapless foliage of the ocean, know   40

Thy voice, and suddenly grow grey with fear,
And tremble and despoil themselves : oh, hear !

(4)

If I were a dead leaf thou mightest bear ;
  If I were a swift cloud to fly with thee ;
A wave to pant beneath thy power, and share   45

The impulse of thy strength, only less free
  Than thou, O uncontrollable !   If even
I were as in my boyhood, and could be

The comrade of thy wanderings over Heaven,
  As then, when to outstrip thy skyey speed   50
Scarce seemed a vision, I would ne'er have striven

As thus with thee in prayer in my sore need.
  Oh, lift me as a wave, a leaf, a cloud !
I fall upon the thorns of life !   I bleed !   54

A heavy weight of hours has chained and bowed
One too like thee : tameless, and swift, and proud.

(5)

Make me thy lyre, even as the forest is :
  What if my leaves are falling like its own !
The tumult of thy mighty harmonies

Will take from both a deep, autumnal tone,   60
  Sweet though in sadness. Be thou, Spirit fierce,
My spirit ! Be thou me, impetuous one !

Drive my dead thoughts over the universe
  Like withered leaves to quicken a new birth !
And, by the incantation of this verse,   65

Scatter, as from an unextinguished hearth
  Ashes and sparks, my words among mankind !
Be through my lips to unawakened earth

The trumpet of a prophecy ! O Wind,
If Winter comes, can Spring be far behind ?   70

P. B. SHELLEY.

276

NATURE AND THE POET

*Suggested by a Picture of Peele Castle in a Storm,
painted by Sir George Beaumont*

I was thy neighbour once, thou rugged Pile !
  Four summer weeks I dwelt in sight of thee :
I saw thee every day ; and all the while
  Thy Form was sleeping on a glassy sea.

So pure the sky, so quiet was the air !   5
  So like, so very like, was day to day !
Whene'er I look'd, thy image still was there ;
  It trembled, but it never pass'd away.

How perfect was the calm ! It seem'd no sleep,
  No mood, which season takes away, or brings :
I could have fancied that the mighty Deep   11
  Was even the gentlest of all gentle things.

Ah ! then if mine had been the Painter's hand
  To express what then I saw ; and add the gleam,
The light that never was on sea or land,   15
  The consecration, and the Poet's dream,—

I would have planted thee, thou hoary Pile,
  Amid a world how different from this !
Beside a sea that could not cease to smile ;
  On tranquil land, beneath a sky of bliss.   20

A picture had it been of lasting ease,
  Elysian quiet, without toil or strife ;
No motion but the moving tide, a breeze,
  Or merely silent Nature's breathing life.

Such, in the fond illusion of my heart,   25
  Such picture would I at that time have made :
And seen the soul of truth in every part,
  A steadfast peace that might not be betray'd.

So once it would have been,—'tis so no more ;
   I have submitted to a new control :   30
A power is gone, which nothing can restore ;
   A deep distress hath humanized my soul.

Not for a moment could I now behold
   A smiling sea, and be what I have been
The feeling of my loss will ne'er be old ;   35
   This, which I know, I speak with mind serene.

Then, Beaumont, Friend ! who would have been
     the Friend
   If he had lived, of him whom I deplore,
This work of thine I blame not, but commend ;
   This sea in anger, and that dismal shore.   40

O 'tis a passionate work !—yet wise and well,
   Well chosen is the spirit that is here ;
That hulk which labours in the deadly swell,
   This rueful sky, this pageantry of fear !

And this huge Castle, standing here sublime,   45
   I love to see the look with which it braves,
—Cased in the unfeeling armour of old time—
   The lightning, the fierce wind, and trampling
     waves.

Farewell, farewell the heart that lives alone,
   Housed in a dream, at distance from the Kind !
Such happiness, wherever it be known,   51
   Is to be pitied ; for 'tis surely blind.

But welcome fortitude, and patient cheer,
   And frequent sights of what is to be borne !
Such sights, or worse, as are before me here :—
   Not without hope we suffer and we mourn.   56

                      W. WORDSWORTH.

277

THE POET'S DREAM

On a poet's lips I slept
Dreaming like a love-adept
In the sound his breathing kept ;
Nor seeks nor finds he mortal blisses,
But feeds on the aerial kisses   5
Of shapes that haunt thought's wildernesses.
He will watch from dawn to gloom
The lake-reflected sun illume
The yellow bees in the ivy-bloom,
  Nor heed nor see what things they be ;
But from these create he can   11
Forms more real than living man,
  Nurslings of immortality !

P. B. SHELLEY.

278

The world is too much with us ; late and soon,
  Getting and spending, we lay waste our powers
  Little we see in Nature that is ours ;
We have given our hearts away, a sordid boon !

This Sea that bares her bosom to the moon,   5
  The winds that will be howling at all hours
  And are up-gather'd now like sleeping flowers,
For this, for everything, we are out of tune ;

It moves us not.—Great God ! I'd rather be
  A Pagan suckled in a creed outworn,   10
So might I, standing on this pleasant lea,

  Have glimpses that would make me less forlorn ;
Have sight of Proteus rising from the sea ;
  Or hear old Triton blow his wreathéd horn.

W. WORDSWORTH.

279

WITHIN KING'S COLLEGE CHAPEL, CAMBRIDGE

Tax not the royal Saint with vain expense,
    With ill-match'd aims the Architect who plann'd
    (Albeit labouring for a scanty band
Of white-robed Scholars only) this immense

And glorious work of fine intelligence !   5
    Give all thou canst ; high Heaven rejects the lore
    Of nicely-calculated less or more :
So deem'd the man who fashion'd for the sense

These lofty pillars, spread that branching roof   9
    Self-poised, and scoop'd into ten thousand cells,
    Where light and shade repose, where music dwells

    Lingering—and wandering on as loth to die ;
Like thoughts whose very sweetness yieldeth proof
    That they were born for immortality.

                  W. WORDSWORTH.

280

YOUTH AND AGE

Verse, a breeze 'mid blossoms straying,
    Where Hope clung feeding, like a bee—
Both were mine ! Life went a-maying
      With Nature, Hope, and Poesy,
        When I was young !   5

When I was young ?—Ah, woeful When !
Ah ! for the change 'twixt Now and Then !
This breathing house not built with hands,
    This body that does me grievous wrong,
O'er aery cliffs and glittering sands   10
    How lightly then it flash'd along :
Like those trim skiffs, unknown of yore,
    On winding lakes and rivers wide,

That ask no aid of sail or oar,
  That fear no spite of wind or tide !   15
Nought cared this body for wind or weather
When Youth and I lived in't together.

Flowers are lovely ; Love is flower-like ;
  Friendship is a sheltering tree ;   19
O ! the joys, that came down shower-like,
  Of Friendship, Love, and Liberty,
    Ere I was old !

Ere I was old ? Ah woeful Ere,
Which tells me, Youth 's no longer here !
O Youth ! for years so many and sweet   25
  'Tis known that Thou and I were one,
I'll think it but a fond conceit—
  It cannot be that thou art gone !
Thy vesper bell hath not yet toll'd :—
And thou wert ay a masker bold !   30
What strange disguise hast now put on
To make believe that thou art gone ?
I see these locks in silvery slips,
  This drooping gait, this alter'd size :
But Springtide blossoms on thy lips,   35
  And tears take sunshine from thine eyes !
Life is but thought : so think I will
That Youth and I are housemates still.

Dew-drops are the gems of morning,
  But the tears of mournful eve !   40
Where no hope is, life 's a warning
  That only serves to make us grieve,
    When we are old :

—That only serves to make us grieve
With oft and tedious taking-leave,   45
Like some poor nigh-related guest
That may not rudely be dismist,
Yet hath outstay'd his welcome while,
And tells the jest without the smile.

S. T. COLERIDGE.

281

THE TWO APRIL MORNINGS

We walk'd along, while bright and red
  Uprose the morning sun ;
And Matthew stopp'd, he look'd, and said,
  ' The will of God be done ! '

A village schoolmaster was he,   5
  With hair of glittering grey ;
As blithe a man as you could see
  On a spring holiday.

And on that morning, through the grass
  And by the steaming rills   10
We travell'd merrily, to pass
  A day among the hills.

' Our work,' said I, ' was well begun ;
  Then, from thy breast what thought,
Beneath so beautiful a sun,   15
  So sad a sigh has brought ? '

A second time did Matthew stop ;
  And fixing still his eye
Upon the eastern mountain-top,
  To me he made reply :   20

' Yon cloud with that long purple cleft
  Brings fresh into my mind
A day like this, which I have left
  Full thirty years behind.

' And just above yon slope of corn   25
  Such colours, and no other,
Were in the sky, that April morn,
  Of this the very brother.

' With rod and line I sued the sport
  Which that sweet season gave,   30
And, to the churchyard come, stopp'd short
  Beside my daughter's grave.

'Nine summers had she scarcely seen,
  The pride of all the vale ;
And then she sang ;—she would have been
  A very nightingale.   36

'Six feet in earth my Emma lay ;
  And yet I loved her more—
For so it seem'd,—than till that day
  I e'er had loved before.   40

'And turning from her grave, I met
  Beside the churchyard yew
A blooming Girl, whose hair was wet
  With points of morning dew.

'A basket on her head she bare ;   45
  Her brow was smooth and white :
To see a child so very fair,
  It was a pure delight !

'No fountain from its rocky cave
  E'er tripp'd with foot so free ;   50
She seem'd as happy as a wave
  That dances on the sea.

'There came from me a sigh of pain
  Which I could ill confine ;
I looked at her, and looked again :   55
  And did not wish her mine !'

—Matthew is in his grave, yet now
  Methinks I see him stand
As at that moment, with a bough
  Of wilding in his hand.   60

                            W. WORDSWORTH.

                   282

              THE FOUNTAIN

              A Conversation

We talk'd with open heart, and tongue
  Affectionate and true,
A pair of friends, though I was young,
  And Matthew seventy-two.

We lay beneath a spreading oak,   5
  Beside a mossy seat ;
And from the turf a fountain broke
  And gurgled at our feet.

' Now, Matthew ! ' said I, ' let us match
  This water's pleasant tune   10
With some old border-song, or catch
  That suits a summer's noon ;

' Or of the church-clock and the chimes
  Sing here beneath the shade
That half-mad thing of witty rhymes   15
  Which you last April made ! '

In silence Matthew lay, and eyed
  The spring beneath the tree :
And thus the dear old man replied,
  The grey-hair'd man of glee :   20

' No check, no stay, this Streamlet fears,
  How merrily it goes !
'Twill murmur on a thousand years
  And flow as now it flows.

' And here, on this delightful day,   25
  I cannot choose but think
How oft, a vigorous man, I lay
  Beside this fountain's brink.

' My eyes are dim with childish tears,
  My heart is idly stirr'd,   30
For the same sound is in my ears
  Which in those days I heard.

' Thus fares it still in our decay :
  And yet the wiser mind
Mourns less for what age takes away,   35
  Than what it leaves behind.

' The blackbird amid leafy trees,
  The lark above the hill,
Let loose their carols when they please,
  Are quiet when they will.   40

'With Nature never do they wage
   A foolish strife ; they see
A happy youth, and their old age
   Is beautiful and free :

'But we are press'd by heavy laws ;   45
   And often, glad no more,
We wear a face of joy, because
   We have been glad of yore.

'If there be one who need bemoan
   His kindred laid in earth,   50
The household hearts that were his own,—
   It is the man of mirth.

'My days, my friend, are almost gone,
   My life has been approved,
And many love me ; but by none   55
   Am I enough beloved.'

'Now both himself and me he wrongs,
   The man who thus complains !
I live and sing my idle songs
   Upon these happy plains :   60

'And, Matthew, for thy children dead
   I'll be a son to thee !'
At this he grasp'd my hand and said,
   'Alas ! that cannot be.'

We rose up from the fountain-side ;   65
   And down the smooth descent
Of the green sheep-track did we glide ;
   And through the wood we went ;

And, ere we came to Leonard's rock,
   He sang those witty rhymes   70
About the crazy old church-clock
   And the bewilder'd chimes.

W. WORDSWORTH.

283

THE RIVER OF LIFE

The more we live, more brief appear
    Our life's succeeding stages :
A day to childhood seems a year,
    And years like passing ages.

The gladsome current of our youth,   5
    Ere passion yet disorders,
Steals lingering like a river smooth
    Along its grassy borders.

But as the careworn cheek grows wan,
    And sorrow's shafts fly thicker,   10
Ye stars, that measure life to man,
    Why seem your courses quicker ?

When joys have lost their bloom and breath,
    And life itself is vapid,
Why, as we reach the Falls of death,   15
    Feel we its tide more rapid ?

It may be strange—yet who would change
    Time's course to slower speeding,
When one by one our friends have gone
    And left our bosoms bleeding ?   20

Heaven gives our years of fading strength
    Indemnifying fleetness ;
And those of youth, a seeming length,
    Proportion'd to their sweetness.

                T. CAMPBELL.

284

THE HUMAN SEASONS

Four seasons fill the measure of the year ;
    There are four seasons in the mind of man :
He has his lusty Spring, when fancy clear
    Takes in all beauty with an easy span :

He has his Summer, when luxuriously   5
  Spring's honey'd cud of youthful thought he loves
To ruminate, and by such dreaming nigh
  His nearest unto heaven : quiet coves

His soul has in its Autumn, when his wings
  He furleth close ; contented so to look   10
On mists in idleness—to let fair things
  Pass by unheeded as a threshold brook :

He has his Winter too of pale misfeature,
Or else he would forgo his mortal nature.

J. KEATS.

285

A LAMENT

O World ! O Life ! O Time !
On whose last steps I climb,
  Trembling at that where I had stood before ;
When will return the glory of your prime ?
    No more—Oh, never more !   5

Out of the day and night
A joy has taken flight :
  Fresh spring, and summer, and winter hoar
Move my faint heart with grief, but with delight
    No more—Oh, never more !   10

P. B. SHELLEY.

286

My heart leaps up when I behold
  A rainbow in the sky :
So was it when my life began,
So is it now I am a man,
So be it when I shall grow old,   5
  Or let me die !
The Child is father of the Man :
And I could wish my days to be
Bound each to each by natural piety.

W. WORDSWORTH.

287

ODE ON INTIMATIONS OF IMMORTALITY FROM RECOLLECTIONS OF EARLY CHILDHOOD

There was a time when meadow, grove, and stream,
  The earth, and every common sight,
    To me did seem
   Apparell'd in celestial light,
The glory and the freshness of a dream.   5
It is not now as it hath been of yore;—
    Turn wheresoe'er I may,
     By night or day,
The things which I have seen I now can see no more.

    The rainbow comes and goes, 10
    And lovely is the rose;
    The moon doth with delight
Look round her when the heavens are bare;
    Waters on a starry night
    Are beautiful and fair; 15
  The sunshine is a glorious birth;
  But yet I know, where'er I go,
That there hath pass'd away a glory from the earth.

Now, while the birds thus sing a joyous song,
  And while the young lambs bound 20
   As to the tabor's sound,
To me alone there came a thought of grief:
A timely utterance gave that thought relief,
   And I again am strong. 24
The cataracts blow their trumpets from the steep,—
 No more shall grief of mine the season wrong:
 I hear the echoes through the mountains throng,
The winds come to me from the fields of sleep,
   And all the earth is gay;
    Land and sea 30
  Give themselves up to jollity,

And with the heart of May
Doth every beast keep holiday ;—
Thou child of joy,
Shout round me, let me hear thy shouts, thou happy
Shepherd-boy !   35

Ye blessèd Creatures, I have heard the call
Ye to each other make ; I see
The heavens laugh with you in your jubilee ;
My heart is at your festival,
My head hath its coronal,   40
The fulness of your bliss, I feel—I feel it all.
O evil day ! if I were sullen
While Earth herself is adorning
This sweet May-morning ;
And the children are culling   45
On every side
In a thousand valleys far and wide
Fresh flowers ; while the sun shines warm,
And the babe leaps up on his mother's arm :—
I hear, I hear, with joy I hear !   50
—But there 's a tree, of many, one,
A single field which I have look'd upon,
Both of them speak of something that is gone :
The pansy at my feet
Doth the same tale repeat :   55
Whither is fled the visionary gleam ?
Where is it now, the glory and the dream ?

Our birth is but a sleep and a forgetting ;
The Soul that rises with us, our life's Star,
Hath had elsewhere its setting,   60
And cometh from afar ;
Not in entire forgetfulness,
And not in utter nakedness,
But trailing clouds of glory do we come
From God, who is our home :   65
Heaven lies about us in our infancy !
Shades of the prison-house begin to close
Upon the growing Boy,

But he beholds the light, and whence it flows,
   He sees it in his joy ;   70
The Youth, who daily farther from the east
  Must travel, still is Nature's priest,
    And by the vision splendid
    Is on his way attended ;
At length the Man perceives it die away, 75
And fade into the light of common day.

Earth fills her lap with pleasures of her own ;
Yearnings she hath in her own natural kind,
And, even with something of a mother's mind
    And no unworthy aim, 80
   The homely nurse doth all she can
To make her foster-child, her inmate, Man,
  Forget the glories he hath known,
And that imperial palace whence he came.

Behold the Child among his new-born blisses,
  A six years' darling of a pigmy size ! 86
  See, where 'mid work of his own hand he lies.
Fretted by sallies of his mother's kisses,
  With light upon him from his father's eyes !
See, at his feet, some little plan or chart, 90
Some fragment from his dream of human life,
Shaped by himself with newly-learnéd art ;
    A wedding or a festival,
    A mourning or a funeral ;
     And this hath now his heart, 95
   And unto this he frames his song :
    Then will he fit his tongue
To dialogues of business, love, or strife ;
    But it will not be long
    Ere this be thrown aside, 100
   And with new joy and pride
The little actor cons another part ;
Filling from time to time his ' humorous stage '
With all the Persons, down to palsied Age,
That life brings with her in her equipage ; 105
    As if his whole vocation
    Were endless imitation.

Thou, whose exterior semblance doth belie
    Thy soul's immensity ;
Thou best Philosopher, who yet dost keep   110
Thy heritage, thou Eye among the blind,
That, deaf and silent, read'st the eternal deep,
Haunted for ever by the eternal Mind,—
       Mighty Prophet ! Seer blest !
      On whom those truths do rest   115
Which we are toiling all our lives to find,
In darkness lost, the darkness of the grave ;
Thou, over whom thy Immortality
Broods like the Day, a Master o'er a Slave,
A Presence which is not to be put by ;   120
Thou little Child, yet glorious in the might
Of heaven-born freedom on thy being's height,
Why with such earnest pains dost thou provoke
The years to bring the inevitable yoke,   124
Thus blindly with thy blessedness at strife ?
Full soon thy Soul shall have her earthly freight,
And custom lie upon thee with a weight
Heavy as frost, and deep almost as life !

      O joy ! that in our embers
        Is something that doth live,   130
      That Nature yet remembers
        What was so fugitive !
The thought of our past years in me doth breed
Perpetual benediction : not indeed
For that which is most worthy to be blest,   135
Delight and liberty, the simple creed
Of Childhood, whether busy or at rest,
With new-fledged hope still fluttering in his
    breast :
      —Not for these I raise
        The song of thanks and praise ;   140
    But for those obstinate questionings
    Of sense and outward things,
    Fallings from us, vanishings,
    Blank misgivings of a creature
Moving about in worlds not realized,   145

High instincts, before which our mortal nature
Did tremble like a guilty thing surprised :
　　But for those first affections,
　　Those shadowy recollections,
　　　　Which, be they what they may,　　150
Are yet the fountain-light of all our day,
Are yet a master-light of all our seeing ;
　　Uphold us, cherish, and have power to make
Our noisy years seem moments in the being
　　Of the eternal silence : truths that wake,　155
　　　　To perish never ;
Which neither listlessness, nor mad endeavour,
　　　　Nor man nor boy
Nor all that is at enmity with joy,
Can utterly abolish or destroy !　　　　160
　　Hence in a season of calm weather
　　　　Though inland far we be,
Our souls have sight of that immortal sea
　　　　Which brought us hither ;
　　　　Can in a moment travel thither—　165
And see the children sport upon the shore,
And hear the mighty waters rolling evermore.

Then, sing ye birds, sing, sing a joyous song !
　　　　And let the young lambs bound
　　　　As to the tabor's sound !　　　　170
　　We, in thought, will join your throng
　　　　Ye that pipe and ye that play,
　　　　Ye that through your hearts to-day
　　　　Feel the gladness of the May !
What though the radiance which was once so
　　bright
Be now for ever taken from my sight,　　176
　　Though nothing can bring back the hour
Of splendour in the grass, of glory in the flower ;
　　　　We will grieve not, rather find
　　　　Strength in what remains behind ;　180
　　　　In the primal sympathy
　　　　Which having been must ever be ;
　　　　In the soothing thoughts that spring

Out of human suffering ;
In the faith that looks through death,
In years that bring the philosophic mind. 186

And O, ye Fountains, Meadows, Hills, and Groves,
Forbode not any severing of our loves !
Yet in my heart of hearts I feel your might ;
I only have relinquish'd one delight   190
To live beneath your more habitual sway ;
I love the brooks which down their channels fret,
Even more than when I tripp'd lightly as they ;
The innocent brightness of a new-born day
          Is lovely yet ;   195
The clouds that gather round the setting sun
Do take a sober colouring from an eye
That hath kept watch o'er man's mortality ;
Another race hath been, and other palms are won.
Thanks to the human heart by which we live,
Thanks to its tenderness, its joys, and fears,   201
To me the meanest flower that blows can give
Thoughts that do often lie too deep for tears.

W. WORDSWORTH.

288

Music, when soft voices die,
Vibrates in the memory—
Odours, when sweet violets sicken,
Live within the sense they quicken.

Rose leaves, when the rose is dead,   5
Are heaped for the beloved's bed ;
And so thy thoughts, when thou art gone,
Love itself shall slumber on.

P. B. SHELLEY.

ADDITIONAL POEMS

ADDITIONAL POEMS

289

I strove with none, for none was worth my strife ;
    Nature I loved, and, next to Nature, Art ;
I warmed both hands before the fire of life
    It sinks, and I am ready to depart.

W. S. LANDOR.

290

ROSE AYLMER

Ah what avails the sceptred race !
    Ah what the form divine !
What every virtue, every grace !
    Rose Aylmer, all were thine.
Rose Aylmer, whom these wakeful eyes   5
    May weep, but never see,
A night of memories and of sighs
    I consecrate to thee.

W. S. LANDOR.

291

THE MAID'S LAMENT

I loved him not ; and yet now he is gone
    I feel I am alone.
I checked him while he spoke ; yet could he speak,
    Alas ! I would not check.
For reasons not to love him once I sought,   5
    And wearied all my thought

To vex myself and him : I now would give
    My love, could he but live
Who lately lived for me, and, when he found
    'Twas vain, in holy ground   10
He hid his face amid the shades of death.
    I waste for him my breath
Who wasted his for me : but mine returns,
    And this lorn bosom burns
With stifling heat, heaving it up in sleep,   15
    And waking me to weep
Tears that had melted his soft heart : for years
    Wept he as bitter tears.
Merciful God! such was his latest prayer,
    These may she never share!   20
Quieter is his breath, his breast more cold,
    Than daisies in the mould,
Where children spell, athwart the churchyard gate,
    His name and life's brief date.
Pray for him, gentle souls, whoe'er you be,   25
    And, O, pray too for me !
                       W. S. LANDOR.

292

TO ROBERT BROWNING

There is delight in singing, tho' none hear
Beside the singer : and there is delight
In praising, tho' the praiser sit alone
And see the praised far off him, far above.
Shakespeare is not our poet, but the world's,   5
Therefore on him no speech ! and brief for thee,
Browning ! Since Chaucer was alive and hale,
No man hath walked along our roads with step
So active, so inquiring eye, or tongue
So varied in discourse. But warmer climes   10
Give brighter plumage, stronger wing : the breeze
Of Alpine heights thou playest with, borne on
Beyond Sorrento and Amalfi, where
The Siren waits thee, singing song for song.
                       W. S. LANDOR.

293

Proud word you never spoke, but you will speak
    Four not exempt from pride some future day.
Resting on one white hand a warm wet cheek
    Over my open volume you will say,
    ' This man loved *me* ! ' then rise and trip away.

W. S. LANDOR.

294

    Well I remember how you smiled
      To see me write your name upon
    The soft sea-sand . . . . ' *O ! what a child !*
      You think you're writing upon stone ! '
I have since written what no tide   5
      Shall ever wash away, what men
Unborn shall read o'er ocean wide
      And find Ianthe's name again.

W. S. LANDOR.

295

TO A WATERFOWL

    Whither, midst falling dew,
While glow the heavens with the last steps of day,
Far, through their rosy depths, dost thou pursue
    Thy solitary way ?

    Vainly the fowler's eye   5
Might mark thy distant flight to do thee wrong,
As, darkly seen against the crimson sky,
    Thy figure floats along.

    Seek'st thou the plashy brink
Of weedy lake, or marge of river wide,   10
Or where the rocking billows rise and sink
    On the chafed ocean side ?

    There is a Power whose care
Teaches thy way along that pathless coast,—
The desert and illimitable air,—   15
    Lone wandering, but not lost.

All day thy wings have fanned,
At that far height, the cold thin atmosphere ;
Yet stoop not, weary, to the welcome land,
　　　Though the dark night is near.　　　　20

And soon that toil shall end ;
Soon shalt thou find a summer home and rest,
And scream among thy fellows ; reeds shall bend,
　　　Soon, o'er thy sheltered nest.

Thou'rt gone, the abyss of heaven　　　25
Hath swallowed up thy form ; yet on my heart
Deeply hath sunk the lesson thou hast given,
　　　And shall not soon depart.

He who, from zone to zone,
Guides through the boundless sky thy certain flight,
In the long way that I must tread alone,　　　31
　　　Will lead my steps aright.
　　　　　　　　　　　W. C. BRYANT.

296
RONDEAU

Jenny kissed me when we met,
　　　Jumping from the chair she sat in ;
Time, you thief, who love to get
　　　Sweets into your list, put that in !
Say I'm weary, say I'm sad,　　　5
　　　Say that health and wealth have missed me,
Say I'm growing old, but add,
　　　Jenny kiss'd me.　　　J. H. LEIGH HUNT.

297
THE WAR SONG OF DINAS VAWR

The mountain sheep are sweeter,
　　　But the valley sheep are fatter ;
We therefore deemed it meeter
　　　To carry off the latter.
We made an expedition ;　　　5
　　　We met a host, and quelled it ;
We forced a strong position,
　　　And killed the men who held it.

On Dyfed's richest valley,
   Where herds of kine were browsing,   10
We made a mighty sally
   To furnish our carousing.
Fierce warriors rushed to meet us ;
   We met them, and o'erthrew them :
They struggled hard to beat us ;   15
   But we conquered them, and slew them.

As we drove our prize at leisure,
   The king marched forth to catch us :
His rage surpassed all measure,
   But his people could not match us.   20
He fled to his hall-pillars ;
   And, ere our force we led off,
Some sacked his house and cellars,
   While others cut his head off.

We there, in strife bewildering,   25
   Spilt blood enough to swim in :
We orphaned many children,
   And widowed many women.
The eagles and the ravens
   We glutted with our foemen ;   30
The heroes and the cravens,
   The spearmen and the bowmen.

We brought away from battle,
   And much their land bemoaned them,
Two thousand head of cattle,   35
   And the head of him who owned them :
Ednyfed, King of Dyfed,
   His head was borne before us ;
His wine and beasts supplied our feasts,
   And his overthrow, our chorus.   40

T. L. PEACOCK.

298

THREE MEN OF GOTHAM

Seamen three !   What men be ye ?
   Gotham's three wise men we be.
Whither in your bowl so free ?
   To rake the moon from out the sea.
The bowl goes trim.   The moon doth shine.
And our ballast is old wine.   6
And your ballast is old wine.

Who art thou, so fast adrift ?
   I am he they call Old Care.
Here on board we will thee lift.   10
   No : I may not enter there.
Wherefore so ?   'Tis Jove's decree,
In a bowl Care may not be.
In a bowl Care may not be.

Fear ye not the waves that roll ?   15
   No : in charméd bowl we swim.
What the charm that floats the bowl ?
   Water may not pass the brim.
The bowl goes trim.   The moon doth shine.
And our ballast is old wine.   20
And your ballast is old wine.

T. L. PEACOCK.

299

THE GRAVE OF LOVE

I dug, beneath the cypress shade,
   What well might seem an elfin's grave ;
And every pledge in earth I laid,
   That erst thy false affection gave.

I pressed them down the sod beneath ;   5
   I placed one mossy stone above ;
And twined the rose's fading wreath
   Around the sepulchre of love.

Frail as thy love, the flowers were dead,
  Ere yet the evening sun was set :   10
But years shall see the cypress spread,
  Immutable as my regret.

T. L. Peacock.

300

A JACOBITE'S EPITAPH

To my true king I offered free from stain
Courage and faith ; vain faith, and courage vain.
For him I threw lands, honours, wealth, away,
And one dear hope, that was more prized than they.
For him I languished in a foreign clime,   5
Grey-haired with sorrow in my manhood's prime ;
Heard on Lavernia Scargill's whispering trees,
And pined by Arno for my lovelier Tees ;
Beheld each night my home in fevered sleep,
Each morning started from the dream to weep ;
Till God, who saw me tried too sorely, gave   11
The resting-place I asked, an early grave.
O thou, whom chance leads to this nameless stone,
From that proud country which was once mine own,
By those white cliffs I never more must see,   15
By that dear language which I spake like thee,
Forget all feuds, and shed one English tear
O'er English dust.   A broken heart lies here.

Lord Macaulay.

301

THE BATTLE OF NASEBY

By Obadiah Bind-their-kings-in-chains-and-their-nobles-with-links-of-iron, serjeant in Ireton's regiment

Oh ! wherefore come ye forth, in triumph from the
    North,
  With your hands, and your feet, and your
    raiment all red ?
And wherefore doth your rout send forth a joyous
    shout ?
  And whence be the grapes of the wine-press
    which ye tread ?

Oh, evil was the root, and bitter was the fruit,   5
   And crimson was the juice of the vintage that we
     trod ;
For we trampled on the throng of the haughty and
     the strong,
   Who sate in the high places, and slew the saints
     of God.

It was about the noon of a glorious day of June,
   That we saw their banners dance and their
     cuirasses shine,   10
And the Man of Blood was there, with his long
     essenced hair,
   And Astley, and Sir Marmaduke, and Rupert of
     the Rhine.

Like a servant of the Lord, with his Bible and his
     sword,
   The General rode along us to form us to the fight,
When a murmuring sound broke out, and swell'd
     into a shout,   15
   Among the godless horsemen upon the tyrant's
     right.

And hark ! like the roar of the billows on the shore,
   The cry of battle rises along their charging line !
For God ! for the Cause ! for the Church ! for the
     Laws !
   For Charles King of England, and Rupert of the
     Rhine !   20

The furious German comes, with his clarions and
     his drums,
   His bravoes of Alsatia, and pages of Whitehall ;
They are bursting on our flanks. Grasp your pikes,
     close your ranks ;
   For Rupert never comes but to conquer or to fall.

They are here ! They rush on ! We are broken !
     We are gone !   25
   Our left is borne before them like stubble on the
     blast.

O Lord, put forth thy might ! O Lord, defend the
    right !
  Stand back to back, in God's name, and fight it to
    the last.

Stout Skippon hath a wound ; the centre hath
    given ground :
  Hark ! hark !—What means the trampling of
    horsemen on our rear ?   30
Whose banner do I see, boys ? 'Tis he, thank God !
    'tis he, boys.
  Bear up another minute : brave Oliver is here.

Their heads all stooping low, their points all in a row,
  Like a whirlwind on the trees, like a deluge on the
    dykes,
Our cuirassiers have burst on the ranks of the
    Accurst,   35
  And at a shock have scattered the forest of his
    pikes.

Fast, fast, the gallants ride, in some safe nook to hide
  Their coward heads, predestined to rot on Temple
    Bar :
And he—he turns, he flies :—shame on those cruel
    eyes
  That bore to look on torture, and dare not look on
    war.   40

Ho ! comrades, scour the plain ; and, ere ye strip
    the slain,
  First give another stab to make your search secure,
Then shake from sleeves and pockets their broad-
    pieces and lockets,
  The tokens of the wanton, the plunder of the poor.

Fools ! your doublets shone with gold, and your
    hearts were gay and bold,   45
  When you kissed your lily hands to your lemans
    to-day ;
And to-morrow shall the fox, from her chambers in
    the rocks,
  Lead forth her tawny cubs to howl above the prey.

Where be your tongues that late mocked at heaven
    and hell and fate,
  And the fingers that once were so busy with your
    blades, 50
Your perfum'd satin clothes, your catches and your
    oaths,
  Your stage-plays and your sonnets, your
    diamonds and your spades?

Down, down, for ever down with the mitre and the
    crown,
  With the Belial of the Court, and the Mammon of
    the Pope;
There is woe in Oxford Halls; there is wail in
    Durham's Stalls: 55
  The Jesuit smites his bosom; the Bishop rends
    his cope.

And She of the seven hills shall mourn her children's
    ills,
  And tremble when she thinks on the edge of
    England's sword;
And the Kings of earth in fear shall shudder when
    they hear
  What the hand of God hath wrought for the
    Houses and the Word. 60

                LORD MACAULAY.

302

BLACKMWORE MAIDENS

The primrwose in the sheäde do blow,
  The cowslip in the zun,
The thyme upon the down do grow,
  The clote where streams do run;
An' where do pretty maïdens grow 5
  An' blow, but where the tow'r
Do rise among the bricken tuns,
  In Blackmwore by the Stour?

If you could zee their comely gaït,
  An' pretty feäces' smiles,   10
A-trippèn on so light o' waïght,
  An' steppèn off the stiles ;
A-gwaïn to church, as bells do swing
  An' ring within the tow'r,
You'd own the pretty maïdens' pleäce   15
  Is Blackmwore by the Stour.

If you vrom Wimborne took your road,
  To Stower or Paladore,
An' all the farmers' housen show'd
  Their daeters at the door ;   20
You'd cry to bachelors at hwome—
  ' Here, come : 'ithin an hour
You'll vind ten maïdens to your mind,
  In Blackmwore by the Stour.'

An' if you looked 'ithin their door,   25
  To zee em in their pleäce,
A-doèn housework up avore
  Their smilèn mother's feäce ;
You'd cry—' Why, if a man would wive
  An' thrive, 'ithout a dow'r,   30
Then let en look en out a wife
  In Blackmwore by the Stour.'

As I upon my road did pass
  A school-house back in Maÿ
There out upon the beäten grass   35
  Wer maïdens at their plaÿ ;
An' as the pretty souls did twile
  An' smile, I cried, ' The flow'r
O' beauty, then, is still in bud
  In Blackmwore by the Stour.'   40

                  W. BARNES.

303

THE WIFE A-LOST

Since I noo mwore do zee your feäce,
  Up steärs or down below,
I'll zit me in the lwonesome pleäce,
  Where flat-bough'd beech do grow;
Below the beeches' bough, my love,   5
  Where you did never come,
An' I don't look to meet ye now,
  As I do look at hwome.

Since you noo mwore be at my zide,
  In walks in zummer het,   10
I'll goo alwone where mist do ride,
  Droo trees a-drippèn wet;
Below the raïn-wet bough, my love,
  Where you did never come,
An' I don't grieve to miss ye now,   15
  As I do grieve at hwome.

Since now bezide my dinner-bwoard
  Your vaïce do never sound,
I'll eat the bit I can avword
  A-vield upon the ground;   20
Below the darksome bough, my love,
  Where you did never dine,
An' I don't grieve to miss ye now,
  As I at hwome do pine.

Since I do miss your vaïce an' feäce   25
  In praÿer at eventide,
I'll praÿ wi' oone sad vaïce vor greäce
  To goo where you do bide;
Above the tree an' bough, my love,
  Where you be gone avore,   30
An' be a-waïtèn vor me now,
  To come vor evermwore.

                    W. BARNES.

304

THE NAMELESS ONE

Roll forth, my song, like the rushing river,
  That sweeps along to the mighty sea ;
God will inspire me while I deliver
    My soul of thee !

Tell thou the world, when my bones lie whitening
  Amid the last homes of youth and eld,   6
That once there was one whose veins ran lightning
    No eye beheld.

Tell how his boyhood was one drear night-hour,
  How shone for him, through his griefs and gloom,
No star of all heaven sends to light our   11
    Path to the tomb.

Roll on, my song, and to after ages
  Tell how, disdaining all earth can give,
He would have taught men, from wisdom's pages,
    The way to live.   16

And tell how trampled, derided, hated,
  And worn by weakness, disease, and wrong,
He fled for shelter to God, who mated
    His soul with song—   20

With song which alway, sublime or vapid,
  Flowed like a rill in the morning-beam,
Perchance not deep, but intense and rapid—
    A mountain stream.

Tell how this Nameless, condemned for years long
  To herd with demons from hell beneath,   26
Saw things that made him, with groans and tears, long
    For even death.

Go on to tell how, with genius wasted,
  Betrayed in friendship, befooled in love,   30
With spirit shipwrecked, and young hopes blasted,
    He still, still strove ;

Till spent with toil, dreeing death for others,
　　And some whose hands should have wrought for
　　　　him
(If children live not for sires and mothers),　　35
　　His mind grew dim ;

And he fell far through that pit abysmal,
　　The gulf and grave of Maginn and Burns,
And pawned his soul for the devil's dismal
　　Stock of returns ;　　　　　　　　　　40

But yet redeemed it in days of darkness,
　　And shapes and signs of the final wrath,
When death, in hideous and ghastly starkness,
　　Stood on his path.

And tell how now, amid wreck and sorrow,　　45
　　And want, and sickness, and houseless nights,
He bides in calmness the silent morrow,
　　That no ray lights.

And lives he still, then ? Yes ! Old and hoary
　　At thirty-nine, from despair and woe,　　50
He lives, enduring what future story
　　Will never know.

Him grant a grave to, ye pitying noble,
　　Deep in your bosoms : there let him dwell !
He, too, had tears for all souls in trouble　　55
　　Here, and in hell.

　　　　　　　　　　　J. C. MANGAN.

305

BRAHMA

If the red slayer think he slays,
　　Or if the slain think he is slain,
They know not well the subtle ways
　　I keep, and pass, and turn again.

Far or forgot to me is near ;　　　　　　5
　　Shadow and sunlight are the same ;
The vanished gods to me appear ;
　　And one to me are shame and fame.

They reckon ill who leave me out ;
  When me they fly, I am the wings ;   10
I am the doubter and the doubt,
  And I the hymn the Brahmin sings.

The strong gods pine for my abode,
  And pine in vain the sacred Seven ;
But thou, meek lover of the good !   15
  Find me, and turn thy back on heaven.

                  R. W. EMERSON.

306

TO EVA

O fair and stately maid, whose eyes
Were kindled in the upper skies
  At the same torch that lighted mine ;
For so I must interpret still
Thy sweet dominion o'er my will,   5
  A sympathy divine.

Ah ! let me blameless gaze upon
Features that seem at heart my own ;
  Nor fear those watchful sentinels,
Who charm the more their glance forbids.   10
Chaste-glowing, underneath their lids,
  With fire that draws while it repels.

                  R. W. EMERSON.

307

AND SHALL TRELAWNY DIE ?

A good sword and a trusty hand !
  A merry heart and true !
King James's men shall understand
  What Cornish lads can do.

And have they fixed the where and when ?
  And shall Trelawny die ?   6
Here's twenty thousand Cornish men
  Will know the reason why !

Out spake their captain brave and bold,
  A merry wight was he :   10
' If London Tower were Michael's hold,
  We'll set Trelawny free !

' We'll cross the Tamar, land to land,
  The Severn is no stay,—
With " one and all," and hand in hand,   15
  And who shall bid us nay ?

' And when we come to London Wall,
  A pleasant sight to view,
Come forth ! Come forth, ye cowards all,
  Here 's men as good as you.   20

' Trelawny he 's in keep and hold
  Trelawny he may die ;—
But here 's twenty thousand Cornish bold
  Will know the reason why ! '

R. S. Hawker.

308

THE SHANDON BELLS

With deep affection,
And recollection,
I often think of
    Those Shandon bells,
Whose sounds so wild would,   5
In the days of childhood,
Fling round my cradle
    Their magic spells.
On this I ponder
Where'er I wander,   10
And thus grow fonder,
    Sweet Cork, of thee ;
With thy bells of Shandon,
That sound so grand on
The pleasant waters   15
    Of the River Lee.

I've heard bells chiming
Full many a clime in,
Tolling sublime in
    Cathedral shrine, 20
While at a glibe rate
Brass tongues would vibrate—
But all their music
    Spoke naught like thine;
For memory, dwelling 25
On each proud swelling
Of thy belfrey knelling
    Its bold notes free,
Made the bells of Shandon
Sound far more grand on 30
The pleasant waters
    Of the River Lee.
I've heard bells tolling
Old Adrian's Mole in,
Their thunder rolling 35
    From the Vatican,
And cymbals glorious
Swinging uproarious
In the gorgeous turrets
    Of Notre Dame; 40
But thy sounds were sweeter
Than the dome of Peter
Flings o'er the Tiber,
    Pealing solemnly;—
O! the bells of Shandon 45
Sound far more grand on
The pleasant waters
    Of the River Lee.
There's a bell in Moscow,
While on tower and kiosk O 50
In Saint Sophia
    The Turkman gets;
And loud in air
Calls men to prayer
From the tapering summit 55
    Of tall minarets.

Such empty phantom
I freely grant them ;
But there is an anthem
　　More dear to me,— 　　　　60
'Tis the bells of Shandon
That sound so grand on
The pleasant waters
　　Of the River Lee.

　　　F. MAHONY (FATHER PROUT).

309

FROM 'SONNETS FROM THE PORTUGUESE'

I thought once how Theocritus had sung
　　Of the sweet years, the dear and wished-for years,
　　Who each one in a gracious hand appears
To bear a gift for mortals, old or young :
And, as I mused it in his antique tongue, 　　　5
　　I saw, in gradual vision through my tears,
　　The sweet, sad years, the melancholy years,
Those of my own life, who by turns had flung
A shadow across me. Straightway I was 'ware,
　　So weeping, how a mystic Shape did move 　　10
Behind me, and drew me backward by the hair ;
　　And a voice said in mastery, while I strove, . . .
' Guess now who holds thee ? '—' Death,' I said.
　　　But there,
　　The silver answer rang, . . . ' Not Death, but
　　　Love.'

310

What can I give thee back, O liberal
　　And princely giver, who hast brought the gold
　　And purple of thine heart, unstained, untold,
And laid them on the outside of the wall
For such as I to take or leave withal, 　　　5
　　In unexpected largesse ? am I cold,
　　Ungrateful, that for these most manifold
High gifts, I render nothing back at all ?

Not so ; not cold,—but very poor instead.
    Ask God who knows. For frequent tears have run
The colours from my life, and left so dead   11
    And pale a stuff, it were not fitly done
To give the same as pillow to thy head.
    Go farther ! let it serve to trample on.

311

Yet love, mere love, is beautiful indeed
    And worthy of acceptation. Fire is bright,
    Let temple burn, or flax. An equal light
Leaps in the flame from cedar-plank or weed.
And love is fire ; and when I say at need   5
    I love thee . . . mark ! . . . *I love thee !* . . . in thy sight
    I stand transfigured, glorified aright,
With conscience of the new rays that proceed
Out of my face toward thine. There 's nothing low
    In love, when love the lowest : meanest creatures
Who love God, God accepts while loving so.   11
    And what I *feel*, across the inferior features
Of what I *am*, doth flash itself, and show
    How that great work of Love enhances Nature's.

312

If thou must love me, let it be for naught
    Except for love's sake only. Do not say
    ' I love her for her smile . . . her look . . . her way
Of speaking gently, . . . for a trick of thought
That falls in well with mine, and certes brought
    A sense of pleasant ease on such a day '—   6
    For these things in themselves, Belovéd, may
Be changed, or change for thee,—and love, so wrought,
May be unwrought so. Neither love me for
    Thine own dear pity's wiping my cheeks dry,—
A creature might forget to weep, who bore
    Thy comfort long, and lose thy love thereby !
But love me for love's sake, that evermore
    Thou mayst love on, through love's eternity.

313

How do I love thee ? Let me count the ways.
  I love thee to the depth and breadth and height
  My soul can reach, when feeling out of sight
For the ends of Being and ideal Grace.
I love thee to the level of every day's   5
  Most quiet need, by sun and candlelight.
  I love thee freely, as men strive for Right ;
I love thee purely, as they turn from Praise.
I love thee with the passion put to use
  In my old griefs, and with my childhood's faith.
I love thee with a love I seemed to lose   11
  With my lost saints,—I love thee with the breath,
Smiles, tears, of all my life !—and, if God choose
  I shall but love thee better after death.

E. B. BROWNING.

314

A MUSICAL INSTRUMENT

What was he doing, the great god Pan,
    Down in the reeds by the river ?
Spreading ruin and scattering ban,
    Splashing and paddling with hoofs of a goat,
    And breaking the golden lilies afloat   5
      With the dragon-fly on the river.

He tore out a reed, the great god Pan,
    From the deep cool bed of the river :
The limpid water turbidly ran,
    And the broken lilies a-dying lay,   10
    And the dragon-fly had fled away,
      Ere he brought it out of the river.

High on the shore sate the great god Pan,
    While turbidly flowed the river ;
And hacked and hewed as a great god can,   15
    With his hard bleak steel at the patient reed,
    Till there was not a sign of a leaf indeed
      To prove it fresh from the river.

He cut it short, did the great god Pan
    (How tall it stood in the river !),   20
Then drew the pith, like the heart of a man,
    Steadily from the outside ring,
    And notched the poor dry empty thing
      In holes, as he sate by the river.

' This is the way,' laughed the great god Pan
    (Laughed while he sate by the river),   26
' The only way, since gods began
    To make sweet music, they could succeed.'
    Then, dropping his mouth to a hole in the reed,
      He blew in power by the river.   30

Sweet, sweet, sweet, O Pan !
    Piercing sweet by the river !
Blinding sweet, O great god Pan !
    The sun on the hill forgot to die,
    And the lilies revived, and the dragon-fly   35
      Came back to dream on the river.

Yet half a beast is the great god Pan,
    To laugh as he sits by the river,
Making a poet out of a man :   39
    The true gods sigh for the cost and pain,—
    For the reed which grows nevermore again
      As a reed with the reeds in the river.
                E. B. BROWNING.

315

THE SLAVE'S DREAM

Beside the ungathered rice he lay,
    His sickle in his hand ;
His breast was bare, his matted hair
    Was buried in the sand.
    Again, in the mist and shadow of sleep,   5
    He saw his Native Land.

Wide through the landscape of his dreams
   The lordly Niger flowed;
Beneath the palm-trees on the plain
   Once more a king he strode;   10
And heard the tinkling caravans
   Descend the mountain-road.

He saw once more his dark-eyed queen
   Among her children stand;
They clasped his neck, they kissed his cheeks,
   They held him by the hand!—   16
A tear burst from the sleeper's lids
   And fell into the sand.

And then at furious speed he rode
   Along the Niger's bank;   20
His bridle-reins were golden chains,
   And, with a martial clank,
At each leap he could feel his scabbard of steel
   Smiting his stallion's flank.

Before him, like a blood-red flag,   25
   The bright flamingoes flew;
From morn till night he followed their flight,
   O'er plains where the tamarind grew,
Till he saw the roofs of Caffre huts,
   And the ocean rose to view.   30

At night he heard the lion roar,
   And the hyena scream,
And the river-horse, as he crushed the reeds
   Beside some hidden stream;
And it passed, like a glorious roll of drums,   35
   Through the triumph of his dream.

The forests, with their myriad tongues,
   Shouted of liberty;
And the Blast of the Desert cried aloud,
   With a voice so wild and free,   40
That he started in his sleep and smiled
   At their tempestuous glee.

He did not feel the driver's whip,
  Nor the burning heat of day ;
For Death had illumined the Land of Sleep,
  And his lifeless body lay   46
A worn-out fetter, that the soul
  Had broken and thrown away !

                    H. W. LONGFELLOW.

316

THE ARSENAL AT SPRINGFIELD

This is the Arsenal. From floor to ceiling,
  Like a huge organ, rise the burnished arms ;
But from their silent pipes no anthem pealing
  Startles the villages with strange alarms.   4

Ah ! what a sound will rise, how wild and dreary,
  When the death-angel touches those swift keys !
What loud lament and dismal Miserere
  Will mingle with their awful symphonies !

I hear even now the infinite fierce chorus,
  The cries of agony, the endless groan,   10
Which, through the ages that have gone before us,
  In long reverberations reach our own.

On helm and harness rings the Saxon hammer,
  Through Cimbric forest roars the Norseman's
    song,
And loud, amid the universal clamour,   15
  O'er distant deserts sounds the Tartar gong.

I hear the Florentine, who from his palace
  Wheels out his battle-bell with dreadful din,
And Aztec priests upon their teocallis   19
  Beat the wild war-drums made of serpent's skin ;

The tumult of each sacked and burning village ;
  The shout that every prayer for mercy drowns ;
The soldiers' revels in the midst of pillage ;
  The wail of famine in beleaguered towns ;

The bursting shell, the gateway wrenched asunder,
   The rattling musketry, the clashing blade ;   26
And ever and anon, in tones of thunder,
   The diapason of the cannonade.

Is it, O man, with such discordant noises,
   With such accursed instruments as these,   30
Thou drownest Nature's sweet and kindly voices,
   And jarrest the celestial harmonies ?

Were half the power that fills the world with terror,
   Were half the wealth bestowed on camps and
      courts,
Given to redeem the human mind from error,   35
   There were no need of arsenals or forts :

The warrior's name would be a name abhorrèd !
   And every nation that should lift again
Its hand against a brother, on its forehead   39
   Would wear for evermore the curse of Cain

Down the dark future, through long generations,
   The echoing sounds grow fainter and then cease ;
And like a bell, with solemn, sweet vibrations,
   I hear once more the voice of Christ say, ' Peace ! '

Peace ! and no longer from its brazen portals   45
   The blast of War's great organ shakes the skies !
But beautiful as songs of the immortals,
   The holy melodies of love arise.

H. W. LONGFELLOW.

317

CHILDREN

Come to me, O ye children !
   For I hear you at your play,
And the questions that perplexed me
   Have vanished quite away.

Ye open the eastern windows,   5
   That look towards the sun,
Where thoughts are singing swallows,
   And the brooks of morning run.

In your hearts are the birds and the sunshine,
  In your thoughts the brooklet's flow ;   10
But in mine is the wind of Autumn,
  And the first fall of the snow.

Ah ! what would the world be to us
  If the children were no more ?
We should dread the desert behind us   15
  Worse than the dark before.

What the leaves are to the forest,
  With light and air for food,
Ere their sweet and tender juices
  Have been hardened into wood,   20

That to the world are children ;
  Through them it feels the glow
Of a brighter and sunnier climate
  Than reaches the trunks below.

Come to me, O ye children !   25
  And whisper in my ear
What the birds and the winds are singing
  In your sunny atmosphere.

For what are all our contrivings,
  And the wisdom of our books,   30
When compared with your caresses,
  And the gladness of your looks ?

Ye are better than all the ballads
  That ever were sung or said ;
For ye are living poems,   35
  And all the rest are dead.

H. W. LONGFELLOW.

318

I do not love thee !—no ! I do not love thee !
And yet when thou art absent I am sad ;
  And envy even the bright blue sky above thee,
Whose quiet stars may see thee and be glad.

I do not love thee !—yet, I know not why,   5
Whate'er thou dost seems still well done, to me :
   And often in my solitude I sigh
That those I do love are not more like thee !

I do not love thee !—yet, when thou art gone,
I hate the sound (though those who speak be dear)
   Which breaks the lingering echo of the tone   1J
Thy voice of music leaves upon my ear.

I do not love thee !—yet thy speaking eyes,
With their deep, bright, and most expressive blue,
   Between me and the midnight heaven arise,   15
Oftener than any eyes I ever knew.

I know I do not love thee ! yet, alas !
Others will scarcely trust my candid heart ;
   And oft I catch them smiling as they pass,
Because they see me gazing where thou art.   20

               CAROLINE E. S. NORTON.

319

RUBÁIYÁT OF OMAR KHAYYÁM OF NAISHÁPÚR

1

Awake ! for Morning in the Bowl of Night
Has flung the Stone that puts the Stars to Flight :
   And Lo ! the Hunter of the East has caught
The Sultan's Turret in a Noose of Light.

2

Dreaming when Dawn's Left Hand was in the Sky
I heard a Voice within the Tavern cry,   6
   ' Awake, my Little ones, and fill the Cup
' Before Life's Liquor in its Cup be dry.'

3

And, as the Cock crew, those who stood before
The Tavern shouted—' Open then the Door !   10
   ' You know how little while we have to stay,
And, once departed, may return no more.'

4

Now the New Year reviving old Desires,
The thoughtful Soul to Solitude retires,
   Where the WHITE HAND OF MOSES on the Bough
Puts out, and Jesus from the ground suspires. 16

5

Irám indeed is gone with all its Rose,
And Jamshýd's Sev'n-ring'd Cup where no one
     knows ;
   But still the Vine her ancient Ruby yields,
And still a Garden by the Water blows.   20

6

And David's Lips are lock't ; but in divine
High-piping Péhleví, with ' Wine ! Wine ! Wine !
   ' *Red* Wine ! '—the Nightingale cries to the Rose
That yellow Cheek of hers to incarnadine.

7

Come, fill the Cup, and in the Fire of Spring   25
The Winter Garment of Repentance fling :
   The Bird of Time has but a little way
To fly—and Lo ! the Bird is on the Wing.

8

And look—a thousand Blossoms with the Day
Woke—and a thousand scatter'd into Clay :   30
   And this first Summer Month that brings the Rose
Shall take Jamshýd and Kaikobád away.

9

But come with old Khayyám, and leave the Lot
Of Kaikobád and Kaikhosrú forgot :
   Let Rustum lay about him as he will,   35
Or Hátim Tai cry Supper—heed them not.

10

With me along some Strip of Herbage strown,
That just divides the desert from the sown,
   Where name of Slave and Sultán scarce is known,
And pity Sultán Máhmúd on his Throne.   40

11

Here with a Loaf of Bread beneath the Bough,
A Flask of Wine, a Book of Verse—and Thou
   Beside me singing in the Wilderness—
And Wilderness is Paradise enow.   44

12

' How sweet is mortal Sovranty ! '—think some :
Others—' How blest the Paradise to come ! '
   Ah, take the Cash in hand and waive the Rest ;
Oh, the brave Music of a *distant* Drum !

13

Look to the Rose that blows about us—' Lo,
' Laughing,' she says, ' into the World I blow :
   ' At once the silken Tassel of my Purse   51
' Tear, and its Treasure on the Garden throw.'

14

The Worldly Hope men set their Hearts upon
Turns Ashes—or it prospers ; and anon,
   Like Snow upon the Desert's dusty Face   55
Lighting a little Hour or two—is gone.

15

And those who husbanded the Golden Grain,
And those who flung it to the Winds like Rain,
   Alike to no such aureate Earth are turn'd
As, buried once, Men want dug up again.   60

16

Think, in this batter'd Caravanserai
Whose Doorways are alternate Night and Day,
   How Sultán after Sultán with his Pomp
Abode his Hour or two, and went his way.

17

They say the Lion and the Lizard keep   65
The Courts where Jamshýd gloried and drank deep:
   And Bahrám, that great Hunter—the Wild Ass
Stamps o'er his Head, and he lies fast asleep.

18

I sometimes think that never blows so red
The Rose as where some buried Caesar bled ; 70
   That every Hyacinth the Garden wears
Dropt in its Lap from some once lovely Head.

19

And this delightful Herb whose tender Green
Fledges the River's Lip on which we lean—
   Ah, lean upon it lightly ! for who knows 75
From what once lovely Lip it springs unseen !

20

Ah, my Belovéd, fill the Cup that clears
To-DAY of past Regrets and future Fears—
   To-morrow ?—Why, To-morrow I may be
Myself with Yesterday's Sev'n Thousand Years.

21

Lo ! some we loved, the loveliest and best 81
That Time and Fate of all their Vintage prest,
   Have drunk their Cup a Round or two before,
And one by one crept silently to Rest.

22

And we, that now make merry in the Room 85
They left, and Summer dresses in new Bloom,
   Ourselves must we beneath the Couch of Earth
Descend, ourselves to make a Couch—for whom ?

23

Ah, make the most of what we yet may spend,
Before we too into the Dust descend ; 90
   Dust into Dust, and under Dust, to lie,
Sans Wine, sans Song, sans Singer, and—sans End !

24

Alike for those who for To-DAY prepare,
And those that after a To-MORROW stare,
   A Muezzín from the Tower of Darkness cries, 95
' Fools ! your Reward is neither Here nor There ! '

25

Why, all the Saints and Sages who discuss'd
Of the Two Worlds so learnedly, are thrust   98
   Like foolish Prophets forth; their Words to Scorn
Are scatter'd and their Mouths are stopt with Dust.

26

Oh, come with old Khayyám, and leave the Wise
To talk; one thing is certain, that Life flies;
   One thing is certain, and the Rest is Lies;
The Flower that once has blown for ever dies.

27

Myself when young did eagerly frequent   105
Doctor and Saint, and heard great Argument
   About it and about: but evermore
Came out by the same Door as in I went.

28

With them the Seed of Wisdom did I sow,
And with my own hand labour'd it to grow: 110
   And this was all the Harvest that I reap'd—
' I came like Water, and like Wind I go.'

29

Into this Universe, and *why* not knowing,
Nor *whence*, like Water willy-nilly flowing:
   And out of it, as Wind along the Waste,   115
I know not *whither*, willy-nilly blowing.

30

What, without asking, hither hurried *whence?*
And, without asking, *whither* hurried hence!
   Another and another Cup to drown
The Memory of this Impertinence!   120

31

Up from Earth's Centre, through the Seventh Gate
I rose, and on the Throne of Saturn sate,
   And many Knots unravel'd by the Road;
But not the Knot of Human Death and Fate.

32

There was a Door to which I found no Key : 125
There was a Veil past which I could not see :
   Some little Talk awhile of ME and THEE
There seem'd—and then no more of THEE and ME.

33

Then to the rolling Heav'n itself I cried,
Asking, ' What Lamp had Destiny to guide 130
   ' Her little Children stumbling in the Dark ? '
And—' A blind Understanding ! ' Heav'n replied.

34

Then to this earthen Bowl did I adjourn
My Lip the secret Well of Life to learn : 134
   And Lip to Lip it murmur'd—' While you live
' Drink !—for once dead you never shall return.'

35

I think the Vessel, that with fugitive
Articulation answer'd, once did live,
   And merry-make ; and the cold Lip I kiss'd,
How many Kisses might it take—and give ! 140

36

For in the Market-place, one Dusk of Day,
I watch'd the Potter thumping his wet Clay :
   And with its all obliterated Tongue
It murmur'd—' Gently, Brother, gently, pray !

37

Ah, fill the Cup :—what boots it to repeat 145
How Time is slipping underneath our Feet :
   Unborn TO-MORROW and dead YESTERDAY,
Why fret about them if TO-DAY be sweet !

38

One Moment in Annihilation's Waste,
One Moment, of the Well of Life to taste— 150
   The Stars are setting and the Caravan
Starts for the Dawn of Nothing—Oh, make haste !

39

How long, how long, in infinite Pursuit
Of This and That endeavour and dispute ?
    Better be merry with the fruitful Grape   155
Than sadden after none, or bitter, Fruit.

40

You know, my Friends, how long since in my House
For a new Marriage I did make Carouse :
    Divorced old barren Reason from my Bed,
And took the Daughter of the Vine to Spouse. 160

41

For ' Is ' and ' Is-not ' though *with* Rule and Line,
And ' Up-and-down ' *without*, I could define,
    I yet, in all I only cared to know,
Was never deep in anything but—Wine.

42

And lately, by the Tavern Door agape,   165
Came stealing through the Dusk an Angel Shape
    Bearing a Vessel on his Shoulder ; and
He bid me taste of it ; and 'twas—the Grape

43

The Grape that can with Logic absolute
The Two-and-Seventy jarring Sects confute :   170
    The subtle Alchemist that in a Trice
Life's leaden Metal into Gold transmute.

44

The mighty Máhmúd, the victorious Lord,
That all the misbelieving and black Horde
    Of Fears and Sorrows that infest the Soul   175
Scatters and slays with his enchanted Sword.

45

But leave the Wise to wrangle, and with me
The Quarrel of the Universe let be :
    And, in some corner of the Hubbub coucht,
Make Game of that which makes as much of Thee.

46

For in and out, above, about, below,   181
'Tis nothing but a Magic Shadow-show,
   Play'd in a Box whose Candle is the Sun,
Round which we Phantom Figures come and go.

47

And if the Wine you drink, the Lip you press,   185
End in the Nothing all Things end in—Yes—
   Then fancy while Thou art, Thou art but what
Thou shalt be—Nothing—Thou shalt not be less.

48

While the Rose blows along the River Brink,
With old Khayyám the Ruby Vintage drink :   190
   And when the Angel with his darker Draught
Draws up to Thee—take that, and do not shrink.

49

'Tis all a Chequer-board of Nights and Days
Where Destiny with Men for Pieces plays :
   Hither and thither moves, and mates, and slays,
And one by one back in the Closet lays.   196

50

The Ball no Question makes of Ayes and Noes,
But Right or Left as strikes the Player goes ;
   And He that toss'd Thee down into the Field,
He knows about it all—HE knows—HE knows !

51

The Moving Finger writes ; and, having writ,
Moves on : nor all thy Piety nor Wit   202
   Shall lure it back to cancel half a Line,
Nor all thy Tears wash out a Word of it.

52

And that inverted Bowl we call The Sky,   205
Whereunder crawling coop't we live and die,
   Lift not thy hands to *It* for help—for It
Rolls impotently on as Thou or I.

53

With Earth's first Clay They did the Last Man's
    knead,
And then of the Last Harvest sow'd the Seed:
    Yea, the first Morning of Creation wrote   211
What the Last Dawn of Reckoning shall read.

54

I tell Thee this—When, starting from the Goal,
Over the shoulders of the flaming Foal
    Of Heav'n Parwín and Mushtara they flung,
In my predestin'd Plot of Dust and Soul   216

55

The Vine had struck a Fibre; which about
If clings my Being—let the Súfi flout;
    Of my Base Metal may be filed a Key,
That shall unlock the Door he howls without. 220

56

And this I know: whether the one True Light
Kindle to Love, or Wrath-consume me quite,
    One glimpse of It within the Tavern caught
Better than in the Temple lost outright.

57

Oh, Thou, who didst with Pitfall and with Gin 225
Beset the Road I was to wander in,
    Thou wilt not with Predestination round
Enmesh me, and impute my Fall to Sin?

58

Oh, Thou, who Man of baser Earth didst make,
And who with Eden didst devise the Snake; 230
    For all the Sin wherewith the Face of Man
Is blacken'd, Man's Forgiveness give—and take!

KÚZA-NÁMA

59

Listen again. One evening at the Close
Of Ramazán, ere the better Moon arose,
    In that old Potter's Shop I stood alone 235
With the clay Population round in Rows.

60

And, strange to tell, among that Earthen Lot
Some could articulate, while others not :
 And suddenly one more impatient cried— 239
' Who *is* the Potter, pray, and who the Pot ? '

61

Then said another—' Surely not in vain
' My Substance from the common Earth was ta'en,
 ' That He who subtly wrought me into Shape
' Should stamp me back to common Earth again.'

62

Another said—' Why, ne'er a peevish Boy, 245
' Would break the Bowl from which he drank in Joy ;
 ' Shall He that *made* the Vessel in pure Love
' And Fancy, in an after Rage destroy ! '

63

None answer'd this ; but after Silence spake
A Vessel of a more ungainly Make : 250
 ' They sneer at me for leaning all awry ;
' What ! did the Hand then of the Potter shake ? '

64

Said one—' Folks of a surly Tapster tell,
' And daub his Visage with the Smoke of Hell ;
 ' They talk of some strict Testing of us—Pish !
' He's a Good Fellow, and 'twill all be well.' 256

65

Then said another with a long-drawn Sigh,
' My Clay with long oblivion is gone dry :
 ' But, fill me with the old familiar Juice,
' Methinks I might recover by and by ! ' 260

66

So while the Vessels one by one were speaking,
One spied the little Crescent all were seeking :
 And then they jogg'd each other, ' Brother,
  Brother !
' Hark to the Porter's Shoulder-knot a-creaking ! '

67

Ah, with the Grape my fading Life provide,   265
And wash my Body whence the Life has died,
  And in a Winding-sheet of Vine-leaf wrapt,
So bury me by some sweet Garden-side.

68

That ev'n my buried Ashes such a Snare
Of Perfume shall fling up into the Air,   270
  As not a True Believer passing by
But shall be overtaken unaware.

69

Indeed the Idols I have loved so long
Have done my Credit in Men's Eye much wrong :
  Have drown'd my Honour in a shallow Cup,
And sold my Reputation for a Song.   276

70

Indeed, indeed, Repentance oft before
I swore—but was I sober when I swore ?
  And then and then came Spring, and Rose-in-hand
My thread-bare Penitence apieces tore.   280

71

And much as Wine has play'd the Infidel,
And robb'd me of my Robe of Honour—well,
  I often wonder what the Vintners buy
One-half so precious as the Goods they sell.   284

72

Alas, that Spring should vanish with the Rose :
That Youth's sweet-scented Manuscript should
      close !
  The Nightingale that in the Branches sang,
Ah, whence, and whither flown again, who knows !

73

Ah, Love ! could thou and I with Fate conspire
To grasp this sorry Scheme of Things entire,   290
  Would not we shatter it to bits—and then
Re-mould it nearer to the Heart's Desire !

74

Ah, Moon of my Delight who know'st no wane,
The Moon of Heav'n is rising once again :
　　How oft hereafter rising shall she look   295
Through this same Garden after me—in vain !

75

And when Thyself with shining Foot shall pass
Among the Guests Star-scatter'd on the Grass,
　　And in thy joyous Errand reach the Spot   299
Where I made one—turn down an empty Glass !

TAMAM SHUD.

E. FITZGERALD.

320

THE CHAMBERED NAUTILUS

This is the ship of pearl, which, poets feign,
　　Sails the unshadowed main,—
　　　The venturous bark that flings
On the sweet summer wind its purpled wings
In gulfs enchanted, where the siren sings,   5
　　And coral reefs lie bare,
Where the cold sea-maids rise to sun their streaming
　　　hair.

Its webs of living gauze no more unfurl ;
　　Wrecked is the ship of pearl !
　　　And every chambered cell,   10
Where its dim dreaming life was wont to dwell,
As the frail tenant shaped his growing shell,
　　Before thee lies revealed—
Its irised ceiling rent, its sunless crypt unsealed !

Year after year beheld the silent toil   15
　　That spread his lustrous coil ;
　　　Still, as the spiral grew,
He left the past year's dwelling for the new,
Stole with soft step its shining archway through,
　　Built up its idle door,   20
Stretched in his last-found home, and knew the old
　　　no more.

Thanks for the heavenly message brought by thee,
　　Child of the wandering sea,
　　Cast from her lap forlorn !
From thy dead lips a clearer note is born　　25
Than ever Triton blew from wreathéd horn !
　　While on mine ear it rings,
Through the deep caves of thought I hear a voice
　　　　that sings :—

Build thee more stately mansions, O my soul,
　　As the swift seasons roll !　　　　　　30
　　Leave thy low-vaulted past !
Let each new temple, nobler than the last,
Shut thee from heaven with a dome more vast,
　　Till thou at length art free,　　　　34
Leaving thine outgrown shell by life's unresting sea.

O. W. HOLMES.

321

THE MEN OF OLD

I know not that the men of old
　　Were better than men now,
Of heart more kind, of hand more bold,
　　Of more ingenuous brow :
I heed not those who pine for force　　5
　　A ghost of Time to raise,
As if they thus could check the course
　　Of these appointed days.

Still it is true, and over true,
　　That I delight to close　　　　　10
This book of life self-wise and new,
　　And let my thoughts repose
On all that humble happiness,
　　The world has since forgone,—
The daylight of contentedness　　15
　　That on those faces shone !

With rights, tho' not too closely scanned,
　　Enjoyed, as far as known,—
With will by no reverse unmanned,—
　　With pulse of even tone,—　　　20

They from to-day and from to-night
    Expected nothing more,
Than yesterday and yesternight
    Had proffered them before.

To them was life a simple art   25
    Of duties to be done,
A game where each man took his part,
    A race where all must run ;
A battle whose great scheme and scope
    They little cared to know,   30
Content, as men at arms, to cope
    Each with his fronting foe.

Man *now* his Virtue's diadem
    Puts on and proudly wears,
Great thoughts, great feelings, came to them,
    Like instincts, unawares :   36
Blending their souls' sublimest needs
    With tasks of every day,
They went about their gravest deeds,
    As noble boys at play.—   40

And what if Nature's fearful wound
    They did not probe and bare,
For that their spirits never swooned
    To watch the misery there,—
For that their love but flowed more fast,   45
    Their charities more free,
Not conscious what mere drops they cast
    Into the evil sea.

A man's best things are nearest him,
    Lie close about his feet,   50
It is the distant and the dim
    That we are sick to greet :
For flowers that grow our hands beneath
    We struggle and aspire,—
Our hearts must die, except they breathe   55
    The air of fresh Desire.

Yet, Brothers, who up Reason's hill
　　Advance with hopeful cheer,—
O ! loiter not, those heights are chill,
　　As chill as they are clear ;　　　　　　60
And still restrain your haughty gaze,
　　The loftier that ye go,
Remembering distance leaves a haze
　　On all that lies below.

LORD HOUGHTON.

322

THE MILLER'S DAUGHTER

It is the miller's daughter,
　　And she is grown so dear, so dear,
That I would be the jewel
　　That trembles at her ear :
For hid in ringlets day and night,　　　　5
I'd touch her neck so warm and white.

And I would be the girdle
　　About her dainty dainty waist,
And her heart would beat against me
　　In sorrow and in rest :　　　　　　　10
And I should know if it beat right,
I'd clasp it round so close and tight.

And I would be the necklace,
　　And all day long to fall and rise
Upon her balmy bosom,　　　　　　　15
　　With her laughter or her sighs,
And I would lie so light, so light,
I scarce should be unclasp'd at night.

LORD TENNYSON.

323

ST. AGNES' EVE

Deep on the convent-roof the snows
 Are sparkling to the moon :
My breath to heaven like vapour goes :
 May my soul follow soon !
The shadows of the convent-towers   5
 Slant down the snowy sward,
Still creeping with the creeping hours
 That lead me to my Lord :
Make Thou my spirit pure and clear
 As are the frosty skies,   10
Or this first snowdrop of the year
 That in my bosom lies.

As these white robes are soil'd and dark,
 To yonder shining ground ;
As this pale taper's earthly spark,   15
 To yonder argent round ;
So shows my soul before the Lamb,
 My spirit before Thee ;
So in mine earthly house I am,
 To that I hope to be.   20
Break up the heavens, O Lord ! and far,
 Thro' all yon starlight keen,
Draw me, thy bride, a glittering star,
 In raiment white and clean.

He lifts me to the golden doors ;   25
 The flashes come and go ;
All heaven bursts her starry floors,
 And strows her lights below,
And deepens on and up ! the gates
 Roll back, and far within   30
For me the Heavenly Bridegroom waits,
 To make me pure of sin.
The sabbaths of Eternity,
 One sabbath deep and wide—
A light upon the shining sea—   35
 The Bridegroom with his bride
        LORD TENNYSON.

324

SIR GALAHAD

My good blade carves the casques of men,
  My tough lance thrusteth sure,
My strength is as the strength of ten,
  Because my heart is pure.
The shattering trumpet shrilleth high,   5
  The hard brands shiver on the steel,
The splinter'd spear-shafts crack and fly,
  The horse and rider reel:
They reel, they roll in clanging lists,
  And when the tide of combat stands,   10
Perfume and flowers fall in showers,
  That lightly rain from ladies' hands.

How sweet are looks that ladies bend
  On whom their favours fall!
For them I battle till the end,   15
  To save from shame and thrall:
But all my heart is drawn above,
  My knees are bow'd in crypt and shrine:
I never felt the kiss of love,
  Nor maiden's hand in mine.   20
More bounteous aspects on me beam,
  Me mightier transports move and thrill;
So keep I fair thro' faith and prayer
  A virgin heart in work and will.

When down the stormy crescent goes,   25
  A light before me swims,
Between dark stems the forest glows,
  I hear a noise of hymns:
Then by some secret shrine I ride;
  I hear a voice, but none are there;   30
The stalls are void, the doors are wide,
  The tapers burning fair.
Fair gleams the snowy altar-cloth,
  The silver vessels sparkle clean,

The shrill bell rings, the censer swings, 35
  And solemn chaunts resound between.

Sometimes on lonely mountain-meres
  I find a magic bark ;
I leap on board : no helmsman steers :
  I float till all is dark. 40
A gentle sound, an awful light !
  Three angels bear the holy Grail :
With folded feet, in stoles of white,
  On sleeping wings they sail.
Ah, blessed vision ! blood of God ! 45
  My spirit beats her mortal bars,
As down dark tides the glory slides,
  And star-like mingles with the stars.

When on my goodly charger borne
  Thro' dreaming towns I go, 50
The cock crows ere the Christmas morn,
  The streets are dumb with snow.
The tempest crackles on the leads,
  And, ringing, springs from brand and mail ;
But o'er the dark a glory spreads, 55
  And gilds the driving hail.
I leave the plain, I climb the height ;
  No branchy thicket shelter yields ;
But blessed forms in whistling storms
  Fly o'er waste fens and windy fields. 60

A maiden knight—to me is given
  Such hope, I know not fear ;
I yearn to breathe the airs of heaven
  That often meet me here.
I muse on joy that will not cease, 65
  Pure spaces clothed in living beams,
Pure lilies of eternal peace,
  Whose odours haunt my dreams ;
And, stricken by an angel's hand,
  This mortal armour that I wear, 70
This weight and size, this heart and eyes,
  Are touch'd, are turn'd to finest air.

The clouds are broken in the sky,
 And thro' the mountain-walls
A rolling organ-harmony
 Swells up, and shakes and falls.
Then move the trees, the copses nod,
 Wings flutter, voices hover clear :
' O just and faithful knight of God !
 Ride on ! the prize is near.'   80
So pass I hostel, hall, and grange ;
 By bridge and ford, by park and pale,
All-arm'd I ride, whate'er betide,
 Until I find the holy Grail.

Lord Tennyson.

325

BREAK, BREAK, BREAK

Break, break, break,
 On thy cold grey stones, O Sea !
And I would that my tongue could utter
 The thoughts that arise in me.

O well for the fisherman's boy,   5
 That he shouts with his sister at play !
O well for the sailor lad,
 That he sings in his boat on the bay !

And the stately ships go on
 To their haven under the hill ; 10
But O for the touch of a vanish'd hand,
 And the sound of a voice that is still !

Break, break, break,
 At the foot of thy crags, O Sea ! 14
But the tender grace of a day that is dead
 Will never come back to me.

Lord Tennyson.

326

THE BROOK

I come from haunts of coot and hern,
    I make a sudden sally
And sparkle out among the fern,
    To bicker down a valley.

By thirty hills I hurry down,   5
    Or slip between the ridges,
By twenty thorps, a little town,
    And half a hundred bridges.

Till last by Philip's farm I flow
    To join the brimming river,   10
For men may come and men may go,
    But I go on for ever.

I chatter over stony ways,
    In little sharps and trebles,
I bubble into eddying bays,   15
    I babble on the pebbles.

With many a curve my banks I fret
    By many a field and fallow,
And many a fairy foreland set
    With willow-weed and mallow.   20

I chatter, chatter, as I flow
    To join the brimming river,
For men may come and men may go,
    But I go on for ever.

I wind about, and in and out,   25
    With here a blossom sailing,
And here and there a lusty trout,
    And here and there a grayling,

And here and there a foamy flake
    Upon me, as I travel   30
With many a silvery waterbreak
    Above the golden gravel,

And draw them all along, and flow
  To join the brimming river,
For men may come and men may go,   35
  But I go on for ever.

I steal by lawns and grassy plots,
  I slide by hazel covers;
I move the sweet forget-me-nots
  That grow for happy lovers.   40

I slip, I slide, I gloom, I glance,
  Among my skimming swallows;
I make the netted sunbeam dance
  Against my sandy shallows.

I murmur under moon and stars   45
  In brambly wildernesses;
I linger by my shingly bars;
  I loiter round my cresses;

And out again I curve and flow
  To join the brimming river,   50
For men may come and men may go,
  But I go on for ever.

              LORD TENNYSON.

327

As thro' the land at eve we went,
  And pluck'd the ripen'd ears,
We fell out, my wife and I,
We fell out, I know not why,
  And kiss'd again with tears.   5

And blessings on the falling out
  That all the more endears,
When we fall out with those we love
  And kiss again with tears!

For when we came where lies the child   10
  We lost in other years,
There above the little grave,
O there above the little grave,
  We kiss'd again with tears.

              LORD TENNYSON.

328

The splendour falls on castle walls
    And snowy summits old in story :
The long light shakes across the lakes,
    And the wild cataract leaps in glory.
Blow, bugle, blow, set the wild echoes flying,   5
Blow, bugle ; answer, echoes, dying, dying, dying.

O hark, O hear ! how thin and clear,
    And thinner, clearer, farther going !
O sweet and far from cliff and scar
    The horns of Elfland faintly blowing !   10
Blow, let us hear the purple glens replying :
Blow, bugle ; answer, echoes, dying, dying, dying.

O love, they die in yon rich sky,
    They faint on hill or field or river :
Our echoes roll from soul to soul,   15
    And grow for ever and for ever.
Blow, bugle, blow, set the wild echoes flying,
And answer echoes, answer dying, dying, dying.

LORD TENNYSON.

329

Tears, idle tears, I know not what they mean,
Tears from the depth of some divine despair
Rise in the heart, and gather to the eyes,
In looking on the happy Autumn-fields,
And thinking of the days that are no more.   5

Fresh as the first beam glittering on a sail,
That brings our friends up from the underworld,
Sad as the last which reddens over one
That sinks with all we love below the verge ;
So sad, so fresh, the days that are no more.   10

Ah, sad and strange as in dark summer dawns
The earliest pipe of half-awaken'd birds

To dying ears, when unto dying eyes   13
The casement slowly grows a glimmering square ;
So sad, so strange, the days that are no more.

   Dear as remember'd kisses after death,
And sweet as those by hopeless fancy feign'd
On lips that are for others ; deep as love,
Deep as first love, and wild with all regret ;
O Death in Life, the days that are no more.   20

LORD TENNYSON.

330

   O Swallow, Swallow, flying, flying South,
Fly to her, and fall upon her gilded eaves,
And tell her, tell her what I tell to thee.

   O tell her, Swallow, thou that knowest each,
That bright and fierce and fickle is the South,   5
And dark and true and tender is the North.

   O Swallow, Swallow, if I could follow, and light
Upon her lattice, I would pipe and trill,
And cheep and twitter twenty million loves.

   O were I thou that she might take me in,   10
And lay me on her bosom, and her heart
Would rock the snowy cradle till I died.

   Why lingereth she to clothe her heart with love,
Delaying as the tender ash delays   14
To clothe herself, when all the woods are green ?

   O tell her, Swallow, that thy brood is flown :
Say to her, I do but wanton in the South,
But in the North long since my nest is made.

   O tell her, brief is life but love is long,
And brief the sun of summer in the North,   20
And brief the moon of beauty in the South.

   O Swallow, flying from the golden woods,
Fly to her, and pipe and woo her, and make her mine,
And tell her, tell her, that I follow thee.

LORD TENNYSON.

331

Now sleeps the crimson petal, now the white ;
Nor waves the cypress in the palace walk ;
Nor winks the gold fin in the porphyry font :
The fire-fly wakens : waken thou with me.

Now droops the milkwhite peacock like a ghost,
And like a ghost she glimmers on to me.   6

Now lies the Earth all Danaë to the stars,
And all thy heart lies open unto me.

Now slides the silent meteor on, and leaves
A shining furrow, as thy thoughts in me.   10

Now folds the lily all her sweetness up,
And slips into the bosom of the lake :
So fold thyself, my dearest, thou, and slip
Into my bosom and be lost in me.

LORD TENNYSON.

332

Come down, O maid, from yonder mountain height:
What pleasure lives in height (the Shepherd sang),
In height and cold, the splendour of the hills ?
But cease to move so near the Heavens, and cease
To glide a sunbeam by the blasted Pine,   5
To sit a star upon the sparkling spire ;
And come, for Love is of the valley, come,
For Love is of the valley, come thou down
And find him ; by the happy threshold, he,
Or hand in hand with Plenty in the maize,   10
Or red with spirted purple of the vats,
Or foxlike in the vine ; nor cares to walk
With Death and Morning on the silver horns,
Nor wilt thou snare him in the white ravine,
Nor find him dropt upon the firths of ice,   15
That huddling slant in furrow-cloven falls
To roll the torrent out of dusky doors :

But follow ; let the torrent dance thee down
To find him in the valley ; let the wild
Lean-headed Eagles yelp alone, and leave   20
The monstrous ledges there to slope, and spill
Their thousand wreaths of dangling water-smoke,
That like a broken purpose waste in air :
So waste not thou ; but come ; for all the vales
Await thee ; azure pillars of the hearth   25
Arise to thee ; the children call, and I
Thy shepherd pipe, and sweet is every sound,
Sweeter thy voice, but every sound is sweet ;
Myriads of rivulets hurrying thro' the lawn,
The moan of doves in immemorial elms,   30
And murmuring of innumerable bees.

LORD TENNYSON.

333

FROM 'IN MEMORIAM'

Ring out, wild bells, to the wild sky,
    The flying cloud, the frosty light :
    The year is dying in the night ;
Ring out, wild bells, and let him die.

Ring out the old, ring in the new,   5
    Ring, happy bells, across the snow :
    The year is going, let him go ;
Ring out the false, ring in the true.

Ring out the grief that saps the mind,
    For those that here we see no more ;   10
    Ring out the feud of rich and poor,
Ring in redress to all mankind.

Ring out a slowly dying cause,
    And ancient forms of party strife ;
    Ring in the nobler modes of life,   15
With sweeter manners, purer laws.

Ring out the want, the care, the sin,
 The faithless coldness of the times ;
 Ring out, ring out my mournful rhymes,
But ring the fuller minstrel in.   20

Ring out false pride in place and blood,
 The civic slander and the spite ;
 Ring in the love of truth and right,
Ring in the common love of good.

Ring out old shapes of foul disease ; 25
 Ring out the narrowing lust of gold ;
 Ring out the thousand wars of old,
Ring in the thousand years of peace.

Ring in the valiant man and free,
 The larger heart, the kindlier hand , 30
 Ring out the darkness of the land,
Ring in the Christ that is to be.

LORD TENNYSON.

334

Come into the garden, Maud,
 For the black bat, night, has flown,
Come into the garden, Maud,
 I am here at the gate alone ;
And the woodbine spices are wafted abroad, 5
 And the musk of the roses blown.

For a breeze of morning moves,
 And the planet of Love is on high,
Beginning to faint in the light that she loves
 On a bed of daffodil sky, 10
To faint in the light of the sun she loves,
 To faint in his light, and to die.

All night have the roses heard
 The flute, violin, bassoon ;
All night has the casement jessamine stirr'd 15
 To the dancers dancing in tune ;
Till a silence fell with the waking bird,
 And a hush with the setting moon.

I said to the lily, ' There is but one
   With whom she has heart to be gay.   20
When will the dancers leave her alone ?
   She is weary of dance and play.'
Now half to the setting moon are gone,
   And half to the rising day;
Low on the sand and loud on the stone   25
   The last wheel echoes away.

I said to the rose, ' The brief night goes
   In babble and revel and wine.
O young lord-lover, what sighs are those,
   For one that will never be thine ?   30
But mine, but mine,' so I sware to the rose,
   ' For ever and ever, mine.'

And the soul of the rose went into my blood,
   As the music clash'd in the hall ;
And long by the garden lake I stood,   35
   For I heard your rivulet fall
From the lake to the meadow and on to the wood,
   Our wood, that is dearer than all ;

From the meadow your walks have left so sweet
   That whenever a March-wind sighs   40
He sets the jewel-print of your feet
   In violets blue as your eyes,
To the woody hollows in which we meet
   And the valleys of Paradise.

The slender acacia would not shake   45
   One long milk-bloom on the tree ;
The white lake-blossom fell into the lake,
   As the pimpernel dozed on the lea ;
But the rose was awake all night for your sake,
   Knowing your promise to me ;   50
The lilies and roses were all awake,
   They sigh'd for the dawn and thee.

Queen rose of the rosebud garden of girls,
   Come hither, the dances are done,

In gloss of satin and glimmer of pearls,   55
   Queen lily and rose in one ;
Shine out, little head, sunning over with curls,
   To the flowers, and be their sun.

There has fallen a splendid tear
   From the passion-flower at the gate.   60
She is coming, my dove, my dear ;
   She is coming, my life, my fate ;
The red rose cries, ' She is near, she is near ;
   And the white rose weeps, ' She is late ; '
The larkspur listens, ' I hear, I hear ; '   65
   And the lily whispers, ' I wait.'

She is coming, my own, my sweet ;
   Were it ever so airy a tread,
My heart would hear her and beat,
   Were it earth in an earthy bed ;   70
My dust would hear her and beat,
   Had I lain for a century dead ;
Would start and tremble under her feet,
   And blossom in purple and red.

LORD TENNYSON.

335

In Love, if Love be Love, if Love be ours,
Faith and unfaith can ne'er be equal powers :
Unfaith in aught is want of faith in all.

It is the little rift within the lute,
That by and by will make the music mute,   5
And ever widening slowly silence all.

The little rift within the lover's lute,
Or little pitted speck in garner'd fruit,
That rotting inward slowly moulders all.

It is not worth the keeping : let it go :   10
But shall it ? answer, darling, answer, no.
And trust me not at all or all in all.

LORD TENNYSON.

336

THE PRIVATE OF THE BUFFS

Some Sikhs and a private of the Buffs having remained behind with the grog carts, fell into the hands
of the Chinese. On the next morning they were
brought before the authorities, and commanded to
perform the *Kotow*. The Sikhs obeyed; but Moyse,
the English soldier, declaring that he would not
prostrate himself before any Chinaman alive, was
immediately knocked upon the head, and his body
thrown on a dunghill.—*The Times*.

Last night, among his fellow roughs,
    He jested, quaffed, and swore,
A drunken private of the Buffs,
    Who never looked before.
To-day, beneath the foeman's frown, 5
    He stands in Elgin's place,
Ambassador from Britain's crown,
    And type of all her race.

Poor, reckless, rude, low-born, untaught,
    Bewildered, and alone, 10
A heart, with English instinct fraught,
    He yet can call his own.
Aye, tear his body limb from limb,
    Bring cord, or axe, or flame :
He only knows, that not through *him* 15
    Shall England come to shame.

Far Kentish hop-fields round him seem'd,
    Like dreams, to come and go ;
Bright leagues of cherry-blossom gleam'd,
    One sheet of living snow ; 20
The smoke, above his father's door,
    In grey soft eddyings hung :
Must he then watch it rise no more,
    Doom'd by himself so young ?

Yes, honour calls !—with strength like steel
   He put the vision by.   26
Let dusky Indians whine and kneel ;
   An English lad must die.
And thus, with eyes that would not shrink,
   With knee to man unbent,   30
Unfaltering on its dreadful brink,
   To his red grave he went.

Vain, mightiest fleets of iron framed ;
   Vain, those all-shattering guns ;
Unless proud England keep, untamed,   35
   The strong heart of her sons.
So, let his name through Europe ring—
   A man of mean estate,
Who died, as firm as Sparta's King,
   Because his soul was great.   40

              Sir F. H. Doyle.

337

A CHRISTMAS HYMN

It was the calm and silent night !—
   Seven hundred years and fifty-three
Had Rome been growing up to might,
   And now was Queen of land and sea !
No sound was heard of clashing wars ;   5
   Peace brooded o'er the hushed domain ;
Apollo, Pallas, Jove and Mars,
   Held undisturbed their ancient reign,
      In the solemn midnight
         Centuries ago !   10

'Twas in the calm and silent night !
   The senator of haughty Rome
Impatient urged his chariot's flight
   From lordly revel rolling home !

Triumphal arches gleaming swell   15
   His breast with thoughts of boundless sway:
What recked the Roman what befell
   A paltry province far away,
     In the solemn midnight
      Centuries ago !   20

Within that province far away
   Went plodding home a weary boor :
A streak of light before him lay,
   Fall'n through a half-shut stable door
Across his path. He passed—for naught   25
   Told what was going on within ;
How keen the stars ! his only thought ;
   The air how calm and cold and thin,
     In the solemn midnight
      Centuries ago !   30

O strange indifference !—low and high
   Drowsed over common joys and cares :
The earth was still—but knew not why ;
   The world was listening—unawares ;
How calm a moment may precede   35
   One that shall thrill the world for ever !
To that still moment none would heed,
   Man's doom was linked no more to sever
     In the solemn midnight
      Centuries ago !   40

It is the calm and solemn night !
   A thousand bells ring out, and throw
Their joyous peals abroad, and smite
   The darkness, charmed and holy now !
The night that erst no name had worn,   45
   To it a happy name is given ;
For in that stable lay new-born
   The peaceful Prince of Earth and Heaven,
     In the solemn midnight
      Centuries ago.   50
                A. DOMETT.

338

The year 's at the spring,
 And day 's at the morn ;
Morning 's at seven ;
 The hill-side 's dew-pearled ;
The lark 's on the wing ;   5
 The snail 's on the thorn :
God 's in his heaven—
 All 's right with the world !

       R. BROWNING.

339

Give her but a least excuse to love me !
  When—where—
How—can this arm establish her above me,
 If fortune fixed her as my lady there,
There already, to eternally reprove me ? 5
  ('Hist !'—said Kate the queen ;
But 'Oh '—cried the maiden, binding her tresses
 ''Tis only a page that carols unseen,
'Crumbling your hounds their messes !')

Is she wronged ?—To the rescue of her honour, 10
  My heart !
Is she poor ?—What costs it to be styled a donor ?
 Merely an earth to cleave, a sea to part.
But that fortune should have thrust all this upon
  her !
  ('Nay, list !'—bade Kate the queen ; 15
And still cried the maiden, binding her tresses,
 ''Tis only a page that carols unseen,
'Fitting your hawks their jesses !')

       R. BROWNING.

340

THE LOST LEADER

Just for a handful of silver he left us,
 Just for a riband to stick in his coat—
Found the one gift of which fortune bereft us,
 Lost all the others she lets us devote ;

They, with the gold to give, doled him out silver,
    So much was theirs who so little allowed :   6
How all our copper had gone for his service !
    Rags—were they purple, his heart had been
      proud !
We that had loved him so, followed him, honoured him,
    Lived in his mild and magnificent eye,   10
Learned his great language, caught his clear accents,
    Made him our pattern to live and to die !
Shakespeare was of us, Milton was for us,
    Burns, Shelley, were with us,—they watch from
      their graves !
He alone breaks from the van and the freemen,
    He alone sinks to the rear and the slaves !   16

We shall march prospering,—not thro' his presence;
    Songs may inspirit us,—not from his lyre ;
Deeds will be done,—while he boasts his quiescence,
    Still bidding crouch whom the rest bade aspire :
Blot out his name, then, record one lost soul more,
    One task more declined, one more footpath untrod,
One more devils'-triumph and sorrow for angels,
    One wrong more to man, one more insult to God!
Life's night begins : let him never come back to us!
    There would be doubt, hesitation, and pain,   26
Forced praise on our part—the glimmer of twilight,
    Never glad confident morning again !
Best fight on well, for we taught him,—strike
      gallantly,
    Menace our heart ere we master his own ;   30
Then let him receive the new knowledge and wait us,
    Pardoned in heaven, the first by the throne !

                  R. BROWNING.

341

HOME-THOUGHTS, FROM ABROAD

Oh, to be in England now that April 's there,
And whoever wakes in England sees, some morn-
    ing, unaware,

That the lowest boughs and the brushwood sheaf
Round the elm-tree bole are in tiny leaf,   4
While the chaffinch sings on the orchard bough
    In England—now!

And after April, when May follows,
And the whitethroat builds, and all the swallows!
Hark, where my blossomed pear-tree in the hedge
  Leans to the field and scatters on the clover
Blossoms and dewdrops—at the bent spray's edge—
  That 's the wise thrush; he sings each song twice
    over,   12
Lest you should think he never could recapture
  The first fine careless rapture!
And though the fields look rough with hoary dew,
All will be gay when noontide wakes anew   16
The buttercups, the little children's dower
—Far brighter than this gaudy melon-flower!

R. BROWNING.

342

HOME-THOUGHTS, FROM THE SEA

Nobly, nobly Cape Saint Vincent to the North-West
  died away;
Sunset ran, one glorious blood-red, reeking into
  Cadiz Bay;
Bluish mid the burning water, full in face Trafalgar
  lay;
In the dimmest North-East distance, dawned
  Gibraltar grand and grey;
'Here and here did England help me: how can I
  help England?'—say,   5
Whoso turns as I, this evening, turn to God to
  praise and pray,
While Jove's planet rises yonder, silent over Africa.

R. BROWNING.

343

MISCONCEPTIONS

This is a spray the Bird clung to,
  Making it blossom with pleasure,
Ere the high tree-top she sprung to,
  Fit for her nest and her treasure.
    Oh, what a hope beyond measure   5
Was the poor spray's, which the flying feet hung to,—
So to be singled out, built in, and sung to!

This is a heart the Queen leant on,
  Thrilled in a minute erratic,
Ere the true bosom she bent on,   10
  Meet for love's regal dalmatic.
    Oh, what a fancy ecstatic
Was the poor heart's, ere the wanderer went on—
Love to be saved for it, proffered to, spent on!

                              R. BROWNING.

344

A WOMAN'S LAST WORD

Let 's contend no more, Love,
    Strive nor weep:
All be as before, Love,
    —Only sleep!

What so wild as words are?   5
    I and thou
In debate, as birds are,
    Hawk on bough!

See the creature stalking
    While we speak!   10
Hush and hide the talking,
    Cheek on cheek!

What so false as truth is,
    False to thee?
Where the serpent's tooth is,   15
    Shun the tree—

Where the apple reddens
  Never pry—
Lest we lose our Edens,
  Eve and I.   20

Be a god and hold me
  With a charm !
Be a man and fold me
  With thine arm !

Teach me, only teach, Love !   25
  As I ought
I will speak thy speech, Love,
  Think thy thought—

Meet, if thou require it,
  Both demands,   30
Laying flesh and spirit
  In thy hands.

That shall be to-morrow
  Not to-night :
I must bury sorrow   35
  Out of sight :

—Must a little weep, Love,
  (Foolish me !)
And so fall asleep, Love,
  Loved by thee.   40
                              R. BROWNING.

345
LIFE IN A LOVE

Escape me ?
  Never—
  Beloved !
While I am I, and you are you,
  So long as the world contains us both,   5
  Me the loving and you the loath,
While the one eludes, must the other pursue.
My life is a fault at last, I fear :

It seems too much like a fate, indeed !
 Though I do my best I shall scarce succeed. 10
But what if I fail of my purpose here ?
It is but to keep the nerves at strain,
 To dry one's eyes and laugh at a fall,
And baffled, get up and begin again,—
 So the chace takes up one's life, that 's all. 15
While, look but once from your farthest bound
 At me so deep in the dust and dark,
No sooner the old hope goes to ground
 Than a new one, straight to the selfsame mark,
  I shape me—   20
  Ever
  Removed !   R. BROWNING.

346

A GRAMMARIAN'S FUNERAL

SHORTLY AFTER THE REVIVAL OF LEARNING IN EUROPE

Let us begin and carry up this corpse,
 Singing together.
Leave we the common crofts, the vulgar thorpes,
 Each in its tether
Sleeping safe on the bosom of the plain, 5
 Cared-for till cock-crow :
Look out if yonder be not day again
 Rimming the rock-row !
That 's the appropriate country ; there, man's thought,
 Rarer, intenser, 10
Self-gathered for an outbreak, as it ought,
 Chafes in the censer.
Leave we the unlettered plain its herd and crop ;
 Seek we sepulture
On a tall mountain, citied to the top, 15
 Crowded with culture !
All the peaks soar, but one the rest excels ;
 Clouds overcome it ;

No, yonder sparkle is the citadel's
  Circling its summit. 20
Thither our path lies ; wind we up the heights :
  Wait ye the warning ?
Our low life was the level's and the night's ;
  He 's for the morning.
Step to a tune, square chests, erect each head, 25
  'Ware the beholders !
This is our master, famous, calm, and dead,
  Borne on our shoulders.

Sleep, crop and herd! sleep, darkling thorpe and croft,
  Safe from the weather ! 30
He, whom we convoy to his grave aloft,
  Singing together,
He was a man born with thy face and throat,
  Lyric Apollo !
Long he lived nameless: how should spring take note
  Winter would follow ? 36
Till lo, the little touch, and youth was gone !
  Cramped and diminished,
Moaned he, ' New measures, other feet anon !
  My dance is finished ' ? 40
No, that 's the world's way: (keep the mountain-side,
  Make for the city !)
He knew the signal, and stepped on with pride
  Over men's pity ;
Left play for work, and grappled with the world
  Bent on escaping : 46
'What's in the scroll,' quoth he, 'thou keepest furled ?
  Show me their shaping,
Theirs, who most studied man, the bard and sage,—
  Give ! '—So, he gowned him, 50
Straight got by heart that book to its last page :
  Learned, we found him.
Yea, but we found him bald too, eyes like lead,
  Accents uncertain :
' Time to taste life,' another would have said, 55
  ' Up with the curtain ! '—
This man said rather, ' Actual life comes next ?
  Patience a moment !

Grant I have mastered learning's crabbed text,
    Still, there's the comment.   60
Let me know all ! Prate not of most or least,
    Painful or easy !
Even to the crumbs I'd fain eat up the feast,
    Aye, nor feel queasy.'
Oh, such a life as he resolved to live,   65
    When he had learned it,
When he had gathered all books had to give !
    Sooner, he spurned it.
Image the whole, then execute the parts—   70
    Fancy the fabric
Quite, ere you build, ere steel strike fire from quartz,
    Ere mortar dab brick !

(Here's the town-gate reached : there's the market-
      place
    Gaping before us.)
Yea, this in him was the peculiar grace   75
    (Hearten our chorus !)
That before living he'd learn how to live—
    No end to learning :
Earn the means first—God surely will contrive
    Use for our earning.   80
Others mistrust and say, ' But time escapes :
    Live now or never !'
He said, 'What's time? leave Now for dogs and apes!
    Man has Forever.'
Back to his book then : deeper drooped his head :
    Calculus racked him :   86
Leaden before, his eyes grew dross of lead :
    Tussis attacked him.
' Now, master, take a little rest !'—not he !
    (Caution redoubled,   90
Step two a-breast, the way winds narrowly !)
    Not a whit troubled,
Back to his studies, fresher than at first,
    Fierce as a dragon
He (soul-hydroptic with a sacred thirst)   95
    Sucked at the flagon.

Oh, if we draw a circle premature,
    Heedless of far gain,
Greedy for quick returns of profit, sure,
    Bad is our bargain !   100
Was it not great ? did not he throw on God,
    (He loves the burthen)—
God's task to make the heavenly period
    Perfect the earthen ?
Did not he magnify the mind, show clear   105
    Just what it all meant ?
He would not discount life, as fools do here,
    Paid by instalment.
He ventured neck or nothing—heaven's success
    Found, or earth's failure :   110
'Wilt thou trust death or not ?' He answered 'Yes!
    Hence with life's pale lure !'
That low man seeks a little thing to do,
    Sees it and does it :
This high man, with a great thing to pursue,   115
    Dies ere he knows it.
That low man goes on adding one to one,
    His hundred 's soon hit :
This high man, aiming at a million,
    Misses an unit.   120
That, has the world here—should he need the next,
    Let the world mind him !
This, throws himself on God, and unperplexed
    Seeking shall find him.
So, with the throttling hands of death at strife,
    Ground he at grammar ;   126
Still, thro' the rattle, parts of speech were rife :
    While he could stammer
He settled *Hoti's* business—let it be !—
    Properly based *Oun*—   130
Gave us the doctrine of the enclitic *De*,
    Dead from the waist down.
Well, here 's the platform, here 's the proper place :
    Hail to your purlieus,
All ye highfliers of the feathered race,   135
    Swallows and curlews !

Here's the top-peak; the multitude below
    Live, for they can, there :
This man decided not to Live but Know—
    Bury this man there ?   140
Here—here's his place, where meteors shoot, clouds
    form,
    Lightnings are loosened,
Stars come and go ! Let joy break with the storm,
    Peace let the dew send !
Lofty designs must close in like effects :   145
    Loftily lying,
Leave him—still loftier than the world suspects,
    Living and dying.

               R. BROWNING.

347

PORPHYRIA'S LOVER

The rain set early in to-night,
    The sullen wind was soon awake,
It tore the elm-tops down for spite,
    And did its worst to vex the lake :
I listened with heart fit to break,   5
When glided in Porphyria ; straight
    She shut the cold out and the storm,
And kneeled and made the cheerless grate
    Blaze up, and all the cottage warm ;
Which done, she rose, and from her form
Withdrew the dripping cloak and shawl,   11
    And laid her soiled gloves by, untied
Her hat and let the damp hair fall,
    And, last, she sat down by my side
And called me.   When no voice replied,   15
She put my arm about her waist,
    And made her smooth white shoulder bare,
And all her yellow hair displaced,
    And, stooping, made my cheek lie there,
And spread o'er all her yellow hair,   20
Murmuring how she loved me—she
    Too weak, for all her heart's endeavour,

To set its struggling passion free
  From pride, and vainer ties dissever,
  And give herself to me for ever. 25
But passion sometimes would prevail,
  Nor could to-night's gay feast restrain
A sudden thought of one so pale
  For love of her, and all in vain:
So, she was come through wind and rain.
Be sure I looked up at her eyes 31
  Happy and proud; at last I knew
Porphyria worshipped me; surprise
  Made my heart swell, and still it grew
While I debated what to do. 35
That moment she was mine, mine, fair
  Perfectly pure and good: I found
A thing to do, and all her hair
  In one long yellow string I wound
Three times her little throat around, 40
And strangled her. No pain felt she;
  I am quite sure she felt no pain.
As a shut bud that holds a bee,
  I warily oped her lids: again
Laughed the blue eyes without a stain. 45
And I untightened next the tress
  About her neck; her cheek once more
Blushed bright beneath my burning kiss:
  I propped her head up as before,
Only, this time my shoulder bore 50
Her head, which droops upon it still:
  The smiling rosy little head,
So glad it has its utmost will,
  That all it scorned at once is fled,
And I, its love, am gained instead! 55
Porphyria's love: she guessed not how
  Her darling one wish would be heard.
And thus we sit together now,
  And all night long we have not stirred,
And yet God has not said a word! 60

R. BROWNING.

348

RABBI BEN EZRA

1

Grow old along with me !
The best is yet to be,
The last of life, for which the first was made :
Our times are in His hand
Who saith ' A whole I planned,   5
Youth shows but half ; trust God : see all, nor be
    afraid ! '

2

Not that, amassing flowers,
Youth sighed ' Which rose make ours,
Which lily leave and then as best recall ? '
Not that, admiring stars,
It yearned ' Nor Jove, nor Mars ;   10
Mine be some figured flame which blends, tran-
    scends them all ! '

3

Not for such hopes and fears
Annulling youth's brief years,
Do I remonstrate : folly wide the mark !   15
Rather I prize the doubt
Low kinds exist without,
Finished and finite clods, untroubled by a spark.

4

Poor vaunt of life indeed,
Were man but formed to feed   20
On joy, to solely seek and find and feast :
Such feasting ended, then
As sure an end to men ;
Irks care the crop-full bird ? Frets doubt the
    maw-crammed beast ?

5

  Rejoice we are allied   25
  To That which doth provide
And not partake, effect and not receive !
  A spark disturbs our clod ;
  Nearer we hold of God
Who gives, than of His tribes that take, I must
   believe.   30

6

  Then, welcome each rebuff
  That turns earth's smoothness rough,
Each sting that bids nor sit nor stand but go !
  Be our joys three-parts pain !
  Strive, and hold cheap the strain ; 35
Learn, nor account the pang ; dare, never grudge
   the throe !

7

  For thence,—a paradox
  Which comforts while it mocks,—
Shall life succeed in that it seems to fail :
  What I aspired to be,   40
  And was not, comforts me :
A brute I might have been, but would not sink i'
   the scale.

8

  What is he but a brute
  Whose flesh hath soul to suit,
Whose spirit works lest arms and legs want play?
  To man, propose this test—   46
  Thy body at its best,
How far can that project thy soul on its lone way ?

9

  Yet gifts should prove their use :
  I own the Past profuse   50
Of power each side, perfection every turn :
  Eyes, ears took in their dole,
  Brain treasured up the whole ;
Should not the heart beat once ' How good to live
   and learn ' ?

10

Not once beat ' Praise be Thine !   55
I see the whole design,
I, who saw power, see now Love perfect too :
Perfect I call Thy plan :
Thanks that I was a man !
Maker, remake, complete,—I trust what Thou
shalt do !'   60

11

For pleasant is this flesh ;
Our soul in its rose-mesh
Pulled ever to the earth, still yearns for rest :
Would we some prize might hold
To match those manifold   65
Possessions of the brute,—gain most, as we did best!

12

Let us not always say
' Spite of this flesh to-day
I strove, made head, gained ground upon the
whole !'
As the bird wings and sings,   70
Let us cry ' All good things
Are ours, nor soul helps flesh more, now, than flesh
helps soul !'

13

Therefore I summon age
To grant youth's heritage,
Life's struggle having so far reached its term :   75
Thence shall I pass, approved
A man, for ay removed
From the developed brute; a God though in the germ.

14

And I shall thereupon
Take rest, ere I be gone   80
Once more on my adventure brave and new :
Fearless and unperplexed,
When I wage battle next,
What weapons to select, what armour to indue.

15

Youth ended, I shall try 85
  My gain or loss thereby ;
Leave the fire ashes, what survives is gold :
  And I shall weigh the same,
  Give life its praise or blame :
Young, all lay in dispute ; I shall know, being old.

16

For note, when evening shuts, 91
  A certain moment cuts
The deed off, calls the glory from the grey :
  A whisper from the west
  Shoots—' Add this to the rest, 95
Take it and try its worth : here dies another day.'

17

So, still within this life,
  Though lifted o'er its strife,
Let me discern, compare, pronounce at last,
  ' This rage was right i' the main, 100
  That acquiescence vain :
The Future I may face now I have proved the Past.'

18

For more is not reserved
  To man, with soul just nerved
To act to-morrow what he learns to-day : 105
  Here, work enough to watch
  The Master work, and catch
Hints of the proper craft, tricks of the tool's true
    play.

19

As it was better, youth
  Should strive, through acts uncouth, 110
Toward making, than repose on aught found made;
  So, better, age, exempt
  From strife, should know, than tempt
Further. Thou waitedst age ; wait death nor be
    afraid !

20

Enough now, if the Right 115
And Good and Infinite
Be named here, as thou callest thy hand thine own,
With knowledge absolute,
Subject to no dispute
From fools that crowded youth, nor let thee feel
alone. 120

21

Be there, for once and all,
Severed great minds from small,
Announced to each his station in the Past !
Was I, the world arraigned,
Were they, my soul disdained, 125
Right ?   Let age speak the truth and give us peace
at last !

22

Now, who shall arbitrate ?
Ten men love what I hate,
Shun what I follow, slight what I receive ;
Ten, who in ears and eyes 130
Match me : we all surmise,
They, this thing, and I, that : whom shall my soul
believe ?

23

Not on the vulgar mass
Called ' work,' must sentence pass,
Things done, that took the eye and had the price ;
O'er which, from level stand, 136
The low world laid its hand,
Found straightway to its mind, could value in a
trice :

24

But all, the world's coarse thumb
And finger failed to plumb, 140
So passed in making up the main account ;
All instincts immature,
All purposes unsure,
That weighed not as his work, yet swelled the man's
amount :

25

Thoughts hardly to be packed 145
 Into a narrow act,
Fancies that broke through language and escaped ;
 All I could never be,
 All, men ignored in me.
This, I was worth to God, whose wheel the pitcher
  shaped. 150

26

Aye, note that Potter's wheel,
 That metaphor ! and feel
Why time spins fast, why passive lies our clay,—
 Thou, to whom fools propound,
 When the wine makes its round, 155
' Since life fleets, all is change ; the Past gone, seize
  to-day ! '

27

Fool ! All that is, at all,
 Lasts ever, past recall ;
Earth changes, but thy soul and God stand sure :
 What entered into thee, 160
 That was, is, and shall be :
Time's wheel runs back or stops ; Potter and clay
  endure.

28

He fixed thee mid this dance
 Of plastic circumstance,
This Present, thou, forsooth, wouldst fain arrest :
 Machinery just meant 166
 To give thy soul its bent,
Try thee and turn thee forth, sufficiently impressed.

29

What though the earlier grooves
 Which ran the laughing loves 170
Around thy base, no longer pause and press ?
 What though, about thy rim,
 Skull-things in order grim
Grow out, in graver mood, obey the sterner stress ?

30

Look not thou down but up!   175
    To uses of a cup,
The festal board, lamp's flash and trumpet's peal,
        The new wine's foaming flow,
        The Master's lips aglow!
Thou, heaven's consummate cup, what needst thou
        with earth's wheel?   180

31

But I need, now as then,
    Thee, God, who mouldest men;
And since, not even while the whirl was worst,
        Did I,—to the wheel of life
        With shapes and colours rife,   185
Bound dizzily,—mistake my end, to slake Thy
        thirst:

32

So, take and use Thy work!
    Amend what flaws may lurk,
What strain o' the stuff, what warpings past the
        aim!
        My times be in Thy hand!   190
        Perfect the cup as planned!
Let age approve of youth, and death complete the
        same!

R. Browning.

349

PROSPICE

Fear death?—to feel the fog in my throat,
        The mist in my face,
When the snows begin, and the blasts denote
        I am nearing the place,
The power of the night, the press of the storm, 5
        The post of the foe;
Where he stands, the Arch Fear in a visible form,
        Yet the strong man must go:

For the journey is done and the summit attained,
    And the barriers fall,   10
Though a battle's to fight ere the guerdon be gained,
    The reward of it all.

I was ever a fighter, so—one fight more,
    The best and the last!
I would hate that death bandaged my eyes, and
    forbore,   15
    And bade me creep past.

No! let me taste the whole of it, fare like my peers
    The heroes of old,
Bear the brunt, in a minute pay glad life's arrears
    Of pain, darkness and cold.   20

For sudden the worst turns the best to the brave,
    The black minute's at end,
And the elements' rage, the fiend-voices that rave,
    Shall dwindle, shall blend,
Shall change, shall become first a peace out of pain,
    Then a light, then thy breast,   26
O thou soul of my soul! I shall clasp thee again,
    And with God be the rest!

R. BROWNING.

350

THE EXECUTION OF MONTROSE

1

Come hither, Evan Cameron!
    Come, stand beside my knee—
I hear the river roaring down
    Towards the wintry sea.
There's shouting on the mountain-side,   5
    There's war within the blast—
Old faces look upon me,
    Old forms go trooping past:
I hear the pibroch wailing
    Amidst the din of fight,   10
And my dim spirit wakes again
    Upon the verge of night.

2

'Twas I that led the Highland host
 Through wild Lochaber's snows,
What time the plaided clans came down 15
 To battle with Montrose.
I've told thee how the Southrons fell
 Beneath the broad claymore,
And how we smote the Campbell clan
 By Inverlochy's shore. 20
I've told thee how we swept Dundee,
 And tamed the Lindsays' pride ;
But never have I told thee yet
 How the great Marquis died.

3

A traitor sold him to his foes ; 25
 O deed of deathless shame !
I charge thee, boy, if e'er thou meet
 With one of Assynt's name—
Be it upon the mountain's side,
 Or yet within the glen, 30
Stand he in martial gear alone,
 Or backed by arméd men—
Face him, as thou wouldst face the man
 Who wronged thy sire's renown ;
Remember of what blood thou art, 35
 And strike the caitiff down !

4

They brought him to the Watergate,
 Hard bound with hempen span,
As though they held a lion there,
 And not a fenceless man. 40
They set him high upon a cart—
 The hangman rode below—
They drew his hands behind his back,
 And bared his noble brow.
Then, as a hound is slipped from leash, 45
 They cheered the common throng,
And blew the note with yell and shout,
 And bade him pass along.

5

It would have made a brave man's heart
 Grow sad and sick that day,   50
To watch the keen malignant eyes
 Bent down on that array.
There stood the Whig west-country lords
 In balcony and bow,
There sat their gaunt and withered dames, 55
 And their daughters all a-row.
And every open window
 Was full as full might be
With black-robed Covenanting carles,
 That goodly sport to see !   60

6

But when he came, though pale and wan,
 He looked so great and high,
So noble was his manly front,
 So calm his steadfast eye ;—
The rabble rout forbore to shout,   65
 And each man held his breath,
For well they knew the hero's soul
 Was face to face with death.
And then a mournful shudder
 Through all the people crept,   70
And some that came to scoff at him
 Now turn'd aside and wept.

7

But onwards—always onwards,
 In silence and in gloom,
The dreary pageant laboured,   75
 Till it reached the house of doom.
Then first a woman's voice was heard
 In jeer and laughter loud,
And an angry cry and a hiss arose
 From the heart of the tossing crowd : 80
Then, as the Graeme looked upwards,
 He saw the ugly smile
Of him who sold his king for gold—
 The master-fiend Argyle !

8

The Marquis gazed a moment,   85
    And nothing did he say,
But the cheek of Argyle grew ghastly pale,
    And he turned his eyes away.
The painted harlot by his side,
    She shook through every limb,   90
For a roar like thunder swept the street,
    And hands were clenched at him ;
And a Saxon soldier cried aloud
    ' Back, coward, from thy place !
For seven long years thou hast not dared   95
    To look him in the face.'

9

Had I been there with sword in hand,
    And fifty Camerons by,
That day through high Dunedin's streets
    Had pealed the slogan-cry.   100
Not all their troops of trampling horse,
    Nor might of mailéd men—
Not all the rebels in the south
    Had borne us backwards then !
Once more his foot on Highland heath   105
    Had trod as free as air,
Or I, and all who bore my name,
    Been laid around him there !

10

It might not be. They placed him next
    Within the solemn hall,   110
Where once the Scottish kings were throned
    Amidst their nobles all.
But there was dust of vulgar feet
    On that polluted floor,
And perjured traitors filled the place   115
    Where good men sate before.
With savage glee came Warristoun
    To read the murderous doom ;
And then uprose the great Montrose
    In the middle of the room.   120

11

'Now, by my faith as belted knight,
    And by the name I bear,
And by the bright Saint Andrew's cross
    That waves above us there—
Yea, by a greater, mightier oath—   125
    And oh, that such should be !—
By that dark stream of royal blood
    That lies 'twixt you and me—
I have not sought in battle-field
    A wreath of such renown,   130
Nor dared I hope on my dying day
    To win the martyr's crown !

12

'There is a chamber far away
    Where sleep the good and brave,
But a better place ye have named for me   135
    Than by my father's grave.
For truth and right, 'gainst treason's might,
    This hand hath always striven,
And ye raise it up for a witness still
    In the eye of earth and heaven.   140
Then nail my head on yonder tower—
    Give every town a limb—
And God who made shall gather them :
    I go from you to Him !'

13

The morning dawned full darkly,   145
    The rain came flashing down,
And the jagged streak of the levin-bolt
    Lit up the gloomy town :
The thunder crashed across the heaven,
    The fatal hour was come ;   150
Yet ay broke in with muffled beat
    The 'larum of the drum.
There was madness on the earth below,
    And anger in the sky,
And young and old, and rich and poor,   155
    Came forth to see him die.

14

Ah, God ! that ghastly gibbet !
    How dismal 'tis to see
The great tall spectral skeleton,
    The ladder, and the tree !   160
Hark ! hark ! it is the clash of arms—
    The bells begin to toll—
' He is coming ! he is coming !
    God's mercy on his soul ! '
One last long peal of thunder—   165
    The clouds are cleared away,
And the glorious sun once more looks down
    Amidst the dazzling day.

15

' He is coming ! he is coming !'
    Like a bridegroom from his room,   170
Came the hero from his prison
    To the scaffold and the doom.
There was glory on his forehead,
    There was lustre in his eye,
And he never walked to battle   175
    More proudly than to die :
There was colour in his visage,
    Though the cheeks of all were wan,
And they marvelled as they saw him pass,
    That great and goodly man !   180

16

He mounted up the scaffold,
    And he turned him to the crowd ;
But they dared not trust the people,
    So he might not speak aloud.
But he looked upon the heavens,   185
    And they were clear and blue,
And in the liquid ether
    The eye of God shone through !
Yet a black and murky battlement
    Lay resting on the hill,   190
As though the thunder slept within—
    All else was calm and still.

17

The grim Geneva ministers
　　With anxious scowl drew near,
As you have seen the ravens flock　　195
　　Around the dying deer.
He would not deign them word nor sign,
　　But alone he bent the knee ;
And veiled his face for Christ's dear grace
　　Beneath the gallows-tree.　　200
Then radiant and serene he rose,
　　And cast his cloak away :
For he had ta'en his latest look
　　Of earth and sun and day.

18

A beam of light fell o'er him,　　205
　　Like a glory round the shriven,
And he climbed the lofty ladder
　　As it were the path to heaven.
Then came a flash from out the cloud,
　　And a stunning thunder-roll ;　　210
And no man dared to look aloft,
　　For fear was on every soul.
There was another heavy sound,
　　A hush and then a groan ;
And darkness swept across the sky—　　215
　　The work of death was done !

W. E. AYTOUN.

351

TUBAL CAIN

Old Tubal Cain was a man of might
　　In the days when Earth was young ;
By the fierce red light of his furnace bright
　　The strokes of his hammer rung ;
And he lifted high his brawny hand　　5
　　On the iron glowing clear,
Till the sparks rushed out in scarlet showers,
　　As he fashioned the sword and spear.

And he sang— Hurra for my handiwork
    Hurra for the spear and sword !   10
Hurra for the hand that shall wield them well,
    For he shall be king and lord ! '

To Tubal Cain came many a one,
    As he wrought by his roaring fire,   14
And each one prayed for a strong steel blade
    As the crown of his desire :
And he made them weapons sharp and strong,
    Till they shouted loud for glee,
And gave him gifts of pearl and gold,
    And spoils of the forest free.   20
And they sang—' Hurra for Tubal Cain,
    Who hath given us strength anew !
Hurra for the smith, hurra for the fire,
    And hurra for the metal true ! '

But a sudden change came o'er his heart,   25
    Ere the setting of the sun,
And Tubal Cain was filled with pain
    For the evil he had done ;
He saw that men, with rage and hate,
    Made war upon their kind,   30
That the land was red with the blood they shed
    In their lust for carnage, blind.
And he said—' Alas ! that ever I made,
    Or that skill of mine should plan,
The spear and the sword for men whose joy   35
    Is to slay their fellow-man.'

And for many a day old Tubal Cain
    Sat brooding o'er his woe ;
And his hand forbore to smite the ore,
    And his furnace smouldered low.   40
But he rose at last with a cheerful face,
    And a bright courageous eye,
And bared his strong right arm for work,
    While the quick flames mounted high.

And he sang—'Hurra for my handicraft!' 45
  And the red sparks lit the air;
'Not alone for the blade was the bright steel
    made.'
  And he fashioned the first ploughshare.

And men, taught wisdom from the past,
  In friendship joined their hands, 50
Hung the sword in the hall, the spear on the wall,
  And ploughed the willing lands;
And sang—'Hurra for Tubal Cain!
  Our stanch good friend is he;
And for the ploughshare and the plough 55
  To him our praise shall be.
But while oppression lifts its head,
  Or a tyrant would be lord,
Though we may thank him for the Plough,
  We'll not forget the Sword!' 60

C. MACKAY.

352

QUA CURSUM VENTUS

As ships, becalmed at eve, that lay
  With canvas drooping, side by side,
Two towers of sail at dawn of day
  Are scarce long leagues apart descried;

When fell the night, upsprung the breeze, 5
  And all the darkling hours they plied,
Nor dreamt but each the self-same seas
  By each was cleaving, side by side:

E'en so—but why the tale reveal 9
  Of those, whom year by year unchanged,
Brief absence joined anew to feel,
  Astounded, soul from soul estranged?

At dead of night their sails were filled,
  And onward each rejoicing steered—
Ah, neither blame, for neither willed, 15
  Or wist, what first with dawn appeared!

To veer, how vain ! On, onward strain,
  Brave barks ! In light, in darkness too,
Through winds and tides one compass guides—
  To that, and your own selves, be true.   20

But O blithe breeze ! and O great seas,
  Though ne'er, that earliest parting past,
On your wide plain they join again,
  Together lead them home at last.

One port, methought, alike they sought,   25
  One purpose hold where'er they fare,—
O bounding breeze, O rushing seas !
  At last, at last, unite them there !

                                A. H. CLOUGH.

                        353

Say not, the struggle naught availeth,
  The labour and the wounds are vain,
The enemy faints not, nor faileth,
  And as things have been they remain.

If hopes were dupes, fears may be liars ;   5
  It may be, in yon smoke concealed,
Your comrades chase e'en now the fliers,
  And, but for you, possess the field.

For while the tired waves, vainly breaking,
  Seem here no painful inch to gain,   10
Far back, through creeks, and inlets making,
  Comes silent, flooding in, the main.

And not by eastern windows only,
  When daylight comes, comes in the light,
In front, the sun climbs slow, how slowly,   15
  But westward, look, the land is bright.

                                A. H. CLOUGH.

354

Where lies the land to which the ship would go?
Far, far ahead, is all her seamen know.
And where the land she travels from? Away,
Far, far behind, is all that they can say.

On sunny noons upon the deck's smooth face, 5
Linked arm in arm, how pleasant here to pace;
Or, o'er the stern reclining, watch below
The foaming wake far widening as we go.

On stormy nights when wild north-westers rave,
How proud a thing to fight with wind and wave!
The dripping sailor on the reeling mast 11
Exults to bear, and scorns to wish it past.

Where lies the land to which the ship would go?
Far, far ahead, is all her seamen know.
And where the land she travels from? Away,
Far, far behind, is all that they can say. 16

A. H. CLOUGH.

355

'O MAY I JOIN THE CHOIR INVISIBLE'

Longum illud tempus, quum non ero, magis me
movet, quam hoc exiguum.—CICERO, *ad Att.* xii. 18.

O may I join the choir invisible
Of those immortal dead who live again
In minds made better by their presence: live
In pulses stirred to generosity,
In deeds of daring rectitude, in scorn 5
For miserable aims that end with self,
In thoughts sublime that pierce the night like stars,
And with their mild persistence urge man's search
To vaster issues.

O

So to live is heaven :
To make undying music in the world, 10
Breathing as beauteous order that controls
With growing sway the growing life of man.
So we inherit that sweet purity
For which we struggled, failed, and agonized
With widening retrospect that bred despair. 15
Rebellious flesh that would not be subdued,
A vicious parent shaming still its child
Poor anxious penitence, is quick dissolved ;
Its discords, quenched by meeting harmonies,
Die in the large and charitable air. 20
And all our rarer, better, truer self,
That sobbed religiously in yearning song,
That watched to ease the burthen of the world,
Laboriously tracing what must be,
And what may yet be better—saw within 25
A worthier image for the sanctuary,
And shaped it forth before the multitude
Divinely human, raising worship so
To higher reverence more mixed with love—
That better self shall live till human Time 30
Shall fold its eyelids, and the human sky
Be gathered like a scroll within the tomb
Unread for ever.
      This is life to come,
Which martyred men have made more glorious
For us who strive to follow.   May I reach 36
That purest heaven, be to other souls
The cup of strength in some great agony,
Enkindle generous ardour, feed pure love,
Beget the smiles that have no cruelty— 40
Be the sweet presence of a good diffused,
And in diffusion ever more intense.
So shall I join the choir invisible
Whose music is the gladness of the world.
                    GEORGE ELIOT.

356
AIRLY BEACON

Airly Beacon, Airly Beacon ;
  Oh the pleasant sight to see
Shires and towns from Airly Beacon,
  While my love climbed up to me !

Airly Beacon, Airly Beacon ;
  Oh the happy hours we lay
Deep in fern on Airly Beacon,
  Courting through the summer's day !

Airly Beacon, Airly Beacon ;
  Oh the weary haunt for me,
All alone on Airly Beacon,
  With his baby on my knee !

C. KINGSLEY.

357
THE SANDS OF DEE

' O Mary, go and call the cattle home,
    And call the cattle home,
    And call the cattle home
  Across the sands of Dee ';
The western wind was wild and dank with foam,
  And all alone went she.

The western tide crept up along the sand,
    And o'er and o'er the sand,
    And round and round the sand,
  As far as eye could see.
The rolling mist came down and hid the land :
  And never home came she.

' Oh ! is it weed, or fish, or floating hair—
    A tress of golden hair,
    A drownéd maiden's hair
  Above the nets at sea ?
Was never salmon yet that shone so fair
  Among the stakes on Dee.'

They rowed her in across the rolling foam,
    The cruel crawling foam,   20
    The cruel hungry foam,
  To her grave beside the sea :
But still the boatmen hear her call the cattle home
  Across the sands of Dee.

              C. KINGSLEY.

358
ODE TO THE NORTH-EAST WIND

    Welcome, wild North-easter !
      Shame it is to see
    Odes to every zephyr ;
      Ne'er a verse to thee.
    Welcome, black North-easter !   5
      O'er the German foam ;
    O'er the Danish moorlands,
      From thy frozen home.
    Tired we are of summer,
      Tired of gaudy glare,   10
    Showers soft and steaming,
      Hot and breathless air.
    Tired of listless dreaming,
      Through the lazy day :
    Jovial wind of winter,   15
      Turn us out to play !
    Sweep the golden reed-beds ;
      Crisp the lazy dyke ;
    Hunger into madness
      Every plunging pike.   20
    Fill the lake with wild-fowl ;
      Fill the marsh with snipe ;
    While on dreary moorlands
      Lonely curlew pipe.
    Through the black fir-forest   25
      Thunder harsh and dry,
    Shattering down the snow-flakes
      Off the curdled sky.
    Hark ! The brave North-easter !
      Breast-high lies the scent,   30

On by holt and headland,
  Over heath and bent.
Chime, ye dappled darlings,
  Through the sleet and snow,
Who can over-ride you ?   35
  Let the horses go !
Chime, ye dappled darlings,
  Down the roaring blast ;
You shall see a fox die
  Ere an hour be past.   40
Go ! and rest to-morrow,
  Hunting in your dreams,
While our skates are ringing
  O'er the frozen streams.
Let the luscious South-wind   45
  Breathe in lovers' sighs,
While the lazy gallants
  Bask in ladies' eyes.
What does he but soften
  Heart alike and pen ?   50
'Tis the hard grey weather
  Breeds hard English men.
What's the soft South-wester ?
  'Tis the ladies' breeze,
Bringing home their trueloves   55
  Out of all the seas :
But the black North-easter,
  Through the snow-storm hurled,
Drives our English hearts of oak
  Seaward round the world.   60
Come, as came our fathers,
  Heralded by thee,
Conquering from the eastward,
  Lords by land and sea.
Come ; and strong within us   65
  Stir the Vikings' blood ;
Bracing brain and sinew ;
  Blow, thou wind of God !

                    C. KINGSLEY.

359

YOUNG AND OLD

When all the world is young, lad,
    And all the trees are green ;
And every goose a swan, lad,
    And every lass a queen ;
Then hey for boot and horse, lad,   5
    And round the world away ;
Young blood must have its course, lad,
    And every dog his day.

When all the world is old, lad,
    And all the trees are brown ;   10
And all the sport is stale, lad,
    And all the wheels run down ;
Creep home, and take your place there,
    The spent and maimed among :
God grant you find one face there,   15
    You loved when all was young.

C. KINGSLEY.

360

O CAPTAIN ! MY CAPTAIN !

O Captain ! my Captain ! our fearful trip is done,
The ship has weather'd every rack, the prize we
    sought is won,
The port is near, the bells I hear, the people all
    exulting,
While follow eyes the steady keel, the vessel grim
    and daring,
        But O heart ! heart ! heart !   5
        O the bleeding drops of red !
            Where on the deck my Captain lies,
            Fallen cold and dead.

O Captain ! my Captain ! rise up and hear the bells;
Rise up—for you the flag is flung—for you the
    bugle trills.   10

For you bouquets and ribbon'd wreaths—for you
    the shores a-crowding,
For you they call, the swaying mass, their eager
    faces turning ;
        Here Captain ! dear father !
        This arm beneath your head !
           It is some dream that on the deck   15
           You've fallen cold and dead.

My Captain does not answer, his lips are pale and
    still,
My father does not feel my arm, he has no pulse
    nor will ;
The ship is anchor'd safe and sound, its voyage
    closed and done,
From fearful trip the victor ship comes in with
    object won ;   20
        Exult, O shores, and ring, O bells !
        But I, with mournful tread,
           Walk the deck my Captain lies,
             Fallen cold and dead.
                WALT WHITMAN.

361

    Playing on the virginals,
        Who but I ! Sae glad, sae free,
    Smelling for all cordials,
        The green mint and marjorie ;
    Set among the budding broom,   5
        Kingcup and daffodilly,
    By my side I made him room :
        O love my Willie !

    ' Like me, love me, girl o' gowd,'
        Sang he to my nimble strain ;   10
    Sweet his ruddy lips o'erflowed
        Till my heartstrings rang again ;
    By the broom, the bonny broom,
        Kingcup and daffodilly,
    In my heart I made him room :   15
        O love my Willie !

'Pipe and play, dear heart,' sang he,
   'I must go, yet pipe and play;
Soon I'll come and ask of thee
   For an answer yea or nay;'   20
And I waited till the flocks
   Panted in yon waters stilly,
And the corn stood in the shocks:
   O love my Willie!

I thought first when thou didst come   25
   I would wear the ring for thee,
But the year told out its sum
   Ere again thou sat'st by me;
Thou hadst naught to ask that day
   By kingcup and daffodilly;   30
I said neither yea nor nay:
   O love my Willie!

          JEAN INGELOW.

362

THE HIGH TIDE ON THE COAST OF LINCOLNSHIRE (1571)

The old mayor climbed the belfry tower,
   The ringers ran by two, by three;
'Pull, if ye never pulled before;
   Good ringers, pull your best,' quoth he.
'Play uppe, play uppe, O Boston bells!   5
Ply all your changes, all your swells,
   Play uppe "The Brides of Enderby."'

Men say it was a stolen tyde—
   The Lord that sent it, He knows all;
But in myne ears doth still abide   10
   The message that the bells let fall:
And there was naught of strange, beside
The flight of mews and peewits pied
   By millions crouched on the old sea wall.

I sat and spun within the doore, 15
  My thread brake off, I raised myne eyes ;
The level sun, like ruddy ore,
  Lay sinking in the barren skies ;
And dark against day's golden death
She moved where Lindis wandereth, 20
My sonne's faire wife, Elizabeth.

'Cusha ! Cusha ! Cusha !' calling,
Ere the early dews were falling,
Farre away I heard her song,
'Cusha ! Cusha !' all along ; 25
Where the reedy Lindis floweth,
  Floweth, floweth,
From the meads where melick groweth
Faintly came her milking song.

'Cusha ! Cusha ! Cusha !' calling, 30
'For the dews will soone be falling ;
Leave your meadow grasses mellow,
  Mellow, mellow ;
Quit your cowslips, cowslips yellow ;
Come uppe Whitefoot, come uppe Lightfoot,
Quit the stalks of parsley hollow, 36
  Hollow, hollow ;
Come uppe Jetty, rise and follow,
  From the clovers lift your head ;
Come uppe Whitefoot, come uppe Lightfoot,
Come uppe Jetty, rise and follow, 41
  Jetty, to the milking shed.'

If it be long, aye, long ago,
  When I beginne to think howe long,
Againe I hear the Lindis flow, 45
  Swift as an arrowe, sharp and strong ;
And all the aire, it seemeth mee,
Bin full of floating bells (sayth shee),
That ring the tune of Enderby.

Alle fresh the level pasture lay, 50
  And not a shadowe mote be seene,

Save where full fyve good miles away
    The steeple towered from out the greene ;
And lo ! the great bell farre and wide
Was heard in all the country side   55
That Saturday at eventide.

The swanherds where their sedges are
    Moved on in sunset's golden breath,
The shepherde lads I heard afarre,
    And my sonne's wife, Elizabeth ;   60
Till floating o'er the grassy sea
Came downe that kyndly message free,
The ' Brides of Mavis Enderby.'

Then some looked uppe into the sky,
    And all along where Lindis flows   65
To where the goodly vessels lie,
    And where the lordly steeple shows.
They sayde, ' And why should this thing be ?
What danger lowers by land or sea ?
They ring the tune of Enderby !   70

' For evil news from Mablethorpe,
    Of pyrate galleys warping down ;
For shippes ashore beyond the scorpe,
    They have not spared to wake the towne :
But while the west bin red to see,   75
And storms be none, and pyrates flee,
Why ring " The Brides of Enderby " ?

I looked without, and lo ! my sonne
    Came riding downe with might and main :
He raised a shout as he drew on,   80
    Till all the welkin rang again,
' Elizabeth ! Elizabeth !'
(A sweeter woman ne'er drew breath
Than my sonne's wife, Elizabeth.)

' The olde sea wall (he cried) is downe,   85
    The rising tide comes on apace,
And boats adrift in yonder towne
    Go sailing uppe the market-place.'

He shook as one that looks on death :
  ' God save you, mother ! ' straight he saith ;
' Where is my wife, Elizabeth ? '   91

' Good sonne, where Lindis winds away,
  With her two bairns I marked her long ;
And ere yon bells beganne to play
  Afar I heard her milking song.'   95
He looked across the grassy lea,
To right, to left, ' Ho Enderby ! '
They rang ' The Brides of Enderby ! '

With that he cried and beat his breast ;
  For, lo ! along the river's bed   100
A mighty eygre reared his crest,
  And uppe the Lindis raging sped.
It swept with thunderous noises loud ;
Shaped like a curling snow-white cloud,
Or like a demon in a shroud.   105

And rearing Lindis backward pressed
  Shook all her trembling bankes amaine ;
Then madly at the eygre's breast
  Flung uppe her weltering walls again.
Then bankes came downe with ruin and rout—
Then beaten foam flew round about—   111
Then all the mighty floods were out.

So farre, so fast the eygre drave,
  The heart had hardly time to beat,
Before a shallow seething wave   115
  Sobbed in the grasses at oure feet :
The feet had hardly time to flee
Before it brake against the knee,
And all the world was in the sea.

Upon the roofe we sate that night,   120
  The noise of bells went sweeping by :
I marked the lofty beacon light
  Stream from the church tower, red and high—
A lurid mark and dread to see ;
And awesome bells they were to mee,   125
That in the dark rang ' Enderby.'

They rang the sailor lads to guide
  From roofe to roofe who fearless rowed ;
And I—my sonne was at my side,
  And yet the ruddy beacon glowed :   130
And yet he moaned beneath his breath,
' O come in life, or come in death !
O lost ¡ my love, Elizabeth.'

And didst thou visit him no more ?
  Thou didst, thou didst, my daughter deare ;
The waters laid thee at his doore,   136
  Ere yet the early dawn was clear.
Thy pretty bairns in fast embrace,
The lifted sun shone on thy face,
Downe drifted to thy dwelling-place.   140

That flow strewed wrecks about the grass,
  That ebbe swept out the flocks to sea ;
A fatal ebbe and flow, alas !
  To manye more than myne and mee :
But each will mourn his own (she saith),   145
And sweeter woman ne'er drew breath
Than my sonne's wife, Elizabeth.

I shall never hear her more
  By the reedy Lindis shore,
' Cusha ! Cusha ! Cusha ! ' calling,   150
  Ere the early dews be falling ;
I shall never hear her song,
' Cusha ! Cusha ! ' all along
Where the sunny Lindis floweth,
    Goeth, floweth ;   155
From the meads where melick groweth,
When the water winding down,
Onward floweth to the town.

I shall never see her more
  Where the reeds and rushes quiver,   160
    Shiver, quiver ;
Stand beside the sobbing river,
Sobbing, throbbing, in its falling
To the sandy lonesome shore ;

I shall never hear her calling,   165
' Leave your meadow grasses mellow,
   Mellow, mellow ;
Quit your cowslips, cowslips yellow ;
Come uppe Whitefoot, come uppe Lightfoot ;
Quit your pipes of parsley hollow,   170
   Hollow, hollow ;
Come uppe Lightfoot, rise and follow ;
   Lightfoot, Whitefoot,
 From your clovers lift the head ;
Come uppe Jetty, follow, follow,   175
  Jetty, to the milking shed.'

                JEAN INGELOW.

363

THE FORSAKEN MERMAN

Come, dear children, let us away :
  Down and away below !
Now my brothers call from the bay ;
  Now the great winds shoreward blow ;
  Now the salt tides seaward flow ;   5
Now the wild white horses play,
Champ and chafe and toss in the spray.
Children dear, let us away !
   This way, this way !

Call her once before you go.   10
   Call once yet.
In a voice that she will know :
  ' Margaret ! Margaret ! '
Children's voices should be dear
(Call once more) to a mother's ear :   15
Children's voices, wild with pain—
Surely she will come again.
Call her once and come away ;
   This way, this way !
' Mother dear, we cannot stay.'   20
The wild white horses foam and fret.
  Margaret ! Margaret !

Come, dear children, come away down !
  Call no more !
One last look at the white-walled town,   25
And the little grey church on the windy shore.
  Then come down.
She will not come though you call all day.
  Come away, come away !

Children dear, was it yesterday   30
We heard the sweet bells over the bay ?
In the caverns where we lay,
Through the surf and through the swell,
The far-off sound of a silver bell ?
Sand-strewn caverns, cool and deep,   35
Where the winds are all asleep ;
Where the spent lights quiver and gleam ;
Where the salt weed sways in the stream ;
Where the sea-beasts ranged all round
Feed in the ooze of their pasture-ground ;   40
Where the sea-snakes coil and twine,
Dry their mail and bask in the brine ;
Where great whales come sailing by,
Sail and sail, with unshut eye,
Round the world for ever and ay ?   45
When did music come this way ?
Children dear, was it yesterday ?

Children dear, was it yesterday
(Call yet once) that she went away ?
Once she sate with you and me,   50
On a red gold throne in the heart of the sea,
And the youngest sate on her knee.
She comb'd its bright hair, and she tended it well,
When down swung the sound of the far-off bell.
She sigh'd, she look'd up through the clear green sea;
She said : ' I must go, for my kinsfolk pray   56
In the little grey church on the shore to-day.
'Twill be Easter-time in the world—ah me !
And I lose my poor soul, Merman, here with thee.'
I said : ' Go up, dear heart, through the waves !   60
Say thy prayer, and come back to the kind sea-caves!'

She smiled, she went up through the surf in the bay.
Children dear, was it yesterday ?

   Children dear, were we long alone ?
' The sea grows stormy, the little ones moan.   65
Long prayers,' I said, ' in the world they say.
Come ! ' I said, and we rose through the surf in the
   bay.
We went up the beach, by the sandy down
Where the sea-stocks bloom, to the white-walled
   town.
Through the narrow paved streets, where all was still,
To the little grey church on the windy hill.   71
From the church came a murmur of folk at their
   prayers,
But we stood without in the cold blowing airs.
We climbed on the graves, on the stones, worn with
   rains,
And we gazed up the aisle through the small-leaded
   panes.   75
She sate by the pillar ; we saw her clear :
' Margaret, hist ! come quick, we are here.
Dear heart,' I said, ' we are long alone.
The sea grows stormy, the little ones moan.'
But, ah, she gave me never a look,   80
For her eyes were sealed to the holy book !
Loud prays the priest ; shut stands the door.
Come away, children, call no more !
Come away, come down, call no more !

   Down, down, down !   85
  Down to the depths of the sea !
She sits at her wheel in the humming town,
  Singing most joyfully.
Hark, what she sings : ' O joy, O joy,   89
For the humming street, and the child with its toy !
For the priest, and the bell, and the holy well—
  For the wheel where I spun,
  And the blessed light of the sun !'
  And so she sings her fill,
  Singing most joyfully,   95

Till the shuttle falls from her hand,
    And the whizzing wheel stands still.
She steals to the window, and looks at the sand,
    And over the sand at the sea ;
And her eyes are set in a stare ;   100
    And anon there breaks a sigh,
And anon there drops a tear,
    From a sorrow-clouded eye,
And a heart sorrow-laden,
    A long, long sigh ;   105
For the cold strange eyes of a little Mermaiden,
    And the gleam of her golden hair.

Come away, away children !
    Come children, come down !
The hoarse wind blows colder ;   110
    Lights shine in the town.
She will start from her slumber
    When gusts shake the door ;
She will hear the winds howling,
    Will hear the waves roar.   115
We shall see, while above us
    The waves roar and whirl,
A ceiling of amber,
    A pavement of pearl.
Singing : ' Here came a mortal,   120
    But faithless was she !
And alone dwell for ever
    The kings of the sea.'

But, children, at midnight,
    When soft the winds blow,   125
When clear falls the moonlight,
    When spring-tides are low ;
When sweet airs come seaward
    From heaths starred with broom,
And high rocks throw mildly   130
    On the blanched sands a gloom ;
Up the still, glistening beaches,
    Up the creeks we will hie,

Over banks of bright seaweed
  The ebb-tide leaves dry.   135
We will gaze, from the sand-hills,
At the white, sleeping town ;
At the church on the hill-side—
  And then come back down.
Singing : ' There dwells a loved one,   140
  But cruel is she !
She left lonely for ever
  The kings of the sea.'

M. ARNOLD.

364

THE SONG OF CALLICLES ON ETNA

Through the black, rushing smoke-bursts,
  Thick breaks the red flame ;
All Etna heaves fiercely
  Her forest-clothed frame.

Not here, O Apollo !   5
  Are haunts meet for thee.
But, where Helicon breaks down
  In cliff to the sea,

Where the moon-silver'd inlets
  Send far their light voice   10
Up the still vale of Thisbe,
  O speed, and rejoice !

On the sward at the cliff-top
  Lie strewn the white flocks ;
On the cliff-side the pigeons   15
  Roost deep in the rocks.

In the moonlight the shepherds,
  Soft lull'd by the rills,
Lie wrapt in their blankets,
  Asleep on the hills.   20

—What forms are these coming
 So white through the gloom ?
What garments out-glistening
 The gold-flower'd broom ?

What sweet-breathing presence   25
 Out-perfumes the thyme ?
What voices enrapture
 The night's balmy prime ?—

'Tis Apollo comes leading
 His choir, the Nine.   30
—The leader is fairest,
 But all are divine.

They are lost in the hollows !
 They stream up again !
What seeks on this mountain   35
 The glorified train ?—

They bathe on this mountain,
 In the spring by their road ;
Then on to Olympus,
 Their endless abode !   40

—Whose praise do they mention ?
 Of what is it told ?—
What will be for ever ;
 What was from of old.

First hymn they the Father   45
 Of all things ;—and then,
The rest of immortals,
 The action of men.

The day in his hotness,
 The strife with the palm ;   50
The night in her silence,
 The stars in their calm.

M. ARNOLD.

365
SHAKESPEARE

Others abide our question—Thou art free !
  We ask and ask—Thou smilest and art still,
    Out-topping knowledge ! So some sovran hill
Who to the stars uncrowns his majesty,
Planting his steadfast footsteps in the sea,   5
  Making the heaven of heavens his dwelling-
      place,
  Spares but the border, often, of his base
To the foil'd searching of mortality ;
And thou, whose head did stars and sunbeams know,
  Self-school'd, self-scann'd, self-honour'd, self-
    secure,   10
Didst walk on earth unguess'd at.—Better so !
  All pains the immortal spirit must endure,
All weakness which impairs, all griefs which bow,
Find their sole voice in that victorious brow.

M. ARNOLD.

366
A SUMMER NIGHT

  In the deserted moon-blanch'd street
How lonely rings the echo of my feet !
  Those windows, which I gaze at, frown,
  Silent and white, unopening down,
  Repellent as the world ;—but see !   5
  A break between the housetops shows
The moon, and, lost behind her, fading dim
Into the dewy dark obscurity
  Down at the far horizon's rim,
  Doth a whole tract of heaven disclose,   10
    And to my mind the thought
    Is on a sudden brought
Of a past night, and a far different scene.
Headlands stood out into the moon-lit deep
    As clearly as at noon ;   15
    The spring-tide's brimming flow
    Heaved dazzlingly between ;

    Houses with long white sweep
      Girdled the glistening bay ;
      Behind, through the soft air,   20
The blue haze-cradled mountains spread away.
      That night was far more fair—
But the same restless pacings to and fro,
And the same vainly throbbing heart was there
      And the same bright calm moon.   25

    And the calm moonlight seems to say :
Hast thou then still the old unquiet breast,
  Which never deadens into rest,
  Nor ever feels the fiery glow
That whirls the spirit from itself away,   30
  But fluctuates to and fro,
  Never by passion quite possess'd,
And never quite benumb'd by the world's sway ?
    And I, I know not if to pray
Still to be what I am, or yield, and be   35
    Like all the other men I see.

For most men in a brazen prison live,
    Where in the sun's hot eye,
With heads bent o'er their toil, they languidly
Their lives to some unmeaning taskwork give, 40
Dreaming of nought beyond their prison-wall.
    And as, year after year,
Fresh products of their barren labour fall
    From their tired hands, and rest
    Never yet comes more near,   45
Gloom settles slowly down over their breast ;
    And while they try to stem
The waves of mournful thought by which they are
        prest,
  Death in their prison reaches them,
Unfreed, having seen nothing, still unblest.   50

      And the rest, a few,
  Escape their prison, and depart
  On the wide ocean of life anew.
There the freed prisoner, where'er his heart
      Listeth, will sail ;   55

Nor doth he know how there prevail,
　　Despotic on that sea,
Trade-winds which cross it from eternity.
Awhile he holds some false way, undebarr'd
　　By thwarting signs, and braves　　　　60
　　The freshening wind and blackening waves.
And then the tempest strikes him ; and between
　　The lightning-bursts is seen
　　Only a driving wreck,
And the pale master on his spar-strewn deck　　65
　　With anguish'd face and flying hair
　　Grasping the rudder hard,
Still bent to make some port he knows not where,
Still standing for some false impossible shore.
　　And sterner comes the roar　　　　70
Of sea and wind, and through the deepening gloom
Fainter and fainter wreck and helmsman loom,
And he too disappears, and comes no more.

　　Is there no life, but these alone ?
　　Madman or slave, must man be one ?　　75

Plainness and clearness without shadow of stain !
　　Clearness divine !
Ye heavens, whose pure dark regions have no sign
Of languor, though so calm, and though so great
Are yet untroubled and unpassionate !　　80
Who, though so noble, share in the world's toil,
And, though so task'd, keep free from dust and soil!
I will not say that your mild deeps retain
A tinge, it may be, of their silent pain
Who have long'd deeply once, and long'd in vain ;
But I will rather say that you remain　　86
A world above man's head, to let him see
How boundless might his soul's horizons be,
How vast, yet of what clear transparency !
How it were good to live there, and breathe free
　　How fair a lot to fill　　　　91
　　Is left to each man still !

　　　　　　　　　　M. ARNOLD.

367

MORALITY

We cannot kindle when we will
  The fire which in the heart resides,
The spirit bloweth and is still,
    In mystery our soul abides ;
      But tasks in hours of insight will'd   5
      Can be through hours of gloom fulfill'd.

With aching hands and bleeding feet
  We dig and heap, lay stone on stone ;
We bear the burden and the heat
    Of the long day, and wish 'twere done.   10
      Not till the hours of light return
      All we have built do we discern.

Then, when the clouds are off the soul,
  When thou dost bask in Nature's eye,
Ask, how *she* view'd thy self-control,   15
    Thy struggling, task'd morality—
      Nature, whose free, light, cheerful air,
      Oft made thee, in thy gloom, despair.

And she, whose censure thou dost dread,
  Whose eye thou wast afraid to seek,   20
See, on her face a glow is spread,
    A strong emotion on her cheek !
      'Ah, child !' she cries, ' that strife divine,
      Whence was it, for it is not mine ?

' There is no effort on *my* brow—   25
  I do not strive, I do not weep ;
I rush with the swift spheres and glow
    In joy, and, when I will, I sleep !
      Yet that severe, that earnest air,
      I saw I felt it once—but where ?   30

' I knew not yet the gauge of time,
    Nor wore the manacles of space ;
I felt it in some other clime !
    I saw it in some other place !
        'Twas when the heavenly house I trod, 35
        And lay upon the breast of God.'

                                        M. ARNOLD.

368

THE FUTURE

A wanderer is man from his birth.
    He was born in a ship
On the breast of the river of Time ;
Brimming with wonder and joy
He spreads out his arms to the light,   5
Rivets his gaze on the banks of the stream.

As what he sees is, so have his thoughts been.
    Whether he wakes
Where the snowy mountainous pass,
Echoing the screams of the eagles,   10
Hems in its gorges the bed
Of the new-born clear-flowing stream ;
Whether he first sees light
Where the river in gleaming rings
Sluggishly winds through the plain ;   15
Whether in sound of the swallowing sea—
    As is the world on the banks,
    So is the mind of the man.

    Vainly does each as he glides
        Fable and dream   20
Of the lands which the river of Time
Had left ere he woke on its breast,
Or shall reach when his eyes have been clos'd.
Only the tract where he sails
He wots of ; only the thoughts,   25
Raised by the objects he passes, are his.

Who can see the green earth any more
As she was by the sources of Time ?
Who imagines her fields as they lay
In the sunshine, unworn by the plough ?   30
 Who thinks as they thought,
The tribes who then roam'd on her breast,
Her vigorous primitive sons ?

 What girl
Now reads in her bosom as clear   35
As Rebekah read, when she sate
At eve by the palm-shaded well ?
 Who guards in her breast
As deep, as pellucid a spring
Of feeling, as tranquil, as sure ?   40

 What bard,
At the height of his vision, can deem
Of God, of the world, of the soul,
 With a plainness as near,
As flashing as Moses felt,   45
When he lay in the night by his flock
On the starlit Arabian waste ?
 Can rise and obey
The beck of the Spirit like him ?

This tract which the river of Time   50
Now flows through with us, is the plain.
Gone is the calm of its earlier shore.
 Border'd by cities, and hoarse
With a thousand cries is its stream.
And we on its breast, our minds   55
Are confused as the cries which we hear,
Changing and shot as the sights which we see.

And we say that repose has fled
For ever the course of the river of Time.
 That cities will crowd to its edge   60
In a blacker incessanter line ;
 That the din will be more on its banks,
Denser the trade on its stream,

Flatter the plain where it flows,
Fiercer the sun overhead.
That never will those on its breast
　　See an ennobling sight,
Drink of the feeling of quiet again.

But what was before us we know not,
And we know not what shall succeed.

Haply, the river of Time,
As it grows, as the towns on its marge
Fling their wavering lights
On a wider, statelier stream—
May acquire, if not the calm
Of its early mountainous shore,
Yet a solemn peace of its own.

And the width of the waters, the hush
Of the grey expanse where he floats,
Freshening its current and spotted with foam
　　As it draws to the Ocean, may strike
Peace to the soul of the man on its breast ;
　　As the pale waste widens around him—
　　As the banks fade dimmer away—
　　As the stars come out, and the night-wind
　　　　Brings up the stream
Murmurs and scents of the infinite Sea.

M. ARNOLD.

69

PHILOMELA

Hark ! ah, the nightingale !
　　The tawny-throated !
Hark ! from that moonlit cedar what a burst !
What triumph ! hark—what pain !

O wanderer from a Grecian shore,
Still, after many years, in distant lands,
Still nourishing in thy bewilder'd brain
That wild, unquench'd, deep-sunken, old-world
　　pain—
　　Say, will it never heal ?

And can this fragrant lawn   10
  With its cool trees, and night,
And the sweet, tranquil Thames,
  And moonshine, and the dew,
To thy rack'd heart and brain
    Afford no balm ?   15

Dost thou to-night behold,
Here, through the moonlight on this English grass,
  The unfriendly palace in the Thracian wild ?
    Dost thou again peruse
    With hot cheeks and sear'd eyes   20
The too clear web, and thy dumb sister's shame ?
    Dost thou once more assay
  Thy flight, and feel come over thee,
  Poor fugitive, the feathery change
Once more, and once more seem to make resound
With love and hate, triumph and agony,   26
Lone Daulis, and the high Cephissian vale ?
    Listen, Eugenia—
How thick the bursts come crowding through the
      leaves !
    Again—thou hearest ?   30
    Eternal passion !
    Eternal pain !

                M. ARNOLD.

370

REQUIESCAT

Strew on her roses, roses,
  And never a spray of yew.
In quiet she reposes ;
  Ah ! would that I did too.

Her mirth the world required ;   5
  She bathed it in smiles of glee.
But her heart was tired, tired,
  And now they let her be.

Her life was turning, turning,
   In mazes of heat and sound ;   10
But for peace her soul was yearning,
   And now peace laps her round.

Her cabin'd, ample spirit,
   It flutter'd and fail'd for breath ;
To-night it doth inherit   15
   The vasty hall of death.

              M. ARNOLD.

371
THE SCHOLAR GIPSY

'There was very lately a lad in the University of Oxford, who was by his poverty forced to leave his studies there ; and at last to join himself to a company of vagabond gipsies. Among these extravagant people, by the insinuating subtilty of his carriage, he quickly got so much of their love and esteem as that they discovered to him their mystery. After he had been a pretty while well exercised in the trade, there chanced to ride by a couple of scholars, who had formerly been of his acquaintance. They quickly spied out their old friend among the gipsies ; and he gave them an account of the necessity which drove him to that kind of life, and told them that the people he went with were not such impostors as they were taken for, but that they had a traditional kind of learning among them, and could do wonders by the power of imagination, their fancy binding that of others : that himself had learned much of their art, and when he had compassed the whole secret, he intended, he said, to leave their company, and give the world an account of what he had learned.'—GLANVIL'S *Vanity of Dogmatizing*, 1661.

Go, for they call you, shepherd, from the hill !
  Go, shepherd, and untie the wattled cotes !
  No longer leave thy wistful flock unfed,
  Nor let thy bawling fellows rack their throats,
    Nor the cropp'd grasses shoot another head !
      But when the fields are still,   6
And the tired men and dogs all gone to rest,
    And only the white sheep are sometimes seen
  Cross and recross the strips of moon-blanch'd green,
  Come, shepherd, and again begin the quest !   10

Here, where the reaper was at work of late—
   In this high field's dark corner, where he leaves
     His coat, his basket, and his earthen cruse,
     And in the sun all morning binds the sheaves,
       Then here, at noon, comes back his stores to
        use—   15
       Here will I sit and wait,
   While to my ear from uplands far away
     The bleating of the folded flocks is borne,
     With distant cries of reapers in the corn—
   All the live murmur of a summer's day.   20

Screen'd is this nook o'er the high, half-reap'd field,
   And here till sun-down, shepherd, will I be !
     Through the thick corn the scarlet poppies peep,
     And round green roots and yellowing stalks I see
       Pale blue convolvulus in tendrils creep ;   25
       And air-swept lindens yield
   Their scent, and rustle down their perfumed
      showers
     Of bloom on the bent grass where I am laid,
     And bower me from the August sun with shade;
   And the eye travels down to Oxford's towers.

And near me on the grass lies Glanvil's book—
   Come, let me read the oft-read tale again !   32
     The story of that Oxford scholar poor,
   Of shining parts and quick inventive brain,
     Who, tired of knocking at preferment's door,
     One summer morn forsook
   His friends, and went to learn the gipsy lore,
     And roam'd the world with that wild brother-
      hood,   38
     And came, as most men deem'd, to little good,
   But came to Oxford and his friends no more.

But once, years after, in the country-lanes,
   Two scholars whom at college erst he knew
     Met him, and of his way of life inquir'd.   43

Whereat he answer'd, that the gipsy crew,
  His mates, had arts to rule as they desired
    The workings of men's brains ;   46
And they can bind them to what thoughts they will.
  'And I,' he said, ' the secret of their art,
    When fully learn'd, will to the world impart ;
But it needs heaven-sent moments for this skill !'

This said, he left them, and return'd no more.—
  But rumours hung about the country-side   52
    That the lost Scholar long was seen to stray,
Seen by rare glimpses, pensive and tongue-tied,
  In hat of antique shape, and cloak of grey,
    The same the gipsies wore.   56
Shepherds had met him on the Hurst in spring ;
  At some lone alehouse in the Berkshire moors,
    On the warm ingle-bench, the smock-frock'd
      boors
Had found him seated at their entering,   60
But, mid their drink and clatter, he would fly ;—
  And I myself seem half to know thy looks,
    And put the shepherds, wanderer, on thy trace;
And boys who in lone wheatfields scare the rooks
  I ask if thou hast pass'd their quiet place ;
    Or in my boat I lie   66
Moor'd to the cool bank in the summer heats,
  Mid wide grass meadows which the sunshine fills,
    And watch the warm green-muffled Cumner hills,
And wonder if thou haunt'st their shy retreats.

For most, I know, thou lov'st retired ground !   71
  Thee, at the ferry, Oxford riders blithe,
    Returning home on summer nights, have met
Crossing the stripling Thames at Bablock-hithe,
  Trailing in the cool stream thy fingers wet,
    As the punt's rope chops round ;   76
And leaning backward in a pensive dream,
  And fostering in thy lap a heap of flowers
    Pluck'd in shy fields and distant Wychwood
      bowers,
And thine eyes resting on the moonlit stream !

And then they land, and thou art seen no more!
 Maidens who from the distant hamlets come
  To dance around the Fyfield elm in May,
 Oft through the darkening fields have seen thee
   roam,
 Or cross a stile into the public way.   85
  Oft thou hast given them store
 Of flowers—the frail-leaf'd, white anemone,
  Dark bluebells drench'd with dews of summer
   eves,
  And purple orchises with spotted leaves—
 But none has words she can report of thee.   90

And, above Godstow Bridge, when hay-time 's here
 In June, and many a scythe in sunshine flames,
  Men who through those wide fields of breezy
   grass
 Where black-wing'd swallows haunt the glittering
   Thames,
  To bathe in the abandon'd lasher pass,   95
  Have often pass'd thee near
 Sitting upon the river bank o'ergrown;
  Mark'd thine outlandish garb, thy figure spare,
  Thy dark vague eyes, and soft abstracted air—
 But, when they came from bathing, thou wert
   gone!   100

At some lone homestead in the Cumner hills,
 Where at her open door the housewife darns,
  Thou hast been seen, or hanging on a gate
 To watch the threshers in the mossy barns.
  Children, who early range these slopes and late
  For cresses from the rills,   106
 Have known thee watching, all an April day,
  The springing pastures and the feeding kine;
  And mark'd thee, when the stars come out and
   shine,
 Through the long dewy grass move slow away.

In autumn, on the skirts of Bagley-wood,   111
 Where most the gipsies by the turf-edged way
  Pitch their smoked tents, and every bush you see

With scarlet patches tagg'd and shreds of grey,
  Above the forest-ground call'd Thessaly—
    The blackbird picking food   116
  Sees thee, nor stops his meal, nor fears at all !
So often has he known thee past him stray
  Rapt, twirling in thy hand a wither'd spray,
And waiting for the spark from Heaven to fall.

And once, in winter, on the causeway chill   121
  Where home through flooded fields foot-travellers
      go,
    Have I not pass'd thee on the wooden bridge
Wrapt in thy cloak and battling with the snow,
  Thy face toward Hinksey and its wintry ridge?
    And thou hast climb'd the hill   126
And gain'd the white brow of the Cumner range ;
  Turn'd once to watch, while thick the snowflakes
      fall,
    The line of festal light in Christ-Church hall—
Then sought thy straw in some sequester'd
      grange.   130

But what—I dream ! Two hundred years are
    flown
  Since first thy story ran through Oxford halls,
    And the grave Glanvil did the tale inscribe
That thou wert wander'd from the studious walls
  To learn strange arts, and join a gipsy tribe.
    And thou from earth art gone   136
Long since, and in some quiet churchyard laid !
  Some country nook, where o'er thy unknown
      grave
    Tall grasses and white flowering nettles wave—
Under a dark red-fruited yew-tree's shade. 140

—No, no, thou hast not felt the lapse of hours !
For what wears out the life of mortal men ?
  'Tis that from change to change their being
      rolls ;
  'Tis that repeated shocks, again, again,
    Exhaust the energy of strongest souls,   145

And numb the elastic powers.
Till having used our nerves with bliss and teen,
And tired upon a thousand schemes our wit,
To the just-pausing Genius we remit   149
Our well-worn life, and are—what we have been!

Thou hast not lived, why shoul'st thou perish, so ?
Thou hadst *one* aim, *one* business, *one* desire !
Else wert thou long since number'd with the
          dead—
Else hadst thou spent, like other men, thy fire !
The generations of thy peers are fled,   155
And we ourselves shall go ;
But thou possessest an immortal lot,
And we imagine thee exempt from age
And living as thou liv'st on Glanvil's page,
Because thou hadst—what we, alas, have not !

For early didst thou leave the world, with powers
Fresh, undiverted to the world without,   162
Firm to their mark, not spent on other things ;
Free from the sick fatigue, the languid doubt,
Which much to have tried, in much been
          baffled, brings.
O life unlike to ours !
Who fluctuate idly without term or scope,   167
Of whom each strives, nor knows for what he
          strives,
And each half lives a hundred different lives;
Who wait like thee, but not, like thee, in hope.   170

Thou waitest for the spark from Heaven: and we,
Light half-believers of our casual creeds,
Who never deeply felt, nor clearly will'd,
Whose insight never has borne fruit in deeds,
Whose vague resolves never have been
          fulfill'd ;   175
For whom each year we see
Breeds new beginnings, disappointments new ;
Who hesitate and falter life away,
And lose to-morrow the ground won to-day—
Ah, do not we, wanderer, await it too ?   180

Yes ! we await it, but it still delays,
   And then we suffer ! and amongst us one,
      Who most has suffer'd, takes dejectedly
His seat upon the intellectual throne ;
      And all his store of sad experience he   185
        Lays bare of wretched days ;
Tells us his misery's birth and growth and signs,
      And how the dying spark of hope was fed,
      And how the breast was soothed, and how the
          head,
And all his hourly varied anodynes.   190

This for our wisest ! and we others pine,
   And wish the long unhappy dream would end,
      And waive all claim to bliss, and try to bear,
With close-lipp'd patience for our only friend,
      Sad patience, too near neighbour to despair ;
        But none has hope like thine !   196
Thou through the fields and through the woods
        dost stray,
   Roaming the country-side, a truant boy,
   Nursing thy project in unclouded joy,
And every doubt long blown by time away. 200

O born in days when wits were fresh and clear,
   And life ran gaily as the sparkling Thames ;
      Before this strange disease of modern life,
With its sick hurry, its divided aims,
      Its heads o'ertax'd, its palsied hearts, was rife—
        Fly hence, our contact fear !   206
Still fly, plunge deeper in the bowering wood !
      Averse, as Dido did with gesture stern
      From her false friend's approach in Hades turn,
Wave us away, and keep thy solitude !   210

Still nursing the unconquerable hope,
   Still clutching the inviolable shade,
      With a free onward impulse brushing through,
By night, the silver'd branches of the glade—
      Far on the forest-skirts, where none pursue,
        On some mild pastoral slope   216

Emerge, and resting on the moonlit pales,
  Freshen thy flowers, as in former years,
  With dew, or listen with enchanted ears,
From the dark dingles, to the nightingales !

But fly our paths, our feverish contact fly !   221
  For strong the infection of our mental strife,
    Which, though it gives no bliss, yet spoils for
      rest ;
  And we should win thee from thy own fair life,
    Like us distracted, and like us unblest !   225
      Soon, soon thy cheer would die,
  Thy hopes grow timorous, and unfix'd thy
      powers,
    And thy clear aims be cross and shifting made;
    And then thy glad perennial youth would fade,
  Fade, and grow old at last, and die like ours.

Then fly our greetings, fly our speech and smiles !
  —As some grave Tyrian trader, from the sea,
  Descried at sunrise an emerging prow
  Lifting the cool-hair'd creepers stealthily,
    The fringes of a southward-facing brow   235
      Among the Aegean isles ;
  And saw the merry Grecian coaster come,
    Freighted with amber grapes, and Chian wine,
    Green bursting figs, and tunnies steep'd in
      brine ;   239
  And knew the intruders on his ancient home,

The young light-hearted masters of the waves ;
  And snatch'd his rudder, and shook out more sail.
    And day and night held on indignantly
  O'er the blue Midland waters with the gale,
    Betwixt the Syrtes and soft Sicily,   245
      To where the Atlantic raves
  Outside the western straits, and unbent sails
    There, where down cloudy cliffs, through
      sheets of foam,
    Shy traffickers, the dark Iberians come ;
  And on the beach undid his corded bales.   250

                  M. ARNOLD.

372
RUGBY CHAPEL
November, 1857

Coldly, sadly descends
The autumn evening ! The field
Strewn with its dank yellow drifts
Of withered leaves, and the elms,
Fade into dimness apace,   5
Silent ;—hardly a shout
From a few boys late at their play !
The lights come out in the street,
In the school-room windows ; but cold,
Solemn, unlighted, austere,   10
Through the gathering darkness, arise
The chapel-walls, in whose bound
Thou, my father ! art laid.

There thou dost lie, in the gloom
Of the autumn evening. But ah !   15
That word, *gloom*, to my mind
Brings thee back in the light
Of thy radiant vigour again !
In the gloom of November we pass'd
Days not of gloom at thy side ;   20
Seasons impair'd not the ray
Of thine even cheerfulness clear.
Such thou wast ! and I stand
In the autumn evening, and think
Of bygone autumns with thee.   25

Fifteen years have gone round
Since thou arosest to tread,
In the summer morning, the road
Of death, at a call unforeseen,
Sudden ! For fifteen years,   30
We who till then in thy shade
Rested as under the boughs
Of a mighty oak, have endured
Sunshine and rain as we might,

Bare, unshaded, alone,   35
Lacking the shelter of thee!

O strong soul, by what shore
Tarriest thou now ?   For that force,
Surely, has not been left vain !
Somewhere, surely, afar,   40
In the sounding labour-house vast
Of being, is practised that strength,
Zealous, beneficent, firm !

Yes, in some far-shining sphere,
Conscious or not of the past,   45
Still thou performest the word
Of the Spirit in whom thou dost live—
Prompt, unwearied, as here !
Still thou upraisest with zeal
The humble good from the ground,   50
Sternly repressest the bad !
Still, like a trumpet, dost rouse
Those who with half-open eyes
Tread the border-land dim
'Twixt vice and virtue ; reviv'st,   55
Succourest !—this was thy work,
This was thy life upon earth.

What is the course of the life
Of mortal men on the earth ?—
Most men eddy about   60
Here and there—eat and drink,
Chatter and love and hate,
Gather and squander, are raised
Aloft, are hurl'd in the dust,
Striving blindly, achieving   65
Nothing ; and then they die—
Perish ! and no one asks
Who or what they have been,
More than he asks what waves,
In the moonlit solitudes mild   70
Of the midmost Ocean, have swell'd,
Foam'd for a moment and gone.

And there are some, whom a thirst
Ardent, unquenchable, fires,
Not with the crowd to be spent—— 75
Not without aim to go round
In an eddy of purposeless dust,
Effort unmeaning and vain.
Ah yes, some of us strive
Not without action to die 80
Fruitless, but something to snatch
From dull oblivion, nor all
Glut the devouring grave !
We, we have chosen our path——
Path to a clear-purposed goal, 85
Path of advance !——but it leads
A long, steep journey, through sunk
Gorges, o'er mountains in snow !
Cheerful, with friends, we set forth——
Then, on the height, comes the storm ! 90
Thunder crashes from rock
To rock, the cataracts reply ;
Lightnings dazzle our eyes ;
Roaring torrents have breach'd
The track——the stream-bed descends 95
In the place where the wayfarer once
Planted his footstep——the spray
Boils o'er its borders ! aloft,
The unseen snow-beds dislodge
Their hanging ruin ;——alas, 100
Havoc is made in our train !
Friends who set forth at our side
Falter, are lost in the storm !
We, we only, are left !
With frowning foreheads, with lips 105
Sternly compress'd, we strain on,
On——and at nightfall, at last,
Come to the end of our way,
To the lonely inn 'mid the rocks ;
Where the gaunt and taciturn host 110
Stands on the threshold, the wind
Shaking his thin white hairs——

Holds his lantern to scan
Our storm-beat figures, and asks :
Whom in our party we bring ?   115
Whom we have left in the snow ?

Sadly we answer : We bring
Only ourselves ! we lost
Sight of the rest in the storm !
Hardly ourselves we fought through,   120
Stripp'd, without friends, as we are !
Friends, companions, and train
The avalanche swept from our side.

But thou would'st not *alone*
Be saved, my father ! *alone*   125
Conquer and come to thy goal,
Leaving the rest in the wild.
We were weary, and we
Fearful, and we, in our march,
Fain to drop down and to die.   130
Still thou turnedst, and still
Beckonedst the trembler, and still
Gavest the weary thy hand !
If, in the paths of the world,
Stones might have wounded thy feet,   135
Toil or dejection have tried
Thy spirit, of that we saw
Nothing ! to us thou wert still
Cheerful, and helpful, and firm.
Therefore to thee it was given   140
Many to save with thyself ;
And, at the end of thy day,
O faithful shepherd ! to come,
Bringing thy sheep in thy hand.

And through thee I believe   145
In the noble and great who are gone ;
Pure souls honour'd and blest
By former ages, who else—
Such, so soulless, so poor,
Is the race of men whom I see—   150

Seem'd but a dream of the heart,
Seem'd but a cry of desire.
Yes ! I believe that there lived
Others like thee in the past,
Not like the men of the crowd   155
Who all round me to-day
Bluster or cringe, and make life
Hideous, and arid, and vile ;
But souls temper'd with fire,
Fervent, heroic, and good,   160
Helpers and friends of mankind.

Servants of God !—or sons
Shall I not call you ? because
Not as servants ye knew
Your Father's innermost mind,   165
His, who unwillingly sees
One of his little ones lost—
Yours is the praise, if mankind
Hath not as yet in its march
Fainted, and fallen, and died !   170

See ! in the rocks of the world
Marches the host of mankind,
A feeble, wavering line !
Where are they tending ?—A God
Marshall'd them, gave them their goal.—
Ah, but the way is so long !   176
Years they have been in the wild !
Sore thirst plagues them ; the rocks,
Rising all round, overawe.
Factions divide them—their host   180
Threatens to break, to dissolve.—
Ah, keep, keep them combined !
Else, of the myriads who fill
That army, not one shall arrive !
Sole they shall stray ; in the rocks   185
Labour for ever in vain,
Die one by one in the waste.

Then, in such hour of need
Of your fainting, dispirited race,
Ye, like angels, appear,   190
Radiant with ardour divine.
Beacons of hope, ye appear !
Languor is not in your heart,
Weakness is not in your word,
Weariness not on your brow.   195
Ye alight in our van ! at your voice,
Panic, despair, flee away.
Ye move through the ranks, recall
The stragglers, refresh the outworn,
Praise, re-inspire the brave !   200
Order, courage, return.
Eyes rekindling, and prayers,
Follow your steps as ye go.
Ye fill up the gaps in our files,
Strengthen the wavering line,   205
Stablish, continue our march,
On, to the bound of the waste,
On, to the City of God !

                                   M. ARNOLD.

                        373

            MIMNERMUS IN CHURCH

You promise heavens free from strife,
    Pure truth, and perfect change of will ;
But sweet, sweet is this human life,
    So sweet, I fain would breathe it still ;
Your chilly stars I can forgo,   5
This warm kind world is all I know.

You say there is no substance here,
    One great reality above :
Back from that void I shrink in fear,
    And childlike hide myself in love :   10
Show me what angels feel. Till then,
I cling, a mere weak man, to men.

You bid me lift my mean desires
  From faltering lips and fitful veins
To sexless souls, ideal quires,   15
  Unwearied voices, wordless strains :
My mind with fonder welcome owns
One dear dead friend's remembered tones.

Forsooth the present we must give
  To that which cannot pass away ;   20
All beauteous things for which we live
  By laws of time and space decay.
But oh, the very reason why
I clasp them, is because they die.
                    W. J. CORY.

374
HERACLITUS

They told me, Heraclitus, they told me you were dead,
They brought me bitter news to hear and bitter
    tears to shed.
I wept, as I remembered, how often you and I
Had tired the sun with talking and sent him down
    the sky.   4

And now that thou art lying, my dear old Carian guest,
A handful of grey ashes, long long ago at rest,
Still are thy pleasant voices, thy nightingales, awake;
For Death, he taketh all away, but them he cannot
    take.   W. J. CORY.

375
AMATURUS

Somewhere beneath the sun,
  These quivering heart-strings prove it,
Somewhere there must be one
  Made for this soul, to move it ;
Some one that hides her sweetness   5
  From neighbours whom she slights,
Nor can attain completeness,
  Nor give her heart its rights ;
Some one whom I could court
  With no great change of manner,   10

Still holding reason's fort,
　Though waving fancy's banner;
A lady, not so queenly
　As to disdain my hand,
Yet born to smile serenely　　　　　　15
　Like those that rule the land;
Noble, but not too proud;
　With soft hair simply folded,
And bright face crescent-browed,
　And throat by Muses moulded;　　　20
And eyelids lightly falling
　On little glistening seas,
Deep-calm, when gales are brawling,
　Though stirred by every breeze:
Swift voice, like flight of dove　　　25
　Through minster arches floating,
With sudden turns, when love
　Gets overnear to doting;
Keen lips, that shape soft sayings
　Like crystals of the snow,　　　　30
With pretty half-betrayings
　Of things one may not know;
Fair hand, whose touches thrill,
　Like golden rod of wonder,
Which Hermes wields at will　　　　35
　Spirit and flesh to sunder;
Light foot, to press the stirrup
　In fearlessness and glee,
Or dance, till finches chirrup,
　And stars sink to the sea.　　　　40

Forth, Love, and find this maid,
　Wherever she be hidden:
Speak, Love, be not afraid,
　But plead as thou art bidden;
And say, that he who taught thee　　45
　His yearning want and pain,
Too dearly, dearly bought thee
　To part with thee in vain.

W. J. CORY.

376

THE MARRIED LOVER

Why, having won her, do I woo ?
  Because her spirit's vestal grace
Provokes me always to pursue,
  But, spirit-like, eludes embrace ;
Because her womanhood is such   5
  That, as on court-days subjects kiss
The Queen's hand, yet so near a touch
  Affirms no mean familiarness ;
Nay, rather marks more fair the height
  Which can with safety so neglect   10
To dread, as lower ladies might,
  That grace could meet with disrespect ;
Thus she with happy favour feeds
  Allegiance from a love so high
That thence no false conceit proceeds   15
  Of difference bridged, or state put by ;
Because, although in act and word
  As lowly as a wife can be,
Her manners, when they call me lord,
  Remind me 'tis by courtesy ;   20
Not with her least consent of will,
  Which would my proud affection hurt,
But by the noble style that still
  Imputes an unattain'd desert ;
Because her gay and lofty brows,   25
  When all is won which hope can ask,
Reflect a light of hopeless snows
  That bright in virgin ether bask ;
Because, though free of the outer court
  I am, this Temple keeps its shrine   30
Sacred to Heaven ; because, in short,
  She's not and never can be mine.
                            C. PATMORE.

377

THE TOYS

My little Son, who look'd from thoughtful eyes
And moved and spoke in quiet grown-up wise,
Having my law the seventh time disobey'd,
    I struck him, and dismiss'd
    With hard words and unkiss'd,   5
  His Mother, who was patient, being dead.
Then, fearing lest his grief should hinder sleep,
    I visited his bed,
    But found him slumbering deep,
With darken'd eyelids, and their lashes yet   10
    From his late sobbing wet.
        And I, with moan,
Kissing away his tears, left others of my own ;
For, on a table drawn beside his head,
    He had put, within his reach,   15
A box of counters and a red-vein'd stone,
A piece of glass abraded by the beach,
    And six or seven shells,
    A bottle with bluebells,
And two French copper coins, ranged there with
        careful art,   20
    To comfort his sad heart.
    So when that night I pray'd
    To God, I wept, and said :
Ah, when at last we lie with trancéd breath,
    Not vexing Thee in death,   25
  And Thou rememberest of what toys
      We made our joys,
    How weakly understood
    Thy great commanded good,
    Then, fatherly not less   30
Than I whom Thou hast moulded from the
    clay,
    Thou'lt leave Thy wrath, and say,
' I will be sorry for their childishness.'

                C. PATMORE.

378

KEITH OF RAVELSTON

The murmur of the mourning ghost
   That keeps the shadowy kine,
' Oh, Keith of Ravelston,
   The sorrows of thy line ! '

Ravelston, Ravelston,   5
   The merry path that leads
Down the golden morning hill,
   And thro' the silver meads ;

Ravelston, Ravelston,
   The stile beneath the tree,   10
The maid that kept her mother's kine,
   The song that sang she !

She sang her song, she kept her kine,
   She sat beneath the thorn,
When Andrew Keith of Ravelston   15
   Rode thro' the Monday morn.

His henchmen sing, his hawk-bells ring,
   His belted jewels shine !
Oh, Keith of Ravelston,
   The sorrows of thy line !   20

Year after year, where Andrew came,
   Comes evening down the glade,
And still there sits a moonshine ghost
   Where sat the sunshine maid.

Her misty hair is faint and fair,   25
   She keeps the shadowy kine ;
Oh, Keith of Ravelston,
   The sorrows of thy line !

I lay my hand upon the stile,
   The stile is lone and cold ;   30
The burnie that goes babbling by
   Says naught that can be told.

Yet, stranger ! here, from year to year,
  She keeps her shadowy kine ;
Oh, Keith of Ravelston,   35
  The sorrows of thy line !

Step out three steps, where Andrew stood—
  Why blanch thy cheeks for fear ?
The ancient stile is not alone,
  'Tis not the burn I hear !   40

She makes her immemorial moan,
  She keeps her shadowy kine ;
Oh, Keith of Ravelston,
  The sorrows of thy line !

S. DOBELL.

379

THE BLESSED DAMOZEL

The blesséd damozel leaned out
  From the gold bar of Heaven ;
Her eyes were deeper than the depth
  Of waters stilled at even ;
She had three lilies in her hand,   5
  And the stars in her hair were seven.

Her robe, ungirt from clasp to hem,
  No wrought flowers did adorn,
But a white rose of Mary's gift,
  For service meetly worn ;   10
Her hair that lay along her back
  Was yellow like ripe corn.

Herseemed she scarce had been a day
  One of God's choristers ;
The wonder was not yet quite gone   15
  From that still look of hers ;
Albeit, to them she left, her day
  Had counted as ten years.

(To one, it is ten years of years.
  . . . . Yet now, and in this place,   20

Surely she leaned o'er me—her hair
    Fell all about my face . . .
Nothing : the autumn fall of leaves.
    The whole year sets apace.)

It was the rampart of God's house   25
    That she was standing on ;
By God built over the sheer depth
    The which is Space begun ;
So high, that looking downward thence
    She scarce could see the sun.   30

It lies in Heaven, across the flood
    Of ether, as a bridge.
Beneath, the tides of day and night
    With flame and darkness ridge
The void, as low as where this earth   35
    Spins like a fretful midge.

Heard hardly, some of her new friends
    Amid their loving games
Spake evermore among themselves
    Their virginal chaste names ;   40
And the souls mounting up to God
    Went by her like thin flames.

And still she bowed herself and stooped
    Out of the circling charm ;
Until her bosom must have made   45
    The bar she leaned on warm,
And the lilies lay as if asleep
    Along her bended arm.

From the fixed place of Heaven she saw
    Time like a pulse shake fierce   50
Through all the worlds. Her gaze still strove
    Within the gulf to pierce
Its path ; and now she spoke as when
    The stars sang in their spheres.

The sun was gone now ; the curled moon   55
    Was like a little feather

Fluttering far down the gulf ; and now
　　She spoke through the still weather.
Her voice was like the voice the stars
　　Had when they sang together.　　　　　　　60

(Ah sweet ! Even now, in that bird's song,
　　Strove not her accents there,
Fain to be hearkened ?　When those bells
　　Possessed the mid-day air,
Strove not her steps to reach my side　　　65
　　Down all the echoing stair ?)

'I wish that he were come to me
　　For he will come,' she said.
'Have I not prayed in Heaven ?—on earth,
　　Lord, Lord, has he not prayed ?　　　　70
Are not two prayers a perfect strength ?
　　And shall I feel afraid ?

'When round his head the aureole clings,
　　And he is clothed in white,
I'll take his hand and go with him　　　　75
　　To the deep wells of light ;
We will step down as to a stream,
　　And bathe there in God's sight.

'We two will stand beside that shrine,
　　Occult, withheld, untrod,　　　　　　　80
Whose lamps are stirred continually
　　With prayer sent up to God ;
And see our old prayers, granted, melt
　　Each like a little cloud.

'We two will lie i' the shadow of　　　　85
　　That living mystic tree,
Within whose secret growth the Dove
　　Is sometimes felt to be,
While every leaf that His plumes touch
　　Saith His Name audibly.　　　　　　　90

'And I myself will teach to him,
　　I myself, lying so,
The songs I sing here ; which his voice
　　Shall pause in, hushed and slow,

And find some knowledge at each pause, 95
  Or some new thing to know.'

(Alas ! We two, we two, thou say'st !
  Yea, one wast thou with me
That once of old. But shall God lift
  To endless unity 100
The soul whose likeness with thy soul
  Was but its love for thee ?)

' We two,' she said, ' will seek the groves
  Where the lady Mary is,
With her five handmaidens, whose names 105
  Are five sweet symphonies,
Cecily, Gertrude, Magdalen,
  Margaret and Rosalys.

' Circlewise sit they, with bound locks
  And foreheads garlanded ; 110
Into the fine cloth white like flame
  Weaving the golden thread,
To fashion the birth-robes for them
  Who are just born, being dead.

' He shall fear, haply, and be dumb : 115
  Then will I lay my cheek
To his, and tell about our love,
  Not once abashed or weak :
And the dear Mother will approve
  My pride, and let me speak. 120

' Herself shall bring us, hand in hand,
  To Him round whom all souls
Kneel, the clear-ranged unnumbered heads
  Bowed with their aureoles :
And angels meeting us shall sing 125
  To their citherns and citoles.

' There will I ask of Christ the Lord
  Thus much for him and me :—
Only to live as once on earth
  With Love,—only to be, 130
As then awhile, for ever now
  Together, I and he.'

She gazed and listened and then said,
　　Less sad of speech than mild,—
' All this is when he comes.'　She ceased.　135
　　The light thrilled towards her, filled
With angels in strong level flight.
　　Her eyes prayed, and she smiled.

(I saw her smile.)　But soon their path
　　Was vague in distant spheres :　　140
And then she cast her arms along
　　The golden barriers,
And laid her face between her hands,
　　And wept.　(I heard her tears.)
　　　　　　　　　　D. G. ROSSETTI.

380

REST

O Earth, lie heavily upon her eyes ;
　　Seal her sweet eyes weary of watching, Earth ;
　　Lie close around her ; leave no room for mirth
With its harsh laughter, nor for sound of sighs.
She hath no questions, she hath no replies,　5
　　Hushed in and curtained with a blesséd dearth
　　Of all that irked her from the hour of birth ;
With stillness that is almost Paradise.
Darkness more clear than noon-day holdeth her,
　　Silence more musical than any song ;　　10
Even her very heart has ceased to stir :
　　Until the morning of Eternity
　　Her rest shall not begin nor end, but be ;
And when she wakes she will not think it long.
　　　　　　　　　　C. G. ROSSETTI.

381

SONG

When I am dead, my dearest,
　　Sing no sad songs for me ;
Plant thou no roses at my head,
　　Nor shady cypress tree :

  Be the green grass above me 5
   With showers and dewdrops wet ;
  And if thou wilt, remember,
   And if thou wilt, forget.

  I shall not see the shadows,
   I shall not feel the rain ; 10
  I shall not hear the nightingale
   Sing on, as if in pain ;
  And dreaming through the twilight
   That doth not rise nor set,
  Haply I may remember, 15
   And haply may forget.
        C. G. ROSSETTI.

382
REMEMBER

Remember me when I am gone away,
 Gone far away into the silent land ;
 When you can no more hold me by the hand,
Nor I half turn to go yet turning stay.
Remember me when no more day by day 5
 You tell me of our future that you planned :
 Only remember me ; you understand
It will be late to counsel then or pray.
Yet if you should forget me for a while
 And afterwards remember, do not grieve : 10
 For if the darkness and corruption leave
 A vestige of the thoughts that once I had,
Better by far you should forget and smile
 Than that you should remember and be sad.
        C. G. ROSSETTI.

383
UP-HILL

Does the road wind up-hill all the way ?
 Yes, to the very end.
Will the day's journey take the whole long day ?
 From morn to night, my friend.

But is there for the night a resting-place ?   5
    A roof for when the slow dark hours begin.
May not the darkness hide it from my face ?
    You cannot miss that inn.

Shall I meet other wayfarers at night ?
    Those who have gone before.   10
Then must I knock, or call when just in sight ?
    They will not keep you standing at that door.

Shall I find comfort, travel-sore and weak ?
    Of labour you shall find the sum.
Will there be beds for me and all who seek ?   15
    Yea, beds for all who come.
                C. G. ROSSETTI.

384

SONG

Oh roses for the flush of youth,
    And laurel for the perfect prime ;
But pluck an ivy branch for me
    Grown old before my time.

Oh violets for the grave of youth,   5
    And bay for those dead in their prime ;
Give me the withered leaves I chose
    Before in the old time.
                C. G. ROSSETTI.

385

A BIRTHDAY

My heart is like a singing bird
    Whose nest is in a watered shoot ;
My heart is like an appletree
    Whose boughs are bent with thickset fruit ;
My heart is like a rainbow shell   5
    That paddles in a halcyon sea ;
My heart is gladder than all these
    Because my love is come to me.

Raise me a dais of silk and down ;
   Hang it with vair and purple dyes ;   10
Carve it in doves, and pomegranates,
   And peacocks with a hundred eyes ;
Work it in gold and silver grapes,
   In leaves, and silver fleurs-de-lys ;
Because the birthday of my life   15
   Is come, my love is come to me.

                C. G. ROSSETTI.

386
BARBARA

On the Sabbath-day,
   Through the churchyard old and grey,
Over the crisp and yellow leaves, I held my rustling
   way ;
And amid the words of mercy, falling on my soul
   like balms,
'Mid the gorgeous storms of music—in the mellow
   organ-calms,   5
'Mid the upward-streaming prayers, and the rich
   and solemn psalms,
   I stood careless, Barbara.

My heart was otherwhere
   While the organ shook the air,
And the priest, with outspread hands, blessed the
   people with a prayer ;   10
But, when rising to go homeward, with a mild and
   saint-like shine
Gleamed a face of airy beauty with its heavenly
   eyes on mine—
Gleamed and vanished in a moment—O that face
   was surely thine
   Out of heaven, Barbara !

O pallid, pallid face !   15
   O earnest eyes of grace
When last I saw thee, dearest, it was in another
   place.

You came running forth to meet me with my
      love-gift on your wrist :
The flutter of a long white dress, then all was lost
      in mist—   19
A purple stain of agony was on the mouth I kissed,
      That wild morning, Barbara.

      I searched, in my despair,
      Sunny noon and midnight air ;
I could not drive away the thought that you were
      lingering there.
O many and many a winter night I sat when you
      were gone,   25
My worn face buried in my hands, beside the fire
      alone—
Within the dripping churchyard, the rain plashing
      on your stone,
      You were sleeping, Barbara.

      'Mong angels, do you think
      Of the precious golden link   30
I clasped around your happy arm while sitting by
      yon brink ?
Or when that night of gliding dance, of laughter
      and guitars,
Was emptied of its music, and we watched, through
      latticed bars,
The silent midnight heaven creeping o'er us with
      its stars,
      Till the day broke, Barbara ?   35

      In the years I've changed ;
      Wild and far my heart hath ranged,
And many sins and errors now have been on me
      avenged ;
But to you I have been faithful, whatsoever good I
      lacked :
I loved you, and above my life still hangs that love
      intact—   40
Your love the trembling rainbow, I the reckless
      cataract—
      Still I love you, Barbara.

Yet, love, I am unblest ;
With many doubts opprest, 44
I wander like a desert wind, without a place of rest.
Could I but win you for an hour from off that starry
shore,
The hunger of my soul were stilled, for Death hath
told you more
Than the melancholy world doth know ; things
deeper than all lore
You could teach me, Barbara.

In vain, in vain, in vain, 50
You will never come again.
There droops upon the dreary hills a mournful
fringe of rain ;
The gloaming closes slowly round, loud winds are
in the tree,
Round selfish shores for ever moans the hurt and
wounded sea,
There is no rest upon the earth, peace is with Death
and thee, 55
Barbara !   A. SMITH.

387

OLD LOVE

'You must be very old, Sir Giles,'
  I said ; he said : 'Yea, very old :'
Whereat the mournfullest of smiles
  Creased his dry skin with many a fold.

'They hammer'd out my basnet point 5
  Into a round salade,' he said,
'The basnet being quite out of joint,
  Natheless the salade rasps my head.'

He gazed at the great fire awhile :
  'And you are getting old, Sir John ;' 10
(He said this with that cunning smile
  That was most sad ;) 'we both wear on.

'Knights come to court and look at me,
  With eyebrows up, except my lord,
And my dear lady, none I see   15
  That know the ways of my old sword.'

(My lady ! at that word no pang
  Stopp'd all my blood.) 'But tell me, John,
Is it quite true that pagans hang
  So thick about the east, that on   20

'The eastern sea no Venice flag
  Can fly unpaid for ?' 'True,' I said,
'And in such way the miscreants drag
  Christ's cross upon the ground, I dread

'That Constantine must fall this year.'   25
  Within my heart : 'These things are small ;
This is not small, that things outwear
  I thought were made for ever, yea, all,

'All things go soon or late ;' I said—
  I saw the duke in court next day ;   30
Just as before, his grand great head
  Above his gold robes dreaming lay,

Only his face was paler ; there
  I saw his duchess sit by him ;
And she—she was changed more ; her hair   35
  Before my eyes that used to swim,

And make me dizzy with great bliss
  Once, when I used to watch her sit—
Her hair is bright still, yet it is
  As though some dust were thrown on it.   40

Her eyes are shallower, as though
  Some grey glass were behind ; her brow
And cheeks the straining bones show through,
  Are not so good for kissing now.

Her lips are drier now she is   45
  A great duke's wife these many years,
They will not shudder with a kiss
  As once they did, being moist with tears.

Also her hands have lost that way
  Of clinging that they used to have ;   50
They look'd quite easy, as they lay
  Upon the silken cushions brave

With broidery of the apples green
  My Lord Duke bears upon his shield.
Her face, alas ! that I have seen   55
  Look fresher than an April field,

This is all gone now ; gone also
  Her tender walking ; when she walks
She is most queenly I well know,
  And she is fair still :—as the stalks   60

Of faded summer-lilies are,
  So is she grown now unto me
This spring-time, when the flowers star
  The meadows, birds sing wonderfully.

I warrant once she used to cling   65
  About his neck, and kiss'd him so,
And then his coming step would ring
  Joy-bells for her,—some time ago.

Ah ! sometimes like an idle dream
  That hinders true life overmuch,   70
Sometimes like a lost heaven, these seem.—
  This love is not so hard to smutch.

W. MORRIS.

388

SHAMEFUL DEATH

There were four of us about that bed ;
  The mass-priest knelt at the side,
I and his mother stood at the head,
  Over his feet lay the bride ;
We were quite sure that he was dead,   5
  Though his eyes were open wide.

He did not die in the night,
  He did not die in the day,
But in the morning twilight
  His spirit pass'd away,   10

When neither sun nor moon was bright,
  And the trees were merely grey.

He was not slain with the sword,
  Knight's axe, or the knightly spear,
Yet spoke he never a word   15
  After he came in here ;
I cut away the cord
  From the neck of my brother dear.

He did not strike one blow,
  For the recreants came behind,   20
In a place where the hornbeams grow,
  A path right hard to find,
For the hornbeam boughs swing so,
  That the twilight makes it blind.

They lighted a great torch then,   25
  When his arms were pinion'd fast,
Sir John the knight of the Fen,
  Sir Guy of the Dolorous Blast,
With knights threescore and ten,
  Hung brave Lord Hugh at last.   30

I am threescore and ten,
  And my hair is all turn'd grey,
But I met Sir John of the Fen
  Long ago on a summer day,   34
And am glad to think of the moment when
  I took his life away.

I am threescore and ten,
  And my strength is mostly pass'd,
But long ago I and my men,
  When the sky was overcast,   40
And the smoke roll'd over the reeds of the fen,
  Slew Guy of the Dolorous Blast.

And now, knights all of you,
I pray you pray for Sir Hugh,
A good knight and a true,   45
And for Alice, his wife, pray too.

                              W. MORRIS.

389

THE HAYSTACK IN THE FLOODS

Had she come all the way for this,
To part at last without a kiss?
Yea, had she borne the dirt and rain
That her own eyes might see him slain
Beside the haystack in the floods?   5

Along the dripping leafless woods,
The stirrup touching either shoe,
She rode astride as troopers do;
With kirtle kilted to her knee,
To which the mud splash'd wretchedly;   10
And the wet dripp'd from every tree
Upon her head and heavy hair,
And on her eyelids broad and fair;
The tears and rain ran down her face.

By fits and starts they rode apace,   15
And very often was his place
Far off from her; he had to ride
Ahead, to see what might betide
When the roads cross'd; and sometimes, when
There rose a murmuring from his men,   20
Had to turn back with promises;
Ah me! she had but little ease;
And often for pure doubt and dread
She sobb'd, made giddy in the head
By the swift riding; while, for cold,   25
Her slender fingers scarce could hold
The wet reins; yea, and scarcely, too,
She felt the foot within her shoe
Against the stirrup: all for this,
To part at last without a kiss   30
Beside the haystack in the floods.

For when they near'd that old soak'd hay,
They saw across the only way
That Judas, Godmar, and the three
Red running lions dismally   35

Grinn'd from his pennon, under which,
In one straight line along the ditch,
They counted thirty heads.

　　　　　　　　So then,
While Robert turn'd round to his men,
She saw at once the wretched end,　　　　　40
And, stooping down, tried hard to rend
Her coif the wrong way from her head,
And hid her eyes ; while Robert said :
' Nay, love, 'tis scarcely two to one,
At Poictiers where we made them run　　　45
So fast—why, sweet my love, good cheer,
The Gascon frontier is so near,
Nought after this.'

　　　　　　　But, ' O,' she said,
' My God ! my God ! I have to tread
The long way back without you ; then　　　50
The court at Paris ; those six men ;
The gratings of the Chatelet ;
The swift Seine on some rainy day
Like this, and people standing by,
And laughing, while my weak hands try　　55
To recollect how strong men swim.
All this, or else a life with him,
For which I should be damned at last,
Would God that this next hour were past ! '

He answer'd not, but cried his cry,　　　60
' St. George for Marny ! ' cheerily ;
And laid his hand upon her rein.
Alas ! no man of all his train
Gave back that cheery cry again ;
And, while for rage his thumb beat fast　　65
Upon his sword-hilts, some one cast
About his neck a kerchief long,
And bound him.

　　　　　　Then they went along
To Godmar ; who said : ' Now, Jehane,
Your lover's life is on the wane　　　　　70

So fast, that, if this very hour
You yield not as my paramour,
He will not see the rain leave off—
Nay, keep your tongue from gibe and scoff,
Sir Robert, or I slay you now.'   75

She laid her hand upon her brow,
Then gazed upon the palm, as though
She thought her forehead bled, and—' No,'
She said, and turn'd her head away,
As there were nothing else to say,   80
And everything were settled : red
Grew Godmar's face from chin to head :
' Jehane, on yonder hill there stands
My castle, guarding well my lands :
What hinders me from taking you,   85
And doing that I list to do
To your fair wilful body, while
Your knight lies dead ? '

                    A wicked smile
Wrinkled her face, her lips grew thin,
A long way out she thrust her chin :   90
' You know that I should strangle you
While you were sleeping ; or bite through
Your throat, by God's help—ah ! ' she said,
' Lord Jesus, pity your poor maid !
For in such wise they hem me in,   95
I cannot choose but sin and sin,
Whatever happens : yet I think
They could not make me eat or drink,
And so should I just reach my rest.'

' Nay, if you do not my behest,   100
O Jehane ! though I love you well,'
Said Godmar, ' would I fail to tell
All that I know ? ' ' Foul lies,' she said.
' Eh ? lies, my Jehane ? by God's head,
At Paris folks would deem them true !   105
Do you know, Jehane, they cry for you,

" Jehane the brown ! Jehane the brown !
Give us Jehane to burn or drown ! "—
Eh—gag me Robert !—sweet my friend,
This were indeed a piteous end   110
For those long fingers, and long feet,
And long neck, and smooth shoulders sweet ;
An end that few men would forget
That saw it—So, an hour yet :
Consider, Jehane, which to take   115
Of life or death ! '

                So, scarce awake,
Dismounting, did she leave that place,
And totter some yards : with her face
Turn'd upward to the sky she lay,
Her head on a wet heap of hay,   120
And fell asleep : and while she slept,
And did not dream, the minutes crept
Round to the twelve again ; but she,
Being waked at last, sigh'd quietly,
And strangely childlike came, and said :   125
' I will not.'   Straightway Godmar's head,
As though it hung on strong wires, turn'd
Most sharply round, and his face burn'd.

For Robert—both his eyes were dry,
He could not weep, but gloomily   130
He seem'd to watch the rain ; yea, too,
His lips were firm ; he tried once more
To touch her lips ; she reach'd out, sore
And vain desire so tortured them,
The poor grey lips, and now the hem   135
Of his sleeve brush'd them.

                With a start
Up Godmar rose, thrust them apart ;
From Robert's throat he loosed the bands
Of silk and mail ; with empty hands
Held out, she stood and gazed, and saw   140
The long bright blade without a flaw
Glide out from Godmar's sheath, his hand

In Robert's hair ; she saw him bend
Back Robert's head ; she saw him send 144
The thin steel down ; the blow told well,
Right backward the knight Robert fell,
And moan'd as dogs do, being half dead,
Unwitting, as I deem : so then
Godmar turn'd grinning to his men,
Who ran, some five or six, and beat 150
His head to pieces at their feet.

Then Godmar turn'd again and said :
' So, Jehane, the first fitte is read !
Take note, my lady, that your way
Lies backward to the Chatelet !' 155
She shook her head and gazed awhile
At her cold hands with a rueful smile,
As though this thing had made her mad.

This was the parting that they had
Beside the haystack in the floods. 160

W. MORRIS.

390

SUMMER DAWN

Pray but one prayer for me 'twixt thy closed lips,
    Think but one thought of me up in the stars.
The summer night waneth, the morning light slips,
    Faint and grey 'twixt the leaves of the aspen,
        betwixt the cloud-bars,
That are patiently waiting there for the dawn : 5
    Patient and colourless, though Heaven's gold
Waits to float through them along with the sun.
Far out in the meadows, above the young corn,
    The heavy elms wait, and restless and cold
The uneasy wind rises ; the roses are dun ; 10
Through the long twilight they pray for the dawn,
Round the lone house in the midst of the corn.
    Speak but one word to me over the corn,
    Over the tender, bowed locks of the corn.

W. MORRIS.

391

As we rush, as we rush in the train,
   The trees and the houses go wheeling back,
But the starry heavens above the plain
   Come flying on our track.

All the beautiful stars of the sky,   5
   The silver doves of the forest of Night,
Over the dull earth swarm and fly,
   Companions of our flight.

We will rush ever on without fear ;
   Let the goal be far, the flight be fleet !   10
For we carry the Heavens with us, dear,
   While the Earth slips from our feet !

                     J. THOMSON.

392

ITYLUS

Swallow, my sister, O sister swallow,
   How can thine heart be full of the spring ?
     A thousand summers are over and dead.
What hast thou found in the spring to follow ?
   What hast thou found in thine heart to sing ?
     What wilt thou do when the summer is shed ?

O swallow, sister, O fair swift swallow,   7
   Why wilt thou fly after spring to the south,
     The soft south whither thine heart is set ?
Shall not the grief of the old time follow ?
   Shall not the song thereof cleave to thy mouth ?
     Hast thou forgotten ere I forget ?   12

Sister, my sister, O fleet sweet swallow,
   Thy way is long to the sun and the south ;
     But I, fulfilled of my heart's desire,   15
Shedding my song upon height, upon hollow,
   From tawny body and sweet small mouth,
     Feed the heart of the night with fire.

I the nightingale all spring through,
  O swallow, sister, O changing swallow,   20
    All spring through till the spring be done,
Clothed with the light of the night on the dew,
  Sing, while the hours and the wild birds follow,
    Take flight and follow and find the sun.

Sister, my sister, O soft light swallow,   25
  Though all things feast in the spring's guest-
        chamber,
    How hast thou heart to be glad thereof yet ?
For where thou fliest I shall not follow,
  Till life forget and death remember,
    Till thou remember and I forget.   30

Swallow, my sister, O singing swallow,
  I know not how thou hast heart to sing.
    Hast thou the heart ? is it all past over ?
Thy lord the summer is good to follow,
  And fair the feet of thy lover the spring :   35
    But what wilt thou say to the spring thy lover?

O swallow, sister, O fleeting swallow,
  My heart in me is a molten ember
    And over my head the waves have met.
But thou wouldst tarry or I would follow,   40
  Could I forget or thou remember,
    Couldst thou remember and I forget.

O sweet stray sister, O shifting swallow,
  The heart's division divideth us.
    Thy heart is light as a leaf of a tree ;   45
But mine goes forth among sea-gulfs hollow
  To the place of the slaying of Itylus,
    The feast of Daulis, the Thracian sea.

O swallow, sister, O rapid swallow,
  I pray thee sing not a little space.   50
    Are not the roofs and the lintels wet ?
The woven web that was plain to follow,
  The small slain body, the flowerlike face,
    Can I remember if thou forget ?

O sister, sister, thy first-begotten !　　　　　55
　　The hands that cling and the feet that follow,
　　　The voice of the child's blood crying yet,
Who hath remembered me ? who hath forgotten ?
　　Thou hast forgotten, O summer swallow,
　　　But the world shall end when I forget.　　60

　　　　　　　　　　A. C. SWINBURNE.

393

THE GARDEN OF PROSERPINE

Here, where the world is quiet ;
　　Here, where all trouble seems
Dead winds' and spent waves' riot
　　In doubtful dreams of dreams ;
I watch the green field growing　　5
For reaping folk and sowing,
For harvest-time and mowing,
　　A sleepy world of streams.

I am tired of tears and laughter,
　　And men that laugh and weep ;　　10
Of what may come hereafter
　　For men that sow to reap :
I am weary of days and hours,
Blown buds of barren flowers,
Desires and dreams and powers　　15
　　And everything but sleep.

Here life has death for neighbour,
　　And far from eye or ear
Wan waves and wet winds labour,
　　Weak ships and spirits steer ;　　20
They drive adrift, and whither
They wot not who make thither ;
But no such winds blow hither,
　　And no such things grow here.

No growth of moor or coppice,   25
  No heather-flower or vine,
But bloomless buds of poppies,
  Green grapes of Proserpine,
Pale beds of blowing rushes,
Where no leaf blooms or blushes   30
Save this whereout she crushes
  For dead men deadly wine.

Pale, without name or number,
  In fruitless fields of corn,
They bow themselves and slumber   35
  All night till light is born ;
And like a soul belated,
In hell and heaven unmated,
By cloud and mist abated
  Comes out of darkness morn.   40

Though one were strong as seven,
  He too with death shall dwell,
Nor wake with wings in heaven,
  Nor weep for pains in hell ;
Though one were fair as roses,   45
His beauty clouds and closes ;
And well though love reposes,
  In the end it is not well.

Pale, beyond porch and portal,
  Crowned with calm leaves, she stands   50
Who gathers all things mortal
  With cold immortal hands ;
Her languid lips are sweeter
Than love's who fears to greet her
To men that mix and meet her   55
  From many times and lands.

She waits for each and other,
  She waits for all men born ;
Forgets the earth her mother,
  The life of fruits and corn ;   60

And spring and seed and swallow
Take wing for her and follow
Where summer song rings hollow
   And flowers are put to scorn.

There go the loves that wither,   65
   The old loves with wearier wings ;
And all dead years draw thither,
   And all disastrous things ;
Dead dreams of days forsaken,
Blind buds that snows have shaken,   70
Wild leaves that winds have taken,
   Red strays of ruined springs.

We are not sure of sorrow,
   And joy was never sure ;
To-day will die to-morrow ;   75
   Time stoops to no man's lure ;
And love, grown faint and fretful,
With lips but half regretful
Sighs, and with eyes forgetful
   Weeps that no loves endure.   80

From too much love of living,
   From hope and fear set free,
We thank with brief thanksgiving
   Whatever gods may be
That no life lives for ever ;   85
That dead men rise up never ;
That even the weariest river
   Winds somewhere safe to sea.

Then star nor sun shall waken,
   Nor any change of light :   90
Nor sound of waters shaken,
   Nor any sound or sight :
Nor wintry leaves nor vernal,
Nor days nor things diurnal ;
Only the sleep eternal   95
   In an eternal night.
                  A. C. SWINBURNE.

394

A FORSAKEN GARDEN

In a coign of the cliff between lowland and highland,
   At the sea-down's edge between windward and lee,
Walled round with rocks as an inland island,
   The ghost of a garden fronts the sea.
A girdle of brushwood and thorn encloses   5
   The steep square slope of the blossomless bed
Where the weeds that grew green from the graves
     of its roses
          Now lie dead.

The fields fall southward, abrupt and broken,
   To the low last edge of the long lone land.   10
If a step should sound or a word be spoken,
   Would a ghost not rise at the strange guest's
     hand?
So long have the grey bare walks lain guestless,
   Through branches and briers if a man make way
He shall find no life but the sea-wind's, restless
         Night and day.   16

The dense hard passage is blind and stifled
   That crawls by a track none turn to climb
To the strait waste place that the years have rifled
   Of all but the thorns that are touched not of
     time.   20
The thorns he spares when the rose is taken;
   The rocks are left when he wastes the plain.
The wind that wanders, the weeds wind-shaken,
        These remain.   24

Not a flower to be pressed of the foot that falls not;
   As the heart of a dead man the seed-plots are dry;
From the thicket of thorns whence the nightingale
     calls not,
   Could she call, there were never a rose to reply.
Over the meadows that blossom and wither
   Rings but the note of a sea-bird's song;   30
Only the sun and the rain come hither
        All year long.

The sun burns sere and the rain dishevels
  One gaunt bleak blossom of scentless breath.
Only the wind here hovers and revels   35
  In a round where life seems barren as death.
Here there was laughing of old, there was weeping,
  Haply, of lovers none ever will know,
Whose eyes went seaward a hundred sleeping
        Years ago.   40

Heart handfast in heart as they stood, 'Look thither,'
  Did he whisper? 'look forth from the flowers
    to the sea;
For the foam-flowers endure when the rose-
    blossoms wither,
  And men that love lightly may die—but we?'
And the same wind sang and the same waves
    whitened,   45
  And or ever the garden's last petals were shed,
In the lips that had whispered, the eyes that had
    lightened,
        Love was dead.

Or they loved their life through, and then went
    whither?
  And were one to the end—but what end who
    knows?
Love deep as the sea as a rose must wither,   51
  As the rose-red seaweed that mocks the rose.
Shall the dead take thought for the dead to love them?
  What love was ever as deep as a grave?
They are loveless now as the grass above them,
        Or the wave.   56

All are at one now, roses and lovers,
  Not known of the cliffs and the fields and the sea.
Not a breath of the time that has been hovers
  In the air now soft with a summer to be.   60
Not a breath shall there sweeten the seasons
    hereafter
Of the flowers or the lovers that laugh now or weep,
When as they that are free now of weeping and
    laughter
        We shall sleep.

Here death may deal not again for ever ;   65
   Here change may come not till all change end.
From the graves they have made they shall rise up
     never,
   Who have left nought living to ravage and rend.
Earth, stones, and thorns of the wild ground
     growing,   69
   While the sun and the rain live, these shall be ;
Till a last wind's breath upon all these blowing
     Roll the sea.

Till the slow sea rise and the sheer cliff crumble,
   Till terrace and meadow the deep gulfs drink,
Till the strength of the waves of the high tides
     humble   75
   The fields that lessen, the rocks that shrink ;
Here now in his triumph where all things falter,
   Stretched out on the spoils that his own hand
     spread,
As a god self-slain on his own strange altar,
     Death lies dead.   80

                    A. C. SWINBURNE.

395

OLIVE

Addressed to Olive Miranda Watts, aged nine years

1

     Who may praise her ?
   Eyes where midnight shames the sun,
   Hair of night and sunshine spun,
   Woven of dawn's or twilight's loom,
   Radiant darkness, lustrous gloom,   5
   Godlike childhood's flowerlike bloom,
   None may praise aright, nor sing
   Half the grace wherewith like spring
     Love arrays her.

2

  Love untold   10
Sings in silence, speaks in light
Shed from each fair feature, bright
Still from heaven, whence toward us, now
Nine years since, she deigned to bow
Down the brightness of her brow,   15
Deigned to pass through mortal birth :
Reverence calls her, here on earth,
   Nine years old.

3

  Love's deep duty,
Even when love transfigured grows   20
Worship, all too surely knows
How, though love may cast out fear,
Yet the debt divine and dear
Due to childhood's godhead here
May by love of man be paid   25
Never ; never song be made
   Worth its beauty.

4

  Nought is all
Sung or said or dreamed or thought
Ever, set beside it ; nought   30
All the love that man may give—
Love whose prayer should be, ' Forgive ! '
Heaven, we see, on earth may live ;
Earth can thank not heaven, we know,
Save with songs that ebb and flow,   35
   Rise and fall.

5

  No man living,
No man dead, save haply one
Now gone homeward past the sun

Ever found such grace as might 40
Tune his tongue to praise aright
Children, flowers of love and light,
Whom our praise dispraises : we
Sing, in sooth, but not as he
    Sang thanksgiving. 45

6

    Hope that smiled,
Seeing her new-born beauty, made
Out of heaven's own light and shade,
Smiled not half so sweetly : love,
Seeing the sun, afar above, 50
Warm the nest that rears the dove,
Sees, more bright than moon or sun,
All the heaven of heavens in one
    Little child.

7

    Who may sing her ? 55
Wings of angels when they stir
Make no music worthy her :
Sweeter sound her shy soft words
Here than songs of God's own birds
Whom the fire of rapture girds 60
Round with light from love's face lit :
Hands of angels find no fit
    Gifts to bring her.

8

    Babes at birth
Wear as raiment round them cast, 65
Keep as witness toward their past,
Tokens left of heaven ; and each,
Ere its lips learn mortal speech,
Ere sweet heaven pass on pass reach,
Bears in undiverted eyes 70
Proof of unforgotten skies
    Here on earth.

9

Quenched as embers
Quenched with flakes of rain or snow
Till the last faint flame burns low,   75
All those lustrous memories lie
Dead with babyhood gone by :
Yet in her they dare not die :
Others fair as heaven is, yet,
Now they share not heaven, forget :   80
  She remembers.

      A. C. SWINBURNE.

396

ODE

We are the music-makers,
 And we are the dreamers of dreams,
Wandering by lone sea-breakers,
 And sitting by desolate streams ;—
World-losers and world-forsakers,   5
 On whom the pale moon gleams :
Yet we are the movers and shakers
 Of the world for ever, it seems.

With wonderful deathless ditties
We build up the world's great cities,   10
 And out of a fabulous story
 We fashion an empire's glory :
One man with a dream, at pleasure,
 Shall go forth and conquer a crown ;
And three with a new song's measure   15
 Can trample a kingdom down.

We, in the ages lying
 In the buried past of the earth,
Built Nineveh with our sighing,
 And Babel itself in our mirth ;   20
And o'erthrew them with prophesying
 To the old of the new world's worth ;
For each age is a dream that is dying,
 Or one that is coming to birth.

A breath of our inspiration   25
Is the life of each generation ;
   A wondrous thing of our dreaming,
   Unearthly, impossible seeming—
The soldier, the king, and the peasant
  Are working together in one,   30
Till our dream shall become their present,
  And their work in the world be done.

They had no vision amazing
Of the goodly house they are raising ;
   They had no divine foreshowing   35
   Of the land to which they are going :
But on one man's soul it hath broken,
  A light that doth not depart ;
And his look, or a word he hath spoken,
  Wrought flame in another man's heart.

And therefore to-day is thrilling   41
With a past day's late fulfilling ;
   And the multitudes are enlisted
   In the faith that their fathers resisted,
And, scorning the dream of to-morrow,   45
  Are bringing to pass, as they may,
In the world, for its joy or its sorrow,
  The dream that was scorned yesterday.

But we, with our dreaming and singing,
   Ceaseless and sorrowless we !   50
The glory about us clinging
   Of the glorious futures we see,
Our souls with high music ringing :
  O men ! it must ever be
That we dwell, in our dreaming and singing,
  A little apart from ye.   56

For we are afar with the dawning
  And the suns that are not yet high,
And out of the infinite morning
  Intrepid you hear us cry—   60

How, spite of your human scorning,
  Once more God's future draws nigh,
And already goes forth the warning
  That ye of the past must die.

Great hail ! we cry to the comers   65
  From the dazzling unknown shore ;
Bring us hither your sun and your summers,
  And renew our world as of yore ;
You shall teach us your song's new numbers,
  And things that we dreamed not before :
Yea, in spite of a dreamer who slumbers, 71
  And a singer who sings no more.

A. W. E. O'SHAUGHNESSY.

397

Out of the night that covers me,
  Black as the pit from pole to pole,
I thank whatever gods may be
  For my unconquerable soul.

In the fell clutch of circumstance   5
  I have not winced nor cried aloud.
Under the bludgeonings of chance
  My head is bloody, but unbowed.

Beyond this place of wrath and tears
  Looms but the Horror of the shade,   10
And yet the menace of the years
  Finds, and shall find, me unafraid.

It matters not how strait the gate,
  How charged with punishments the scroll,
I am the master of my fate :   15
  I am the captain of my soul.

W. E. HENLEY.

398

PIED BEAUTY

Glory be to God for dappled things—
　For skies of couple-colour as a brindled cow ;
　　For rose-moles all in stipple upon trout that
　　　swim ;
Fresh-firecoal chestnut-falls ; finches' wings ;
　Landscape plotted and pieced—fold, fallow, and
　　plough ; 5
　　And áll trádes, their gear and tackle and trim.

All things counter, original, spare, strange ;
　Whatever is fickle, freckled (who knows how ?)
　　With swift, slow ; sweet, sour ; adazzle, dim ;
He fathers-forth whose beauty is past change : 10
　　Praise Him.
　　　　　　　　　GERARD MANLEY HOPKINS.

399

THE STARLIGHT NIGHT

Look at the stars ! look, look up at the skies !
　O look at all the fire-folk sitting in the air !
　The bright boroughs, the circle-citadels there !
Down in dim woods the diamond delves ! the
　　elves'-eyes !
The grey lawns cold where gold, where quickgold
　　lies ! 5
　Wind-beat whitebeam ! airy abeles set on a flare !
　Flake-doves sent floating forth at a farmyard
　　scare !—
Ah well ! it is all a purchase, all is a prize.

Buy then ! bid then !—What ?—Prayer, patience,
　　alms, vows.
Look, look : a May-mess, like on orchard boughs !
　Look ! March-blown, like on mealed-with-yellow
　　sallows ! 11

These are indeed the barn ; withindoors house
The shocks.   This piece-bright paling shuts the
    spouse
   Christ home, Christ and His mother and all His
    hallows.

GERARD MANLEY HOPKINS.

400

FROM 'MODERN LOVE'

In our old shipwrecked days there was an hour,
When in the firelight steadily aglow,
Joined slackly, we beheld the red chasm grow
Among the clicking coals.   Our library-bower
That eve was left to us : and hushed we sat   5
As lovers to whom Time is whispering.
From sudden-opened doors we heard them sing :
The nodding elders mixed good wine with chat.
Well knew we that Life's greatest treasure lay
With us, and of it was our talk.   ' Ah, yes !   10
Love dies ! ' I said : I never thought it less.
She yearned to me that sentence to unsay.
Then when the fire domed blackening, I found
Her cheek was salt against my kiss, and swift
Up the sharp scale of sobs her breast did lift :— 15
Now am I haunted by that taste ! that sound.

Mark where the pressing wind shoots javelin-like
Its skeleton shadow on the broad-backed wave !
Here is a fitting spot to dig Love's grave ;
Here where the ponderous breakers plunge and
    strike,   20
And dart their hissing tongues high up the sand :
In hearing of the ocean, and in sight
Of those ribbed wind-streaks running into white.
If I the death of Love had deeply planned,
I never could have made it half so sure,   25
As by the unblest kisses which upbraid
The full-waked sense ; or failing that, degrade !
'Tis morning : but no morning can restore

What we have forfeited.   I see no sin :
The wrong is mixed.   In tragic life, God wot,   30
No villain need be ! Passions spin the plot :
We are betrayed by what is false within.

We saw the swallows gathering in the sky,
And in the osier-isle we heard them noise.
We had not to look back on summer joys,   35
Or forward to a summer of bright dye :
But in the largeness of the evening earth
Our spirits grew as we went side by side.
The hour became her husband and my bride.
Love, that had robbed us so, thus blessed our
　　　　dearth !   40
The pilgrims of the year waxed very loud
In multitudinous chatterings, as the flood
Full brown came from the West, and like pale blood
Expanded to the upper crimson cloud.
Love, that had robbed us of immortal things,   45
This little moment mercifully gave,
Where I have seen across the twilight wave
The swan sail with her young beneath her wings.

Thus piteously Love closed what he begat :
The union of this ever-diverse pair !   50
These two were rapid falcons in a snare,
Condemned to do the flitting of the bat.
Lovers beneath the singing sky of May,
They wandered once ; clear as the dew on flowers :
But they fed not on the advancing hours :   55
Their hearts held cravings for the buried day.
Then each applied to each that fatal knife,
Deep questioning, which probes to endless dole.
Ah, what a dusty answer gets the soul
When hot for certainties in this our life !—   60
In tragic hints here see what evermore
Moves dark as yonder midnight ocean's force,
Thundering like ramping hosts of warrior horse,
To throw that faint thin line upon the shore !
　　　　　　　　　　GEORGE MEREDITH.

401

A BALLAD TO QUEEN ELIZABETH

OF THE SPANISH ARMADA

King Philip had vaunted his claims ;
　　He had sworn for a year he would sack us ;
With an army of heathenish names
　　He was coming to fagot and stack us ;
　　Like the thieves of the sea he would track us, 5
And shatter our ships on the main ;
　　But we had bold Neptune to back us,—
And where are the galleons of Spain ?

His carackes were christened of dames
　　To the kirtles whereof he would tack us ;　　10
With his saints and his gilded stern-frames,
　　He had thought like an egg-shell to crack us ;
　　Now Howard may get to his Flaccus,
And Drake to his Devon again,
　　And Hawkins bowl rubbers to Bacchus,—　　15
For where are the galleons of Spain ?

Let his Majesty hang to St. James
　　The axe that he whetted to hack us ;
He must play at some lustier games
　　Or at sea he can hope to out-thwack us ;　　20
　　To his mines of Peru he would pack us
To tug at his bullet and chain ;
　　Alas ! that his Greatness should lack us !—
But where are the galleons of Spain ?

Envoy

Gloriana ! the Don may attack us　　　　　　25
Whenever his stomach be fain ;
　　He must reach us before he can rack us, . . .
And where are the galleons of Spain ?

AUSTIN DOBSON.

402

GIRD ON THY SWORD

Gird on thy sword, O man, thy strength endue,
In fair desire thine earth-born joy renew.
Live thou thy life beneath the making sun
Till Beauty, Truth, and Love in thee are one.

Thro' thousand ages hath thy childhood run :   5
On timeless ruin hath thy glory been :
From the forgotten night of loves fordone
Thou risest in the dawn of hopes unseen.

Higher and higher shall thy thoughts aspire,
Unto the stars of heaven, and pass away,   10
And earth renew the buds of thy desire
In fleeting blooms of everlasting day.

Thy work with beauty crown, thy life with love ;
Thy mind with truth uplift to God above :
For whom all is, from whom was all begun,   15
In whom all Beauty, Truth, and Love are one.

ROBERT BRIDGES.

403

I HAVE LOVED FLOWERS THAT FADE

I have loved flowers that fade,
Within whose magic tents
Rich hues have marriage made
With sweet unmemoried scents :
A honeymoon delight,—   5
A joy of love at sight,
That ages in an hour :—
My song be like a flower !

I have loved airs, that die
Before their charm is writ   10
Along a liquid sky
Trembling to welcome it.
Notes, that with pulse of fire
Proclaim the spirit's desire,
Then die, and are nowhere :-   15
My song be like an air !

Die, song, die like a breath,
And wither as a bloom :
Fear not a flowery death,
Dread not an airy tomb ! 20
Fly with delight, fly hence !
'Twas thine love's tender sense
To feast ; now on thy bier
Beauty shall shed a tear.

ROBERT BRIDGES.

404

NIGHTINGALES

Beautiful must be the mountains whence ye come,
And bright in the fruitful valleys the streams, wherefrom
Ye learn your song :
Where are those starry woods ? O might I wander there,
Among the flowers, which in that heavenly air 5
Bloom the year long !

Nay, barren are those mountains and spent the streams :
Our song is the voice of desire, that haunts our dreams,
A throe of the heart,
Whose pining visions dim, forbidden hopes profound, 10
No dying cadence nor long sigh can sound,
For all our art.

Alone, aloud in the raptured ear of men
We pour our dark nocturnal secret ; and then,
As night is withdrawn 15
From these sweet-springing meads and bursting boughs of May,
Dream, while the innumerable choir of day
Welcome the dawn.

ROBERT BRIDGES.

405

IN MEMORIAM F. A. S.

Yet, O stricken heart, remember, O remember
  How of human days he lived the better part.
April came to bloom and never dim December
  Breathed its killing chills upon the head or heart.

Doomed to know not Winter, only Spring, a being
  Trod the flowery April blithely for a while,   6
Took his fill of music, joy of thought and seeing,
  Came and stayed and went, nor ever ceased to
    smile.

Came and stayed and went, and now when all is
  finished,
  You alone have crossed the melancholy stream,
Yours the pang, but his, O his, the undiminished
  Undecaying gladness, undeparted dream.   12

All that life contains of torture, toil and treason,
  Shame, dishonour, death, to him were but a name.
Here, a boy, he dwelt through all the singing season
  And ere the day of sorrow departed as he came.
                   R. L. STEVENSON.

406

UNTO US A SON IS GIVEN

Given, not lent,
And not withdrawn—once sent,
This Infant of mankind, this One,
Is still the little welcome Son.

New every year,   5
New born and newly dear,
He comes with tidings and a song,
The ages long, the ages long;

Even as the cold
Keen winter grows not old,   10
As childhood is so fresh, foreseen,
And spring in the familiar green.

Sudden as sweet
Come the expected feet.
All joy is young, and new all art,   15
And He, too, whom we have by heart.

ALICE MEYNELL.

407

VENERATION OF IMAGES

Thou man, first-comer, whose wide arms entreat,
    Gather, clasp, welcome, bind,
Lack, or remember ; whose warm pulses beat
    With love of thine own kind :—

Unlifted for a blessing on yon sea,   5
    Unshrined on this highway,
O flesh, O grief, thou too shalt have our knee,
    Thou rood of every day !

ALICE MEYNELL.

408

IN ROMNEY MARSH

As I went down to Dymchurch Wall,
    I heard the South sing o'er the land ;
I saw the yellow sunlight fall
    On knolls where Norman churches stand.

And ringing shrilly, taut and lithe,   5
    Within the wind a core of sound,
The wire from Romney town to Hythe
    Alone its airy journey wound.

A veil of purple vapour flowed
    And trailed its fringe along the Straits ;   10
The upper air like sapphire glowed ;
    And roses filled Heaven's central gates.

Masts in the offing wagged their tops ;
    The swinging waves peal'd on the shore ;
The saffron beach, all diamond drops   15
    And beads of surge, prolonged the roar.

As I came up from Dymchurch Wall,
  I saw above the Downs' low crest
The crimson brands of sunset fall,
  Flicker and fade from out the west.   20

Night sank : like flakes of silver fire
  The stars in one great shower came down ;
Shrill blew the wind ; and shrill the wire
  Rang out from Hythe to Romney town.

The darkly shining salt sea drops   25
  Streamed as the waves clashed on the shore ;
The beach, with all its organ stops
  Pealing again, prolonged the roar.

JOHN DAVIDSON.

409

EPITAPH ON AN ARMY OF MERCENARIES

These, in the day when heaven was falling,
  The hour when earth's foundations fled,
Followed their mercenary calling
  And took their wages and are dead.

Their shoulders held the sky suspended ;   5
  They stood, and earth's foundations stay ;
What God abandoned, these defended,
  And saved the sum of things for pay.

A. E. HOUSMAN.

410

' IN NO STRANGE LAND '

'The Kingdom of God is within you.'

O world invisible, we view thee,
O world intangible, we touch thee,
O world unknowable, we know thee,
Inapprehensible, we clutch thee !

Does the fish soar to find the ocean,   5
The eagle plunge to find the air—
That we ask of the stars in motion
If they have rumour of thee there ?

Not where the wheeling systems darken,
And our benumbed conceiving soars !— 10
The drift of pinions, would we hearken,
Beats at our own clay-shuttered doors.

The angels keep their ancient places ;—
Turn but a stone, and start a wing !
'Tis ye, 'tis your estrangèd faces, 15
That miss the many-splendoured thing.

But (when so sad thou canst not sadder)
Cry ;—and upon thy so sore loss
Shall shine the traffic of Jacob's ladder
Pitched betwixt Heaven and Charing Cross. 20

Yea, in the night, my Soul, my daughter,
Cry,—clinging Heaven by the hems ;
And lo, Christ walking on the water,
Not of Gennesareth, but Thames !

FRANCIS THOMPSON.

411

DRAKE'S DRUM

Drake he's in his hammock an' a thousand mile
 away,
 (Capten, art tha sleepin' there below ?)
Slung atween the round shot in Nombre Dios Bay,
 An' dreamin' arl the time o' Plymouth Hoe.
Yarnder lumes the Island, yarnder lie the ships, 5
 Wi' sailor lads a-dancin' heel-an'-toe,
An' the shore-lights flashin', an' the night-tide
 dashin',
 He sees et arl so plainly as he saw et long ago.

Drake he was a Devon man, an' rüled the Devon seas,
 (Capten, art tha sleepin' there below ?), 10
Rovin' tho' his death fell, he went wi' heart at ease,
 An' dreamin' arl the time o' Plymouth Hoe.
'Take my drum to England, hang et by the shore,
 Strike et when your powder 's runnin' low ;
If the Dons sight Devon, I'll quit the port o' Heaven,
 An' drum them up the Channel as we drummed
 them long ago.' 16

Drake he 's in his hammock till the great Armadas
    come,
    (Capten, art tha sleepin' there below ?),
Slung atween the round shot, listenin' for the drum,
    An' dreamin' arl the time o' Plymouth Hoe. 20
Call him on the deep sea, call him up the Sound,
    Call him when ye sail to meet the foe ;
Where the old trade 's plyin' an' the old flag flyin'
    They shall find him ware an' wakin', as they
      found him long ago !

SIR HENRY NEWBOLT.

412

UNWELCOME

We were young, we were merry, we were very very
    wise,
    And the door stood open at our feast,
When there passed us a woman with the West in her
    eyes,
    And a man with his back to the East.

O, still grew the hearts that were beating so fast,   5
    The loudest voice was still.
The jest died away on our lips as they passed,
    And the rays of July struck chill.

The cups of red wine turn'd pale on the board,
    The white bread black as soot.   10
The hound forgot the hand of her lord,
    She fell down at his foot.

Low let me lie, where the dead dog lies,
    Ere I sit me down again at a feast,
When there passes a woman with the West in her
    eyes,   15
    And a man with his back to the East.

MARY COLERIDGE.

413

THE LAKE ISLE OF INNISFREE

I will arise and go now, and go to Innisfree,
And a small cabin build there, of clay and wattles
    made ;
Nine bean rows will I have there, a hive for the
    honey bee,
And live alone in the bee-loud glade.

And I shall have some peace there, for peace comes
    dropping slow,   5
Dropping from the veils of the morning to where
    the cricket sings ;
There midnight's all a-glimmer, and noon a purple
    glow,
And evening full of the linnet's wings.

I will arise and go now, for always night and day
I hear lake water lapping with low sounds by the shore;
While I stand on the roadway, or on the pavements
    gray,   11
I hear it in the deep heart's core.

W. B. YEATS.

414

THE FOLLY OF BEING COMFORTED

One that is ever kind said yesterday :
' Your well-beloved's hair has threads of grey,
And little shadows come about her eyes ;
Time can but make it easier to be wise
Though now it seem impossible, and so   5
Patience is all that you have need of.' No,
I have not a crumb of comfort, not a grain ;
Time can but make her beauty over again :
Because of that great nobleness of hers
The fire that stirs about her, when she stirs   10
Burns but more clearly. O she had not these ways,
When all the wild summer was in her gaze,
O heart ! O heart ! if she'd but turn her head,
You'd know the folly of being comforted.

W. B. YEATS.

415

THE COWARD

I could not look on Death, which being known,
Men led me to him, blindfold and alone.

RUDYARD KIPLING.

416

THE LAST CHANTEY

Thus said The Lord in the Vault above the Cheru-
    bim,
  Calling to the Angels and the Souls in their
    degree :
     ' Lo ! Earth has pass'd away
     On the smoke of Judgement Day.
  That Our word may be established shall We
    gather up the sea ? '   5

Loud sang the souls of the jolly, jolly mariners :
  ' Plague upon the hurricane that made us furl
    and flee !
    But the war is done between us,
    In the deep the Lord hath seen us—
  Our bones we'll leave the barracout', and God
    may sink the sea ! '   10

Then said the soul of Judas that betrayèd Him :
  ' Lord, hast Thou forgotten Thy covenant with
    me ?
    How once a year I go
    To cool me on the floe ?
  And Ye take my day of mercy if Ye take away
    the sea ! '   15

Then said the soul of the Angel of the Off-shore
    Wind :
  (He that bits the thunder when the bull-mouthed
    breakers flee) :
    ' I have watch and ward to keep
    O'er Thy wonders on the deep,
  And Ye take mine honour from me if Ye take
    away the sea ! '   20

Loud sang the souls of the jolly, jolly mariners :
  ' Nay, but we were angry, and a hasty folk are
       we !
     If we worked the ship together
     Till she foundered in foul weather,
   Are we babes that we should clamour for a
      vengeance on the sea ? '   25

Then said the souls of the slaves that men threw
     overboard :
   ' Kennelled in the picaroon a weary band were
      we ;
     But Thy arm was strong to save,
     And it touched us on the wave,
   And we drowsed the long tides idle till Thy
      Trumpets tore the sea.'   30

Then cried the soul of the stout Apostle Paul to
     God :
   ' Once we frapped a ship, and she laboured
      woundily.
     There were fourteen score of these,
     And they blessed Thee on their knees,
   When they learned Thy Grace and Glory under
      Malta by the sea ! '   35

Loud sang the souls of the jolly, jolly mariners,
   Plucking at their harps, and they plucked un-
     handily :
     ' Our thumbs are rough and tarred,
     And the tune is something hard—
   May we lift a Deepsea Chantey such as seamen
      use at sea ? '   40

Then said the souls of the gentlemen-adventurers—
   Fettered wrist to bar all for red iniquity :
     ' Ho, we revel in our chains
     O'er the sorrow that was Spain's ;
   Heave or sink it, leave or drink it, we were
      masters of the sea ! '   45

Up spake the soul of a gray Gothavn 'speckshioner—
   (He that led the flinching in the fleets of fair
      Dundee) :
     ' Oh, the ice-blink white and near,
     And the bowhead breaching clear !
Will Ye whelm them all for wantonness that
     wallow in the sea ?'   50

Loud sang the souls of the jolly, jolly mariners,
   Crying : ' Under Heaven, here is neither lead
     nor lea !
     Must we sing for evermore
     On the windless, glassy floor ?
Take back your golden fiddles and we'll beat to
     open sea !'   55

Then stooped the Lord, and He called the good sea
   up to Him,
And 'stablished his borders unto all eternity,
     That such as have no pleasure
     For to praise the Lord by measure,
They may enter into galleons and serve Him on
     the sea.   60

Sun, wind, and cloud shall fail not from the face of it,
Slinging, ringing spindrift, nor the fulmar flying
   free ;
     And the ships shall go abroad
     To the Glory of the Lord
Who heard the silly sailor-folk and gave them back
     their sea !   65
               RUDYARD KIPLING.

417
RECESSIONAL
June 22, 1897

God of our fathers, known of old,
   Lord of our far-flung battle-line,
Beneath whose awful Hand we hold
   Dominion over palm and pine—
Lord God of Hosts, be with us yet,   5
Lest we forget—lest we forget !

The tumult and the shouting dies ;
	The captains and the kings depart :
Still stands Thine ancient sacrifice,
	An humble and a contrite heart.			10
Lord God of Hosts, be with us yet,
Lest we forget—lest we forget !

Far-called, our navies melt away ;
	On dune and headland sinks the fire :
Lo, all our pomp of yesterday				15
	Is one with Nineveh and Tyre !
Judge of the Nations, spare us yet,
Lest we forget—lest we forget !

If, drunk with sight of power, we loose
	Wild tongues that have not Thee in awe,		20
Such boastings as the Gentiles use,
	Or lesser breeds without the Law—
Lord God of Hosts, be with us yet,
Lest we forget—lest we forget !

For heathen heart that puts her trust		25
	In reeking tube and iron shard,
All valiant dust that builds on dust,
	And guarding, calls not Thee to guard,
For frantic boast and foolish word—
Thy Mercy on Thy People, Lord !			30

						RUDYARD KIPLING.

418

CADGWITH

My windows open to the autumn night,
In vain I watched for sleep to visit me ;
How should sleep dull mine ears, and dim my sight,
Who saw the stars, and listened to the sea ?

Ah, how the City of our God is fair !			5
If, without sea, and starless though it be,
For joy of the majestic beauty there,
Men shall not miss the stars, nor mourn the sea.

						LIONEL JOHNSON.

419

FOR THE FALLEN

With proud thanksgiving, a mother for her children,
England mourns for her dead across the sea.
Flesh of her flesh they were, spirit of her spirit,
Fallen in the cause of the free.

Solemn the drums thrill : Death august and royal
Sings sorrow up into immortal spheres.   6
There is music in the midst of desolation
And a glory that shines upon our tears.

They went with songs to the battle, they were
     young,
Straight of limb, true of eye, steady and aglow. 10
They were staunch to the end against odds un-
     counted,
They fell with their faces to the foe.

They shall grow not old, as we that are left grow
     old :
Age shall not weary them, nor the years condemn.
At the going down of the sun and in the morning
We will remember them.   16

They mingle not with their laughing comrades
     again ;
They sit no more at familiar tables of home ;
They have no lot in our labour of the day-time ;
They sleep beyond England's foam.   20

But where our desires are and our hopes profound,
Felt as a well-spring that is hidden from sight,
To the innermost heart of their own land they are
     known
As the stars are known to the Night ;

As the stars that shall be bright when we are dust,
Moving in marches upon the heavenly plain,   26
As the stars that are starry in the time of our
     darkness,
To the end, to the end, they remain.
                         LAURENCE BINYON.

420

SWEET STAY-AT-HOME

Sweet Stay-at-Home, sweet Well-content,
Thou knowest of no strange continent :
Thou hast not felt thy bosom keep
A gentle motion with the deep ;
Thou hast not sailed in Indian seas,   5
Where scent comes forth in every breeze.
Thou hast not seen the rich grape grow
For miles, as far as eyes can go.
Thou hast not seen a summer's night
When maids could sew by a worm's light ;   10
Nor the North Sea in spring send out
Bright hues that like birds flit about
In solid cages of white ice—
Sweet Stay-at-Home, sweet Love-one-place.
Thou hast not seen black fingers pick   15
White cotton when the bloom is thick,
Nor heard black throats in harmony ;
Nor hast thou sat on stones that lie
Flat on the earth, that once did rise
To hide proud kings from common eyes,   20
Thou hast not seen plains full of bloom
Where green things had such little room
They pleased the eye like fairer flowers—
Sweet Stay-at-Home, all these long hours.
Sweet Well-content, sweet Love-one-place,   25
Sweet, simple maid, bless thy dear face ;
For thou hast made more homely stuff
Nurture thy gentle self enough.
I love thee for a heart that 's kind—
Not for the knowledge in thy mind.—   30

W. H. DAVIES.

421

TREES

Of all the trees in England,
　　Her sweet three corners in,
Only the Ash, the bonnie Ash
　　Burns fierce while it is green.

Of all the trees in England, 5
　　From sea to sea again,
The Willow loveliest stoops her boughs
　　Beneath the driving rain.

Of all the trees in England,
　　Past frankincense and myrrh, 10
There 's none for smell, of bloom and smoke,
　　Like Lime and Juniper.

Of all the trees in England,
　　Oak, Elder, Elm, and Thorn,
The Yew alone burns lamps of peace 15
　　For them that lie forlorn.

WALTER DE LA MARE.

422

ARABIA

Far are the shades of Arabia,
　　Where the Princes ride at noon,
'Mid the verdurous vales and thickets,
　　Under the ghost of the moon ;
And so dark is that vaulted purple 5
　　Flowers in the forest rise
And toss into blossom 'gainst the phantom stars
　　Pale in the noonday skies.

Sweet is the music of Arabia
　　In my heart, when out of dreams 10
I still in the thin clear mirk of dawn
　　Descry her gliding streams ;

Hear her strange lutes on the green banks
   Ring loud with the grief and delight
Of the dim-silked, dark-haired Musicians   15
   In the brooding silence of night.

They haunt me—her lutes and her forests ;
   No beauty on earth I see
But shadowed with that dream recalls
   Her loveliness to me :   20
Still eyes look coldly upon me,
   Cold voices whisper and say—
' He is crazed with the spell of far Arabia,
   They have stolen his wits away.'

              WALTER DE LA MARE.

423

BEFORE THE ROMAN CAME TO RYE

Before the Roman came to Rye or out to Severn
   strode,
The rolling English drunkard made the rolling
   English road.
A reeling road, a rolling road, that rambles round
   the shire,
And after him the parson ran, the sexton and the
   squire ;
A merry road, a mazy road, and such as we did tread
The night we went to Birmingham by way of
   Beachy Head.   6

I knew no harm of Bonaparte and plenty of the
   Squire,
And for to fight the Frenchman I did not much
   desire ;
But I did bash their baggonets because they
   came arrayed
To straighten out the crooked road an English
   drunkard made,   10

Where you and I went down the lane with ale-mugs
    in our hands,
The night we went to Glastonbury by way of Good-
    win Sands.

His sins they were forgiven him ; or why do flowers
    run
Behind him; and the hedges all strengthening in
    the sun ?
The wild thing went from left to right and knew not
    which was which,   15
But the wild rose was above him when they found
    him in the ditch.
God pardon us, nor harden us ; we did not see so
    clear
The night we went to Bannockburn by way of
    Brighton Pier.

My friends, we will not go again or ape an ancient
    rage,
Or stretch the folly of our youth to be the shame of
    age,   20
But walk with clearer eyes and ears this path that
    wandereth,
And see undrugged in evening light the decent inn
    of death ;
For there is good news yet to hear and fine things
    to be seen,
Before we go to Paradise by way of Kensal Green.
G. K. CHESTERTON.

424

SEA-FEVER

I must down to the seas again, to the lonely sea
    and the sky,
And all I ask is a tall ship and a star to steer her by,
And the wheel's kick and the wind's song and the
    white sail's shaking,
And a grey mist on the sea's face and a grey dawn
    breaking.

I must down to the seas again, for the call of the
    running tide   5
Is a wild call and a clear call that may not be
    denied ;
And all I ask is a windy day with the white clouds
    flying,
And the flung spray and the blown spume, and the
    sea-gulls crying.

I must down to the seas again, to the vagrant
    gypsy life,
To the gull's way and the whale's way where the
    wind 's like a whetted knife ;   10
And all I ask is a merry yarn from a laughing
    fellow-rover,
And quiet sleep and a sweet dream when the long
    trick 's over.

JOHN MASEFIELD.

425

ADLESTROP

Yes. I remember Adlestrop—
The name, because one afternoon
Of heat the express-train drew up there
Unwontedly. It was late June.

The steam hissed. Some one cleared his throat. 5
No one left and no one came
On the bare platform. What I saw
Was Adlestrop—only the name

And willows, willow-herb, and grass,
And meadowsweet, and haycocks dry,   10
No whit less still and lonely fair
Than the high cloudlets in the sky.

And for that minute a blackbird sang
Close by, and round him, mistier,
Farther and farther, all the birds   15
Of Oxfordshire and Gloucestershire.
EDWARD THOMAS.

426

MARGARET'S SONG

Too soothe and mild your lowland airs
    For one whose hope is gone :
I'm thinking of a little tarn,
    Brown, very lone.

Would now the tall swift mists could lay   5
    Their wet grasp on my hair,
And the great natures of the hills
    Round me friendly were.

In vain !—For taking hills your plains
    Have spoilt my soul, I think,   10
But would my feet were going down
    Towards the brown tarn's brink.
LASCELLES ABERCROMBIE.

427

A TOWN WINDOW

Beyond my window in the night
    Is but a drab inglorious street,
Yet there the frost and clean starlight
    As over Warwick woods are sweet.

Under the grey drift of the town   5
    The crocus works among the mould
As eagerly as those that crown
    The Warwick spring in flame and gold.

And when the tramway down the hill
    Across the cobbles moans and rings,   10
There is about my window-sill
    The tumult of a thousand wings.
JOHN DRINKWATER.

428

THE GOLDEN JOURNEY TO SAMARKAND

PROLOGUE

We who with songs beguile your pilgrimage
   And swear that Beauty lives though lilies die,
We Poets of the proud old lineage
   Who sing to find your hearts, we know not why,—

What shall we tell you ? Tales, marvellous tales 5
   Of ships and stars and isles where good men rest,
Where nevermore the rose of sunset pales,
   And winds and shadows fall toward the West :

And there the world's first huge white-bearded kings,
   In dim glades sleeping, murmur in their sleep, 10
And closer round their breasts the ivy clings,
   Cutting its pathway slow and red and deep.

II

And how beguile you ? Death has no repose
   Warmer and deeper than that Orient sand
Which hides the beauty and bright faith of those 15
   Who made the Golden Journey to Samarkand.

And now they wait and whiten peaceably,
   Those conquerors, those poets, those so fair :
They know time comes, not only you and I,
   But the whole world shall whiten, here or there ;

When those long caravans that cross the plain 21
   With dauntless feet and sound of silver bells
Put forth no more for glory or for gain,
   Take no more solace from the palm-girt wells ;

When the great markets by the sea shut fast   25
　　All that calm Sunday that goes on and on ;
When even lovers find their peace at last,
　　And Earth is but a star, that once had shone.

JAMES ELROY FLECKER.

429

AFTER RONSARD

When you are old, and I—if that should be—
　　Lying afar in undistinguished earth,
And you no more have all your will of me,
　　To teach me morals, idleness, and mirth,
But, curtained from the bleak December nights, 5
　　You sit beside the else-deserted fire
And 'neath the glow of double-polèd lights,
　　Till your alert eyes and quick judgement tire,
Turn some new poet's page, and to yourself
　　Praise his new satisfaction of new need,   10
Then pause and look a little toward the shelf
　　Where my books stand which none but you shall
　　　　read :
And say : ' I too was not ungently sung
When I was happy, beautiful, and young.'

CHARLES WILLIAMS.

430

THE SOLDIER

If I should die, think only this of me :
　　That there 's some corner of a foreign field
That is for ever England. There shall be
　　In that rich earth a richer dust concealed ;
A dust whom England bore, shaped, made aware, 5
　　Gave, once, her flowers to love, her ways to roam,
A body of England's, breathing English air,
　　Washed by the rivers, blest by suns of home.

And think, this heart, all evil shed away,
  A pulse in the eternal mind, no less   10
      Gives somewhere back the thoughts by England
        given ;
Her sights and sounds ; dreams happy as her day ;
  And laughter, learnt of friends ; and gentleness,
    In hearts at peace, under an English heaven.
                RUPERT BROOKE.

431

EVERYONE SANG

Everyone suddenly burst out singing ;
And I was filled with such delight
As prisoned birds must find in freedom
Winging wildly across the white
Orchards and dark-green fields ; on ; on ; and out
    of sight.   5

Everyone's voice was suddenly lifted,
And beauty came like the setting sun.
My heart was shaken with tears ; and horror
Drifted away . . . O but every one
Was a bird ; and the song was wordless ; the
    singing will never be done.   10
                SIEGFRIED SASSOON.

432

ALMSWOMEN

At Quincey's moat the squandering village ends,
And there in the almshouse dwell the dearest friends
Of all the village, two old dames that cling
As close as any trueloves in the spring.
Long, long ago they passed threescore-and-ten,   5
And in this doll's house lived together then ;
All things they have in common, being so poor,
And their one fear, Death's shadow at the door.
Each sundown makes them mournful, each sunrise
Brings back the brightness in their failing eyes.   10

How happy go the rich fair-weather days
When on the roadside folk stare in amaze
At such a honeycomb of fruit and flowers
As mellows round their threshold ; what long hours
They gloat upon their steepling hollyhocks,   15
Bee's balsams, feathery southernwood, and stocks,
Fiery dragon's-mouths, great mallow leaves
For salves, and lemon-plants in bushy sheaves,
Shagged Esau's-hands with five green finger-tips.
Such old sweet names are ever on their lips.   20
As pleased as little children where these grow
In cobbled pattens and worn gowns they go,
Proud of their wisdom when on gooseberry shoots
They stuck eggshells to fright from coming fruits
The brisk-billed rascals ; pausing still to see   25
Their neighbour owls saunter from tree to tree,
Or in the hushing half-light mouse the lane
Long-winged and lordly.
               But when those hours wane,
Indoors they ponder, scared by the harsh storm
Whose pelting saracens on the window swarm,   30
And listen for the mail to clatter past
And church clock's deep bay withering on the blast ;
They feed the fire that flings a freakish light
On pictured kings and queens grotesquely bright,
Platters and pitchers, faded calendars   35
And graceful hour-glass trim with lavenders.

Many a time they kiss and cry, and pray
That both be summoned in the selfsame day,
And wiseman linnet tinkling in his cage
End too with them the friendship of old age,   40
And all together leave their treasured room
Some bell-like evening when the may's in bloom.
                   EDMUND BLUNDEN.

433
AFTER LONDON

London Bridge is broken down ;
  Green is the grass on Ludgate Hill ;
I know a farmer in Camden Town
  Killed a brock by Pentonville.

I have heard my grandam tell   5
  How some thousand years ago
Houses stretched from Camberwell
  Right to Highbury and Bow.

Down by Shadwell's golden meads
  Tall ships' masts would stand as thick 10
As the pretty tufted reeds
  That the Wapping children pick.

All the kings from end to end
  Of all the world paid tribute then,
And meekly on their knees would bend   15
  To the King of the Englishmen.

Thinks I while I dig my plot,
  What if your grandam's tales be true ?
Thinks I, be they true or not,
  What 's the odds to a fool like you ?   20

Thinks I, while I smoke my pipe
  Here beside the tumbling Fleet,
Apples drop when they are ripe,
  And when they drop are they most sweet.
                    J. D. C. PELLOW.

434

A PRAYER FOR MY SON

Bid a strong ghost stand at the head
That my Michael may sleep sound,
Nor cry, nor turn in the bed
Till his morning meal come round;
And may departing twilight keep   5
All dread afar till morning's back,
That his mother may not lack
Her fill of sleep.

Bid the ghost have sword in fist:
Some there are, for I avow   10
Such devilish things exist,
Who have planned his murder, for they know
Of some most haughty deed or thought
That waits upon his future days,
And would through hatred of the bays   15
Bring that to nought.

Though You can fashion everything
From nothing every day, and teach
The morning stars to sing,
You have lacked articulate speech   20
To tell Your simplest want, and known,
Wailing upon a woman's knee,
All of that worst ignominy
Of flesh and bone;

And when through all the town there ran 25
The servants of Your enemy,
A woman and a man,
Unless the Holy Writings lie,
Hurried through the smooth and rough
And through the fertile and waste,   30
Protecting, till the danger past,
With human love.

W. B. YEATS.

435

THE HAWK

'Call down the hawk from the air;
Let him be hooded or caged
Till the yellow eye has grown mild,
For larder and spit are bare,
The old cook enraged,   5
The scullion gone wild.'

'I will not be clapped in a hood,
Nor a cage, nor alight upon wrist,
Now I have learnt to be proud
Hovering over the wood   10
In the broken mist
Or tumbling cloud.'

'What tumbling cloud did you cleave,
Yellow-eyed hawk of the mind,
Last evening? that I, who had sat   15
Dumbfounded before a knave,
Should give to my friend
A pretence of wit.'

W. B. YEATS.

436

BYZANTIUM

The unpurged images of day recede;
The Emperor's drunken soldiery are abed;
Night resonance recedes, night-walkers' song
After great cathedral gong;
A starlit or a moonlit dome disdains   5
All that man is,
All mere complexities,
The fury and the mire of human veins.

Before me floats an image, man or shade,
Shade more than man, more image than a shade;
For Hades' bobbin bound in mummy-cloth   11
May unwind the winding path;

A mouth that has no moisture and no breath
Breathless mouths may summon;
I hail the superhuman;   15
I call it death-in-life and life-in-death.

Miracle, bird or golden handiwork,
More miracle than bird or handiwork,
Planted on the star-lit golden bough,
Can like the cocks of Hades crow,   20
Or, by the moon embittered, scorn aloud
In glory of changeless metal
Common bird or petal
And all complexities of mire or blood.

At midnight on the Emperor's pavement flit 25
Flames that no faggot feeds, nor steel has lit,
Nor storm disturbs, flames begotten of flame,
Where blood-begotten spirits come
And all complexities of fury leave,
Dying into a dance,   30
An agony of trance,
An agony of flame that cannot singe a sleeve.

Astraddle on the dolphin's mire and blood,
Spirit after spirit! The smithies break the flood,
The golden smithies of the Emperor!   35
Marbles of the dancing floor
Break bitter furies of complexity,
Those images that yet
Fresh images beget,
That dolphin-torn, that gong-tormented sea. 40
                    W. B. YEATS.

437

THE DELPHIC ORACLE UPON PLOTINUS

Behold that great Plotinus swim,
Buffeted by such seas;
Bland Rhadamanthus beckons him,
But the Golden Race looks dim,
Salt blood blocks his eyes.   5

Scattered on the level grass
Or winding through the grove
Plato there and Minos pass,
There stately Pythagoras
And all the choir of Love.   10

W. B. YEATS.

438

TWO SONGS OF A FOOL II

I slept on my three-legged stool by the fire,
The speckled cat slept on my knee;
We never thought to enquire
Where the brown hare might be,
And whether the door were shut.   5
Who knows how she drank the wind
Stretched up on two legs from the mat,
Before she had settled her mind
To drum with her heel and to leap?
Had I but awakened from sleep   10
And called her name, she had heard,
It may be, and had not stirred,
That now, it may be, has found
The horn's sweet note and the tooth of the hound.

W. B. YEATS.

439

FROM THE 'ANTIGONE'

Overcome—O bitter sweetness,
Inhabitant of the soft cheek of a girl—
The rich man and his affairs,
The fat flocks and the fields' fatness,
Mariners, rough harvesters;   5
Overcome Gods upon Parnassus;
Overcome the Empyrean; hurl
Heaven and Earth out of their places,

That in the same calamity
Brother and brother, friend and friend, 10
Family and family,
City and city may contend,
By that great glory driven wild.

Pray I will and sing I must,
And yet I weep—Oedipus' child 15
Descends into the loveless dust.

W. B. YEATS.

See also Nos. 413, 414.

440

LAMENT OF THE FRONTIER GUARD

(translated from Rihaku)

By the North Gate, the wind blows full of sand,
Lonely from the beginning of time until now!
Trees fall, the grass goes yellow with autumn.
I climb the towers and towers
    to watch out the barbarous land: 5
Desolate castle, the sky, the wide desert.
There is no wall left to this village.
Bones white with a thousand frosts,
High heaps, covered with trees and grass;
Who brought this to pass? 10
Who has brought the flaming imperial anger?
Who has brought the army with drums and with
    kettle-drums?
Barbarous kings.
A gracious spring, turned to blood-ravenous
    autumn,
A turmoil of wars-men, spread over the middle
    kingdom, 15
Three hundred and sixty thousand,
And sorrow sorrow like rain.
Sorrow to go, and sorrow, sorrow returning.
Desolate, desolate fields,
And no children of warfare upon them, 20

No longer the men for offence and defence.
Ah, how shall you know the dreary sorrow at the
    North Gate,
With Rihoku's name forgotten,
And we guardsmen fed to the tigers.

EZRA POUND.

441

VILLANELLE: THE PSYCHOLOGICAL HOUR

I

I had over-prepared the event,
    that much was ominous.
With middle-ageing care
    I had laid out just the right books.
I had almost turned down the pages.   5

    Beauty is so rare a thing.
    So few drink of my fountain.

So much barren regret,
So many hours wasted!
And now I watch, from the window,   10
    the rain, the wandering buses.
'Their little cosmos is shaken'—
    the air is alive with that fact.
In their parts of the city
    they are played on by diverse forces.   15
How do I know?
    Oh, I know well enough.
For them there is something afoot.
    As for me;
I had over-prepared the event—   20

    Beauty is so rare a thing.
    So few drink of my fountain.

Two friends: a breath of the forest . . .
Friends? Are people less friends
    because one has just, at last, found them?
Twice they promised to come.   26

'Between the night and morning'

Beauty would drink of my mind.
   Youth would awhile forget
      my youth is gone from me.   30

II

('Speak up! You have danced so stiffly?
   Some one admired your works,
   And said so frankly.

   'Did you talk like a fool,
   The first night?   35
   The second evening?'

'*But* they promised again:
      "To-morrow at tea-time."')

III

Now the third day is here—
   no word from either;
No word from her nor him,
Only another man's note: 40
      'Dear Pound, I am leaving England.'
           EZRA POUND.

442

GERONTION

Thou hast nor youth nor age
But as it were an after dinner sleep
Dreaming on both.

Here I am, an old man in a dry month,
Being read to by a boy, waiting for rain.
I was neither at the hot gates
Nor fought in the warm rain
Nor knee deep in the salt marsh, heaving a cutlass,
Bitten by flies, fought.   6

My house is a decayed house,
And the jew squats on the window sill, the owner,
Spawned in some estaminet of Antwerp,
Blistered in Brussels, patched and peeled in
  London.   10
The goat coughs at night in the field overhead;
Rocks, moss, stonecrop, iron, merds.
The woman keeps the kitchen, makes tea,
Sneezes at evening, poking the peevish gutter.
      I an old man, 15
A dull head among windy spaces.

Signs are taken for wonders. 'We would see a
  sign!'
The word within a word, unable to speak a word,
Swaddled with darkness. In the juvescence of the
  year
Came Christ the tiger   20
In depraved May, dogwood and chestnut, flowering
  judas,
To be eaten, to be divided, to be drunk
Among whispers; by Mr. Silvero
With caressing hands, at Limoges
Who walked all night in the next room; 25

By Hakagawa, bowing among the Titians;
By Madame de Tornquist, in the dark room
Shifting the candles; Fraülein von Kulp
Who turned in the hall, one hand on the door.
  Vacant shuttles   30
Weave the wind. I have no ghosts,
An old man in a draughty house
Under a windy knob.

After such knowledge, what forgiveness? Think
  now
History has many cunning passages, contrived
  corridors   35
And issues, deceives with whispering ambitions
Guides us by vanities. Think now

She gives when our attention is distracted
And what she gives, gives with such supple con-
    fusions
That the giving famishes the craving. Gives too
    late   40
What's not believed in, or if still believed,
In memory only, reconsidered passion. Gives too
    soon
Into weak hands, what's thought can be dispensed
    with
Till the refusal propagates a fear. Think
Neither fear nor courage saves us. Unnatural vices
Are fathered by our heroism. Virtues   46
Are forced upon us by our impudent crimes.
These tears are shaken from the wrath-bearing
    tree.

The tiger springs in the new year. Us he devours.
    Think at last   50
We have not reached conclusion, when I
Stiffen in a rented house. Think at last
I have not made this show purposelessly
And it is not by any concitation
Of the backward devils.   55
I would meet you upon this honestly.
I that was near your heart was removed therefrom
To lose beauty in terror, terror in inquisition.
I have lost my passion: why should I need to keep it
Since what is kept must be adulterated?   60
I have lost my sight, smell, hearing, taste and
    touch:
How should I use them for your closer contact?

These with a thousand small deliberations
Protract the profit of their chilled delirium,
Excite the membrane, when the sense has cooled,
With pungent sauces, multiply variety   66
In a wilderness of mirrors. What will the spider do,
Suspend its operations, will the weevil
Delay? De Bailhache, Fresca, Mrs. Cammel,
    whirled

Beyond the circuit of the shuddering Bear 70
In fractured atoms. Gull against the wind, in the
windy straits
Of Belle Isle, or running on the Horn,
White feathers in the snow, the Gulf claims,
And an old man driven by the Trades
To a sleepy corner.

Tenants of the house, 75
Thoughts of a dry brain in a dry season.

T. S. ELIOT.

443

WHISPERS OF IMMORTALITY

Webster was much possessed by death
And saw the skull beneath the skin;
And breastless creatures under ground
Leaned backward with a lipless grin.

Daffodil bulbs instead of balls 5
Stared from the sockets of the eyes!
He knew that thought clings round dead limbs
Tightening its lusts and luxuries.

Donne, I suppose, was such another
Who found no substitute for sense; 10
To seize and clutch and penetrate,
Expert beyond experience,

He knew the anguish of the marrow
The ague of the skeleton;
No contact possible to flesh 15
Allayed the fever of the bone.

. . . . .

Grishkin is nice: her Russian eye
Is underlined for emphasis;
Uncorseted, her friendly bust
Gives promise of pneumatic bliss. 20

The crouched Brazilian jaguar
Compels the scampering marmoset
With subtle effluence of cat;
Grishkin has a maisonette;

The sleek Brazilian jaguar 25
Does not in its arboreal gloom
Distil so rank a feline smell
As Grishkin in a drawing-room.

And even the Abstract Entities
Circumambulate her charm; 30
But our lot crawls between dry ribs
To keep our metaphysics warm.

T. S. ELIOT.

444

ANIMULA

'Issues from the hand of God, the simple soul'
To a flat world of changing lights and noise,
To light, dark, dry or damp, chilly or warm;
Moving between the legs of tables and of chairs,
Rising or falling, grasping at kisses and toys, 5
Advancing boldly, sudden to take alarm,
Retreating to the corner of arm and knee,
Eager to be reassured, taking pleasure
In the fragrant brilliance of the Christmas tree,
Pleasure in the wind, the sunlight and the sea; 10
Studies the sunlit pattern on the floor
And running stags around a silver tray;
Confounds the actual and the fanciful,
Content with playing-cards and kings and queens,
What the fairies do and what the servants say. 15
The heavy burden of the growing soul
Perplexes and offends more, day by day;
Week by week, offends and perplexes more
With the imperatives of 'is and seems'
And may and may not, desire and control. 20
The pain of living and the drug of dreams
Curl up the small soul in the window seat

Behind the *Encyclopaedia Britannica*.
Issues from the hand of time the simple soul
Irresolute and selfish, misshapen, lame,   25
Unable to fare forward or retreat,
Fearing the warm reality, the offered good,
Denying the importunity of the blood,
Shadow of its own shadows, spectre in its own gloom,
Leaving disordered papers in a dusty room;   30
Living first in the silence after the viaticum.

Pray for Guiterriez, avid of speed and power,
For Boudin, blown to pieces,
For this one who made a great fortune,
And that one who went his own way.   35
Pray for Floret, by the boarhound slain between
    the yew trees,
Pray for us now and at the hour of our birth.

T. S. ELIOT.

445

NECROLOGICAL

The friar had said his paternosters duly
And scourged his limbs, and afterwards would
    have slept;
But with much riddling his head became unruly,
He arose, from the quiet monastery he crept.

Dawn lightened the place where the battle had
    been won.   5
The people were dead—it is easy, he thought, to
    die—
Those dead remained, but the living all were gone,
Gone with the wailing trumps of victory.

The dead men wore no raiment against the air,
Bartholomew's men had spoiled them where they
    fell;   10
In defeat the heroes' bosoms were whitely bare,
The field was white like meads of asphodel.

Not all were white; some gory and fabulous
Whom the sword had pierced and then the grey
    wolf eaten;
But the brother reasoned that heroes' flesh was
    thus,   15
Flesh fails, and the postured bones lie weather-
    beaten.

The lords of chivalry were prone and shattered,
The gentle and the body-guard of yeomen;
Bartholomew's stroke went home—but little it
    mattered,
Bartholomew went to be stricken of other foemen.

Beneath the blue ogive of the firmament   21
Was a dead warrior, clutching whose mighty
    knees
Was a leman, who with her flame had warmed his
    tent,
For him enduring all men's pleasantries.

Close by the sable stream that purged the plain
Lay the white stallion and his rider thrown.   26
The great beast had spilled there his little brain,
And the little groin of the knight was spilled by a
    stone.

The youth possessed him then of a crooked blade
Deep in the belly of a lugubrious knight;   30
He fingered it well, and it was cunningly made;
But strange apparatus was it for a Carmelite.

Then he sat upon a hill and hung his head,
Riddling, riddling, and lost in a vast surmise,
And so still that he likened himself unto those dead
Whom the kites of Heaven solicited with sweet
    cries.   36
                    JOHN CROWE RANSOM.

446

CAPTAIN CARPENTER

Captain Carpenter rose up in his prime
Put on his pistols and went riding out
But had got wellnigh nowhere at that time
Till he fell in with ladies in a rout.

It was a pretty lady and all her train   5
That played with him so sweetly but before
An hour she'd taken a sword with all her main
And twined him of his nose for evermore.

Captain Carpenter mounted up one day
And rode straightway into a stranger rogue   10
That looked unchristian but be that as may
The Captain did not wait upon prologue.

But drew upon him out of his great heart
The other swung against him with a club
And cracked his two legs at the shinny part   15
And let him roll and stick like any tub.

Captain Carpenter rode many a time
From male and female took he sundry harms
He met the wife of Satan crying 'I'm   19
The she-wolf bids you shall bear no more arms.'

Their strokes and counters whistled in the wind
I wish he had delivered half his blows
But where she should have made off like a hind
The bitch bit off his arms at the elbows.

And Captain Carpenter parted with his ears   25
To a black devil that used him in this wise
O Jesus ere his threescore and ten years
Another had plucked out his sweet blue eyes.

Captain Carpenter got up on his roan
And sallied from the gate in hell's despite   30
I heard him asking in the grimmest tone
If any enemy yet there was to fight?

'To any adversary it is fame
If he risk to be wounded by my tongue
Or burnt in two beneath my red heart's flame 35
Such are the perils he is cast among.

'But if he can he has a pretty choice
From an anatomy with little to lose
Whether he cut my tongue and take my voice
Or whether it be my round red heart he choose.'

It was the neatest knave that ever was seen 41
Stepping in perfume from his lady's bower
Who at this word put in his merry mien
And fell on Captain Carpenter like a tower.

I would not knock old fellows in the dust 45
But there lay Captain Carpenter on his back
His weapons were the old heart in his bust
And a blade shook between rotten teeth alack.

The rogue in scarlet and grey soon knew his mind
He wished to get his trophy and depart 50
With gentle apology and touch refined
He pierced him and produced the Captain's heart.

God's mercy rest on Captain Carpenter now
I thought him Sirs an honest gentleman
Citizen husband soldier and scholar enow 55
Let jangling kites eat of him if they can.

But God's deep curses follow after those
That shore him of his goodly nose and ears
His legs and strong arms at the two elbows
And eyes that had not watered seventy years. 60

The curse of hell upon the sleek upstart
Who got the Captain finally on his back
And took the red red vitals of his heart
And made the kites to whet their beaks clack clack.
                              JOHN CROWE RANSOM.

447

FUTILITY

Move him into the sun—
Gently its touch awoke him once,
At home, whispering of fields unsown.
Always it woke him, even in France,
Until this morning and this snow.   5
If anything might rouse him now
The kind old sun will know.

Think how it wakes the seeds,—
Woke, once, the clays of a cold star.
Are limbs, so dear-achieved, are sides,   10
Full-nerved—still warm—too hard to stir?
Was it for this the clay grew tall?
—O what made fatuous sunbeams toil
To break earth's sleep at all?

WILFRED OWEN.

448

STRANGE MEETING

It seemed that out of battle I escaped
Down some profound dull tunnel, long since
    scooped
Through granites which titanic wars had groined.
Yet also there encumbered sleepers groaned,
Too fast in thought or death to be bestirred.   5
Then, as I probed them, one sprang up, and stared
With piteous recognition in fixed eyes,
Lifting distressful hands as if to bless.
And by his smile, I knew that sullen hall,
By his dead smile I knew we stood in Hell.   10
With a thousand pains that vision's face was
    grained;
Yet no blood reached there from the upper ground,
And no guns thumped, or down the flues made
    moan.
'Strange friend,' I said, 'here is no cause to mourn.'
'None,' said the other, 'save the undone years,   15

The hoplessness. Whatever hope is yours,
Was my life also; I went hunting wild
After the wildest beauty in the world,
Which lies not calm in eyes, or braided hair,
But mocks the steady running of the hour,   20
And if it grieves, grieves richlier than here.
For by my glee might many men have laughed,
And of my weeping something had been left,
Which must die now. I mean the truth untold,
The pity of war, the pity war distilled.
Now men will go content with what we spoiled.
Or, discontent, boil bloody, and be spilled.
They will be swift with swiftness of the tigress,
None will break ranks, though nations trek from
    progress.
Courage was mine, and I had mystery,   30
Wisdom was mine, and I had mastery;
To miss the march of this retreating world
Into vain citadels that are not walled.
Then, when much blood had clogged their chariot-
    wheels
I would go up and wash them from sweet wells, 35
Even with truths that lie too deep for taint.
I would have poured my spirit without stint
But not through wounds; not on the cess of war.
Foreheads of men have bled where no wounds were.
I am the enemy you killed, my friend.   40
I knew you in this dark; for so you frowned
Yesterday through me as you jabbed and killed.
I parried; but my hands were loath and cold.
Let us sleep now. . . .'
WILFRED OWEN.

449

THE FLIGHT

Sing we the two lieutenants, Parer and M'Intosh,
After the War wishing to hie them to Australia,
Planned they would take a high way, a hazardous
    crazy air-way:

Death their foregone conclusion, a flight headlong
    to failure,
We said. For no silver posh   5
Plane was their pigeon, no dandy dancer quick-
    stepping through heaven,
But a craft of obsolete design, a condemned D.H.
    nine;
Sold for a song it was, patched up though to write
    an heroic
Line across the world as it reeled on its obstinate
    stoic
Course to that southern haven.   10

On January 8, 1920, their curveting wheels kissed
England goodbye. Over Hounslow huddled in
    morning mist
They rose and circled like buzzards while we rubbed
    our sleepy eyes:
Like a bird scarce-fledged they flew, whose flying
    hours are few—
Still dear is the nest but deeper its desire unto the
    skies—   15
And they left us to our sleeping.
They felt earth's warning tug on their wings: vain
    to advance
Asking a thoroughfare through the angers of the air
On so flimsy a frame: but they pulled up her nose
    and the earth went sloping
Away, and they aimed for France.   20

Fog first, a wet blanket, a kill-joy, the primrose-of-
    morning's blight,
Blotting out the dimpled sea, the ample welcome of
    land,
The gay glance from the bright
Cliff-face behind, snaring the sky with treachery,
    sneering
At hope's loss of height. But they charged it,
    flying blind;   25
They took a compass-bearing against that dealer of
    doubt,

As a saint when the field of vision is fogged gloriously
 steels
His spirit against the tainter of air, the elusive
 taunter:
They climbed to win a way out,
Then downward dared till the moody waves snarled
 at their wheels. 30

Landing at last near Conteville, who had skimmed
 the crest of oblivion
They could not rest, but rose and flew on to Paris,
 and there
Trivially were delayed—a defective petrol feed—
Three days: a time hung heavy on
Hand and heart, till they leapt again to the upper air,
Their element, their lover, their angel antagonist. 36
Would have taken a fall without fame, but the
 sinewy framework the wrist
Of steel the panting engine wrestled well: and they
 went
South while the going was good, as a swallow that
 guide nor goad
Needs on his sunny scent. 40

At Lyons the petrol pump failed again, and forty-
 eight hours
They chafed to be off, the haughty champions whose
 breathing-space
Was an horizon span and the four winds their fan.
Over Italy's shores
A reverse, the oil ran out and cursing they turned
 about 45
Losing a hundred miles to find a landing place.
Not a coast for a castaway this, no even chance of
 alighting
On sward or wind-smooth sand:
A hundred miles without pressure they flew, the
 engine fighting
For breath, and its heart nearly burst before they
 dropped to land. 50

And now the earth they had spurned rose up
   against them in anger,
Tier upon tier it towered, the terrible Apennines:
No sanctuary there for wings, not flares nor land-
   ing-lines,
No hope of floor and hangar.
Yet those iced-tipped spears that disputed the
   passage set spurs   55
To their two hundred and forty horse power;
   grimly they gained
Altitude, though the hand of heaven was heavy
   upon them,
The downdraught from the mountains: though
   desperate eddies spun them
Like a coin, yet unkindly tossed their luck came
   uppermost
And mastery remained.   60

Air was all ambushes round them, was avalanche
   earthquake
Quicksand, a funnel deep as doom, till climbing
   steep
They crawled like a fly up the face of perpendicular
   night
And levelled, finding a break
At fourteen thousand feet. Here earth is shorn
   from sight: 65
Deadweight a darkness hangs on their eyelids, and
   they bruise
Their eyes against a void: vindictive the cold airs
   close
Down like a trap of steel and numb them from
   head to heel;
Yet they kept an even keel,
For their spirit reached forward and took the con-
   trols while their fingers froze.   70

They had not heard the last of death. When the
   mountains were passed,
He raised another crest, the long crescendo of pain
Kindled to climax, the plane

Took fire. Alone in the sky with the breath of their
    enemy
Hot in their face they fought: from three thousand
    feet they tilted   75
Over, side-slipped away—a trick for an ace, a race
And running duel with death: flame streamed out
    behind,
A crimson scarf of, as life-blood out of a wound,
    but the wind
Of their downfall staunched it; death wilted,
Lagged and died out in smoke—he could not stay
    their pace.   80

A lull for a while. The powers of hell rallied their
    legions.
On Parer now fell the stress of the flight; for the
    plane had been bumped,
Buffeted, thrashed by the air almost beyond repair:
But he tinkered and coaxed, and they limped
Over the Adriatic on into warmer regions.   85
Erratic their course to Athens, to Crete: coolly they
    rode her
Like a tired horse at the water-jumps, they jockeyed
    her over seas,
Till they came at last to a land whose dynasties of sand
Had seen Alexander, Napoleon, many a straddling
    invader,
But never none like these. . . .   90
                      C. DAY LEWIS.

450

DESCRIPTION OF A VIEW

Well boiled in acid and then laid on glass
(A labelled strip) the specimen of building,
Though concrete, was not sure what size it was,
And was so large as to compare with nothing.
High to a low and vulnerable sky   5
It rose, and could have scraped it if it chose;
But, plain, and firm, and cleanly, like stretched
    string,

It would not think of doing such a thing;
On trust, it did not try.
My eye walked up the ladder of its windows.   10

Stretched in the crane's long pencil of a stalk
(Whose dry but tough metal brown of grass
Flowered its salted down on this tall chalk)
Sole as the bridge Milton gave death to pass
The beam of Justice as in doubt for ever   15
Hung like a Zeppelin over London river;
Its lifted sealine impiously threatened deluge,
Fixed, like a level rainbow, to the sky;

Whose blue glittered with a frosted silver
Like palace walls in Grimm papered with needles 20
The sands all shining in its larger concrete
A dome compact of all but visible stars.

WILLIAM EMPSON.

451

NOTE ON LOCAL FLORA

There is a tree native in Turkestan,
Or further east towards the Tree of Heaven,
Whose hard cold cones, not being wards to time,
Will leave their mother only for good cause;
Will ripen only in a forest fire;   5
Wait, to be fathered as was Bacchus once,
Through men's long lives, that image of time's end.
I knew the Phoenix was a vegetable.
So Semele desired her deity
As this in Kew thirsts for the Red Dawn.   10

WILLIAM EMPSON.

452

OUT ON THE LAWN

To Geoffrey Hoyland

Out on the lawn I lie in bed,
Vega conspicuous overhead

In the windless nights of June;
Forests of green have done complete
The day's activity; my feet 5
  Point to the rising moon.

Lucky, this point in time and space
Is chosen as my working place;
  Where the sexy air of summer,
The bathing hours and the bare arms, 10
The leisured drives through a land of farms,
  Are good to the newcomer.

Equal with colleagues in a ring
I sit on each calm evening,
  Enchanted as the flowers 15
The opening light draws out of hiding
From leaves with all its dove-like pleading
  Its logic and its powers.

That later we, though parted then
May still recall these evenings when 20
  Fear gave his watch no look;
The lion griefs loped from the shade
And on our knees their muzzles laid,
  And Death put down his book.

Moreover, eyes in which I learn 25
That I am glad to look, return
  My glances every day;
And when the birds and rising sun
Waken me, I shall speak with one
  Who has not gone away. 30

Now North and South and East and West
Those I love lie down to rest;
  The moon looks on them all:
The healers and the brilliant talkers,
The eccentrics and the silent walkers, 35
  The dumpy and the tall.

She climbs the European sky;
Churches and power stations lie
   Alike among earth's fixtures:
Into the galleries she peers,   40
And blankly as an orphan stares
   Upon the marvellous pictures.

To gravity attentive, she
Can notice nothing here; though we
   Whom hunger cannot move,   45
From gardens where we feel secure
Look up, and with a sigh endure
   The tyrannies of love:

And, gentle, do not care to know,
Where Poland draws her Eastern bow,   50
   What violence is done;
Nor ask what doubtful act allows
Our freedom in this English house,
   Our picnics in the sun.

The creepered wall stands up to hide   55
The gathering multitudes outside
   Whose glances hunger worsens;
Concealing from their wretchedness
Our metaphysical distress,
   Our kindness to ten persons.   60

And now no path on which we move
But shows already traces of
   Intentions not our own,
Thoroughly able to achieve
What our excitement could conceive,   65
   But our hands left alone.

For what by nature and by training
We loved, has little strength remaining:
   Though we would gladly give
The Oxford colleges, Big Ben,   70
And all the birds in Wicken Fen,
   It has no wish to live.

Soon through the dykes of our content
The crumpling flood will force a rent,
   And, taller than a tree,   75
Hold sudden death before our eyes
Whose river-dreams long hid the size
   And vigours of the sea.

But when the waters make retreat
And through the black mud first the wheat   80
   In shy green stalks appears;
When stranded monsters gasping lie,
And sounds of riveting terrify
   Their whorled unsubtle ears:

May this for which we dread to lose   85
Our privacy, need no excuse
   But to that strength belong;
As through a child's rash happy cries
The drowned voice of his parents rise
   In unlamenting song.   90

After discharges of alarm,
All unpredicted may it calm
   The pulse of nervous nations;
Forgive the murderer in his glass,
Tough in its patience to surpass   95
   The tigress her swift motions.

W. H. AUDEN.

453

LOOK, STRANGER

Look, stranger, at this island now
The leaping light for your delight discovers,
Stand stable here
And silent be,
That through the channels of the ear   5
May wander like a river
The swaying sound of the sea.

Here at the small field's ending pause
Where the chalk wall falls to the foam, and its tall
　　ledges
Oppose the pluck　　　　　　　　　　　　　　10
And knock of the tide,
And the shingle scrambles after the suck-
ing surf, and the gull lodges
A moment on its sheer side.

Far off like floating seeds the ships　　　　　　15
Diverge on urgent voluntary errands;
And the full view
Indeed may enter
And move in memory as now these clouds do,
That pass the harbour mirror　　　　　　　　20
And all the summer through the water saunter.

W. H. AUDEN.

454

A SHILLING LIFE

A shilling life will give you all the facts:
How Father beat him, how he ran away,
What were the struggles of his youth, what acts
Made him the greatest figure of his day:
Of how he fought, fished, hunted, worked all night,
Though giddy, climbed new mountains; named a
　　sea:
Some of the last researchers even write
Love made him weep his pints like you and me.

With all his honours on, he sighed for one
Who, say astonished critics, lived at home;　　10
Did little jobs about the house with skill
And nothing else; could whistle; would sit still
Or potter round the garden; answered some
Of his long marvellous letters but kept none.

W. H. AUDEN.

455

SPRING VOICES

The small householder now comes out warily
Afraid of the barrage of sun that shouts cheerily,
Spring is massing forces, birds wink in air,
The battlemented chestnuts volley green fire,
The pigeons banking on the wind, the hoots of
    cars,   5
Stir him to run wild, gamble on horses, buy cigars;
Joy lies before him to be ladled and lapped from his
    hand—
Only that behind him, in the shade of his villa,
    memories stand
Breathing on his neck and muttering that all this
    has happened before,
Keep the wind out, cast no clout, try no un-
    warranted jaunts untried before,   10
But let the spring slide by nor think to board its car
For it rides West to where the tangles of scrap-iron
    are;
Do not walk, these voices say, between the bucking
    clouds alone
Or you may loiter into a suddenly howling crater,
    or fall, jerked back, garrotted by the sun.
                   LOUIS MACNEICE.

456

TRAPEZE

Beyond the dykes of cloud and steel spikes of air
The sun's breathing golden prickling fur
Over a vibrant belly warned us
Leap the beast will some time
Breaking every bridge of the well-worn thorough-
    fare   5
Of the zodiac. Gone the fawning yawning purr
Changed for a foam-flash. Gone the indolent in-
    dustry

That padded round the treadmill, raised the crops
And helped to work the tides. Look up and see
Fiery now . . . how he angrily   10
Flicks his tongue hungry around his chops.

Blood slavers over the evening sky;
Bees are at compline, not knowing that soon
An end is set to respectability.
On the skyline shaggy spears of grass   15
Itch ominously and the moon
Limps on a crutch whose ferrule taps to us
Doom (if rightly we decodify).

Still we are happy even if our nerves
Twitch now and again as the grasses do.   20
We know that we only live on sufferance
And that however well this star-seat serves
Our purpose as trapezists for this once,
In any case the rope is wearing through.
Tom Tom Terry, Tom Tom Terry.   25
The glutton tit swings in the cocoanut
In the equinoctial gale.
This circus-job means death sooner or later
From wild beasts or fire among the tinsel.
Tom Tom Terry, Tom Tom Terry.   30

Louis MacNeice.

457

HOW STRANGELY THIS SUN

How strangely this sun reminds me of my love!
Of my walk alone at evening, when like the cottage
    smoke
Hope vanished, written amongst red wastes of sky.
I remember my strained listening to his voice
My staring at his face and taking the photograph 5

With the river behind and the woods touched by
    Spring;
Till the identification of a morning—
Expansive sheets of blue rising from fields

Roaring movements of light observed under
    shadow—
With his figure leaning over a map, is now com-
    plete.   10

What is left of that smoke which the wind blew
    away?
I corrupted his confidence and his sunlike happiness
So that even now in his turning of bolts or driving
    a machine
His hand will show error. That is for him.
For me this memory which now I behold,   15
When, from the pasturage, azure rounds me in rings
And the lark ascends, and his voice still rings, still
    rings.

                STEPHEN SPENDER.

458
NEW YEAR

Here at the centre of the turning year,
The turning Polar North,
The frozen streets, and the black fiery joy
Of the Child launched again forth,
I ask that all the years and years   5
Of future disappointment, like a snow
Chide me at one fall now.

I leave him who burns endlessly
In the brandy pudding crowned with holly,
And I ask that Time should freeze my skin   10
And all my fellow travellers harden
Who are not flattered by this town
Nor up its twenty storeys whirled
To prostitutes without infection.

Cloak us in accidents and in the failure   15
Of the high altar and marital adventure;
In family disgrace, denunciation
Of bankers, a premier's assassination.

From the government windows
Let heads of headlines watch depart,   20
Strangely depart by staying, those
Who build a new world in their heart.

Where scythe shall curve but not upon our neck
And lovers proceed to their forgetting work,
Answering the harvests of obliteration.   25
After the frozen years and streets
Our tempered will shall plough across the nations.
The engine hurrying through the lucky valley
The hand that moves to guide the silent lines
Effect their beauty without robbery.   30

STEPHEN SPENDER.

459

THE SEAL BOY

See he slips like insinuations
Into the waves and sidles
Across breakers, diving under
The greater tidals,

Plunging, a small plane   5
Down dark altitudes,
Trailing bubbles like aerial bombs
Or a balloon's broods.

O moving ecstatic boy
Sliding through the gloomy seas   10
Who bring me pearls to enjoy
Rarer than to be found in these seas—

Between the fixed bars of your lips
Darts the kiss like silver
Fish, and in my wild grip   15
You harbour, for ever.

GEORGE BARKER.

460

THE CHIMERA

A chimera with a mane of rainbows flowing
Pursues me in my swiftest flight,
Or when I stand
Tenderly touches my perspiring hand,
And follows my going.   5

No space of crossing possible
I essay, but thrown ahead of me
Shown on the profile lines of lands
This figure stands
Exultant and beguiling and beautiful.   10

Like fields the annual fleece surges
With energy animal and human,
Five silver seas bear
This body, the stellar seven's despair,
And the eyes are tidal with celestial urges.   15

Whose form if not the world's we see,
Of whom the glittering feet if not
The oceans as wings of the world Mercury?
And larches and tulips the limbs, and the eyes
Flower indeed from the seeds of the starred skies. 20
                                        GEORGE BARKER.

461

WHEN ONCE THE TWILIGHT

When once the twilight locks no longer
Locked in the long worm of my finger
Nor dammed the sea that sped about my fist,
The mouth of time sucked, like a sponge,
The milky acid on each hinge,   5
And swallowed dry the waters of the breast.

When the galactic sea was sucked
And all the dry seabed unlocked,
I sent my creature scouting on the globe,
That globe itself of hair and bone   10
That, sewn to me by nerve and brain,
Had stringed my flask of matter to his rib.

My fuses timed to charge his heart,
He blew like powder to the light
And held a little sabbath with the sun,   15
But when the stars, assuming shape,
Drew in his eyes the straws of sleep,
He drowned his father's magics in a dream.

All issue armoured, of the grave,
The redhaired cancer still alive,   20
The cataracted eyes that filmed their cloth;
Some dead undid their bushy jaws,
And bags of blood let out their flies;
He had by heart the Christ-cross-row of death.

Sleep navigates the tides of time;   25
The dry Sargasso of the tomb
Gives up its dead to such a working sea;
And sleep rolls mute above the beds
Where fishes' food is fed the shades
Who periscope through flowers to the sky.   30

The hanged who lever from the limes
Ghostly propellers for their limbs,
The cypress lads who wither with the cock,
These, and the others in sleep's acres,
Of dreaming men make moony suckers,   35
And snipe the fools of vision in the back.

When once the twilight screws were turned,
And mother milk was stiff as sand,
I sent my own ambassador to light;
By trick or chance he fell asleep   40
And conjured up a carcase shape
To rob me of my fluids in his heart.

Awake, my sleeper, to the sun,
A worker in the morning town,
And leave the poppied pickthank where he lies; 45
The fences of the light are down,
All but the briskest riders thrown,
And worlds hang on the trees.

DYLAN THOMAS.

462

THIS BREAD I BREAK

This bread I break was once the oat,
This wine upon a foreign tree
Plunged in its fruit;
Man in the day or wind at night
Laid the crops low, broke the grape's joy.   5

Once in this wind the summer blood
Knocked in the flesh that decked the vine,
Once in this bread
The oat was merry in the wind;
Man broke the sun, pulled the wind down.   10

This flesh you break, this blood you let
Make desolation in the vein,
Were oat and grape
Born of the sensual root and sap;
My wine you drink, my bread you snap.   15

DYLAN THOMAS.

NOTES TO

THE GOLDEN TREASURY

BY FRANCIS TURNER PALGRAVE

SUMMARY OF BOOK FIRST

THE Elizabethan Poetry, as it is rather vaguely termed, forms the substance of this Book, which contains pieces from Wyatt under Henry VIII to Shakespeare midway through the reign of James I, and Drummond who carried on the early manner to a still later period. There is here a wide range of style ;—from simplicity expressed in a language hardly yet broken in to verse,—through the pastoral fancies and Italian conceits of the strictly Elizabethan time,—to the passionate reality of Shakespeare : yet a general uniformity of tone prevails. Few readers can fail to observe the natural sweetness of the verse, the single-hearted straightforwardness of the thoughts :—nor less, the limitation of subject to the many phases of one passion which then characterized our lyrical poetry,—unless when, as with Drummond and Shakespeare, the ' purple light of Love ' is tempered by a spirit of sterner reflection.

It should be observed that this and the following Summaries apply in the main to the Collection here presented, in which (besides its restriction to Lyrical Poetry) a strictly representative or historical Anthology has not been aimed at. Great excellence, in human art as in human character, has from the beginning of things been even more uniform than Mediocrity, by virtue of the closeness of its approach to Nature :—and so far as the standard of Excellence kept in view has been attained in this volume, a comparative absence of extreme or temporary phases in style, a similarity of tone and manner, will be found throughout :—something neither modern nor ancient, but true in all ages, and, like the works of Creation, perfect as on the first day.

PAGE NO.

1   2   l. 4. *Rouse Memnon's mother* : Awaken the Dawn from the dark Earth and the clouds where she is resting. Aurora in the old mythology is mother of Memnon (the East), and wife of Tithonus (the appearances of Earth and Sky during the last hours of Night). She leaves him every morning in renewed youth, to prepare the way for Phoebus (the Sun), whilst Tithonus remains in perpetual old age and greyness.

2   —   l. 27. *by Peneüs' streams* : Phoebus loved the Nymph Daphne whom he met by the river Peneüs in the vale of Tempe. This legend expressed the attachment of the Laurel (Daphne) to the Sun, under whose heat the tree both fades and flourishes.

It has been thought worth while to explain these allusions, because they illustrate the character of the Grecian Mythology which arose in the Personification of natural phenomena, and was totally free from those debasing and ludicrous ideas with which, through Roman and later misunderstanding or perversion, it has been associated.

2   —   l. 31. *Amphion's lyre* : He was said to have built the walls of Thebes to the sound of his music.

—   —   l. 39. *Night like a drunkard reels* : Compare *Romeo and Juliet*, Act II, Scene 3 : ' The grey-eyed morn smiles,' etc.

3   4   l. 10. *Time's chest* : in which he is figuratively supposed to lay up past treasures. So in *Troilus*, Act III, Scene 3, ' Time hath a wallet at his back,' etc.

4   5   A fine example of the highwrought and conventional Elizabethan Pastoralism,

PAGE NO.

which it would be ludicrous to criticize on the ground of the unshepherdlike or unreal character of some images suggested. Stanza 6 was probably inserted by Izaak Walton.

6   9   This Poem, with 25 and 94, is taken from Davison's *Rhapsody*, first published in 1602. One stanza has been here omitted, in accordance with the principle noticed in the Preface. Similar omissions occur in 45, 87, 100, 128, 160, 165, 227, 235. The more serious abbreviation by which it has been attempted to bring Crashaw's ' Wishes ' and Shelley's ' Euganean Hills ' within the limits of lyrical unity is commended with much diffidence to the judgement of readers acquainted with the original pieces.

10   15   This charming little poem, truly ' old and plain, and dallying with the innocence of love ' like that spoken of in *Twelfth Night*, is taken, with 5, 17, 20, 34, and 40, from the most characteristic collection of Elizabeth's reign, *England's Helicon*, first published in 1600.

—   16   Readers who have visited Italy will be reminded of more than one picture by this gorgeous Vision of Beauty, equally sublime and pure in its Paradisaical naturalness. Lodge wrote it on a voyage to ' the Islands of Terceras and the Canaries ' ; and he seems to have caught, in those southern seas, no small portion of the qualities which marked the almost contemporary Art of Venice,—the glory and the glow of Veronese, or Titian, or Tintoret when he most resembles Titian, and all but surpasses him.

—   —   l. 1. *The clear* is the crystalline or outermost heaven of the old cosmography. For *resembling* (l. 7) other copies give *refining*: the correct reading is perhaps *revealing*.

11   —   l. 43. *for a fair there's fairer none* : If you desire a Beauty, there is none more beautiful than Rosalynde.

13   18   l. 10. *that fair thou owest* : that beauty thou ownest.

PAGE NO.

15   22   l. 9. *my . . . thy* is here conjecturally
printed for 'thy . . . my.' A very few
similar corrections of (it is presumed)
misprints have been made : as *men* for *me*,
41. l. 3 ; *dome* for *doom*, 275. l. 25 ; with
two or three more less important.

15   23   ll. 7, 8. *the star . . . Whose worth's unknown, although his height be taken* : apparently, Whose stellar influence is uncalculated
although his angular altitude from the plane
of the astrolabe or artificial horizon used by
astrologers has been determined.

17   27   l. 9. *keel* : skim.

19   29   l. 8. *expense* : waste.

—   30   l. 5. *Nativity, once in the main of light* :
when a star has risen and entered on the
full stream of light ;—another of the astro-
logical phrases no longer familiar.

—   —   l. 7. *Crooked* eclipses : as coming athwart
the Sun's apparent course.

Wordsworth, thinking probably of the
Venus and the *Lucrece,* said finely of Shakespeare : 'Shakespeare *could* not have
written an Epic ; he would have died of
plethora of thought.' This prodigality of
nature is exemplified equally in his Sonnets.
The copious selection here given (which,
from the wealth of the material, required
greater consideration than any other
portion of the Editor's task) contains many
that will not be fully felt and understood without some earnestness of thought
on the reader's part. But he is not likely
to regret the labour.

20   31   l. 11. *upon misprision growing* : either,
granted in error, or, on the growth of
contempt.

—   32   With the tone of this Sonnet compare
Hamlet's ' Give me that man That is not
passion's slave,' etc. Shakespeare's writings show the deepest sensitiveness to
passion :—hence the attraction he felt in
the contrasting effects of apathy.

PAGE NO.

21   33   l. 4. *grame* : sorrow. It was long before English Poetry returned to the charming simplicity of this and a few other poems by Wyatt.

22   34   l. 23. Pandion in the ancient fable was father to Philomela.

24   38   l. 4. *ramage* : confused noise.

—   39   l. 4. *censures* : judges.

25   40   By its style this beautiful example of old simplicity and feeling may be referred to the early years of Elizabeth.

—   —   l. 3. *late* : lately.

26   41   l. 9. *haggards* : the least tameable hawks.

27   44   l. 2. *cypres* or cyprus,—used by the old writers for *crape* ; whether from the French *crespe* or from the Island whence it was imported. Its accidental similarity in spelling to *cypress* has, here and in Milton's *Penseroso*, probably confused readers.

29 46–47 'I never saw anything like this funeral dirge,' says Charles Lamb, 'except the ditty which reminds Ferdinand of his drowned father in *The Tempest*. As that is of the water, watery ; so this is of the earth, earthy. Both have that intenseness of feeling, which seems to resolve itself into the element which it contemplates.'

31   51   l. 8. *crystal* : fairness.

32   53   This 'Spousal Verse' was written in honour of the Ladies Elizabeth and Katherine Somerset. Although beautiful, it is inferior to the *Epithalamion* on Spenser's own marriage,—omitted with great reluctance as not in harmony with modern manners.

33   —   l. 27. *feateously* : elegantly.

35   —   l. 121. *shend* : put out.

36   —   l. 145. *a noble peer* : Robert Devereux, second Lord Essex, then at the height of his brief triumph after taking Cadiz : hence the allusion following to the Pillars of

PAGE NO.

Hercules, placed near Gades by ancient
legend.

36   53   l. 157. *Eliza* : Elizabeth.

—   —   l. 173. *twins of Jove* : the stars Castor and
Pollux.

—   —   l. 174. *baldric*, belt ; the zodiac.

39   57   A fine example of a peculiar class of
Poetry ;—that written by thoughtful men
who practised this Art but little. Wotton's,
72, is another. Jeremy Taylor, Bishop
Berkeley, Dr. Johnson, Lord Macaulay,
have left similar specimens.

SUMMARY OF BOOK SECOND

THIS division, embracing the latter eighty years of the
seventeenth century, contains the close of our Early
poetical style and the commencement of the Modern.
In Dryden we see the first master of the new : in Milton,
whose genius dominates here as Shakespeare's in the
former book,—the crown and consummation of the
early period. Their splendid Odes are far in advance
of any prior attempts, Spenser's excepted : they exhibit
the wider and grander range which years and experience
and the struggles of the time conferred on Poetry. Our
Muses now give expression to political feeling, to
religious thought, to a high philosophic statesmanship
in writers such as Marvell, Herbert, and Wotton ; whilst
in Marvell and Milton, again, we find the first noble
attempts at pure description of nature, destined in our
own ages to be continued and equalled. Meanwhile the
poetry of simple passion, although before 1660 often
deformed by verbal fancies and conceits of thought,
and afterward by levity and an artificial tone, produced in Herrick and Waller some charming pieces of
more finished art than the Elizabethan : until in the
courtly compliments of Sedley it seems to exhaust
itself, and lie almost dormant for the hundred years
between the days of Wither and Suckling and the days
of Burns and Cowper.—That the change from our early
style to the modern brought with it at first a loss of

nature and simplicity is undeniable : yet the far bolder and wider scope which Poetry took between 1620 and 1700, and the successful efforts then made to gain greater clearness in expression, in their results have been no slight compensation.

PAGE NO.

44   62   l. 64. *whist* : hushed.

—   —   l. 89. *Pan* : used here for the Lord of all.

47   —   l. 191. *Lars and Lemures* : household gods and spirits of relations dead.

—   —   l. 194. *Flamens* : Roman priests.

—   —   l. 199. *that twice-batter'd god* : Dagon.

48   —   l. 213. *Osiris*, the Egyptian god of Agriculture (here, perhaps by confusion with Apis, figured as a Bull), was torn to pieces by Typho and embalmed after death in a sacred chest. This myth, reproduced in Syria and Greece in the legends of Thammuz, Adonis, and perhaps Absyrtus, represents the annual death of the Sun or the Year under the influences of the winter darkness. Horus, the son of Osiris, as the New Year, in his turn overcomes Typho.—It suited the genius of Milton's time to regard this primeval poetry and philosophy of the seasons, which has a further reference to the contest of Good and Evil in Creation, as a malignant idolatry. Shelley's Chorus in *Hellas*, ' Worlds on worlds,' treats the subject in a larger and sweeter spirit.

—   —   l. 215. *unshower'd* : as watered by the Nile only.

51   64   *The Late Massacre* : the Vaudois persecution, carried on in 1655 by the Duke of Savoy. This ' collect in verse,' as it has been justly named, is the most mighty Sonnet in any language known to the Editor. Readers should observe that, unlike our sonnets of the sixteenth century, it is constructed on the original Italian or Provençal model,—unquestionably far superior to the imperfect form employed by Shakespeare and Drummond.

PAGE NO.
51   65   Cromwell returned from Ireland in 1650. Hence the prophecies, not strictly fulfilled, of his deference to the Parliament, in ll. 81–96.

This Ode, beyond doubt one of the finest in our language, and more in Milton's style than has been reached by any other poet, is occasionally obscure from imitation of the condensed Latin syntax. The meaning of st. 5 is ' rivalry or hostility are the same to a lofty spirit, and limitation more hateful than opposition.' The allusion in st. 11 is to the old physical doctrines of the non-existence of a vacuum and the impenetrability of matter :—in st. 18 to the omen traditionally connected with the foundation of the Capitol at Rome. The ancient belief that certain years in life complete natural periods and are hence peculiarly exposed to death, is introduced in st. 26 by the word *climacteric*.

55   66   *Lycidas*. The person lamented is Milton's college friend Edward King, drowned in 1637 whilst crossing from Chester to Ireland.

Strict Pastoral Poetry was first written or perfected by the Dorian Greeks settled in Sicily : but the conventional use of it, exhibited more magnificently in *Lycidas* than in any other pastoral, is apparently of Roman origin. Milton, employing the noble freedom of a great artist, has here united ancient mythology with what may be called the modern mythology of Camus and Saint Peter,—to direct Christian images. —The metrical structure of this glorious poem is partly derived from Italian models.

—   —   l. 15. *Sisters of the sacred well* : the Muses, said to frequent the fountain Helicon on Mount Parnassus.

56   —   l. 54. *Mona* : Anglesea, called by the Welsh Inis Dowil or the Dark Island, from its dense forests.

—   —   l. 55. *Deva* : the Dee, a river which

probably derived its magical character from
Celtic traditions : it was long the boundary
of Briton and Saxon.—These places are
introduced, as being near the scene of the
shipwreck.

56   66   l. 58. *Orpheus* was torn to pieces by
Thracian women.

57   —   ll. 68, 69. *Amaryllis* and *Neaera* : names
used here for the love-idols of poets : as
Damoetas previously for a shepherd.

—   —   l. 75. *the blind Fury* : Atropos, fabled to
cut the thread of life.

—   —   ll. 85, 86. *Arethuse* and *Mincius* : Sicilian
and Italian waters here alluded to as
synonymous with the pastoral poetry of
Theocritus and Virgil.

—   —   l. 88. *oat* : pipe, used here like Collins'
oaten stop, No. 146, l. 1, for *Song*.

—   —   l. 96. *Hippotades* : Aeolus, god of the
Winds.

—   —   l. 99. *Panope* : a Nereid. The names of
local deities in the Hellenic mythology
express generally some feature in the
natural landscape, which the Greeks studied
and analysed with their usual unequalled
insight and feeling. *Panope* represents the
boundlessness of the ocean-horizon when
seen from a height, as compared with the
limited horizon of the land in hilly countries
such as Greece or Asia Minor.

—   —   l. 103. *Camus* : the Cam ; put for King's
University.

—   —   l. 106. *that sanguine flower* : the Hyacinth
of the ancients ; probably our Iris.

58   —   l. 109. *The pilot* : Saint Peter, figuratively
introduced as the head of the Church on
earth, to foretell ' the ruin of our corrupted
clergy, then in their heighth ' under Laud's
primacy.

—   —   l. 128. *the wolf* : Popery.

—   —   l. 132. *Alpheus* : a stream in Southern
Greece, supposed to flow underseas to join
the Arethuse.

58 66 l. 138. *swart star*: the Dogstar, called swarthy because its heliacal rising in ancient times occurred soon after mid-summer.

59 — l. 159. *moist vows*: either tearful prayers, or prayers for one at sea.

— — l. 160. *Bellerus*: a giant, apparently created here by Milton to personify Bellerium, the ancient title of the Land's End.

— — l. 161. *the great Vision*: the story was that the Archangel Michael had appeared on the rock by Marazion in Mount's Bay which bears his name. Milton calls on him to turn his eyes from the south homeward, and to pity Lycidas, if his body has drifted into the troubled waters off the Land's End. Finisterre being the land due south of Marazion, two places in that district (then by our trade with Corunna probably less unfamiliar to English ears) are named,—*Namancos* now Mujio in Galicia, *Bayona* north of the Minho, or perhaps a fortified rock (one of the *Cies* Islands) not unlike Saint Michael's Mount, at the entrance of Vigo Bay.

— — l. 170. *ore*: rays of golden light.

60 — l. 189. *Doric*: Sicilian, pastoral.

62 70 *The assault* was an attack on London expected in 1642, when the troops of Charles I reached Brentford. 'Written on his door' was in the original title of this sonnet. Milton was then living in Aldersgate Street.

— — l. 10. *The Emathian conqueror*: When Thebes was destroyed (B.C. 335) and the citizens massacred by thousands, Alexander ordered the house of Pindar to be spared. He was as incapable of appreciating the Poet as Lewis XIV of appreciating Racine: but even the narrow and barbarian mind of Alexander could understand the advantage of a showy act of homage to Poetry.

— — ll. 12, 13. *the repeated air Of sad Electra's*

PAGE NO.

> *poet* : Amongst Plutarch's vague stories, he
> says that when the Spartan confederacy in
> 404 B.C. took Athens, a proposal to demolish
> it was rejected through the effect produced
> on the commanders by hearing part of a
> chorus from the Electra of Euripides sung
> at a feast. There is, however, no apparent
> congruity between the lines quoted (167–8,
> ed. Dindorf) and the result ascribed to them.

64   73   This high-toned and lovely Madrigal is
quite in the style, and worthy of, the ' pure
Simonides.'

65   75   Vaughan's beautiful though quaint verses
should be compared with Wordsworth's
great Ode, No. 287.

66   76   l. 6. *Favonius* : the spring wind.

67   77   l. 2. *Themis* : the goddess of justice.
Skinner was grandson by his mother to Sir
E. Coke :—hence, as pointed out by Mr.
Keightley, Milton's allusion to the *bench*.

—   —   l. 8. Sweden was then at war with
Poland, and France with the Spanish
Netherlands.

69   79   l. 28. *Sidneian showers* : either in allusion
to the conversations in the *Arcadia*, or to
Sidney himself as a model of ' gentleness '
in spirit and demeanour.

73   84   *Elizabeth of Bohemia* : daughter to
James I, and ancestor to Sophia of Han-
over. These lines are a fine specimen of
gallant and courtly compliment.

74   85   Lady M. Ley was daughter to Sir J. Ley,
afterwards Earl of Marlborough, who died
March, 1628–9, coincidently with the
dissolution of the third Parliament of
Charles's reign. Hence Milton poetically
compares his death to that of the Orator
Isocrates of Athens, after Philip's victory
in 328 B.C.

78–79 92–93   These are quite a Painter's poems.

82   99   *From Prison* : to which his active support
of Charles I twice brought the high-spirited
writer.

PAGE NO.

87 105   Inserted in Book II as written in the character of a Soldier of Fortune in the seventeenth century.

88 106   *waly waly*: an exclamation of sorrow, the root and the pronunciation of which are preserved in the word *caterwaul*. *Brae*, hillside: *burn*, brook: *busk*, adorn. *Saint Anton's Well*: at the foot of Arthur's Seat by Edinburgh. *Cramasie*, crimson.

89 107   l. 7. *burd*, maiden.

90 108   *corbies*, crows: *fail*, turf: *hause*, neck: *theek*, thatch.—If not in their origin, in their present form this and the two preceding poems appear due to the seventeenth century, and have therefore been placed in Book II.

92 111   The remark quoted in the note to No. 47 applies equally to these truly wonderful verses, which, like *Lycidas*, may be regarded as a test of any reader's insight into the most poetical aspects of Poetry. The general differences between them are vast: but in imaginative intensity Marvell and Shelley are closely related.—This poem is printed as a translation in Marvell's works: but the original Latin is obviously his own. The most striking verses in it, here quoted as the book is rare, answer more or less to stanzas 2 and 6 :—

> Alma Quies, teneo te! et te, Germana Quietis
> Simplicitas! vos ergo diu per Templa, per urbes,
> Quaesivi, Regum perque alta Palatia frustra.
> Sed vos Hortorum per opaca silentia longe
> Celarant Plantae virides, et concolor Umbra.

94, 98 112   *L'Allegro* and *Il Penseroso*. It is a
        113   striking proof of Milton's astonishing power that these, the earliest pure Descriptive Lyrics in our language, should still remain the best in a style which so many great poets have since attempted. The Bright and the Thoughtful aspects of Nature are their subjects : but each is preceded by a mytho-

logical introduction in a mixed Classical and Italian manner. The meaning of the first is that Gaiety is the child of Nature ; of the second, that Pensiveness is the daughter of Sorrow and Genius.

94 112 l. 2. Perverse ingenuity has conjectured that for *Cerberus* we should read *Erebus*, who in the Mythology is brother at once and husband of Night. But the issue of that union is not Sadness, but Day and Aether :— completing the circle of primary Creation, as the parents are both children of Chaos, the first-begotten of all things. (Hesiod.)

95 — l. 36. *the mountain nymph* ; compare Wordsworth's Sonnet, No. 210.

96 — l. 62. is in *apposition* to the preceding, by a grammatical license not uncommon with Milton.

— — l. 67. *tells his tale* : counts his flock.

— — l. 80. *Cynosure* : the Pole Star.

— — ll. 83 *sqq. Corydon, Thyrsis*, etc. : shepherd names from the old Idylls.

97 — l. 132. *Jonson's learned sock* : the gaiety of our age would find little pleasure in his elaborate comedies.

98 — l. 136. *Lydian airs* : a light and festive style of ancient music.

98 113 l. 3. *bestead* : avail.

99 — l. 19. *starr'd Ethiop queen* : Cassiopeia, the legendary Queen of Ethiopia, and thence translated amongst the constellations.

100 — l. 59. *Cynthia* : the Moon : her chariot is drawn by dragons in ancient representations.

— — l. 88. *Hermes*, called Trismegistus, a mystical writer of the Neo-Platonist school.

101 — l. 99. *Thebes*, etc. : subjects of Athenian Tragedy.

— — l. 102. *buskin'd* : tragic.

— — l. 104. *Musaeus* : a poet in Mythology.

— — l. 109. *him that left half-told* : Chaucer, in his incomplete 'Squire's Tale.'

PAGE NO.

101 113   l. 116. *great bards* : Ariosto, Tasso, and Spenser are here intended.

— —   l. 123. *frounced* : curled.

— —   l. 124. *the Attic Boy* : Cephalus.

103 114   Emigrants supposed to be driven towards America by the Government of Charles I.

— —   ll. 23–4. *But apples*, etc. A fine example of Marvell's imaginative hyperbole.

104 115   l. 6. *concent* : harmony.

SUMMARY OF BOOK THIRD

IT is more difficult to characterize the English Poetry of the eighteenth century than that of any other. For it was an age not only of spontaneous transition, but of bold experiment : it includes not only such divergences of thought as distinguish the *Rape of the Lock* from the *Parish Register*, but such vast contemporaneous differences as lie between Pope and Collins, Burns and Cowper. Yet we may clearly trace three leading moods or tendencies :—the aspects of courtly or educated life represented by Pope and carried to exhaustion by his followers ; the poetry of Nature and of Man, viewed through a cultivated, and at the same time an impassioned frame of mind by Collins and Gray :—lastly, the study of vivid and simple narrative, including natural description, begun by Gay and Thomson, pursued by Burns and others in the north, and established in England by Goldsmith, Percy, Crabbe, and Cowper. Great varieties in style accompanied these diversities in aim : poets could not always distinguish the manner suitable for subjects so far apart : and the union of the language of courtly and of common life, exhibited most conspicuously by Burns, has given a tone to the poetry of that century which is better explained by reference to its historical origin than by naming it, in the common criticism of our day, artificial. There is, again, a nobleness of thought, a courageous aim at high and, in a strict sense, manly excellence in many of the writers :—nor can that period be justly termed tame and wanting in originality, which produced poems such as Pope's *Satires*, Gray's *Odes* and *Elegy*, the ballads of Gay and Carey, the songs of Burns and Cowper. In truth Poetry at this as at all times was a more or less unconscious mirror of the genius of the age : and the brave and admirable spirit of inquiry which made the eighteenth century the turning-time in European civilization is reflected faithfully in its verse. An intelligent reader will find the influence of Newton as markedly in the poems of Pope, as of Elizabeth in the plays of Shakespeare. On this great subject, however, these indications must here be sufficient.

PAGE NO.

115 123 *The Bard.* This Ode is founded on a fable that Edward I, after conquering Wales, put the native Poets to death.— After lamenting his comrades (st. 2, 3) the Bard prophesies the fate of Edward II and the conquests of Edward III (4) : his death and that of the Black Prince (5) : of Richard II, with the wars of York and Lancaster, the murder of Henry VI (the *meek usurper*), and of Edward V and his brother (6). He turns to the glory and prosperity following the accession of the Tudors (7), through Elizabeth's reign (8) : and concludes with a vision of the poetry of Shakespeare and Milton.

— — l. 13. *Glo'ster* : Gilbert de Clare, son-in-law to Edward. *Mortimer,* one of the Lords Marchers of Wales.

116 — l. 35. *Arvon* : the shores of Carnarvon-shire opposite Anglesey.

— — l. 57. *She-wolf* : Isabel of France, adulterous Queen of Edward II.

117 — l. 87. *towers of Julius* : the Tower of London, built in part, according to tradition, by Julius Caesar.

— — l. 93. *bristled boar* : the badge of Richard III.

— — l. 99. *Half of thy heart* : Queen Eleanor died soon after the conquest of Wales.

118 — l. 109. *Arthur* : Henry VII named his

eldest son thus, in deference to British feeling and legend.

119 125   l. 5. The Highlanders called the battle of Culloden, Drumossie.

120 126   *lilting*, singing blithely : *loaning*, broad lane : *bughts*, pens : *scorning*, rallying : *dowie*, dreary : *daffing* and *gabbing*, joking and chatting : *leglin*, milk-pail : *shearing*, reaping : *bandsters*, sheaf-binders : *runkled*, wrinkled : *lyart*, grizzled : *fleeching*, coaxing : *gloaming*, twilight : *bogle*, ghost : *dool*, sorrow.

122 128   The Editor has found no authoritative text of this poem, in his judgement superior to any other of its class in melody and pathos. Part is probably not later than the seventeenth century : in other stanzas a more modern hand, much resembling Scott's, is traceable. Logan's poem (127) exhibits a knowledge rather of the old legend than of the old verses.—*Hecht*, promised — the obsolete *hight* : *mavis*, thrush : *ilka*, every : *lav'rock*, lark : *haughs*, valley-meadows : *twined*, parted from : *marrow*, mate : *syne*, then.

123 129   The Royal George, of 108 guns, whilst undergoing a partial careening in Portsmouth Harbour, was overset about 10 A.M. Aug. 29, 1782. The total loss was believed to be near 1000 souls.

126 131   A little masterpiece in a very difficult style : Catullus himself could hardly have bettered it. In grace, tenderness, simplicity, and humour it is worthy of the Ancients ; and even more so, from the completeness and unity of the picture presented.

130 136   Perhaps no writer who has given such strong proofs of the poetic nature has left less satisfactory poetry than Thomson. Yet he touched little which he did not beautify : and this song, with ' Rule, Britannia ' and a few others, must make us

regret that he did not more seriously apply himself to lyrical writing.

132 140 l. 1. *Aeolian lyre*: the Greeks ascribed the origin of their Lyrical Poetry to the Aeolis in Asia Minor.

— — l. 17. *Thracia's hills*: supposed a favourite resort of Mars.

133 — l. 21. *feather'd king*: the Eagle of Jupiter, admirably described by Pindar in a passage here imitated by Gray.

— — l. 27. *Idalia* in Cyprus, where *Cytherea* (Venus) was especially worshipped.

— — l. 53. *Hyperion*: the Sun. St. 6–8 allude to the Poets of the islands and mainland of Greece, to those of Rome and of England.

135 — l. 115. *Theban Eagle*: Pindar.

138 141 l. 75. *chaste-eyed Queen*: Diana.

139 142 l. 5. *Attic warbler*: the nightingale.

141 144 *sleekit*, sleek: *bickering brattle*, flittering flight: *laith*, loath: *pattle*, ploughstaff: *whiles*, at times: *a daimen-icker*, a corn-ear now and then: *thrave*, shock: *lave*, rest: *foggage*, aftergrass: *snell*, biting: *but hald*, without dwelling-place: *thole*, bear: *cranreuch*, hoarfrost: *thy lane*, alone: *a-gley*, off the right line, awry.

145 147 Perhaps the noblest stanzas in our language.

149 148 *stoure*, dust-storm: *braw*, smart.

150 149 *scaith*, hurt: *ent*, guard: *steer*, molest.

151 151 *drumlie*, muddy: *birk*, birch.

153 152 *greet*, cry: *daurna*, dare not.—There can hardly exist a poem more truly tragic in the highest sense than this: nor, except Sappho, has any Poetess known to the Editor equalled it in excellence.

— 153 *fou*, merry with drink: *coost*, carried: *unco skeigh*, very proud: *garl*, forced: *abeigh*, aside: *Ailsa Craig*, a rock in the Firth of Clyde: *grat his een bleert*, cried till his eyes were bleared: *lowpin*, leaping: *linn*, waterfall: *sair*, sore: *smoor'd*, smothered : *crouse and canty*, blithe and gay.

154 154 Burns justly named this ' one of the most beautiful songs in the Scots or any other language.' One verse, interpolated by Beattie, is here omitted :—it contains two good lines, but is quite out of harmony with the original poem. *Bigonet*, little cap— probably altered from *beguinette* : *thraw*, twist : *caller*, fresh.

156 155 *airts*, quarters : *row*, roll : *shaw*, small wood in a hollow, spinney : *knowes*, knolls.

157 156 *jo*, sweetheart : *brent*, smooth : *pow*, head.

— 157 *leal*, faithful : *fain*, happy.

158 158 Henry VI founded Eton.

164 161 The Editor knows no Sonnet more re-markable than this, with 162, records Cowper's gratitude to the lady whose affectionate care for many years gave what sweetness he could enjoy to a life radically wretched. Petrarch's sonnets have a more ethereal grace and a more perfect finish ; Shakespeare's more passion ; Milton's stand supreme in stateliness, Wordsworth's in depth and delicacy. But Cowper's unites with an exquisiteness in the turn of thought which the Ancients would have called Irony, an intensity of pathetic tenderness peculiar to his loving and ingenuous nature.—There is much mannerism, much that is unimportant or of now exhausted interest in his poems : but where he is great, it is with that elementary greatness which rests on the most universal human feelings. Cowper is our highest master in simple pathos.

166 163 l. 19. *fancied green* : cherished garden.

167 164 Little more than his name appears recoverable with regard to the author of this truly noble poem. It should be noted as exhibiting a rare excellence—the climax of simple sublimity.

It is a lesson of high instructiveness to examine the essential qualities which give first-rate poetical rank to lyrics such as 'To-morrow' or 'Sally in our Alley,' when compared with poems written (if the phrase may be allowed) in keys so different as the subtle sweetness of Shelley, the grandeur of Gray and Milton, or the delightful Pastoralism of the Elizabethan verse. Intelligent readers will gain hence a clear understanding of the vast imaginative range of Poetry ;—through what wide oscillations the mind and the taste of a nation may pass ;—how many are the roads which Truth and Nature open to Excellence.

SUMMARY OF BOOK FOURTH

IT proves sufficiently the lavish wealth of our own age in Poetry, that the pieces which, without conscious departure from the standard of Excellence, render this Book by far the longest, were with very few exceptions composed during the first thirty years of the nineteenth century. Exhaustive reasons can hardly be given for the strangely sudden appearance of individual genius : but none, in the Editor's judgement, can be less adequate than that which assigns the splendid national achievements of our recent poetry to an impulse from the follies and wars that at the time disgraced our foreign neighbours. The first French Revolution was rather, in his opinion, one result, and in itself by no means the most important, of that far wider and greater spirit which through inquiry and doubt, through pain and triumph, sweeps mankind round the circles of its gradual development : and it is to this that we must trace the literature of modern Europe. But, without more detailed discussion on the motive causes of Scott, Wordsworth, Campbell, Keats, and Shelley, we may observe that these Poets, with others, carried to further perfection the later tendencies of the century preceding, in simplicity of narrative, reverence for human Passion and Character in every sphere, and impassioned love of Nature :—that, whilst maintaining on the whole the advances in art made since the Restoration, they renewed the half-forgotten melody and depth of tone which marked the best Elizabethan writers :—that, lastly, to what was thus inherited they added a richness in language and a variety in metre, a force and fire in narrative, a tenderness and bloom in feeling, an insight into the finer passages of the Soul and the inner meanings of the landscape, a larger and wiser Humanity,—hitherto hardly attained, and perhaps unattainable even by predecessors of not inferior individual genius. In a word, the nation which, after the Greeks in their glory, has been the most gifted of all nations for Poetry, expressed in these men the highest strength and prodigality of its nature. They interpreted the age to itself—hence the many phases of thought and style they present :—to sympathize with each, fervently and impartially, without fear and without fancifulness, is no doubtful step in the higher education of the Soul. For, as with the Affections and the Conscience, Purity in Taste is absolutely proportionate to Strength :—and when once the mind has raised itself to grasp and to delight in Excellence, those who love most will be found to love most wisely.

PAGE	NO.	
169	166	l. 11. *stout Cortez* : History requires here *Balboa* : (A. T.) It may be noticed that to find in Chapman's Homer the ' pure serene ' of the original, the reader must bring with him the imagination of the youthful poet ;—he must be ' a Greek himself,' as Shelley finely said of Keats.
173	169	The most tender and true of Byron's smaller poems.
174	170	This Poem, with 236, exemplifies the peculiar skill with which Scott employs proper names :—nor is there a surer sign of high poetical genius.
191	191	The Editor in this and in other instances has risked the addition (or the change) of a Title, that the aim of the verses following

may be grasped more clearly and immediately.

197 198   l. 4. *nature's Eremite*: like a solitary thing in Nature.—This beautiful Sonnet was the last word of a poet deserving the title 'marvellous boy' in a much higher sense than Chatterton. If the fulfilment may ever safely be prophesied from the promise, England appears to have lost in Keats one whose gifts in Poetry have rarely been surpassed. Shakespeare, Milton, and Wordsworth, had their lives been closed at twenty-five, would (so far as we know) have left poems of less excellence and hope than the youth who, from the petty school and the London surgery, passed at once to a place with them of 'high collateral glory.'

199 201   It is impossible not to regret that Moore has written so little in this sweet and genuinely national style.

— 202   A masterly example of Byron's command of strong thought and close reasoning in verse :—as the next is equally characteristic of Shelley's wayward intensity, and 204 of the dramatic power, the vital identification of the poet with other times and characters, in which Scott is second only to Shakespeare.

209 209   Bonnivard, a Genevese, was imprisoned by the Duke of Savoy in Chillon on the lake of Geneva for his courageous defence of his country against the tyranny with which Piedmont threatened it during the first half of the seventeenth century.—This noble Sonnet is worthy to stand near Milton's on the Vaudois massacre.

209 210   Switzerland was usurped by the French under Napoleon in 1800 : Venice in 1797 (211).

212 215   This battle was fought Dec. 2, 1800, between the Austrians under Archduke John and the French under Moreau, in a

forest near Munich. *Hohen Linden* means *High Limetrees*.

216   218   After the capture of Madrid by Napoleon, Sir J. Moore retreated before Soult and Ney to Corunna, and was killed whilst covering the embarkation of his troops. His tomb, built by Ney, bears this inscription—' John Moore, leader of the English armies, slain in battle, 1809.'

229   229   The Mermaid was the club-house of Shakespeare, Ben Jonson, and other choice spirits of that age.

—   230   *Maisie* : Mary. Scott has given us nothing more complete and lovely than this little Song, which unites simplicity and dramatic power to a wildwood music of the rarest quality. No moral is drawn, far less any conscious analysis of feeling attempted :— the pathetic meaning is left to be suggested by the mere presentment of the situation. Inexperienced critics have often named this, which may be called the Homeric manner, superficial, from its apparent simple facility : but first-rate excellence in it (as shown here, in 196, 156, and 129) is in truth one of the least common triumphs of Poetry.—This style should be compared with what is not less perfect in its way, the searching out of inner feeling, the expression of hidden meanings, the revelation of the heart of Nature and of the Soul within the Soul,—the Analytical method, in short,—most completely represented by Wordsworth and by Shelley.

235   234   *correi* : covert on a hillside ; *cumber* : trouble.

—   235   Two intermediate stanzas have been here omitted. They are very ingenious, but, of all poetical qualities, ingenuity is least in accordance with pathos.

247   243   This Poem has an exaltation and a glory, joined with an exquisiteness of expression, which place it in the highest rank amongst

PAGE NO.

the many masterpieces of its illustrious Author.

257   252   l. 24. *interlunar swoon* : interval of the Moon's invisibility.

263   256   l. 11. *Calpe* : Gibraltar.

—   —   l. 21. *Lofoden* : the Maelstrom whirlpool off the N.W. coast of Norway.

264   257   This lovely Poem refers here and there to a ballad by Hamilton on the subject better treated in 127 and 128.

277   268   l. 10. *Arcturi* : seemingly used for *northern stars.*

—   —   l. 21. *And wild roses,* etc. Our language has no line modulated with more subtle sweetness. A good poet *might* have written *And roses wild,*—yet this slight change would disenchant the verse of its peculiar beauty.

280   270   l. 81. *Ceres' daughter* : Proserpine.

—   —   l. 82. *God of Torment* : Pluto.

281   271   This impassioned Address expresses Shelley's most rapt imaginations, and is the direct modern representative of the feeling which led the Greeks to the worship of Nature.

290   274   The leading idea of this beautiful description of a day's landscape in Italy is expressed with an obscurity not unfrequent with its author. It appears to be,—On the voyage of life are many moments of pleasure, given by the sight of Nature, who has power to heal even the worldliness and the uncharity of man.

291   —   l. 58. Amphitrite was daughter to Ocean.

292   —   l. 76. *Sun-girt* City : It is difficult not to believe that the correct reading is *Seagirt.* Many of Shelley's poems appear to have been printed in England during his residence abroad : others were printed from his manuscripts after his death. Hence probably the text of no English Poet after 1600 contains so many errors. See the Note on No. 9.

PAGE NO.

296 275   l. 21. *Maenad*: a frenzied Nymph, attendant on Dionysus in the Greek mythology.

—   —   l. 39. Plants under water sympathize with the seasons of the land, and hence with the winds which affect them.

298 276   Written soon after the death, by shipwreck, of Wordsworth's brother John. This Poem should be compared with Shelley's following it. Each is the most complete expression of the innermost spirit of his art given by these great Poets :—of that Idea which, as in the case of the true Painter (to quote the words of Reynolds), ' subsists only in the mind : The sight never beheld it, nor has the hand expressed it ; it is an idea residing in the breast of the artist, which he is always labouring to impart, and which he dies at last without imparting.'

299   —   l. 50. *the Kind* : the human race.

300 278   l. 13. Proteus represented the everlasting changes, united with ever-recurrent sameness, of the Sea.

301 279   l. 1. *the royal Saint* : Henry VI.

INDEX OF WRITERS

WITH DATES OF BIRTH AND DEATH, FIRST LINES
OF THE POEMS, AND TITLES

THE END

PRINTED IN GREAT BRITAIN
AT THE UNIVERSITY PRESS, OXFORD
BY VIVIAN RIDLER
PRINTER TO THE UNIVERSITY

THE
GOLDEN TREASURY
OF THE BEST SONGS AND LYRICAL
POEMS IN THE ENGLISH LANGUAGE

Selected and arranged by
FRANCIS TURNER PALGRAVE

With Additional Poems

A. Jones

LONDON
OXFORD UNIVERSITY PRESS

FRANCIS TURNER PALGRAVE

Born, Great Yarmouth, 28 September 1824
Died, South Kensington, 24 October 1897

The Golden Treasury of the best Songs and
Lyrical Poems in the English language *was first
published in* 1861. *In* The World's Classics *it
was first published, with additional Poems, in* 1907
and reprinted six times. New edition 1914, *reprinted eighteen times. Enlarged edition, with
poems by contemporary writers,* 1928, *reprinted
eight times. Further poems (bringing the additions
up to the date of publication) were included in*
1941; *reprinted ten times and again in* 1959, 1960
and 1963 (*twice*).

PRINTED IN GREAT BRITAIN